AF379999

Seize the City, Undo the State

Seize the City, Undo the State

The Inception of Russia's War on Ukraine

SERHIY KUDELIA

OXFORD
UNIVERSITY PRESS

Oxford University Press is a department of the University of Oxford.
It furthers the University's objective of excellence in research, scholarship,
and education by publishing worldwide. Oxford is a registered trade mark of
Oxford University Press in the UK and in certain other countries.

Published in the United States of America by Oxford University Press
198 Madison Avenue, New York, NY 10016, United States of America.

© Oxford University Press 2025

All rights reserved. No part of this publication may be reproduced, stored in a retrieval system,
transmitted, used for text and data mining, or used for training artificial intelligence, in any form or
by any means, without the prior permission in writing of Oxford University Press, or as expressly
permitted by law, by license or under terms agreed with the appropriate reprographics rights
organization. Inquiries concerning reproduction outside the scope of the above should be sent
to the Rights Department, Oxford University Press, at the address above.

You must not circulate this work in any other form
and you must impose this same condition on any acquirer.

Library of Congress Cataloging-in-Publication Data
Names: Kudelia, Serhiy, author.
Title: Seize the city, undo the state: the inception of Russia's war on Ukraine / Serhiy Kudelia,
Associate Professor of Political Science, Baylor University.
Description: Oxford ; New York : Oxford University Press, [2025] |
Includes bibliographical references and index.
Identifiers: LCCN 2024038477 (print) | LCCN 2024038478 (ebook) |
ISBN 9780197795538 | ISBN 9780197795545 (pbk) | ISBN 9780197795569 (epub) |
ISBN 9780197795576
Subjects: LCSH: Russo-Ukrainian War, 2014—Campaigns—Ukraine—Donbas (Region) |
Separatist movements—Ukraine—Donbas (Region)—History—21st century. |
Donbas (Ukraine : Region)—Politics and government—21st century.
Classification: LCC DK5479.D65 K83 2025 (print) | LCC DK5479.D65 (ebook) |
DDC 947.706/2—dc23/eng/20241202
LC record available at https://lccn.loc.gov/2024038477
LC ebook record available at https://lccn.loc.gov/2024038478

DOI: 10.1093/9780197795576.001.0001

Cover image: The abandoned city council building in Toretsk, Donetsk oblast, which
was ravaged during the street fighting between Ukrainian soldiers and militants
on July 21, 2014. Photo by Serhiy Kudelia (November, 2018)

Paperback printed by Integrated Books International, United States of America
Hardback printed by Bridgeport National Bindery, Inc., United States of America

The manufacturer's authorised representative in the EU for product safety is Oxford University Press España S.A. of El Parque Empresarial
San Fernando de Henares, Avenida de Castilla, 2 – 28830 Madrid (www.oup.es/en or product.safety@oup.com). OUP España S.A. also acts as
importer into Spain of products made by the manufacturer.

For Mlada

Contents

List of Figures

List of Tables

List of Abbreviations

ATO	anti-terrorist operation
DCFTA	Deep and Comprehensive Free Trade Agreement
DND	Voluntary People's Patrol
DNR	Donetsk People's Republic
EU	European Union
FSB	Federal Security Service of the Russian Federation
GRU	Main Intelligence Directorate of the Russian Federation
KPU	Communist Party of Ukraine
LNR	Luhansk People's Republic
MAP	Membership Action Plan
MD	Mariupol Patrol
MGB	Ministry of State Security of Donetsk People's Republic
NATO	North Atlantic Treaty Organization
NOD	People's Militia of Donbas
NSDC	National Security and Defense Council of Ukraine
OM	Odesa Militia
OUN	Organization of Ukrainian Nationalists
PM	People's Militia of Odesa
PMR	Transnistrian Moldovan Republic
PR	Party of Regions
RF	Russian Federation
RNBO	National Security and Defence Council of Ukraine
RS	Right Sector
RU	Russian Unity
SBU	Security Service of Ukraine
UPA	Ukrainian Insurgent Army

Preface

We set up a meeting in a small hipster café located on the corner of Peace Boulevard and Greek Street, right in the heart of Mariupol. Its name, The Reading Hut (Izba Chytalnia), perfectly matched the interior—shelves of old used books, a large sofa, a black piano attached to the wall and, next to it, a painted silhouette of a saxophone player. "All you can IMAGINE is real," a spraypainted slogan declared. It was a perfect student hangout—a place to spend long hours reading or writing. But I was there to meet a Ukrainian Security Service operative who investigated the separatist takeover of the city four years earlier. Once I ordered hot tea, my cell started ringing. It was him.

"I am not coming. I just got a call from a local journalist who said he knew about our meeting. Why did you tell him?" He was clearly irked; I was baffled. No one else could know about the interview or its location. "Is this how he wants to avoid talking to me? But why come up with this absurd pretext?" I thought for a second. Determined to interview him, I took a conciliatory tone: "I have no idea why this person would say that. But I can meet at any other place—just tell me where to go." After a short pause he concurred: "Okay, go to my apartment. But make sure to take a taxi there and see that no one is following you. I will be waiting outside."

The cab crossed the river Kalmius into the left-bank district of Mariupol. In the darkness of the night only the spotlit pipes of the steel factory Azovstal could be seen sputtering large clouds of white smoke. When I approached the building, my interlocutor was already outside. Despite a tense exchange minutes earlier, he greeted me with a disarming smile and a firm handshake. Known to me only under his pen name, Ivan, he immediately got to the main topic: "It is easy to find my place. I am the only one with the large Ukrainian flag on my balcony. I like to drive local 'separs' nuts."[1]

We sat at the kitchen table stacked with sliced sausage, lard, pickled cucumbers, tomatoes, and other traditional chasers for the main dish: a bottle of Ukrainian pepper vodka. Over the next hour we discussed how the city

---

[1] *Separ* is Ukrainian slang for "separatist."

had turned into a separatist stronghold in spring 2014 and why many were still "waiting" for Russia to come even four years later. His kitchen wall was covered with signatures and greetings of Ukrainian soldiers who were fighting on the front lines just a few miles from where we sat. "If it were not for them, Russia would be here today," Ivan told me.

At the time neither of us expected that in less than four years Russia would arrive in Mariupol, following months of ferocious bombardment and street fights. Much less surprising was that my interviewee, who turned out to be Vasyl Volodymyrovych Bohach, a lieutenant colonel of the Security Service of Ukraine (SBU), did not leave. Together with the remaining city defenders he hid in the underground tunnels of Azovstal to continue repelling Russian attacks. Bohach was killed on May 8, 2022, after a Russian bomb struck one of the underground bunkers. He was merely 42 years old. On July 12, 2023, Ukrainian president Volodymyr Zelensky posthumously awarded Bohach the Golden Star and the title Hero of Ukraine.[2]

This book tells the stories of hundreds of men and women like Bohach, who considered it their duty to speak out or act against the takeover of their land. But it also tells the stories of hundreds who led or abated this takeover, who encouraged others to join it, and who intimidated and killed those who tried to stop it. These stories are mainly based on my interviews with participants or observers of the rising confrontation, some of whom were on opposite sides in spring 2014. Their names have remained largely unknown to the wider public, even in Ukraine. Most will be mentioned publicly in the following pages for the first time.

This book stands apart from all existing accounts of the war in Donbas, most of which rely on secondary sources or direct recollections of those on only one of the warring sides. As a result, they often produce biased or incomplete narratives which cannot fully account for the logic behind the behavior of conflicting actors. This book, by contrast, relies on multiple perspectives on the conflict and reveals views and perceptions in rival camps. It examines slogans and grievances articulated by individuals at rallies at the time; dives into the firsthand accounts of participants; seeks to compare their motives and objectives, understand their emotions and calculations—all crucial elements of a broader explanation for the insurgency.

[2] "Ukaz Prezydenta Ukrainy N326/2023: Pro prysvoennia V. Bohachu zvannia Heroi Ukrainy," Official Website of the President of Ukraine, June 12, 2023, https://www.president.gov.ua/documents/3262023-47029.

This books also provides an alternative to panoramic accounts of the armed conflict, which analyze it in broad strokes and often intermix geopolitical and domestic factors. Instead, this book moves from general to a particular—first, outlining Russia's strategies regarding Ukraine since 1991, then identifying specific methods used by Russian agents to seize Ukrainian territories in early 2014—and, in its core chapters, by examining how the Ukrainian state was dismantled in individual towns, mostly by the very people who lived there.

The micro-level analysis developed in the book draws on data collected during my multiple trips to two dozen towns in Donbas, as well as two major cities outside the region, Kharkiv and Odesa. By using this approach, I reveal specific mechanisms through which the seizure of Sloviansk on April 12, 2014, the starting point of the conflict, triggered the unraveling of the Ukrainian state in towns nearby and across the region in the following weeks—but not in other regional centers, such as Kharkiv or Odesa. Crucially, this approach allows me to compare the relative contribution of Russian and local actors to this unraveling—a point of considerable debate in the literature on the origins of the conflict.

Finally, this book shifts the analytical focus from state-level elites, usually at the center of most studies of this war, to ordinary residents who lived in the towns of Donbas in spring of 2014. Their actions over this short period proved as consequential for their localities as the decisions made by political leaders in Moscow or Kyiv. Many of them had no prior experience in politics but instead had pursued careers in business, education, or journalism; others worked in public administration on the local level and never dealt with issues of national or international significance; yet others were politically active but never had to choose between life and death.

Each of them, however, made choices which, ultimately, altered not only their lives but the history of their region, the well-being of their communities, and the future of the country they once called their own. If they joined local militia units, guarded checkpoints, addressed rallies, organized a separatist referendum, raised separatist symbols, or assaulted town residents supportive of Ukraine, their actions contributed to removing the Ukrainian state presence. If they displayed blue-and-yellow flags, rallied for Ukraine's unity, countered separatist demonstrators, joined volunteer units, and fought Russian mercenaries or local militants, they reinforced Ukraine's sovereignty. As the book shows, the cumulative effect of their competing choices often tipped the scales in each town already prior to the onset of the large-scale armed conflict.

The profiles of regular town residents offered in this book draws on over one hundred in-depth interviews I conducted between December 2014, my first visit to Sloviansk, and August 2021. In some respects, each interview was a leap of faith on the part of a person already traumatized by the conflict but still finding it important and meaningful to share their individual experience. My interviewees trusted my integrity as a scholar and ability as a writer to tell their stories and tie them together without distortions or misrepresentations. They also believed in my ability to see the project through completion—a belief that kept me going during the most difficult phases of writing. I am deeply grateful for their trust and inspiration and take responsibility for any failures they may find in the book.

During my field research I also benefited from the insights of numerous individuals who guided me across Donbas, a region I had never visited prior to 2014. I was fortunate to complete the first round of town visits and individual interviews between September and December 2018 with the invaluable assistance of an outstanding Ukrainian journalist and scholar, Yulia Abibok. She helped me with data collection and shared her local knowledge of the region during our joint trips there. I conducted the group survey of residents of eight towns of Donetsk and Luhansk oblast in May through June 2015 together with Ukrainian scholars, activists, and journalists: Anastasia Lykholat, Svitlana Nidzvetska, Nina Potarska, Halya Rusanevich, Anton Pechenkin, and Serhiy Solodko. The results of this survey offered important insights into the drivers behind the varied local response to the armed conflict in Donbas and informed my subsequent research. Baylor University funded both this survey and the book research and writing phases by granting two research leaves. I am grateful to my university and Departmental colleagues who believed in this project from the start and encouraged me to see it through. Peter Campbell read the book proposal and gave valuable advice on how to communicate my ideas to the publisher. I also greatly appreciate the unwavering endorsement I received at various stages of my research from the Political Science Department chair David Clinton whose own meticulous scholarship set a notable example to follow. The data and digital scholarship director at Baylor University, Joshua Been, offered his time and assistance with generating visual representations of urban agglomerations in Donbas. I completed writing most parts of the book as a fellow of the Ukrainian Research in Switzerland program at the University of Basel and would like to thank its director, Benjamin Schenk, and program coordinator, Oliver Göhler, for the warm welcome and tremendous support they offered throughout my stay. Basel became a place where this book found its narrative structure and key arguments.

My special gratitude also goes to several scholars of the region, whose work I have long admired and sought to emulate, in particular, my doctoral advisor, Bruce Parrott; my postdoctoral mentors Jeffrey Kopstein, Henry Hale, and Lucan Way; and the first American political science professor I met as an undergraduate student in Lviv, now a renowned scholar of Ukraine, Paul D'Anieri. I am indebted to numerous other scholars, from whom I learned over the years and whose insights I value greatly despite our occasional disagreements. They include, among many others, Dominique Arel, Keith Darden, Yevhen Finkel, Elise Giuliano, Erik Herron, David Marples, Kimitaka Matsuzato, Mitchell Orenstein, Jessica Pisano, Oxana Shevel, and Gerard Toal. I am particularly thankful to the first readers of my manuscript, Bruce Parrott, Jesse Driscoll, and two anonymous reviewers, who expressed enthusiasm for the project and offered pointed suggestions on how to sharpen its arguments. I also appreciate the careful review of the manuscript and commitment to having it published from Oxford University Press team, particularly its executive editor David McBride and manuscript editor Judith Hoover. All the responsibility for the remaining flaws of this work remains solely with me.

Finally, my most profound gratitude goes to my parents—my mother, Lyudmyla, and my late father, Yuliy—for their boundless dedication and sacrifice. They taught me the most important lessons in life. These same lessons I try to convey now to my daughter, Mlada, who was born the day before the armed conflict in Donbas began. She was with me during all phases of this project, growing from a toddler into a preteen, generously afforded me writing time, and offered the most powerful motivation for its completion: her love. I dedicate this book to her and the promise of peace that she embodies.

SK
St Andrews, Scotland
April, 2024

Introduction

In the beginning was the city. In fact, dozens of cities and smaller towns fell almost simultaneously, often quietly, one after the other. It happened as if from a series of minor earthquakes that hit sequentially each part of the region. That region—Donbas—would soon become synonymous with war and suffering, with heroism and betrayal, with love and death.[1] For many inside and outside the region, the cities fell under external control because of temporary weakness of the Ukrainian state and Russia's meddling. For some regional locals, the cities did not fall at all—rather they broke away in a hurried rush of emotional defiance. For a group of outsiders from Russia, the capture of the cities was just the first step in the determined march to complete dismemberment of the Ukrainian state.

This book tells about the start of the war in Donbas, or the first stage of the wider Russo-Ukrainian war, by comparing the experience of individual towns of the region. It identifies actors who risked or sacrificed their lives and those who sought to save them. It describes acts of courage and valor displayed by regular citizens as well as cowardice and betrayal by those vested with power and responsibility. It uncovers crimes committed in active conflict zones and on quiet city streets; and explains why perpetrators and enablers of these crimes often shared a homeland with their victims. It reveals the exact role that the Russian agents played in the swift breakdown of the Ukrainian state in Donbas in spring of 2014 and ways in which locals also contributed it. Ultimately, the book demonstrates that momentous geopolitical events are not just the outcome of decision-making by a handful of political leaders but also the product of everyday choices of regular residents from towns large and small.

---

[1] Throughout the book, the toponym Donbas refers to the region within administrative borders of Donetsk and Luhansk oblasts (provinces) of Ukraine. It was initially coined to identify an area south of the river Siverskiy Donets rich in coal deposits and industrialized in the late nineteenth to early twentieth century. Since then, Donbas has been widely used not just as a geographic or economic marker but also as a social and political signifier of a larger region within administrative borders of the two eastern Ukrainian oblasts.

Seize the City, Undo the State. Serhiy Kudelia, Oxford University Press. © Oxford University Press (2025).
DOI: 10.1093/9780197795576.003.0001

One such town is Bakhmut.[2] During my visit there in October 2018, it felt like a place filled with hope that the worst period of the war was well behind it. The sporadic exchange of fire between the Ukrainian armed forces and Russia-backed separatist units continued just several miles south of the city, but it hardly affected the daily life of its residents. Markets were bustling with activity; coffee shops were filled with young people; taxi drivers were seeking customers to tour the cellars of Artemivsk winery or the tunnels of Soledar salt mine, just a short ride away. As I walked the quiet streets of this quaint town covered with brown and yellow leaves and lit with warm autumn sun, I could not help feeling that the violence it experienced in 2014 could never come back.

Four years after my visit, Bakhmut and Soledar became the main targets of Russia's offensive operations and the site of the longest battle in the first year of full-scale war. Both cities were ruined after months of incessant bombing. Bakhmut's name came to symbolize the tenacity of Ukrainian resistance. In his address to the U.S. Congress in December 2022 Ukraine's President Volodymyr Zelensky compared the fight for Bakhmut with the eighteenth-century battle for Saratoga in the American Revolutionary War and declared that it would "change the trajectory of our war for independence and freedom."[3] When the last Ukrainian soldiers withdrew from Bakhmut at the end of May 2023, it had been ten months since Russian troops started their assault on the city.

In spring of 2014, the loss of Ukraine's sovereign control over Bakhmut happened in a matter of weeks and was barely noticed even outside the city, let alone the rest of the world. Instead of tens of thousands of Russian regular army units and paramilitary fighters, the city came under the control of several dozen militants, mostly town natives. Instead of putting up resistance, town police sided with the militants as the Ukrainian military remained camped in its base. Although the militants removed Ukrainian state symbols from all municipal buildings, the city administrators continued governing the city from their offices. The mayor and other local administrators held meetings with separatist activists as city council deputies invited them to

---

[2] Bakhmut is an original name for a town, which became Artemivsk under the Soviet rule. It reverted to its original name following the decision of the Ukrainian parliament in 2016, which changed all geographic names in Ukraine associated with the communist regime. All town names mentioned in this book are based on their current official Ukrainian usage (so Toretsk rather than Dzerzhynsk, Pokrovsk rather Krasnoarmiysk, Myrnohrad rather than Dymytrov and Lyman rather than Krasnyi Lyman).

[3] Official Website of the President of Ukraine, "Address by Volodymyr Zelenskyy in a Joint Meeting of the US Congress," December 22, 2022, https://www.president.gov.ua/en/news/mi-stoyimo-boremos-i-vigrayemo-bo-mi-razom-ukrayina-amerika-80017.

council sessions. And even though the Ukrainian government recognized that the city came under separatist control, it continued transferring public funds to cover its operating expenses.

The similar experience of dozens of other towns across Donbas provided the initial impetus for this book and raised the questions it seeks to answer: How did a heavily urbanized and industrialized region with over six million inhabitants quickly fall under control of a handful of militants? How could militants rule over these towns without replacing city administration or dispersing local police? And why did separatists fail to seize some smaller towns in the region despite quick success in the largest ones?

By addressing these questions, the book makes both theoretical and empirical contributions. Theoretically, I engage three broad topics in the study of asymmetric armed conflict: (1) how external interventions contribute to the outbreak of separatist insurgency; (2) how urban density enables the spread of an insurgent campaign; and (3) how governance models vary under insurgent rule. Empirically, I offer new town-level data from the start of the armed conflict in Donbas, compare mechanisms of separatist takeover of individual towns, identify actors who enabled militants, and trace the varied responses of municipal authorities to the separatist challenge. The evidence presented also puts Moscow's decision to launch a full-scale invasion of Ukraine in February 2022 in a new light. It reveals how the combined effect of coercive pressure and pro-Russian mobilization may induce cooperation of local authorities, trigger defections within the security agencies, and create preconditions for quick seizure and sustained control of large urban centers. Since Russia's covert intervention in 2014 left a large part of Donbas under its de facto control, Russian leaders might have expected that an open invasion on a much larger scale would have enabled the seizure of other major cities and territories through the same set of mechanisms. The failure of these plans could be attributed to the profound transformation of Ukrainian society and the state in the ensuing eight years, largely unnoticed in the Kremlin.

Why the Conflict in Donbas?

The existing academic studies of the armed conflict in Donbas fall into three broad categories. One set of accounts focuses on the role of foreign powers. Various scholars view it as an example of Russia's expansionist policies, a response to internal developments in Ukraine, or an extension of a geopolitical competition between Russia and the West.[4] Common to this approach is the view that the armed conflict in Donbas was manufactured by Russian proxies on Moscow's direct or indirect command. Separatist units that participated in the fighting are dismissed as artificial formations without grassroots support. The second approach attributes causal significance to variables internal to Ukraine or Donbas. It pays particular attention to the mechanisms through which violence emerged and escalated to the level of war.[5] Scholars using this approach explore the effects of the weakened Ukrainian state following the Euromaidan revolution and the polarized discourses that the revolution produced, the economic structure of the region and its ties to Russia, interests and strategies of regional political and business actors, clashing identity choices, and heightened grievances of its residents. Some studies taking this approach define the conflict as a civil war with genuine and substantial local involvement; others argue that it combines characteristics of interstate and intrastate conflicts.

The third set of accounts recognizes the importance of Russia's actors in triggering or sustaining the conflict but views the escalation as the outcome of an interactive dynamic emerging out of actions of Russian agents, such as Igor Girkin and Aleksandr Borodai, and local actors each pursing their own objectives.[6] These process-based studies analyze the unfolding

---

[4] Examples of this approach include Paul D'Anieri, *Ukraine and Russia: From Civilized Divorce to Uncivil War* (Cambridge: Cambridge University Press, 2023); Lawrence Freedman, *Ukraine and the Art of Strategy* (Oxford: Oxford University Press, 2019); Tetyana Malyarenko and Stefan Wolff, *The Dynamics of Emerging De-Facto States: Eastern Ukraine in the Post-Soviet Space* (New York: Routledge, 2019); Samuel Charap and Timothy J. Colton, *Everyone Loses: The Ukraine Crisis and Ruinous Contest for Post-Soviet Eurasia* (London: IISS, 2017); Taras Kuzio, *Putin's War against Ukraine: Revolution, Nationalism, and Crime* (Independently published by CreateSpace, 2017); Vlad Mykhnenko, "Causes and Consequences of the War in Eastern Ukraine: An Economic Geography Perspective," *Europe-Asia Studies* 72, no. 3 (April 2020): 528–560; Andrew Wilson, "The Donbas in 2014: Explaining Civil Conflict Perhaps, but Not Civil War," *Europe-Asia Studies* 68, no. 4 (2016): 631–652.

[5] For examples of this argument, see Dominique Arel and Jesse Driscoll, *Ukraine's Unnamed War: Before the Russian Invasion of 2022* (Cambridge: Cambridge University Press, 2022); Daria Platonova, *The Donbas Conflict in Ukraine: Elites, Protest, and Partition* (New York: Routledge, 2021); Anna Matveeva, *Through Times of Trouble: Conflict in Southeastern Ukraine Explained from Within* (London: Lexington Books, 2017); Ivan Katchanovski, "The Separatist War in Donbas: A Violent Break-up of Ukraine?," *European Politics and Society* 17, no. 6 (2016): 473–489; Yuri Zhukov, "Trading Hard Hats for Combat Helmets: The Economics of Rebellion in Eastern Ukraine," *Journal of Comparative Economics* 44, no. 1 (2016): 1–15.

[6] For examples, see Anna Aratyunyan, *Hybrid Warriors: Proxies, Freelances and Moscow's Struggle for Ukraine* (London: Hurst, 2022); Denys Kazansky and Maryna Vorotyntseva, *Yak Ukraina Vtrachala Donbas* (Kyiv: Chorna Hora, 2020); Silviya Nitsova, "Why the Difference? Donbas, Kharkiv and Dnipropetrovsk after Ukraine's Euromaidan Revolution," *Europe-Asia Studies* 73, no. 10 (2021):

of the conflict sequentially and examine the cumulative effect that individual choices of conflict participants in Donetsk, Luhansk, or Sloviansk had on conflict escalation. Scholars using this approach may differ on the relative significance of external and internal actors in producing the insurgency, but they all attribute greater weight to human agency over international or domestic structural factors.

This book relies on the process-based method of analysis but shifts its focus from decision-makers on the national or regional level to actors who operated in towns across the region. The town-centered approach allows us to trace the actual progression of the insurgency from its origins and identify the mechanisms through which it happened.[7] Seizing smaller towns was a crucial initial objective for the militants. The two provinces of Donbas—Donetska and Luhanska oblasts—are the most densely urbanized in Ukraine.[8] This made the population of both provinces more dispersed across multiple large and midsize towns than anywhere else in the country. Only 6% of Donetsk oblast residents and 5% of Luhansk oblast residents lived in regional capitals before 2014.[9] The visible presence of militants in Donetsk and Luhansk was, thus, insufficient to claim success for their secessionist project. They needed to extend their control to most of the region before they could stage an independence referendum for two self-proclaimed separatist units—Donetsk People's Republic (DNR) and Luhansk People's Republic (LNR). Moreover, given that Donbas had eleven towns with over 100,000 residents, even faking a region-wide referendum required substantial human and organizational resources. In Crimea, with a population almost three times smaller than in Donbas, this task was accomplished through swift deployment of Russian troops and defection of local officials and the Ukrainian security personnel to the Russian side. In Donbas, however, there was neither comparable defection among local elites nor any sizable military force backing separatist leaders. Hence,

1832–1856; Kimitaka Matsuzato, "The Donbass War: Outbreak and Deadlock," *Demokratizatsiya: The Journal of Post-Soviet Democratization* 25, no. 2 (Spring 2017): 175–200.

[7] On the significance of studying mechanisms and processes for explaining episodes of political change, see Charles Tilly, "Mechanisms in Political Processes," *Annual Review of Political Science* 4 (2001): 21–41.

[8] Six out of thirteen of the largest urban agglomerations of Ukraine were in Donbas as of 2013. See World Bank Group, *Cities in Europe and Central Asia: Ukraine* (Washington, DC: World Bank Group, 2013), 4.

[9] This is far below the share of oblast residents living in other major regional capitals of Ukraine, such as Kyiv (34%), Kharkiv (20.6%), and Odesa (13.1%). See Delphine Alberta Hamilton, *Ukraine—Urbanization Review* (Washington, DC: World Bank Group, 2015), 24.

the militant coercive presence was unevenly distributed across the region and was concentrated in major towns. Only a more granular analysis of town dynamics could reveal the exact mechanisms through which separatist leaders in Donetsk and Luhansk managed to put the entire region under their control in a single month, from the capture of municipal buildings on April 7 to the holding of the May 11 referendum. The book's town-centered approach also adds new evidence to the debate on the primacy of external versus internal causes of conflict. It is based on the first systematic collection and comparison of the data on the militant presence and sources of separatist support from across over a dozen towns of the region. It uncovers variation in the level of militant control over individual towns, not recognized by scholars of the conflict up to now. It also reveals patterns in grassroots mobilization on behalf of the separatist project and instances of successful civic resistance to separatist rule. This allows us to establish, with greater precision, the relative weight of external and internal drivers behind the extension of separatist control over the entire region.

Going Micro

A micro-level approach to examining the origins and dynamics of wars represents a recent turn in conflict studies long dominated by the focus on macro-level variables.[10] In contrast to an earlier preoccupation with state-level characteristics, it views "the individual, the household, the group, and the community" as units central to the "processes and dynamics of violent conflict."[11] It is premised on the recognition that group conflict is not merely the product of national policies or structural changes but emerges out of an interaction between "individuals, their families, and their social networks" that constitute groups.[12] Hence, the agency of individuals seemingly on the margins of social processes, particularly their individual choices and actions,

[10] Roos Haer, Johannes Vüllers, and Nils Weidmann, "Studying Micro Dynamics in Civil Wars: Introduction," *Zeitschrift für Friedens und Konfliktforschung* 8 (2019): 151–159; Philip Verwimp, Patricia Justino, and Tilman Brück, "The Analysis of Conflict: A Micro-level Perspective," *Journal of Peace Research* 46, no. 3 (2009): 307–314.

[11] Patricia Justino, Tilman Brück, and Philip Verwimp, "Micro-level Dynamics of Conflict, Violence, and Development: A New Analytical Framework," in *A Micro-level Perspective on the Dynamics of Conflict, Violence, and Development*, ed. Patricia Justino, Tilman Brück, and Philip Verwimp (Oxford: Oxford University Press, 2013), 4. For one of the pioneering micro-level analyses of insurgency, see Roger D. Petersen, *Resistance and Rebellion: Lessons from Eastern Europe* (Cambridge: Cambridge University Press, 2001).

[12] Justino, Brück, Verwimp, "Micro-level Dynamics of Conflict...", 6.

have an independent effect on the outbreak, the course, and the outcome of conflict. Agents' causal significance can be established through temporal and spatial disaggregation of the conflict to the level of single localities. The first type of disaggregation allows us to identify variation in the intensity of violence and its types over time and the roles of individual community members and social networks at different conflict stages and to establish linkages between violence cycles. Through spatial disaggregation, scholars compare conflict dynamics in different localities, connect a particular violence type to a specific area, and identify any variation of civilian responses to conflict and violence across localities.

The utility of micro-level studies has been demonstrated by the breadth of new findings and conceptualizations. In an early, groundbreaking contribution, Kalyvas identified territorial control as the key predictor of the type of violence used in different localities in Greece during its civil war.[13] Another important early work by Petersen outlined mechanisms that led individuals to move between different forms of resistance by comparing towns in Soviet-occupied Lithuania.[14] Later contributions used micro-level analysis to study how party competition led to violence, how prior institutions shaped insurgent governance, or how information-sharing patterns affected the sustainability of the insurgency.[15]

Despite demonstrated advances in the study of conflict, a micro-level approach also imposes several limitations on researchers. One of these stems from reliance on single-case studies, which limits generalizability of the findings.[16] Another arises out of the nature of micro-level research, which often excludes macro-level variables from consideration and may bias ultimate findings regarding the causality of the conflict. Data collection may also prove challenging.[17] Since micro-level research requires acquiring granular data from small localities, its availability may be limited if the conflict is ongoing or historically distant. Even in the case of a recent conflict,

---

[13] Stathis Kalyvas, *The Logic of Violence in Civil War* (Cambridge: Cambridge University Press, 2006).

[14] Petersen, *Resistance and Rebellion*.

[15] See Jeffrey Kopstein and Jason Wittenberg, *Intimate Violence: Anti-Jewish Pogroms on the Eve of the Holocaust* (Ithaca, NY: Cornell University Press, 2018); Ana Arjona, *Rebelocracy: Social Order in the Colombian Civil War* (Cambridge: Cambridge University Press, 2016); Janet Lewis, *How Insurgency Begins: Rebel Group Formation in Uganda and Beyond* (Cambridge: Cambridge University Press, 2020).

[16] Hauer, Vüllers, Weidmann, "Studying Micro Dynamics in Civil Wars: Introduction."

[17] Santiago Sossa, "The Micro-dynamics of Conflict and Peace: Evidence from Colombia," *International Interactions: Empirical and Theoretical Research in International Relations* 49, no. 2 (2023): 165.

collecting data from primary sources may be impeded by legal, ethical, and political constraints. This leads to excessive use of secondary sources, raising bias and reliability concerns.

Here I seek to remedy some of these methodological deficiencies in several ways. First, I recognize the effects of macro-level variables, particularly of Russia's policies and strategic choices of its leaders, in explaining the genesis of the Donbas conflict. Chapters 2 and 3 offer a detailed examination of their effects and demonstrate some of the limitations of an exclusive focus on external variables. Second, my field research in almost two dozen localities allowed me to collect town-specific data from primary and secondary sources, which I use as complementary to my analysis. I rely on secondary sources, such as news reports, primarily to establish the timeline of events and relevant actors and examine their contemporaneous framing. My primary sources, often event participants or observers, add a lot of nuance to how the events unfolded, as well as the exact relationship between multiple actors and their motives and expectations. Many of the figures discussed in the book operated covertly and, hence, were often omitted from local reporting. The reports on those who took a more public role have been limited and, often, censored. No available open-source information could thus approximate the range of data collected while visiting the field. Still, I am aware of the biases that my interviewees may exhibit. Following the best practices in the field, I am transparent regarding both my sources and my estimation of information veracity, especially on sensitive topics, such as collaboration or responsibility for violence.[18] Finally, even though the book is based on the single-case study of Donbas, its analysis has theoretical implications beyond this case.

Summary of the Case

In spring of 2014 the region of Donbas became the target of multiple, competing claims from internal and external actors. One set of claims, articulated in Russia, was irredentist in nature.[19] From this standpoint, Donbas, like

---

[18] Mehmet Arslan et al., "Trends in Civil War Data: Geography, Organizations, and Events," in *What Do We Know about Civil Wars?*, ed. T. David Mason and Sara McLaughlin Mitchell (Lanham, MD: Rowman & Littlefield, 2023): 249 – 262.

[19] Following Chazan, "irredentism" refers here to "attempts by existing states to annex adjacent lands and the people who inhabit them in the name of historical, cultural, religious, linguistic or geographic affinity." See Naomi Chazan, "Conclusion: Irredentism, Separatism, and Nationalism,"

Crimea, was part of Russia's historic territory and populated by people with Russian identity characteristics.[20] Putin amplified these claims during his April 2014 press conference. By describing southeastern regions of Ukraine, including Donbas, as Novorossia ("New Russia") he revived a historical label, which has long been an object of revisionist fascination in nationalist and neo-imperial circles. In the words of the political scientist Gerard Toal, the mention of Novorossia "conveyed public legitimacy upon a separatist cause at the very moment armed pro-Russian filibuster groups were fighting under its banner in the Donbas."[21] Putin's insistence that Ukraine received the region from Russia only in the 1920s for "unclear" reasons signaled an interest in contesting its membership in the Ukrainian state.

The second set of claims on Donbas originated from internal actors and was secessionist in nature.[22] They ranged from demands for regional autonomy, particularly in economic and cultural affairs, to calls for complete separation from Ukraine. The main premise for these claims was the right of self-determination of the region's residents, which would have to be realized through a referendum on its future status. The secessionist nature of these demands, however, did not mean that these actors engaged in claim-making independently from any external influence. In fact, as Horowitz observes, irredentism and secessionism are often interrelated, especially if they represent the strategy of an external power. Irredentist states often seek to achieve their objectives by "encouraging movements by groups located in antagonistic states."[23]

The third set of claims came from the new government in Kyiv and its supporters in the region and represented a defensive reaction to Russia's expansionism. They rested on Ukraine's recognized right as a sovereign state

in *Irredentism and International Politics*, ed. Naomi Chazan (Boulder, CO: Lynne Rienner, 1991), 139.

[20] One Russian participant in the Donbas conflict, Aleksandr Zhuchkovskiy, defined it as a "Russian irredenta or a struggle of the Russian people of Ukraine, Belorussia, Kazakhstan, the Baltics and of other 'sovereigns' for reunification in the single Russian state." See Aleksandr Zhuchkovskiy, *85 dnei Slavianska* (Nizhniy Novgorod: Chernaia Sotnia, 2018), 13.

[21] Gerard Toal, *Near Abroad: Putin, the West, and the Contest over Ukraine and the Caucasus* (Oxford: Oxford University Press, 2017), 262.

[22] As Horowitz notes, the definitions of "separatist" and "secession" should be inclusive enough to account for the elasticity of demands on the state from those seeking autonomy or full independence of the region. Thus, any movements "seeking any territorially defined political change" aimed at changing the status of the group should be viewed as separatist. See Donald Horowitz, "Patterns of Ethnic Separatism," *Comparative Studies of Society and History* 23, no. 2 (1981), 168.

[23] Donald L. Horowitz, "Irredentas and Secessions: Adjacent Phenomena, Neglected Connections," in *Irredentism and International Politics*, ed. Naomi Chazan (Boulder, CO: Lynne Rienner, 1991), 15.

to maintain its territorial integrity and defend its borders. They were buttressed by support from the majority of the international community that warned against attempts to alter Ukraine's borders and refused to recognize any alteration of the status of the Autonomous Republic of Crimea.[24] The armed conflict in Donbas resulted from the confluence of these competing claims, which partially explains the difficulty of classifying it as an interstate or intrastate war.[25]

The initial phase of the armed conflict, from April to July 2014, took the form of irregular warfare between the Ukrainian state and affiliated substate actors, on one hand, and a broad range of militant formations pursuing separatist or irredentist objectives, on the other.[26] According to Balcells and Kalyvas, the main characteristics of irregular warfare include (1) asymmetry in the military capacity of the warring sides, (2) concentration of lightly armed challengers in specific localities, and (3) challengers' use of incursions and ambushes as primary fighting tactics.[27] The armed conflict in Donbas, at least in the first five months, fulfills each of these three classification criteria. Until August Ukrainian fighters outnumbered the militants of the conflict by a ratio of at least 2 to 1, while in key contested areas, like the Sloviansk agglomeration, this ratio was at least 5 to 1.[28] The Ukrainian

[24] *UN News*, "Backing Ukraine's Territorial Integrity, UN Assembly Declares Crimea Referendum Invalid," March 27, 2014, https://news.un.org/en/story/2014/03/464812.

[25] For the debate on proper classification of the conflict, see Jesse Driscoll, "Ukraine's Civil War: Would Accepting This Terminology Help Resolve the Conflict?," Policy Memo No. 572, Washington, DC: PONARS Eurasia, February 2019, https://www.ponarseurasia.org/ukraine-s-type-4-conflict-why-is-it-important-to-study-terminology-before-changing-it/; Tymofiy Brik, "Ukraine's 'Type 4' Conflict: Why Is It Important to Study Terminology before Changing It?," Policy Memo No. 575, Washington, DC: PONARS Eurasia, February 2019, https://www.ponarseurasia.org/wp-content/uploads/attachments/Pepm575_Brik_Feb2019-1.pdf.

[26] The term "militant" is used in the book to describe a broad range of actors, from local civilians to foreign mercenaries, who directly participated in the armed resistance to the Ukrainian state. Other terms to denote armed opposition, such as "rebels" and "insurgents," are used synonymously with "militants."

[27] Laia Balcells and Stathis Kalyvas, "Does Warfare Matter? Severity, Duration, and Outcomes of Civil Wars," *Journal of Conflict Resolution* 58, no. 8 (2014): 1390–1418.

[28] The Ukrainian forces deployed in the anti-terrorist operation (ATO) included the Armed Forces of Ukraine, the National Guard of Ukraine, the Security Service of Ukraine, the Border Guard, the Interior Ministry units, and volunteer battalions. According to the official Ministry of Defense data, by July 2014 in the entire area of the "counter-terrorism operation" there were 24,500 soldiers of the Armed Forces of Ukraine in addition to thousands of other security personnel for at least 30,000 in total. See A. Syrotenko, ed., *Voenni Aspekty Protydii "Hibrydnii" Ahresii* (Kyiv: National Defense University of Ukraine, 2020), 31. By mid-August, Ukraine had deployed about 40,000 troops, including 32,000 from the Armed Forces of Ukraine, up to 3,000 National Guard, up to 3,000 State Border Guard Service soldiers, and up to 2,000 personnel of Ukraine's Security Service. By contrast, the official Ukrainian government estimates of the militant forces amounted to 15,000 in July and 17,000 in August. See Ukraine Ministry of Defense, *Zbroini Syly Ukrainy, White Paper-2015* (Kyiv: Ukraine Ministry of Defense, 2015), 10. In the main area of operations around the Sloviansk agglomerations in early June there were at least 10,000 Ukrainian troops fighting about 1,500 militants. By early July the number of Ukrainian troops in the Sloviansk agglomeration increased to

forces consisted mostly of the regular trained army units under centralized command. Militants, by contrast, consisted of dozens of smaller battalions and groups, often staffed by local recruits without any prior military training and led by warlord commanders who eschewed any outside control.[29] Only in July, after local recruits incurred substantial losses, did more trained mercenaries and "vacationing" military personnel start arriving from Russia to maintain the fighting capacity of the militants.[30] The deployment of unmarked regular Russian troops to Donbas happened later, in August.

At first, a retired Russian FSB officer, Igor Girkin, tried to act as the supreme commander of these ragtag forces in Donetsk, but some key commanders, like retired Russian army officer Igor Bezler and the defector and SBU officer Oleksandr Khodakovsky, refused to follow his orders. Similarly, numerous individual armed groups in the Luhansk region resisted any centralized control from the self-proclaimed minister of defense Ihor Plotnitsky and pursued their own objectives. Insurgent units were dispersed in towns across the regions, but they lacked coordination and failed to form a contiguous front line. From the outset of the war, the Ukrainian forces deployed heavy military equipment, tanks and other armored vehicles, large-caliber artillery systems, multiple-launch rocket systems, and military aviation in the conflict area. This far surpassed the light armaments initially used by the militants, who started receiving small amounts of mechanized equipment and advanced munitions from Russia only in June.[31] The casualties

17,000, while the number of militants there increased to about 2,500. See Zhuchkovskiy, *85 dnei Slavianska*, 221–222. According to Girkin, the entire armed formation in the Sloviansk-Kramatorsk agglomeration totaled 2,000 people in July. There were also up to 400 militants under Igor Bezler's command in the Horlivka agglomeration. Cited in Anatoliy Tsyganok, *Donbass: Neokonchennaia voina. Grazhdanskaia voina na Ukraine (2014–2016): Russkiy vzgliad* (Moscow: AIRO-XXI, 2017), 352–353.

[29] The prevalence of local recruits in the insurgency was confirmed by the Ukrainian authorities. For example, the acting head of the Presidential Administration at the time of the conflict outbreak, Serhiy Pashynskyi, stated in June 2014, "There is a myth, which we created, about some arrived Russian terrorists who are fighting against Ukraine. There are certainly Russian mercenaries present, but they are not the main moving force of those processes, which are happening in Donbas. The local people are the main moving force." Sergei Ruzhynskiy, "Sergei Pashynskiy: My perestali byt natsiei rabov. My stali silnoi, dinamichnoi, russko-ukrainoiazychnoi natsiei," iPress, June 27, 2014, https://ipress.ua/ru/articles/sergey_pashynskyy_mi_perestaly_bit_natsyey _rabov_mi_staly_sylnoy_dynamychnoy_russkoukraynoyazichnoy_natsyey_72025.html.

[30] Ukraine Ministry of Defense, *Zbroini Syly Ukrainy*, 28.

[31] Michael Kofman et al., *Lessons from Russia's Operations in Crimea and Eastern Ukraine* (Santa Monica, CA: RAND, 2017), 44. Even the best equipped Sloviansk brigade during its operation between April and July 2014 had nineteen armored military vehicles (armored personnel carriers and infantry fighting vehicles), three self-propelled 120mm mortar guns 2S9 NONA, sixteen 82mm and 120mm mortars, one mobile short-range surface-to-air missile system Strela-10, five 23mm anti-aircraft guns ZU-32-2, five portable surface-to-air systems Igla, ten heavy machine guns, thirteen

on the pro-government side resulted from militant ambushes of Ukrainian military convoys, assaults on military bases or other infrastructure, such as airports, and strikes against combat aircrafts using man-portable surface-to-air missiles or rocket-propelled grenades.[32] These actions further reveal the use of tactics characteristic of insurgent forces. The fundamental asymmetry between the two sides allowed for a swift return of militant-controlled or contested towns in Donbas under Ukraine's control. From the start of the active phase of the government's counterinsurgency operation in May until late August, the Ukrainian forces cleared over two-thirds of the territories in Donetsk and Luhansk oblasts.[33]

Outline of the Argument

The initial success of the insurgency campaign depends on the ability of insurgents to achieve two primary objectives: (1) establish coercive control over a territory and (2) acquire the power to set rules and administer the region on behalf of its residents. Since secessionist insurgencies usually seek to form a new polity on top of the preexisting state, the first stage is conceptualized here as a *state-founding* phase. It requires a militant organization to gain a comparative coercive advantage in a particular locality and issue a competing sovereign claim over it. The second stage is conceptualized as a *state-building* process. It involves the use of preexisting and the development of new institutions for the purpose of governance over a defined locality.[34] While coercive dominance is usually a precondition for the militants' ability to govern, the two stages may overlap, especially if insurgents face resistance from a target state.

In Donbas, the *state-founding* stage started on April 6 with the capture of government buildings in Donetsk and Luhansk and the proclamation of

grenade launchers, five dozen short-range rocket launchers of various types, and up to 2,200 rifles, carbines, and machine guns. See Zhuchkovskiy, *85 dnei Slavianska*, 346.

[32] Ukraine Ministry of Defense, *The White Book of Anti-Terrorist Operation in the East of Ukraine in 2014–2016* (Kyiv: Ukraine Ministry of Defense, 2017), https://nuou.org.ua/assets/journals/bila_knyga/white-book-ato.pdf.

[33] Ibid., 30. The asymmetry in military capacity of the warring sides was corrected with the deployment of 4,000 Russian troops on August 24, 2014. They quickly stopped the Ukrainian advance and reversed some Ukrainian gains, which resulted in the signing of the Minsk Accords on September 5, 2014.

[34] Mazzuca distinguishes between these two stages in analyzing the success and failure of early Latin American states. See Sebastian Mazzuca, *Latecomer State Formation: Political Geography and Capacity Failure in Latin America* (New Haven, CT: Yale University Press, 2021).

two entities—the DNR and the LNR—on the territory of two preexisting Ukrainian provinces. The holding of a pseudo-referendum on independence in small and large towns of Donbas on May 11, contrary to the rulings of the Ukrainian government, demonstrated militant success in gaining coercive dominance across the region. The *state-building* phase started shortly after Girkin's capture of Sloviansk on April 12 with attempts to replace or subordinate municipal authorities to local militant leaders. The announcement of DNR and LNR governments in mid-May accelerated the takeover of the administration of most towns of the region by separatist activists and repurposing of existing governance institutions for their needs.

The Ukrainian government recognized the loss of control over most of Donbas on its first official map of the "anti-terrorist operation" (ATO) issued on May 20.[35] According to the government's own estimates, however, the total number of militants there ranged from 2,500 in April to 7,000 in May.[36] This was a minuscule number for a territory consisting of at least eight large urban agglomerations with over five million residents.[37] Neither an external capture by outside agents nor local armed mobilization can explain such a sudden removal of Ukraine's sovereign presence from the region.

This book argues that the completion of each of the two stages of secessionist insurgency in Donbas became possible through a cooperative effort of outside actors from Russia, local militants, and local civilians, such as party and civic activists, business entrepreneurs, and municipal authorities. Any civilian opposition to insurgent control within the region was quickly suppressed through the joint efforts of the locals and Russian coercive agents. The book's micro-level approach to the study of the conflict allows us to identify four main mechanisms of the separatist capture of Donbas. First, militants engaged in assaults on symbols of state coercive dominance, such as police stations, SBU offices, prosecutor general offices, and military bases, located within towns. The insurgency started with the capture of SBU buildings in Donetsk and Luhansk on April 6, followed by the seizure of police stations and the SBU office in Sloviansk on April 12. This allowed militants to capture thousands of firearms and stockpiles of

---

[35] See ATO map from May 20, 2014, prepared by the National Security and Defense Council, https://media.slovoidilo.ua/maps/nsdc/2014/05/large/map-nsdc-2014-05-20-uk-w3000.jpg.

[36] Ukraine Ministry of Defense, *Zbroini Syly Ukrainy*.

[37] For the list of urban agglomerations in Donbas, see World Bank Group, *Cities in Europe and Central Asia*; Hryhoriy Pidhrushnyi and Oleksandr Vrublevskyi, "Miski Aglomeratsii Donbasu," in *Aglomeratsii: Mizhnarodnyi Dosvid, Tendentsii, Vysnovky dlia Ukrainy. Analitychna Zapyska*, ed. Nina Natalenko (Kyiv: Instytut Hromadianskoho Suspilstva, 2017), 81–103.

ammunition.[38] In some towns, like Lyman, militants abstained from capturing police stations but pressured local police chiefs to let them inside and to surrender available arms. In others, like the SBU building in Kramatorsk, the security personnel preemptively moved out of their offices, which militants then used as their operational bases. The second mechanism was pressuring local law enforcement to endorse militants and acquiesce to their rule. To this end, there were joint press conferences of police chiefs and militant leaders, while the police and militants organized joint street patrols and together guarded checkpoints under separatist banners. Third, checkpoints became ubiquitous throughout the region in April and May. As sites of random searches and interrogations of local civilians, they became symbols of coercive dominance and consolidation of territorial control by separatist rulers. Widespread compliance with their demands also signaled the acceptance of militants' newly acquired coercive power by the wider public. The final mechanism was the use of local civilians to pressure Ukrainian military units. This included obstructing the movement of Ukrainian military columns, blocking the exits of military bases to prevent the deployment of troops, and picketing weapons depots to prevent the transfer of arms.

As I detail in Chapter 3, Russian actors made a crucial contribution at the stage of *state founding*, particularly in consolidating separatist control over the towns outside two capital cities. Densely urbanized terrain became an enabling factor that allowed a small number of militants to exercise influence over towns where they had minimal or no permanent presence. The proximity of towns clustered in Donbas in urban agglomerations increased militants' mobility and created a contagion effect that led to emulation of separatist tactics across multiple localities.[39] At the same time, friction associated with greater distance impeded the spread of insurgent control.[40] The book shows that there was no sustained and sizable militant presence in those areas that were further away from the main militant strongholds or from the border with Russia. Localities in Donbas

---

[38] Only in Luhansk did SBU militants acquire 2,000 automatic firearms and 2.5 million bullets. See Mykola Lytvyn, *Linia Rozmezhuvannia* (Kyiv: Hamzyn, 2019), 218.

[39] On the significance of geographic proximity for contagion, see Mark Beissinger, "Structure and Example in Modular Political Phenomenon: The Diffusion of Bulldozer/Rose/Orange/Tulip Revolutions," *Perspective on Politics* 5, no. 2 (June 2007): 259–276.

[40] On friction of the terrain as an obstacle to state-making, see James C. Scott, *The Art of Not Being Governed: An Anarchist History of Upland Southeast Asia* (New Haven, CT: Yale University Press, 2009).

that remained outside militant control included Svatove, on the border with Kharkiv oblast, and the Pokrovsk agglomeration, on the border with Dnipropetrovsk oblast. They witnessed the rise of grassroots anti-separatist resistance, which stopped separatist challenges.

In most urban agglomerations where militant coercive dominance was successfully established, however, the state-building stage immediately imposed governing challenges on the militants. They suddenly needed to ensure continuity in performing a variety of tasks, such as provision of public goods and services, operation of utilities, and timely payment of benefits and wages to pensioners and public employees. To achieve long-term coercive dominance, they had to acquire credibility in governance. Although, as I demonstrate in Chapter 3, Russian agents contributed to setting up basic institutions of the two self-declared states in Donetsk and Luhansk, they lacked region-specific knowledge or expertise in running dozens of towns across the region. The primary responsibility for this fell on municipal authorities and other local elites familiar with the specifics of town governance. As detailed in Chapter 6, town leaders adopted various strategies in response to the expectations of continued administration under militant control. The cooperative responses ranged from enthusiastic collaboration to a more cautious hedging, while noncooperative strategies ranged from sabotage to active resistance. Finally, exit became another tactic for some town leaders. Their response was conditioned by how much militants controlled their town. In cases of full or partial control, local administrators were more likely to adopt a cooperative response. Where militant presence was absent, as Chapter 8 shows, local administrators initiated or supported resistance against a potential separatist challenge. The success of the *state-founding* stage, achieved under the guidance of Russian agents, was a critical precondition for the start of the *state-building* stage.

Contribution and Implications

The book seeks to contribute both to existing studies of the armed conflict in Donbas and broader literature on external intervention and intrastate conflict. It adds to earlier studies of Russia's role in starting the insurgency in Donbas by identifying the exact mechanisms through which Russian agents influenced the early course of the conflict. The existing accounts explain Russia's causal primacy by focusing on individual subversive actors, like Girkin, their possible ties to the Russian government, and Moscow's assistance from the start of the conflict.[41] This, however, provides inconclusive evidence of Russia's contribution since there is also substantial evidence of the prevalence of locals among militants in other towns motivated by internally generated grievances.[42] Through a micro-level investigation of the conflict dynamics in urban agglomerations of Donbas, this book shows the broader impact of Russian agents beyond the agglomeration centers where they were stationed. Although the locals prevailed among insurgent recruits, Russian agents were decisive in exerting and maintaining coercive pressure on local elites, establishing the command-and-control structure of militant units, assigning roles and responsibilities to local commanders, and operational planning and execution. The arrival of Russian actors in early April was crucial in reviving the waning separatist mobilization. As the book documents, despite the initial strength of anti-Kyiv grievances among Donbas locals, the first phase of protests was demobilized through an accommodative strategy of local elites. Meanwhile, Girkin's intervention in April led to a noticeable reversal in the rhetoric of some town leaders from endorsing a united Ukraine to articulating separatist demands. The resolutions of some city councils, which endorsed the holding of the secessionist referendum, were adopted only in April under pressure from armed separatists. Russian agents then spearheaded the second mobilization wave in April and May 2014.

The book offers new evidence regarding the role of subnational elites, particularly municipal authorities, in smaller towns targeted by the militants. It conclusively shows that local elites neither responded to insurgency in a coordinated fashion nor sought to mobilize residents against Kyiv as part of bargaining with the new government.[43] Instead of pursuing an intentional confrontational strategy at the start, local elites were reactive to protest outbreaks and sought to demobilize them through token concessions. Moreover, once faced with an armed challenge, their responses ranged from collaboration to resistance to exit. My research yielded no evidence of

---

[41] See Wilson, "The Donbas in 2014"; Jakob Hauter, "Forensic Conflict Studies: Making Sense of War in the Social Media Age," *Media, War & Conflict* 16, no. 2 (2023): 153–172.

[42] This point is made particularly clearly in Arel and Driscoll, *Ukraine's Unnamed War*. Also see Matveeva (2017) and Zhukov, "Trading Hard Hats for Combat Helmets."

[43] For arguments about the centrality of elite bargaining to explaining the conflict, see Arel and Driscoll, *Ukraine's Unnamed War*; Platonova (2021); Martin Laryš and Emil Souleimanov, "Delegated Rebellions as an Unwanted Byproduct of Subnational Elites' Miscalculation: A Case Study of Donbas," *Problems of Post-Communism* 69, no. 2 (2022): 155–165.

attempts to coordinate elite actions across towns and, instead, found that their behavior was conditioned by factors endogenous to their localities, such as the strength of the militant coercive presence. Furthermore, current studies of elite impact on the conflict focus mainly on major business players, like Rinat Akhmetov and Ihor Kolomoiskyi, or prominent political figures, like Viktor Yanukovych, Oleksandr Yefremov, and Henadiy Kernes.[44] By contrast, this book points to town-level elite actors as vital in either assisting or preventing separatist state-building. These individuals were unknown at the national or even regional level, and their impact has not been recognized in the academic literature on the conflict.[45]

The book extends arguments from the literature on asymmetric conflict, secessionist insurgencies, and internationalized civil wars. First, it builds on prior findings regarding geographic aspects of the conflict, particularly the role of population concentration, to show how clustering of the population in several major closely located urban agglomerations facilitates a quick capture of the region.[46] Proximity of urban centers increases mobility of militants, lowers their transportation costs, and allows them to exercise indirect coercive influence over neighboring towns without being physically present. Second, the book contributes to the burgeoning literature on urban insurgencies to identify conditions under which urban insurgency survives.[47] It shows that highly urbanized terrain may enable quick diffusion of insurgent activities from one town to another, but sustaining insurgent control requires establishing an alliance with local administrators or sympathetic elite actors. Third, while most of the existing studies of external interventions examine the impact of third parties on ongoing armed conflicts, this book investigates their contribution to the conflict's outbreak.[48] It identifies Russia's role in tactical and ideological preparation of the militants,

---

[44] Quentin Buckholz, "The Dogs That Didn't Bark: Elite Preferences and the Failure of Separatism in Kharkiv and Dnipropetrovsk," *Problems of Post-Communism* 66, no. 3 (2019): 151–160; Nitsova, "Why the Difference?"

[45] One notable exception is Kimitaka Matsuzato, "The Donbas War and the Politics in Cities on the Front: Mariupol and Kramatorsk," *Nationalities Papers* 46, no. 6 (2018): 1008–1027.

[46] Monica Duffy Toft, "Indivisible Territory, Geographic Concentration, and Ethnic War," *Security Studies* 12, no. 2 (2002): 82–119; Nils Weidmann, "Geography as Motivation and Opportunity: Group Concentration and Ethnic Conflict," *Journal of Conflict Resolution* 53, no. 4 (2009): 526–543.

[47] Pioneering treatment of urban insurgency is Paul Staniland's "Cities on Fire: Social Mobilization, State Policy, and Urban Insurgency," *Comparative Political Studies* 43, no. 12 (2010): 1623–1649; for a recent study, see Anthony King, *Urban Warfare in the Twenty-First Century* (London: Polity, 2021).

[48] For critical evaluation of this aspect of scholarship on external intervention, see Patrick Regan, "Interventions into Civil War: A Retrospective Survey with Prospective Ideas," *Civil Wars* 12, no. 4 (2010): 456–476.

consolidation of territorial control and coercive dominance, and separatist institution-building.

Finally, the book engages the literature on rebel governance by showing how rebels structure their interaction with local officials as well as political and civic activists to establish a new political order.[49] It examines ways in which militants dealt with governance tasks in towns under their control, explores how they used preexisting institutions or created new ones to meet their goals, outlines strategies of elite actors in response to the separatist challenge, and distinguishes between resulting governing arrangements. These arrangements varied mainly in how much rebels played a leading or supplementary role in governance and allowed civilian actors to maintain autonomy in decision-making. The book, thus, reinforces the notion that rebel-controlled space may still exhibit competing or complementary types of authority exercised simultaneously by multiple actors.[50] At the same time, the book shows that the level of insurgent coercive control restricted the range of strategies available to local elites. In most cases, by establishing coercive control, militants acquired some administrative control too. In contrast, in those towns where rebels failed to dominate coercively, local elites opted for sabotage or resistance to rebel rule. Overall, the choices of elite and civic actors were conditioned by the strength of the militant presence in their localities. Yet they showed an independent capacity to constrain or even undermine militants during both *state-founding* and *state-building* stages.

Data Collection

The centrality of urban centers and their spatial characteristics for the onset of insurgency in Donbas dictated my field research strategies and data collection process. During my field research I visited sixteen towns in Donetsk oblast and five towns in Luhansk oblast, which belonged to six urban

---

[49] For recent examples of rebel governance studies, see Zachariah Mampilly, *Rebel Rulers: Insurgent Governance and Civilian Life during War* (Ithaca, NY: Cornell University Press, 2011); Paul Staniland, "States, Insurgents, and Wartime Political Orders," *Perspectives on Politics* 10, no. 2 (2012): 243 – 264; Arjona, *Rebelocracy*; Reyko Huang, *The Wartime Origins of Democratization: Civil War, Rebel Governance, and Political Regimes* (Cambridge: Cambridge University Press, 2016); Nelson Kasfir, Georg Frerks, and Niels Terpstra, "Introduction: Armed Groups and Multi-layered Governance," *Civil Wars* 19, no. 3 (2017): 257–278. For a literature review, see Cyanne E. Loyle et al., "New Directions in Rebel Governance Research," *Perspectives on Politics* 21, no. 1 (March 2023): 264–276.

[50] Loyle et al., "New Directions in Rebel Governance Research," 266.

agglomerations.[51] They were all under Ukraine's control during the time of my field research.[52] While I was aware of the variation in the intensity of separatist presence in some of these towns prior to the start of research, I learned about the precise strength of collaboration or resistance there only during my research in the field. Hence, while my sample of towns included those where I expected to see variation in the behavior of local authorities and residents, my goal was to collect primary data on all urban agglomerations in Ukraine-controlled area of Donbas at the time of research.

The exclusion of towns under separatist control from the sample should not affect its main findings regarding the origins and dynamics of the insurgency campaign. The prewar protest mobilization occurred similarly across the region; the locus of fighting, at the outset, was in Sloviansk and neighboring towns examined closely in the book. The territorial control of the *state-founding* stage was first established by militants in the Sloviansk agglomeration and spread to neighboring agglomerations from there. Apart from Donbas, I conducted additional research in Odesa and Kharkiv—two other Ukrainian cities outside Donbas with strong pro-Russian mobilization in 2014. Despite successful early organization and street actions, separatist groups failed to seize control of these cities. I will analyze the reasons for this failure by comparing background conditions, mobilization dynamics, Russia's strategies, and local elite choices in these two cities and the towns of Donbas seized by separatists.

Between December 2014 and July 2019, I made over a dozen research trips to the towns of Donetsk and Luhansk provinces. During my visits I gathered detailed information about the recent political history of each town, its socioeconomic characteristics, and key political and economic actors involved in its governance. I have also created town-specific timelines of main events preceding the outbreak of the conflict and the developments there once the separatist uprising began. My focus was on the initial episodes of popular mobilization, such as rallies, marches, pickets, or self-defense initiatives, their organizers and participants, and the change in their narrative

---

[51] During my field research, conducted between December 2014 and July 2019, I gathered data in the following towns: (1) in Donetsk oblast: Sloviansk, Kramatorsk, Druzhkivka, Kostiantynivka, Lyman, Siversk, Toretsk, Bakhmut, Soledar, Chasiv Yar, Dobropillia, Pokrovsk, Myrnohrad, Novohrodivka, Selydove, Mariupol; (2) in Luhansk oblast: Lysychansk, Sieverodonetsk, Rubizhne, Svatove, Starobilsk.

[52] Since the start of the full-scale Russian invasion on February 24, 2022, eleven of these towns have come under occupation of the Russian troops (Lyman, Bakhmut, Soledar, Mariupol, Novohrodivka, Selydove, Lysychansk, Sieverodonetsk, Rubizhne, Svatove, Starobilsk). As of November 1, 2024, only one—Lyman—had been liberated by the Ukrainian army.

structures and demands. I paid particular attention to the timing and mechanisms of their militarization; their initial use of violence and its perpetrators; their tactics and selection of targets; and the response of the local public, local authorities, law enforcement, and political activists. I also examined symbolic ways in which they asserted control; the use of separatist imagery in government buildings, local media, and official celebrations; and the presence of separatist leaders during local council or executive committee meetings. I further investigated the role of external actors before and during the insurgency and the ways they and other armed actors interacted with local civilians and administrators. Finally, I explored patterns of resistance to separatist activities, their organizers and tactics, sources of support, and overall impact.

Most of the data on individual towns was collected from primary sources through in-person or online unstructured interviews. As a bilingual citizen of Ukraine, I used Ukrainian and Russian languages interchangeably depending on the preferences of my interlocutors. This was particularly important given local sensitivity regarding language choice, which is often viewed through the political prism. It also helped to establish direct rapport with the interviewees and overcome some unease given my affiliation with a U.S. university. Before the trip to each town, I gathered information about journalists or civic activists and politicians and municipal officials who played a visible role during the insurgency's mobilization and armed phases. After my meetings with them I used the snowball method to identify and approach relevant individuals mentioned during the interviews. For each town I conducted in-depth interviews with seven to ten individuals, each of whom observed the events from different vantage points. This allowed me to form a more multifaceted understanding of the developments and include divergent perspectives in my analysis. Although most of the people interviewed for the book backed the Ukrainian side, at least a third were either openly supportive of the separatist movement or took a neutral stance at the start of the armed conflict.

My interviewees can be grouped into five distinct categories. The first category included individuals who worked at various levels of local government, from mayors and their deputies to town council members. The second category included public-sector employees, such as schoolteachers and school principals and various public servants. The third category included civil society representatives, such as journalists, employees of nongovernmental organizations, and volunteers. The fourth category included business owners, entrepreneurs, and workers in private enterprises. The fifth category included representatives of political parties and other activists affiliated with political organizations.

Since most of the interviews were conducted at least four years after the start of the armed conflict, many interviewees had difficulty providing the exact timeline or sequence of events. Still, they offered detailed recollections about developments in their cities in 2014, explained motives for their actions, identified key actors on opposing sides and their roles, and described shifting perceptions about the level of government or separatist control. For most respondents the start of the armed conflict was a highly consequential and emotional event, which was more likely to form durable memories and make them immune to distortions.[53] Still, the media coverage and intense political debates about the nature of these events might have induced greater selectivity or introduced bias in their recollections.[54] Hence, I sought to cross-check testimonies among respondents and with contemporaneous news reports to establish the exact sequence of events and positions of decision-makers. I also gathered hundreds of videos from each town posted on YouTube by local users at the time or shared with me during my field visits.[55] Video recordings became a critical supplement to news reports, which were usually light on details. They allowed me to observe rallies, marches, council meetings, and other gatherings where participants articulated their views and demands. They also helped to estimate the scale of mobilization and composition of mass gatherings and to identify organizers and main speakers, their use of political symbols, the framing of their appeals, and their interactions with others. I also looked for a paper trail behind these events left in local newspapers or in official documents archived by local governments, such as city council resolutions, reports on city council meetings, and statements of key local officials. Finally, I relied on Ukrainian- and Russian-language memoirs and recollections of key decision-makers and event participants included in books or published in the media.

[53] M. A. Conway, et al., "The Formation of Flashbulb Memories," *Memory & Cognition* 22 (1994): 326–343; U. Hepp et al., "Inconsistency in Reporting Potentially Traumatic Events," *British Journal of Psychiatry* 188 (2006): 278–283.

[54] L. Kvavilashvili et al., "Consistency of Flashbulb Memories of September 11 over Long Delays: Implications for Consolidation and Wrong Time Slice Hypothesis," *Journal of Memory and Language* 61 (2009): 556–572.

[55] The supplementary materials, including videos, collected during research for this book are stored in Harvard Dataverse, dataverse.harvard.edu/dataverse/kudelia.

Overview of the Book

My arguments and evidence are presented in nine chapters. Chapter 1 outlines the conceptual framework of the book, distinguishing between two stages of the secessionist insurgency—acquiring monopoly or comparative advantage in the use of violence (state founding) and imposition of rules and institutions necessary for governance (state building). It then offers a detailed analysis of the impact of urban terrain on the spread of the insurgency and relates it to the methodology of this study based on micro-level investigation of conflict dynamics in individual towns in Donbas.

Chapter 2 focuses on the reasons for Russia's armed intervention in Ukraine in 2014, which is analyzed in the context of the literature on external interventions in armed conflicts. It argues that Moscow's choice to launch covert occupation of parts of Ukraine and instigate separatist uprisings should be viewed as an outcome of a long-term interstate rivalry. This rivalry was rooted in the refusal of Russian political elites and the public to accept Ukraine's state boundaries and its sovereign agency following Soviet disintegration.

Chapter 3 extends the focus on Moscow's decision-making by examining the mechanisms of the Russian occupation of Crimea and their adaptation in Donbas. It identifies both continuities and discontinuities in tactics and actors across the two regions.[56] It shows that Russian agents came to play a decisive role in establishing coercive dominance over most of Donbas. They also prevailed in the newly created governance structures of the two self-proclaimed republics. Still, the small number of Russian coercive agents among militia and their reliance on incumbent municipal authorities suggest that local actors, at the very least, helped to sustain the insurgency campaign. This sets the stage for subsequent chapters, which shift the book's focus to the choices and strategies of municipal elites and local activists.

Chapter 4 examines the goals and motives behind pro-Russian mobilization across the region in February through May 2014. The chapter demonstrates that violence by separatist activists became a common tactic used against pro-Ukrainian demonstrations before the arrival of pro-Russian agents in the region and accelerated in intensity afterward. Chapter 5 traces the origins of separatist militia to the initial formation of self-defense groups under patronage of municipal authorities in January and February 2014.

---

[56] Toal, *Near Abroad*, 251 points to the shared "theatrics of secession" in Crimea and Donbas based on the same "script" but avoids giving specifics on the differences in the implementation of the two "scripts."

The chapter also explores how violence against pro-Ukrainian activists and local officials opposed to the separatist movement was used as a signaling device to show coercive dominance of the militants. Chapter 6 sheds greater light on the strategies of municipal elites faced with the separatist challenge. It examines how their public rhetoric changed in response to perceived power shifts and shows that there was no single coordinated strategy that local elites adopted. Rather, it depended on the level of coercive control exercised in towns by militants. Elites adopted cooperative strategies in areas where militants had a clear coercive dominance. They were more likely to engage in sabotage or resistance in towns where militants were either small in number or absent altogether.

Chapter 7 shifts attention from coercive to administrative control and explores how militants sought to subordinate existing state institutions to the needs of separatist governance. It shows that police and media were the two institutions that militants managed to capture successfully across all cases where they had coercive control, but the extent to which they controlled other institutions varied significantly. While in some cases local administrators agreed to govern together with the militants in a power-sharing mode, in others, militants and local administrators formed parallel governance structures, which rarely intersected. In yet other cases, the town leaders continued governing without any significant interference on the part of the militants in what I characterize as governance by default. In rare cases, militant leaders also assumed the main administrative responsibilities. Local officials proved indispensable for consolidation of separatist rule, but in several towns they either sabotaged separatist initiatives or openly defied and resisted them.

Chapter 8 offers an in-depth analysis of the examples of elite resistance and sabotage, which either destabilized separatist rule or prevented the town's capture. In some instances, this resistance was led by municipal leaders; in others it was initiated by local community members. The capacity to use force against separatists, however, was crucial, for preventing the loss of Ukraine's sovereign control over towns.

Chapter 9 moves the analysis to Kharkiv and Odesa, which experienced the strongest pro-Russian mobilization outside Donbas. It explores separatists' failure to pose a credible challenge by examining the combined effect of different background conditions, such as geography and public preferences, and agency-level choices. In the conclusion I summarize the book's main findings regarding the relative impact of external and internal variables at various stages of the secessionist insurgency in Donbas.

Chapter 1
How Was Donbas Occupied?

Mariupol, a port city of almost half a million people located on the Azov Sea, became one of the first targets of the invading Russian army in February 2022. The simultaneous advance of the Russian troops from three sides led to the city's full encirclement by early March. The two-month siege of Mariupol resulted in the demolition of its residential areas and of the entire economic infrastructure. By preliminary estimates, at least twenty-five thousand residents were killed or died due to malnutrition, cold, or lack of access to medical services.[1] Even after Russian forces took control of the city, over three hundred Ukrainian fighters continued their resistance from within the city's metallurgical plant, Azovstal. Their negotiated extraction from the plant began only on May 16.

The intensity and duration of the fighting for Mariupol in spring of 2022 stood in stark contrast to its quick separatist takeover eight years earlier. Then the city fell under de facto separatist control in less than a month of demonstrations and altercations with the police and Ukrainian military units. In April 2014, local separatist leaders and activists first seized the city council and forced most administrators out of the building. They then staged assaults on the Ukrainian military base and police station, which resulted in the withdrawal of most Ukrainian forces from the city in May. Militants subordinated the remaining police units and attempted to take over the reins of administrative power. Yet they failed to subordinate local government or prevent the nationwide presidential elections in the city on May 24. Hence, Mariupol remained a contested city in which separatists acquired coercive dominance but could not influence its administration. Their presence in Mariupol proved short-lived. In early June, a small contingent of Ukrainian forces brought Mariupol back under Ukraine's control after several hours of sporadic fighting.

---

[1] An AP investigation suggested that the actual death toll might be three times higher. See Lori Hinnat, Vasilisa Stepanenko, Sarah El Deeb, and Elizaveta Tilna, "Russia Scrubs Mariupol's Ukraine Identity, Builds on Death," *Associated Press*, December 22, 2022, https://apnews.com/article/russia-ukraine-war-erasing-mariupol-499dceae43ed77f2ebfe750ea99b9ad9.

Seize the City, Undo the State. Serhiy Kudelia, Oxford University Press. © Oxford University Press (2025).
DOI: 10.1093/9780197795576.003.0002

The example of Mariupol illustrates some of the main arguments of the book. First, in 2014 the ability of a small number of poorly equipped militants to quickly capture towns the size of Mariupol rested on the vacuum of coercive power that emerged in urban centers across the region. Police forces either were passive and demoralized or enthusiastically sided with the militants. Second, the seizure of the region by militants entailed two distinct stages: (1) establishing coercive dominance on behalf of the self-proclaimed republics and (2) exercising administrative control in accordance with the new rules and ideology. In some towns militants completed both stages; in others they succeeded in only one; elsewhere they could not finalize either of the two. Third, while the role of local actors varied in each town, their availability and active collaboration with Russian agents was a crucial precondition for the success of the separatist challenge. Fourth, the high urban density of Donbas meant that towns became primary targets for separatist challengers. Full control over several centrally positioned towns allowed them to exert influence over neighboring areas and gave the insurgency its spatial breadth. Proximity to key separatist strongholds, such as Sloviansk and Horlivka, also proved crucial for effective militant coordination and increased the strength of the separatist presence there.

This book argues that the success of the armed uprising in Donbas in 2014 required both the provision of material and ideational assistance from Russia *and* organizational capacity within the region to launch and sustain the separatist challenge. The limited intervention of small mercenary groups led by Russian agents would have failed to put the region, entirely or even partially, under separatist control had they failed to mobilize a larger insurgent campaign. To achieve this, they relied on networks of civic groups and activists that became the movement's "social basis."[2] They also depended on the reciprocal response of local municipal authorities who had to ensure administrative continuity. Separatist militias, for their part, had no centralized coordination or sufficient resource base to sustain their challenge over the longer term. They relied on strong vertical ties to their respective communities but lacked horizontal ties needed to conduct an insurgency campaign across a large region. They depended on Russian actors to resolve the collective action problem and overcome a factionalized command structure that often put them at odds with each other.

---

[2] Staniland defines social bases as "structures of collective action and social interaction in a society." See Paul Staniland, *Networks of Rebellion: Explaining Insurgent Cohesion and Collapse* (Ithaca, NY: Cornell University Press, 2014), ch. 2, p. 17.

The absence of any visible defection among municipal authorities or local businesses at the onset of the conflict posed another problem to separatist leaders. There were no prominent political figures or experienced government officials in the governments of self-proclaimed republics. Their two public leaders—thirty-two-year-old Denis Pushylin in Donetsk and forty-four-year-old Valeriy Bolotov in Luhansk—were minor entrepreneurs who had never been involved in politics prior to 2014. The same was true for little-known separatist activists in other towns across Donbas. Even if some town mayors might have sympathized with their demands, they had no reason to share power with them.

Russian intervention thus helped to solve three central problems of the separatist movement in Donbas: coordination, organization, and mobilization. First, Russian militia commanders, like Girkin in Sloviansk and Bezler in Horlivka, became focal points for coordinating smaller, preexisting separatist groups from multiple towns.[3] They also provided replicable action templates for removing Ukraine's sovereign presence on the town level. Second, Russian mercenaries and undercover agents possessed crucial organizational and military skills to turn protest actions into an armed insurgency. Third, their appearance in Donbas raised public expectations about the likelihood of a low-cost secession from Ukraine following the Crimean example. This, in turn, encouraged recruitment into the insurgency and participation in separatist initiatives, like the referendum. No less important, however, was the backdrop of the insurgent campaign.

The arrival of Girkin's armed unit in Sloviansk moved the locus of separatist uprising westward, from administrative capitals like Donetsk and Luhansk to a peripheral, midsize town further away from the Russian border. This was a risky and unconventional strategy. The longer distance to Russia complicated both provision of arms and escape routes. Its proximity to government-controlled regions of Kharkiv and Dnipropetrovsk made it more vulnerable to Ukrainian government forces. Prior to Girkin's arrival, Sloviansk also lacked a large and well-organized separatist movement. The few rallies held there in March attracted several hundred people, mainly

---

[3] Igor Girkin (also known by his nom de guerre, Igor Strelkov) was a Russian citizen who, from 1993, served in the Russian armed forces and, from 1996, in the Federal Security Service. He retired at the rank of FSB colonel in 2013. See Khronika 'Russkoi Vesny', "Biografia Igoria Ivanovicha Strelkova," February 23, 2016, https://istrelkov.ru/9-biografiya-igorya-ivanovicha-strelkova.html. Igor Bezler (also known under his call sign, "Bes") was a Russian citizen and a career officer of the Russian armed forces. He was educated in the Russian Military Academy in Moscow in the early 1990s and stationed in military bases across Russia. He moved to Horlivka in Donetsk oblast after his retirement in 2003 but never received Ukrainian citizenship. See RIA Novosti, "Biografia Igoria Bezlera," August 28, 2014, https://ria.ru/20140828/1021803991.html.

local Communist Party activists. The scale of public mobilization there was significantly lower than in Donetsk or even nearby Kramatorsk. The Sloviansk mayor, Nelia Shtepa, distanced herself from communist-led separatist rallies and did not endorse their demands. The town's main advantage for Russian insurgency organizers was its proximity to other towns and urban agglomerations in Donbas. This proved essential for upscaling the separatist challenge from an insurrection based in two administrative centers to a regional revolt engulfing dozens of towns across the region.

Seizing Territory

Russia's initial limited intervention in Donbas led by only several dozen skilled individuals could not, by itself, accomplish the central task of an insurgent campaign: establishing control over the territory.[4] Mampilly defines it as the "ability of a rebel group to exert its power over a defined territorial space and to induce collaboration from the civilian population living within this area."[5] Territorial control is crucial for achieving three main objectives of the successful insurgency. First, since insurgency represents "a process of competitive state-building," having control of the terrain is a precondition for removal of the state's sovereign authority, in both symbolic and physical terms, and assertion of the insurgent group's coercive dominance.[6] Second, a sustained insurgency campaign requires collaboration or, at the least, compliance of the local populace. Full territorial control increases the likelihood that local residents will collaborate with the dominant side.[7] Third, control is a prerequisite for insurgents to form new governance structures or convert the existing ones for their purposes.[8] Effective governance requires the ability to enforce new rules of political and social order, provide basic services to civilians, and fulfill financial obligations to public-sector employees and pensioners.[9]

The high urban density of the Donbas region was another factor that enabled quick extension of militant rule across localities. Two Donbas

---

[4] Kalyvas, *The Logic of Violence in Civil War*.
[5] Mampilly, *Rebel Rulers*, 59.
[6] Kalyvas, *The Logic of Violence in Civil War*, 218.
[7] Ibid., ch. 4.
[8] Mampilly, *Rebel Rulers*, 63.
[9] Hence, rebel governance is defined as "the set of actions insurgents engage in to regulate the social, political, and economic life of non-combatants during war." See Ana Arjona, Nelson Kasfir, and Zachariah Mampilly, eds., *Rebel Governance in Civil War* (Cambridge: Cambridge University Press, 2015), 3.

provinces—Donetsk and Luhansk—constitute over 52,000 square kilometers; their total population prior to the conflict was about six and a half million people. Based on studies of external interventions, establishing effective population security and control in the region by a foreign power would have required stationing at least 100,000 troops there.[10] In a peaceful context, even basic policing tasks under the occupation regime would have required at least thirty thousand security personnel. But in a dense urban environment with a supportive or neutral population and indifferent police forces, a handful of militants acting simultaneously in each of the neighboring towns could seize a large area. This tactic was adopted in Donbas. As Oleksandr Turchynov, an acting president of Ukraine in spring 2014, explained in his recollections, "Since Donbas consisted of numerous towns, creeping separatism turned into a major problem for us. In a town with residents sympathetic to separatists ten militants captured the mayor's office or police stations facing no resistance and raised [the] Russian flag—and that's it, the media reported that the town joined 'DNR' or 'LNR.'"[11]

The exact mechanisms of establishing control might have differed across towns. In some, such as Sloviansk and Kramatorsk, it started with the storming of police stations. In others, such as Mariupol and Donetsk, it started with the capture of municipal government buildings. In Toretsk, Lysychansk, and yet other cases, there was no capture of buildings, but town authorities and law enforcement colluded with the militants and engaged in close collaboration with them. Overall, the separatist claims of control over the entire region of Donbas depended on their successful seizure and governance of its urban agglomerations.

Insurgency as State Creation

A secessionist insurgency is an attempt to replace a state's sovereign authority over a particular territory through violent means. Its ultimate objective is the formation of a new state that will exist and govern in its place. Unless

[10] The standard ratio for maintaining external occupation regime is 20 troops per 1,000 residents, which would have put the size of the military contingent required in Donbas at over 120,000. See James Quinlivan, "Burden of Victory: The Painful Arithmetic of Stability Operations," *RAND Review* 27, no. 2 (Summer 2003): 29.

[11] Oleksandr Turchynov, "Zapadnye diplomaty ne verili, chto my vystoim," *Babel*, August 23, 2021, https://babel.ua/ru/texts/68499-zapadnye-diplomaty-ne-verili-chto-my-vystoim-aleksandr-turchinov-rasskazyvaet-kak-vesnoy-letom-2014-goda-zanyal-vse-vysshie-posty-v-ukraine-zanovo-stroil-vlast-i-nachal-ato.

they are guided by irredentist goals of joining the existing state, insurgent leaders need to complete two stages of political development: *state founding* and *state building*.[12] The former, based on the Weberian view of the state, requires replacing the monopoly of a preexisting state with militant coercive control over a contiguous territory. The latter, by contrast, requires acquiring capacity to govern this territory by building new state institutions and repurposing old ones to serve militant needs. There is often a symbiotic relationship between the two stages. As Mampilly observed, "[T]he complicated relationship between rebel governance efforts and the incumbent state is predicated on the struggle for territorial control."[13] Given that lack of coercive resources often constrains insurgent leaders, they tend to prioritize control over certain towns or areas. This leads to uneven distribution of territorial control and to varied patterns of state building or governance arrangements across insurgent-held territory.

The Ukrainian state's low coercive capacity allowed for rapid proliferation of small separatist militia groups in towns across the region. However, until the arrival of Girkin's unit, they lacked centralized control and refrained from challenging or removing the state's coercive monopoly. Even assaults on security service headquarters in Luhansk and Donetsk in early April did not result in attempts to subordinate the remaining police forces in these towns. Only with the armed seizure of Sloviansk police station and its SBU office on April 12, 2014, did the *state founding* stage begin. The Sloviansk agglomeration became the first area in the region where militants monopolized violence in all its major towns. Their capacity to exercise territorial control became, initially, visible with the emergence of barricades inside the city and checkpoints at its entrances. These delineated the de facto boundaries of the new separatist unit.

The main initial limitation to the expansion of separatist territorial control was variation in the scale of civilian collaboration. In the towns closest to Sloviansk, Girkin could recruit from the social networks supportive of the separatist cause. Those towns witnessed the formation of self-defense groups and the staging of separatist rallies already in late February. In other towns, by contrast, there were no visible signs of separatist organization, while individual activists were marginal and detached from larger social groups. As a result, once the challenge to the state turned violent, some of the towns with

---

[12] Mazzuca, *Latecomer State Formation* differentiates between state formation and state building.
[13] Mampilly, *Rebel Rulers*, 59.

preexisting separatist networks, like Lyman and Druzhkivka, quickly fell under militant control. Others, like Dobropillia or Svatove, had neither an organized separatist presence nor a civilian population sufficiently responsive to their appeals. If those towns were also less accessible from militant centers and had Ukrainian armed units deployed nearby, as in Pokrovsk, they were more likely to turn into contested areas or remain under the government's control.

The proximity of towns in my sample to four initial militant strongholds—Sloviansk, Horlivka, Donetsk, Luhansk—influenced the strength of separatist influence there. The example of Sloviansk illustrates this relationship clearly (Figure 1.1). In towns located further than 40 kilometers (about 25 miles) from Sloviansk, local separatists either failed to assert their control or required constant reinforcements from the closest militant strongholds. Mariupol is the only town that does not fit this pattern. It was the furthest town from Sloviansk and other strongholds where armed insurgency still took hold. As I document in Chapter 5, the militants' emergence and

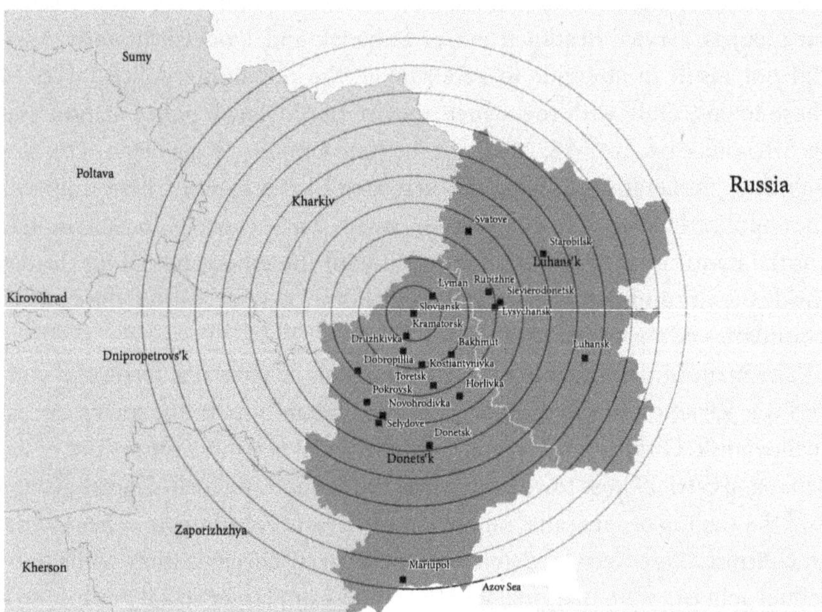

Figure 1.1 The proximity of towns discussed in the book to the separatist stronghold of Sloviansk, from the closest, Kramatorsk and Lyman, to the most distant, Mariupol. Distance between two concentric circles is at the scale 5 mm:20 km.

brief success there could be attributed to Russia's patronage exercised independently from the rest of the region due to the proximity of the Russian border—just 60 kilometers from the city.

The second stage of secessionist state development—*state building*—requires not just the capacity to use force but also the capacity to govern. Given that rebels usually lack any administrative experience or skills, they need to rely on the collaboration of municipal elites to prevent the quick collapse of the city's administration. The strength of preexisting institutions further limits the range of governance choices available to rebels.[14] But strong institutions also offer rebels an interim solution to a governance challenge. According to one comparative study of insurgencies, at the outset of a conflict rebel groups are more likely to rely on preexisting institutions and engage in "little institution building."[15]

Town Mayors as a Lynchpin of Local Governance

Once the state authority in Ukraine imploded, town councils and mayors in Donbas became the last remaining institutions residents of the region still viewed as legitimate. Being the only directly elected executives in Ukraine apart from the president, mayors derived their legitimacy from the popular support of town residents. Most mayors in Donbas in early 2014 were members of the Party of Regions (PR), dominant there for the preceding decade. It was not just a political force but a large clientelist pyramid of national and local officials and businesspeople subordinated to the few strongmen at the top, led by President Yanukovych.

Town mayors performed several important tasks for PR leadership. They engaged in targeted distribution of goods to the party's key voting blocks, such as pensioners, factory workers, and public-sector employees. They provided favorable treatment to local factories owned by major PR donors or party leaders. They ensured positive coverage of the party in local media outlets. They also mobilized locals for rallies in the regional capitals and Kyiv. In return, many of the mayors received informal access to local economic assets and used municipal funds to support their family business. In Bakhmut, for

---

[14] Arjona, *Rebelocracy* analyzes the constraining effects of preexisting institutions based on their two characteristics: legitimacy and effectiveness.

[15] Based on the study of 127 cases of civil wars for the period between 1950 and 2006, the mean number of new institutions was 3.6 per rebel organization. See Huang, *The Wartime Origins of Democratization*, 71.

example, the mayor's family owned a company that paved roads and a chain of gas stations with exclusive rights to operate within the city.[16] In Toretsk, the mayor's son-in-law owned the bread manufacturing company that supplied its products to all public-sector institutions.[17] Through such schemes, mayors benefited from their positions and often accumulated substantial wealth over their years in power.

The armed insurgents' appearance in towns across Donbas posed a political threat to mayors and created major risks for their economic assets and enrichment schemes. Hence, it should have turned most mayors into natural allies of the Ukrainian state. Yet antagonism of the new authorities in Kyiv to remaining PR officials, especially those tied to Donetsk elites, similarly posed a threat to their political longevity. Moreover, the weakness of the Ukrainian state was clearly exposed by the Russian occupation of Crimea and the government's failure to defend it. Hence, siding with Kyiv at the time might have been a losing bet for them. The mayors also had to show sensitivity to the demands of town residents, expressed during the rallies held under the Russian flag. As the book shows, collaboration of municipal authorities depended on the strength of the militant presence in their towns. During the nonviolent mobilization stage in March local elites sought to accommodate separatist demands through talks and token concessions. But when they suddenly faced their armed challengers, they responded with one of five strategies. The two possible cooperative responses were collaboration and hedging; noncooperation was expressed in sabotage, resistance, and exit.

Collaboration required public collusion with insurgents and explicit endorsement of their cause. It represented open defection to the separatist side based on personal convictions or pragmatic expectations about the outcome of the conflict. Hedging entailed limited cooperation with insurgents on the technical aspects of governance, usually in private, but avoidance of explicit public backing or any other supportive actions. It was an attempt to walk a fine line between mitigating personal risks from the militant presence and remaining outwardly loyal to the Ukrainian state. The path of sabotage meant dismissing or ignoring separatist demands and undermining their attempts to organize parallel governance structures. While it did not preclude interaction with the separatists, it represented a more

[16] Interview with Dmytro Kononets, September 17, 2018.
[17] Interview with Andriy Hrudkin, November 7, 2018.

decisive, even if inconsistent, pushback against some of their demands. The path of resistance meant direct support for counterinsurgent forces and pro-Ukrainian locals to expel separatists from the city. It was often expressed in public rejection of separatist demands and backing of local resistance efforts. Those who chose the path of exit delegated their responsibilities to other officials and fled to government-controlled parts of Ukraine. This choice was based on the recognition that any noncooperative strategies posed significant short-term risks to one's physical safety. Cooperative response, on the other hand, required readiness to cut all ties to Ukraine or face the long-term risk of prosecution. These strategies were sometimes adopted sequentially by mayors and other municipal administrators. One could move from hedging at the start of the conflict to collaborating or exiting at a later stage. Still, the strategies conditioned ways in which militants could participate in governance. Whether separatist leaders could swiftly expand their administrative rule across Donbas rested on the municipal authorities' cooperation.

Two Types of Control

This book compares attempted *state founding* and *state building* by militants in six urban agglomerations of Donbas. To measure their progress at each of the stages I distinguish between two types of control: coercive and administrative. Coercive control reflects the extent to which separatist actors managed to subordinate local law enforcement and other state security agents in a selected area and acquired exclusive power to coerce residents. It is a measure of success in *state founding*. Administrative control measures the extent to which separatist actors subordinated municipal authorities and acquired exclusive power to make and enforce rules for governing these territories. It denotes progress in *state building*.

In my analysis I further distinguish between instances of full control, partial control, and lack of control. Full coercive and administrative control indicates that separatist actors acquired decisive influence in all matters related to maintaining order and town governance. Partial coercive or administrative control indicates that separatists acquired some influence over state actors (police or administration) but could advance their preferred policies only through negotiation with these actors rather than unilateral imposition. Lack of coercive and administrative control indicates that separatists were excluded from any decision-making in administrative or security spheres and lacked any ability to advance their preferred policies.

In most cases reviewed for this book, establishing full or partial coercive control was a prerequisite for acquiring administrative control. Between April and August 2014, out of the sample of seventeen towns selected for the comparative study (see Table 1.1), nine were under full administrative and coercive control of the separatist militia and five were under partial coercive or administrative control. In three towns separatists failed to acquire administrative or coercive control.

Militant capacity to establish coercive control over towns influenced the strategy that local elites adopted in response to insurgent presence. In towns under the full or partial coercive control of insurgents, elites adopted mostly cooperative strategies.[18] This, in turn, allowed militants to further establish full or partial administrative control over target towns (see Figure 1.2).

Table 1.1 Types of Insurgent Control and Elite Strategies in Sample Towns of Donetsk and Luhansk Provinces, April–July 2014

Sample Town	Rebel Coercive Control	Local Elite Response Strategy	Rebel Administrative Control
Sloviansk	Complete	Collaboration	Complete
Lyman	Complete	Hedging/Collaboration	Complete
Kramatorsk	Complete	Hedging/Exit	Complete
Druzhkivka	Complete	Collaboration	Complete
Kostiantynivka	Complete	Hedging/Exit	Complete
Bakhmut	Partial	Hedging/Sabotage	Partial
Toretsk	Complete	Collaboration	Complete
Pokrovsk	Absent	Sabotage	Absent
Dobropillia	Absent	Resistance	Absent
Novohrodivka	Complete	Collaboration	Complete
Selydove	Partial	Hedging/Collaboration	Partial
Mariupol	Partial	Hedging/Sabotage	Partial
Lysychansk	Complete	Collaboration	Complete
Sieverodonetsk	Complete	Collaboration	Complete
Rubizhne	Partial	Hedging	Partial
Starobilsk	Partial	Hedging	Partial
Svatove	Absent	Resistance	Absent

[18] One exception was Kostiantynivka, where both the mayor and the secretary of the city council left the city once militants established their coercive presence. In Bakhmut local authorities sought to

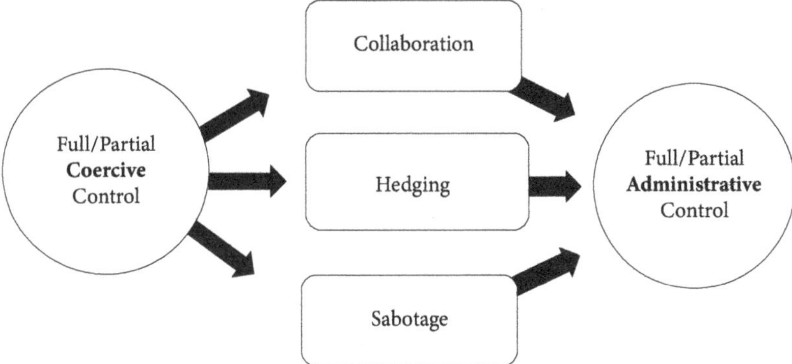

Figure 1.2 Elite strategies and governance outcomes under coercive control by militants.

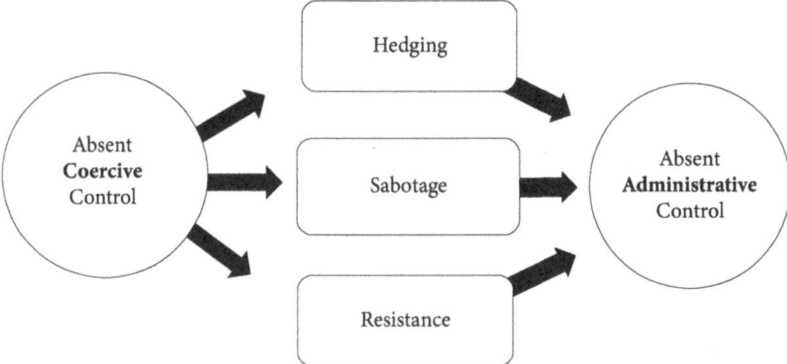

Figure 1.3 Elite strategies and governance outcomes in the absence of coercive control by militants.

By contrast, in towns where insurgents failed to establish any coercive presence local elites were more likely to pursue noncooperative strategies of sabotage or resistance.[19] As a result, militants also had no influence over the town's administration (see Figure 1.3).

The ability of rebels to signal coercive predominance in individual towns was crucial for the subsequent task of imposing new rules on the community and exercising political influence over it. Due to the initial weakness

sabotage some of the separatist initiatives despite partial coercive control over the town established by the militants.

[19] The only town in the sample where local elites collaborated with insurgents in the absence of complete control of militants was Selydove. In this case, however, the decisive factor that influenced cooperative response might have been the town's proximity to the militants' base in Donetsk.

of armed separatist units in most towns, militant leaders could establish administrative control over the region only if they could gain influence beyond their immediate base. This makes one structural characteristic of Donbas—the high density of its urban agglomerations—a key opportunity factor enabling a small number of foreign-led militants to seize the region.

Urbanization and Insurgency

Earlier studies of armed conflict argued that the rural areas were more favorable for the development of insurgent campaigns.[20] Based on their logic, successful insurgency requires rebels to avoid detection and escape preemptive attacks by government forces. This can be achieved only in poorly accessible or distant areas of the country, far away from major urban settlements. Since the state's policing capacity and terrain control are usually diminished outside the cities, particularly in mountainous regions, the government has difficulty getting precise enough information about rebel plans and whereabouts to detect and disrupt nascent insurgent networks.[21] One quantitative study of civil wars concluded that low levels of urbanization and population density "inhibit government capability."[22] As a result, the training and preparation of insurgents is more likely to happen in sparsely populated areas.[23] An urban environment, by contrast, creates opportunities for anonymous denunciation, which favors government's counterinsurgency efforts.[24] As a result, the countryside often becomes the arena of prolonged fighting, while "the capture of cities tends to be the end point" of an insurgent campaign.[25]

Scholars of civil wars have only recently started exploring possible causal links between patterns of urban settlement and the likelihood of armed conflict outbreak.[26] Staniland was among the first scholars to identify urban

---

[20] See James D. Fearon and David D. Laitin, "Ethnicity, Insurgency and Civil War," *American Political Science Review* 97, no. 1 (February 2003); 75–90; Kalyvas, *The Logic of Violence in Civil War.*

[21] Lewis, *How Insurgency Begins.*

[22] Paul Collier and Anke Hoeffler, "Greed and Grievance in Civil War," *Oxford Economic Papers* 56, no. 4 (October 2004): 570.

[23] Dani Nedal, Megan Stewart, and Michael Weintraub, "Urban Concentration and Civil War," *Journal of Conflict Resolution* 64, no. 6 (2020): 1146–1171.

[24] Fearon and Laitin, "Ethnicity, Insurgency and Civil War."

[25] Jo Beall, Tom Goodfellow, and Dennis Rodgers, "Cities and Conflict in Fragile States in the Developing World," *Urban Studies* 50, no. 15 (November 2013): 3074.

[26] Emma Elfversson and Kristine Höglund, "Are Armed Conflicts Becoming More Urban?," *Cities* 119 (2021): 1–10.

insurgency as a distinct type of insurgent campaign waged by "nonstate actors heavily located in urban areas."[27] He argues that "robust community structures" in the cities formed around shared identity or social and kinship ties provide a "social infrastructure for mobilization," which makes sustained insurgency possible. Other authors recognize that cities in densely urbanized countries may represent a "valuable asset" both for the government and for the rebels.[28] Their capture would mean gaining control over most of the urban population and wealth and may, hence, decide the outcome of the conflict. One analysis of revolutionary episodes between 1900 and 2014 offers further quantitative evidence that the urban setting offers better chances of success for armed rebels than rural areas.[29] Hence, the conditions for the success of urban insurgencies need to be reexamined.

Existing studies of uprisings and civil wars have so far outlined four mechanisms through which an urban environment may facilitate armed collective action. First, it allows actors to claim control over a large area by capturing symbolic centers of power in the cities, like municipal government buildings or police stations. This quickly communicates insurgent strength to the government and demonstrates to the people the credibility of their claim to rule.[30] As Raleigh notes, seized cities become the "physical representation of an opposition's group strength and support."[31] Beissinger attributes the effectiveness of urban uprisings to their disruptive effect on governments due to their proximity to power centers.[32]

Second, an urban setting aids recruitment into the insurgency by tapping into preexisting community structures and mobilization of people with prior social ties.[33] In this context, civic groups and organizations may become vehicles for forming the initial activist core and further consolidating public opinion behind the insurgent cause. The urban organizational milieu

---

[27] Staniland, "Cities on Fire," 1624.

[28] Nedal, Stewart, and Weintraub, "Urban Concentration and Civil War."

[29] Beissinger estimates that urban revolts that involved violence had almost twice the probability of success compared to all rural revolts (.44 vs. .26). While exclusively armed rebellions in urban contexts have a slightly lower probability of success than rural revolts (.20), they represented a minority of all urban revolutionary episodes (9%). Mark Beissinger, *Revolutionary City: Urbanization and the Global Transformation of Rebellion* (Princeton, NJ: Princeton University Press, 2022), 156.

[30] Clionadh Raleigh, "Urban Violence Patterns across African States," *International Studies Review* 17 (2015): 90–160; Karen Büscher, "African Cities and Violent Conflict: The Urban Dimension of Conflict and Post Conflict Dynamics in Central and Eastern Africa," *Journal of Eastern African Studies* 12, no. 2 (2018): 193–210.

[31] Raleigh, "Urban Violence Patterns across African States," 94.

[32] Beissinger, *Revolutionary City*, 15.

[33] Staniland, *Networks of Rebellion*.

and community structure thus offer unique solutions to the collective action problem that are not readily available in a rural setting.

Third, the concentration of capital and productive economic assets in the cities provides insurgents with funding sources for their operations. It also offers them additional leverage in dealing with the government, which may view these assets as critical for its own economic solvency. Fourth, towns enhance the defensive capabilities of the militants and promise them a better chance of survival. This is particularly relevant for smaller insurgent groups, which cannot engage in lineal frontal warfare. As King observes, an urban environment restrains the government's use of force out of fear of domestic or international backlash.[34] This makes it more likely that a government will choose containment over annihilation as a dominant counterinsurgent strategy. As a result, as Sassen puts it, "[T]he physical and human features of the city are an obstacle for conventional armies—an obstacle wired into urban space itself."[35] Towns may, thus, shield insurgents from conventional military operations even more effectively than rural or mountainous terrain.

This study points to the significance of another variable—*urban agglomeration density*—which represents proximity of urban agglomerations in a particular region. It examines how the spatial location of urban agglomerations in relation to each other enables insurgent takeover. By tracing the process of establishing control over individual towns across Donbas this study identifies four key advantages that high urban agglomeration density offers to insurgents. First, it lowers the costs of capture and control of the territories by allowing rebels to exercise indirect coercive influence over proximate urban centers. The seizure of the police stations in the agglomeration centers of Sloviansk and Kramatorsk, for example, allowed rebels to compel collaboration of the local authorities in neighboring towns. Second, urban agglomeration density allows insurgent activities to turn into a modular process. It enables emulation of tactics through the perception of similarity in structural conditions and a heightened perception of success.[36] High mobility across towns enables militants to quickly spread tactical know-how and encourage its adoption by local activists. Third, proximity of urban agglomerations compensates for the scarcity of recruits in one area by drawing on the recruitment pool in other areas. Economic, political, or

---

[34] King *Urban Warfare in the Twenty-First Century.*

[35] Saskia Sassen, "When the City Itself Becomes a Technology of War," *Theory, Culture & Society* 27, no. 6 (2010): 39.

[36] Beissinger, "Structure and Example in Modular Political Phenomenon," 265.

cultural particularities of every agglomeration may impose constraints on insurgent recruitment in certain urban centers and foster recruitment in others. For example, towns with declining industries or bankrupt factories may produce a greater supply of recruits from among former workers than towns with more efficient manufacturing and a better economic outlook. Similarly, developed patronage networks based on economic or political ties in certain towns may enhance the ability of insurgent leaders to mobilize people for rallies in neighboring cities where these networks might not exist. Fourth, urban agglomeration density offers a particular advantage to insurgencies led or organized by foreign actors. Due to their large population size, urban agglomerations may provide foreign actors with anonymity or invisibility, which is impossible to achieve in rural environments with close familiarity between residents. This allows foreign actors to operate without immediate detection and offers an opportunity for undercover mobilization of their supporters from abroad if they share key cultural characteristics with the locals.

Insurgents may capitalize on proximity of urban agglomerations, however, only under conditions of eroding state capacity. As Beissinger observes, for the balance of forces to favor the challengers, the state's ability to penetrate territory must weaken.[37] This would require defection of the police, tasked with maintaining public order, and realignment of local authorities behind separatist challengers. It also requires some support from the local population, which should, at minimum, abstain from mounting active resistance to insurgents across urban terrain. The weakness of the state is also crucial for the ability of external actors to provide support to the rebels. Porous state borders allow for easy transfer of military equipment, deployment of undercover agents, and military training of locals who would need to move back and forth across state lines. This offers an important extension to the argument about the effect of state weakness on the likelihood of civil war. Low state capacity may create favorable conditions for insurgents operating not only in rough terrain or from a rural base, as Fearon and Laitin showed, but also in densely urbanized areas with multiple urban centers near each other.[38]

Urban terrain became an important backdrop for popular mobilization across Donbas. The region had, historically, the highest density and level of

---

[37] Beissinger, *Revolutionary City*, 166.
[38] Fearon and Laitin, "Ethnicity, Insurgency and Civil War."

urbanization of all oblasts in Ukraine, with over 80% of its six and a half million residents living in cities.[39] Prior to the conflict outbreak, the region had a total of eighty-three towns, which constituted 26% of all urban settlements in Ukraine.[40] Some urban clusters in the region developed as agglomerations with integrated towns neighboring each other and closely tied socially and economically. This was spurred by intense industrialization of the two oblasts from the 1930s to the 1950s, when new towns emerged next to newly built industrial plants or coal mining companies. As a result, Donbas transformed into the region with the largest number of highly integrated urban centers in Ukraine, which encompass cities and connected midsize or small townships forming town agglomerations.[41] Overall, Donbas had twelve urban agglomerations located close to each other and connected through roads and the railway.[42] They were also one of the most populous in Ukraine—of the thirteen largest urban agglomerations in Ukraine by population size, six were in Donbas.[43] Moreover, the two oblasts had more towns with a population over fifty thousand than any other Ukrainian province. Due to high density, 80% of the population of Donetsk oblast resided in six urban agglomerations, which encompassed 53.9% of the oblast territory.[44] In Luhansk oblast the density of urban population was even higher; its six urban agglomerations took up 39% of the oblast territory but contained 85.5% of its population. By establishing control over the largest urban agglomerations insurgents were thus bringing most of the region's residents under their rule.

The Spatial Dimension of Research

During my field research I traveled across six urban agglomerations discussed in the book, collected data, and interviewed residents in each of them (see Figure 1.4).

[39] Mykhailo Kushnirenko, "Znachenie sotsiologicheskikh obsledovaniy v gradostroitelnom proektrirovanii na uroven gorodskoi i raionnoi planirovki Donbassa," *Dosvid ta Perpspektyvy Rozvytku Mist Ukrainy*, no. 25 (2013): 60.

[40] Ibid.

[41] For a definition of "agglomeration," see Chuangling Fang and Danlin Yu, "Urban Agglomeration: An Evolving Concept of an Emerging Phenomenon," *Landscape and Urban Planning* 162 (2017): 126–136.

[42] Kushnirenko, "Znachenie sotsiologicheskikh obsledovaniy v gradostroitelnon proektrirovanii na uroven gorodskoi i raionnoi planirovki Donbassa."

[43] These six agglomeration centers included Donetsk (1,506,202), Alchevsk (447,975), Luhansk (432,483), Horlivka (353,497), Kramatorsk (297,665), and Sieverodonetsk (281,903). See Delphine Alberta Hamilton, *Ukraine: Urbanization Review* (Washington, DC: World Bank Group, 2015): 30.

[44] Based on the data in Pidhrushnyi and Vrublevskyi, "Miski Aglomeratsii Donbasu."

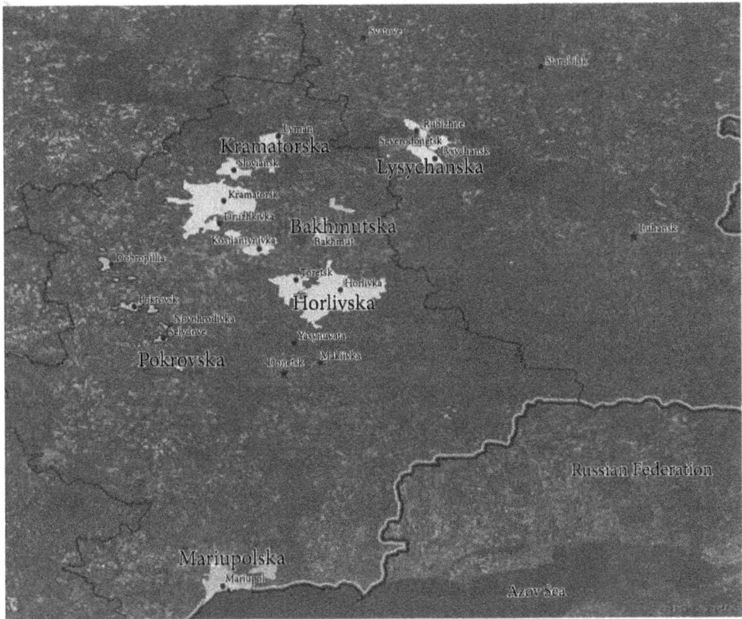

Figure 1.4 Six urban agglomerations discussed in the book with centers in Kramatorsk, Lysychansk, Horlivka, Bakhmut, Pokrovsk, and Mariupol.

In addition, I visited two towns in Luhansk oblast—Svatove and Starobilsk—which are not part of the urban agglomerations but played a significant role during the separatist mobilization and countermobilization in the region. My secondary research sites were Kyiv, Kharkiv, Odesa, and Moscow, where I also interviewed relevant actors and collected data on the dynamics of separatist mobilization outside of Donbas.

The experience of personal travel across Donetsk and Luhansk oblasts was crucial to understanding the spatial dimension of the insurgency and the opportunities and obstacles the terrain offered insurgents. The layout of the town itself contained important clues about the challenges that militants faced. In Sloviansk, their initial targets—the police station, the city council building, and the SBU office—were located steps from each other. This allowed for simultaneous capture of the town's governing and coercive centers. The central part of the town, which became the epicenter of the insurgency for the first three months, was surrounded by four major thoroughfares: Tsentralna, Shovkovychna, Bankivska, and Poshtova. They formed a trapezoid easy for militants to reinforce and defend. By contrast, the police station in neighboring Kramatorsk, also targeted by the militants, was a mile from the central square. One needed to pass blocks of Stalin-era buildings in the old part of town and the sumptuous Pushkin Park in order to reach it. But the police station lay next to the main road that connected the city with Sloviansk. It remained contested by the Ukrainian forces for the duration of the fighting in the area. This may explain why militants only raided the police station in Kramatorsk on several occasions but never sought to turn it into their base.

The dull gray four-story city council building in Kramatorsk faces a large square dominated by the monumental culture palace,[45] a white neoclassical building with dozens of columns, two large wings, and a triangular façade. The first separatist rallies in Kramatorsk were held right on its steps. This posed a challenge to the local authorities due to its proximity to the city council. Visible from any front window of the municipal building, the rallies communicated separatists' power to mobilize large groups of people without approaching municipal leaders directly. By contrast, another town in the agglomeration, Lyman, was divided in half by railway tracks. Its municipal government offices were in the larger half, connected to Sloviansk through the main road, T 0514. This connection turned it into an easy target for Strelkov-led militants, who arrived there almost immediately after the takeover of Sloviansk.

Equally important to the research was exploring the geographic terrain. On the map, the towns of Lysychansk and Sieverodonetsk may seem like immediate neighbors separated only by the river Siverskyi Donets. However, a visit to the area reveals a more complex juxtaposition. The riverbank on Lysychansk's side rises steeply, creating a natural barrier for any advancing force. The main road from the railway station at the foot of the slope to the city center curves several times before it reaches the plateau at the top. Lysychansk itself has an elongated rectangular form, as if imitating the river's shape. Its main district consists of several parallel streets that stretch for miles. By contrast, Sieverodonetsk has a circular and compact shape with a clearly delineated center. The shape of Sieverodonetsk and the flat terrain around it make the town easily accessible from multiple directions. The difficulty of its defense led to the early withdrawal of the separatist forces in

---

[45] "Culture Palaces," one of the prominent Soviet legacies, functioned as a community center that staged performances, offered extracurricular activities for children and other recreational opportunities for town residents. For further discussion, see Karl Schlögel, *The Soviety Century: Archeology of a Lost World* (Princeton, NJ: Princeton University Press, 2021): Ch. 19.

July 2014 and a quick retreat of the Ukrainian forces during 2022 Russian offensive. Lysychansk held on for several more weeks in 2014 and sustained a more serious shelling from long-range artillery.

The experience of traveling from one town to another by car across the region exposes the intensity of distance decay even between the proximate cities.[46] Take Sloviansk and Pokrovsk agglomerations, located nearby on a map. The linear distance between their two nearest towns—Kramatorsk and Dobropillia—is about thirty miles. However, it could take at least an hour to travel from one town to another. The only road connecting them was replete with large cracks and potholes that required driving at extremely low speed. Poor transportation infrastructure increased travel costs and intensified the sense of separation between the two agglomerations. In spring of 2014 the weak connection and the friction of the terrain prevented militants in Sloviansk from projecting coercive influence in urban centers located to the south. This, in turn, allowed pro-Ukrainian activists in the Pokrovsk agglomeration to stage a successful anti-separatist resistance campaign.

The urban design of Donbas towns has several recurring features. Their centerpiece is usually a large square surrounded by municipal government offices, a culture palace that offered recreational opportunities, and educational institutions. In Novohrodivka, the vast culture palace with twelve massive columns at its entrance faced a long central square lined with trees and coffee shops. At its opposite end was a much less prominent city council building. The executive council in Mariupol faced a Greek square with two small fountains and university buildings behind it. In Rubizhne the city council building and the culture palace faced each other across the vast Volodymyrska Square. The layout, an open public place next to the government building, offered a major advantage for protest mobilization. Apart from protesters' greater visibility, their presence next to the local power center became "a physical expression of the dual sovereignty that lies at the heart of revolutionary claims."[47] When separatist mobilization started in Donbas in February and March 2014, the central squares in towns of the region turned into staging grounds for anti-Kyiv rallies and, later, became launching pads for militant assaults on the town's municipal

---

[46] Distance decay represents the weakening of interactions between geographic places as the separation between them increases. See Lenka Hasova and Levi Wolf, "Proximity and Distance Decay," in *The Geographic Information Science & Technology Body of Knowledge* (2022 edition), ed. John P. Wilson, https://doi.org/10.22224/gistbok/2022.2.3.

[47] Beissinger, *Revolutionary City*, 253.

buildings. In some towns, they also became the sites of direct confrontation between pro-Russian and pro-Ukrainian demonstrators—initially peaceful, but increasingly violent as mobilization continued.

Researching Urban Agglomerations

When Girkin's unit arrived in Sloviansk on the morning of April 12, 2014, it found itself in one of the largest urban agglomerations in the region. Centered in Kramatorsk, the agglomeration included three smaller towns—Druzhkivka and Kostiantynivka, located to the southeast, and Lyman, northeast from Sloviansk. Each of the towns in the agglomeration was a thirty-minute drive away from the other. Lyman (called Krasnyi Lyman prior to the war) is a major railway juncture connecting Donbas with Kharkiv oblast and the rest of Central Ukraine. Its intercity road running from Sloviansk to Lysychansk, the two rebel strongholds in the summer of 2014, amplified its strategic significance for the militants. In 2022, Lyman changed hands twice, first occupied by the Russian troops in March and later liberated by Ukrainian forces in September.

The other four towns in the agglomeration are connected by the single major thoroughfare (N20) and by the railroad that provides fast train service to Kyiv. Located on the C-shaped axis from Sloviansk through Kramatorsk and Druzhkivka to Kostiantynivka, the four towns represented one of the most tightly connected and industrialized urban areas in Ukraine. Kramatorsk is the largest town in the agglomeration, with a population of 160,000 in 2014, a large number of whom worked at the two major factories in the agglomeration—Novokramatorsk machine building enterprise and Energomashspetsstal. Half an hour's drive from Kramatorsk is Druzhkivka, a town of about sixty thousand people, which expanded with the post–World War II industrial boom. Its largest factories—a machine-building factory that produces mining equipment and a hardware plant that produces bolts, nuts, and fasteners—have been part of the industrial holding owned by Ukraine's wealthiest oligarch, Rinat Akhmetov. Ten miles further south lies Kostiantynivka, the fifth town of the agglomeration. The railroad cuts the town into almost equal halves. On the north side is the manufacturing district, with a metallurgical equipment factory, a glassmaking company, and a popular chocolate maker. Residential buildings, hospitals, and schools are located to the south of the railway tracks. The three major roads leading out of Kostiantynivka go to towns in three other urban agglomerations discussed in the book. The closest is Toretsk, located about fifteen miles southeast and part of the Horlivka agglomeration. About twenty miles northeast is Bakhmut, which is the center of its own urban agglomeration. And about thirty-five miles southwest lies Pokrovsk, another urban agglomeration center.

A local called Toretsk a "dead-end" town due to its location and economic structure.[48] Black gob piles and rusty drill rigs signal the transition from heavy industry to mining country. Coal mines have long been the main source of jobs and funds for the city. The decline in coal production in the 1990s triggered an outflow of people from Toretsk to neighboring cities. In contrast to Toretsk, Bakhmut remained a bustling town with several major industrial plants and a thriving service sector. Two smaller towns in its agglomeration were Soledar, famous for its salt production, and Chasiv Yar.

Pokrovsk is the center of an urban agglomeration located on the western side of Donetsk oblast and bordering Dnipropetrovsk oblast. It includes the towns of Dobropillia to the north, Myrnohrad to the east, and Novohrodivka and Selydove to the south. Neither of the two militant strongholds—Sloviansk and Horlivka—had a direct road to Pokrovsk, and a trip through the towns in between, Kramatorsk and Kostiantynivka, could take over two hours via dilapidated roads. From a small village, Pokrovsk grew into a town of over sixty thousand residents with the increase in coal production. By 2014 the city's two major coal mines—Pokrovske and Krasnolymanska—accounted for 90% of its total industrial production.[49]

Twenty miles north from Pokrovsk is another mining town, Dobropillia. Its population together with three satellite towns—Novodonetske, Bilozerske, and Bilytske—totaled around sixty thousand in 2014. The five mines that operated in the area were part of the mine holding Dobropilliavuhillia. Although it was a state-owned holding at the time, the mines were leased and operated by Akhmetov's holding company DTEK. Dobropillia's direct road to Kramatorsk made it the closest town within the Pokrovsk agglomeration to the insurgent stronghold in the spring of 2014. The trip by car, however, would take more than an hour traversing open fields with little cover. This hindered militants stationed in Sloviansk from reinforcing their comrades there.

---

[48] Interview with Grudkin, 2018.
[49] Investment passport of Pokrovsk: https://pokrovsk-rada.gov.ua/uk/page/investicijnij-pasport-english-version.

Mariupol, on the southern tip of Donetsk oblast, was the city most distant from all major militant strongholds. Still, its proximity to the Russian border allowed local separatists to travel there for supplies and training. Mariupol has been one of Ukraine's largest industrial hubs, with two major metallurgical plants—Ilyicha and Azovstal—located within the city proper. They provided jobs for up to seventy thousand people and formed a service infrastructure that included food markets and drugstores, healthcare facilities, childcare centers, and resorts. At least a third of Mariupol residents owed their livelihood to the operation of the plants. This gave their owner, Akhmetov, outsized political and social influence over the town's governance.

My research in Luhansk oblast focused on one major agglomeration, its center in Lysychansk and two smaller towns to the north—Svatove and Starobilsk. The Lysychansk agglomeration also included Sieverodonetsk and Rubizhne. It was the closest agglomeration in Luhansk oblast to Sloviansk, which made it vital in the first months of the conflict. Lysychansk became a major transfer hub for ammunition supplies from the Russian border to Sloviansk and a base for Russian volunteers on their way to join Girkin's unit. Both towns are among the oldest in Donbas. Lysychansk was founded in 1795, just ten years after the founding of Sloviansk. It became the location of the region's first coal mine, which gave the city a claim to being the "cradle of Donbas." This unofficial title is carved on a black stone erected next to the city's mining college. The population of Lysychansk was slightly over 100,000 at the start of the conflict, making it the third most populous city in Luhansk oblast and on par with neighboring Sieverodonetsk. It was also one of the towns in Donbas most affected by the economic crisis following the Soviet collapse. Out of seven mines that were once part of the holding company Lysychanskvuhillia only four remained operational and only one was profitable in 2014.[50] The second largest oil-processing factory in Ukraine, Lysychansk NPZ, struggled to turn a profit and ceased most operations by 2012.[51] Another major industrial asset, the Lysychansk soda plant, was acquired by Russian investors in 2007. It ceased operations in 2010 after failing to cover its energy expenses, and by 2013 most of the physical plant was dismantled for scrap metal. The closure of the city's largest

[50] Interview with Serhiy Apryshkin, May 4, 2021.
[51] Interview with Olena Nizhelska, June 14, 2019.

factories led to the shrinking of its share in the GDP of Luhansk oblast, from 32% in 2004 to 5.1% in 2013.[52]

Several bridges across Siverskiy Donets lead directly into another industrial town—Sieverodonetsk. Following World War II, it turned into one of the centers of chemical production in the Soviet Union, while its flagship company, Azot, became the largest manufacturer of ammonium nitrate in Ukraine. The third town in the agglomeration, Rubizhne, witnessed the bankruptcies of most of its factories in the 1990s. The only factory that still operated there in 2014 was Zarya, the largest producer of explosives in Ukraine. Two other towns in Luhansk oblast discussed in the book, Svatove and Starobilsk, lay outside any urban agglomerations. Founded as Cossack settlements at the turn of the eighteenth century, they were integrated into the industrial economy of Donbas only after World War II. Still, the economies of both cities were dominated by agricultural production. This made them less attractive to the region's industrial groups and gave local landowners and large farmers the most influence over local governance.

Anatomy of a Conflict

In contrast to earlier studies of the Donbas conflict, this book seeks to establish its causes by tracing the conflict development from the bottom up. Following other micro-level studies of war, it disaggregates the initial phase of the conflict "by actors, time and space."[53] Rather than viewing the entire region of Donbas as a single unit of analysis, this study compares the experience of individual towns there targeted by the militants. This allows us to uncover variation in the responsiveness to separatist demands among various actors and across the region. Instead of focusing on major events at the start of the conflict, such as the capture of government buildings in oblast centers or the arrival of Strelkov in Sloviansk, this study devotes equal attention to the daily flow of events unfolding in these towns since the start of the Euromaidan revolution in Kyiv in November 2013.

---

[52] *Zaraz*, "Lisichanskiy zavod RTI unichtozhaetsia kak Donetskiy aeroport, no bez voiny," October 20, 2017, https://zaraz.info/lisichanskij-zavod-rti-unichtozhaetsya-kak-donetskij-aeroport-no-bez-vojny-foto/.

[53] Roos Hauer, Johannes Vüllers, and Nils Weidmann. "Studying Micro Dynamics in Civil Wars: Introduction," *Zeitschrift für Friedens und Konfliktforschung* 8 (2019): 153.

The rise of a separatist insurgency is viewed here as a multistage process, in which less prominent events, such as a protest gathering or a council resolution, may be as significant as major outbreaks of violence. In a similar vein, a focus on prominent actors leading the insurgency or speaking on its behalf misses numerous actors who contributed to its rise and escalation in less visible ways. Hence, this study shifts attention from well-known figures, such as Strelkov and Borodai, to local town officials and civic activists who led, aided, or counteracted the separatist mobilization in spring 2014.

The book's methodological approach, which uses towns as units of observation, does not neglect the impact of external actors, particularly the Russian state and its agents. In fact, this micro-level study offers new and compelling evidence of specific ways in which Russian agents facilitated the rise of separatism in Donbas and coordinated the armed challenge to the Ukrainian state. It also provides analytical clarity regarding the exact mechanisms through which Russian actors managed to remove the Ukrainian sovereign presence in Donbas and contributed to the formation of two separatist quasi-states. The next chapter starts with the examination of Russia's long rivalry with Ukraine and explains why it resulted in military intervention in Crimea and Donbas. Chapter 3 moves the analysis from the level of interstate relations to the level of individual action with a focus on specific Russian agents who organized and led the insurgent campaign.

Chapter 2
Rivalry, Revolution, and Russia's Intervention

When on April 11, 2014, the Russian citizen Igor Girkin with four dozen armed men approached the Ukrainian border, the separatist whirlwind had long engulfed Donbas. Government buildings in Donetsk and Luhansk were already under the control of many separatist groups with conflicting demands. Some wanted to see Donbas gain broad autonomous powers within federalized Ukraine; others sought its secession or integration into Russia. In smaller towns of the region, locals had been for weeks staging rallies and questioning the legitimacy of the new Ukrainian authorities. Many publicly called on Russian leadership to intervene on their behalf and proudly waved Russian flags. Local self-defense groups established checkpoints near town entrances and conducted regular street patrols jointly with the police. Town officials held meetings with separatist leaders and provided them with office space. Girkin's own guides who met him at the border were activists from Sloviansk already plotting resistance to the Ukrainian authorities.

Still, at the time of Girkin's arrival, the separatist challenge to Kyiv remained sporadic and restrained. Clashes between pro-Russian and pro-Ukrainian activists in Donetsk in March led to the killing of a young local Maidan supporter. But any systematic armed mobilization was absent. Local witnesses of separatist actions recalled that they initially resembled a fringe activity unlikely to have any serious repercussions.[1] The capture of the police station and SBU office in Sloviansk on April 12 added qualitatively new dynamics to the mobilization process. It marked the forceful removal of Ukraine's sovereign control over the entire town and the emergence of the first organized nonstate armed unit openly challenging the Ukrainian state. Predictably, the Ukrainian government responded with an armed counter-mobilization accompanied by an assault on the rebel bases under Girkin's

[1] Interview with Konstantin Savinov, July 23, 2019.

Seize the City, Undo the State. Serhiy Kudelia, Oxford University Press. © Oxford University Press (2025).
DOI: 10.1093/9780197795576.003.0003

command. By May 5, or just over three weeks later, the intensity of these altercations reached the level of a minor armed conflict.[2] By mid-July the conflict had produced over one thousand casualties, the minimum threshold for classifying it as a war.[3]

The debate on the correct term to describe the conflict has been inconclusive for two reasons. First, there was disagreement regarding the significance of Russian and local forces for starting the conflict. While the presence of the Russian agents was obvious, their relative weight within the insurgency, in terms of both physical numbers and ideational leadership, remained a matter of dispute. Those who privileged Russia's role denied the independent agency of rebel groups in Donbas and emphasized the interstate dimension of the conflict.[4] Others viewed Moscow's actions as reactive and attributed the main causal significance to local actors, characterizing the conflict as a "civil war."[5] Since the two sides conveniently picked the evidence suited to their arguments, the disagreement between them could not be resolved by gathering more data. Second, the debate acquired strong political overtones given the embrace of the term "civil war" by the Russian officials and propaganda. Hence, even those who insisted on the appropriateness of the term did so with various caveats.[6]

One compromise term comes from the UCDP/PRIO data set, the standard academic source on organized violence, which identifies the war in Donbas as an "internationalized internal armed conflict." However, it also denotes that the conflict began as a civil war but experienced outside involvement at a later stage. Empirically, this sequencing is inaccurate. While Girkin claimed to have made the decision to enter the conflict in Donbas independently from the Kremlin, throughout his presence in the region he and his key allies maintained close communication with Russian officials. There is also evidence of Russian undercover activities in other parts of the region at the time the separatist movement emerged. The first high-casualty

---

[2] Author's calculations based on open-source information regarding the casualties among Ukrainian forces, insurgents, and civilians. By May 5 over twenty-five people were killed as part of the conflict. This surpassed the minimum threshold normally used for identifying a violent confrontation as an armed conflict. For an exact list of casualties, see Appendix. The categories and coding criteria are based on Therese Pettersson, "UCDP/PRIO Armed Conflict Dataset Codebook v 24.1 (https://ucdp.uu.se/downloads/)," 2024.

[3] The casualties data is based on the Report on Office of the United Nations High Commissioner for Human Rights, "Human Rights Situation in Ukraine," July 15, 2014, https://www.ohchr.org/sites/default/files/Documents/Countries/UA/HRMMUReport15June2014.pdf. The category coding is based on Pettersson, "UCDP/PRIO Armed Conflict Dataset… ."

[4] Jakob Hauter, "Delegated Interstate War: Introducing an Addition to Armed Conflict Typologies," *Journal of Strategic Studies* 12, no. 4 (2019): 90–103.

[5] Arel and Driscoll, *Ukraine's Unnamed War*; Nicholas Sambanis, Stergios Skaperdas, and William Wohlforth, "External Intervention, Identity, and Civil War," *Comparative Political Studies* 53, no. 14 (2020): 2155–2182; Zhukov, "Trading Hard Hats for Combat Helmets."

[6] Driscoll, "Ukraine's Civil War."

battle of the war, the storming of the airport in Donetsk on May 26, 2014, occurred with the participation of the newly arrived contingent from Russia. Among over fifty militants killed during this battle the majority, at least thirty-one, were Russian citizens.[7]

In this book, I identify the initial phase of the armed conflict in Donbas as a foreign-led insurgency campaign. The use of the term "insurgency" reflects three broadly accepted elements of the Donbas conflict at its early stage. First, it points to its asymmetric nature in which one of the sides, the Ukrainian armed forces, substantially outnumbered the other, used more sophisticated weapons systems, and had access to a much larger arsenal of weapons. Second, it suggests that most participants on one of the sides were nonstate actors since they were not part of any state's official military formations or state-run command-and-control structures. Third, most fighters among the militants were locals and, as Ukrainian citizens, subject to the same authority as their opponents at the start of the hostilities. Yet, as I document in the next chapter, the key units of the insurgency were organized and directed by Russian agents, received ideological guidance from Russian citizens, and relied on arms supplies and financial assistance from Russia. This is sufficient to identify the insurgency as a "foreign-led" campaign, which sought to advance the interests not only of the region's residents but also of the Russian state.

This chapter outlines the broader objectives that Russia has long pursued in Ukraine and traces Moscow's gradual shift from relying on noncoercive means of influence to using military force. It starts with a conceptual discussion of the ways in which foreign actors influenced the insurgencies and intervened in armed conflicts. I argue that Russia's intervention is a clear example of third-party involvement that preceded the outbreak of armed conflict and pursued, foremost, strategic goals. Rather than an expression of solidarity with perceived ethnic kin, Russia's support for the insurgency should be understood in the context of Moscow's long-standing rivalry with the Ukrainian state rooted in its resentment over the terms of disintegration of the Soviet state.

Interventions and Insurgency

The literature on internal armed conflicts has long recognized the significance of external interventions for explaining a conflict's dynamics and

---

[7] Zhuchkovskiy, *85 dnei Slavianska*, 170.

outcomes.[8] In an extensive analysis of outside support for rebel groups in the first decade since the end of the Cold War, Byman et al. find that external states played a "major role in initiating, sustaining, [and] bringing to victory over half of post–Cold War insurgencies (44 out of 74)."[9] They conclude that external backing has the greatest impact at the initial stage of an insurgency, when "the relative power balance between government forces and those of the insurgents tends to heavily favor the regime."[10]

Still, third-party involvement in civil wars has been analyzed primarily as a choice made in response to an ongoing insurgency rather than an attempt to promote or organize one.[11] In order to trace foreign interventions at the initial stage, Regan and Meachum collected data on foreign interventions in risk-prone countries over a period of fifty years.[12] They found that external military interventions prior to conflict onset increase the likelihood of civil war. Given that the most usual form of military intervention in their data set was the provision of arms, external interveners could provoke conflict by increasing the capacity of a rebel group to act against the state. Only a handful of scholars focused exclusively on the actions of external powers to explain war's outbreak. The causal mechanisms outlined in their studies can be grouped based on the causal primacy given to individual cognition, identity (grievances), and strategic calculations (or perception of opportunity). Scholars who emphasize cognition look at how foreign powers, often inadvertently, affect the perceptions and calculations of potential warring parties. For example, rebels may lower their expected costs of starting a rebellion in anticipation of foreign intervention.[13] Governments may also underestimate the expected costs of suppressing the rebellion due to a lack of reliable information regarding the scale of external support.[14] External powers, however, may act out of a sense of ethnic solidarity with a minority

[8] Karen Rasler, "Internationalized Civil War: A Dynamic Analysis of the Syrian Intervention in Lebanon," *Journal of Conflict Resolution* 27, no. 3 (1987): 421–456.

[9] Daniel Byman et al., *Trends in Outside Support for Insurgent Movements* (Santa Monica, CA: RAND, 2001), 2.

[10] Ibid., 105.

[11] For Regan, this was an "artifact of data-gathering process" that narrows observations to the civil wars already underway. Regan, "Interventions into Civil War," 471. See also Noel Anderson, "Competitive Intervention, Protracted Conflict, and the Global Prevalence of Civil War," *International Studies Quarterly* 63, no. 3 (2019): 692–706.

[12] The authors identified states that experienced political instability associated with potential conflict in the period between 1957 and 2007. They found that foreign actors conducted 449 separate interventions in 1,443 observed years-at-risk, with provision of arms being the most common form of intervention and accounting for over half of the cases (230). Patrick Regan and M. Scott Meachum, "Data on Interventions during Periods of Political Instability," *Journal of Peace Research* 51, no. 1 (2014): 127–135.

[13] Timothy Crawford, "Moral Hazard, Intervention and Internal War: A Conceptual Analysis," *Ethnopolitics* 4, no. 2 (2005): 175–193.

[14] Idean Salehyan, *Rebels without Borders: Transnational Insurgencies in World Politics* (Ithaca, NY: Cornell University Press, 2009).

group.[15] This may be the result of growing animosity between the group and the national government, triggered by exclusionary or assimilationist policies.[16] The external power could then intervene in defense of the rights of an aggrieved kinship group. Such an intervention may be particularly likely if an external power also harbors irredentist designs regarding the territory where its kinship minority group resides.[17] The decision of an external power to intervene may also result from strategic calculations unrelated to group identity but driven by relations with the target state.[18] Interstate rivalries may even have an independent effect on the expectations of the challengers and the host government response if a country neighbors its rival.[19] They radicalize domestic challengers, raise expectations of external assistance, incentivize the government's coercive response, and increase the costs of a negotiated settlement given its geopolitical implications. San-Akca combines strategic and ideational motives in her model of state-rebel interaction.[20] She finds that the highest likelihood of external state support occurs when rebels target a perceived adversary (strategic motive), but states may back groups based on shared identity and ideational affinity irrespective of material interests.

Drivers of Russia's Intervention

Academic accounts of Russia's military intervention in Ukraine privilege either identity or strategic concerns. Some scholars argue that Russia's

---

[15] Stephen Saideman, "Explaining the International Relations of Secessionist Conflicts: Vulnerability versus Ethnic Ties," *International Organization* 51, no. 4 (1997): 721–753; Kristian Skrede Gleditsch, "Transnational Dimensions of Civil War," *Journal of Peace Research* 44, no. 3 (2007): 293–309; Lars-Erik Cederman, Seraina Rüegger, and Guy Schvitz, "Redemption through Rebellion: Border Change, Lost Unity, and Nationalist Conflict," *American Journal of Political Science* 66, no. 1 (2022): 24–42.

[16] Brubaker offered one of the first conceptualizations of the impact of kinship ties on the outbreak of armed conflict by pointing to the role of a "triadic configuration": a nationalizing state, a national minority in this state, and an external national homeland. Rogers Brubaker, "National Minorities, Nationalizing States, and External National Homelands in the New Europe: Notes toward a Relational Analysis," *Reihe Politikwissenschaft*, no. 11 (1993): 3–21.

[17] In the analysis of transborder ethnic groups since 1945, Cederman, Rüegger, and Schvitz, "Redemption through Rebellion" find that the risk of conflict increases with the rise in territorial fractionalization of an ethnic group.

[18] For example, Salehyan, Gleditsch, and Cunningham suggest that external intervention may be motivated by the goal of weakening a specific regime. Hence, external powers are more likely to intervene on behalf of "strong rebel organizations with clear, centralized organizational structures" that exhibit a high degree of "preference congruence" with intervening powers. Idean Salehyan, Kristian Skrede Gleditsch, and David Cunningham, "Explaining External Support for Insurgent Groups," *International Organization* 65, no. 4 (2011): 715.

[19] Mark Toukan, "International Politics by Other Means: External Sources of Civil War," *Journal of Peace Research* 56, no. 6 (2019): 812–826.

[20] Belgin San-Akca, *States in Disguise: Causes of State Support for Rebel Groups* (Oxford: Oxford University Press, 2016).

actions in Donbas resulted from ethnonationalist resentments that emerged after territorial fragmentation of ethnic Russians with the collapse of the USSR.[21] They attribute the conflict's outbreak to the rising grievances among "Russian Ukrainians" in Donbas against their new "host state" of Ukraine and mirror resentments of coethnics in the "homeland state," the Russian Federation. Another account of the Kremlin's decision-making emphasizes the ethical obligations that Russia felt to "protect Russians and those gravitating to Russia in the former Soviet region."[22]

Geopolitical motives, by contrast, are usually viewed through the prism of an earlier exclusion of Russia from the post–Cold War security arrangement in Europe and the history of "low-grade competition" between the West and Russia in post-Soviet Eurasia.[23] This produced, in the words of Charap and Colton, a "negative-sum interaction," which culminated in the clash over Ukraine. Mearsheimer puts responsibility for the conflict more directly on the West, which pursued NATO enlargement to enter "Russia's backyard" and threaten its "core strategic interests."[24] In a similar vein, Malyarenko and Wolff view Russia's intervention as a defense of its role as a "regional power" and aimed against Western encroachment into its "zone of influence."[25] To bridge the two approaches, Sambanis, Skaperdas, and Wohlforth examine the events preceding the armed conflict in Donbas sequentially.[26] The first sequence consists of political interventions by "competitive external actors" (EU/United States and Russia), which culminated in the Euromaidan revolution. These interventions affected the relationship between identity groups, making polarization between them "more salient." In the second sequence, Russia intervened militarily to "support alienated groups in Crimea and the Donetsk coal basin."[27] Geopolitical confrontation thus set the stage for Russia's identity-driven military intervention.

---

[21] Manuel Vogt, Kristian Skrede Gleditsch, and Lars-Erik Cederman, "From Claims to Violence: Signaling, Outbidding, and Escalation in Ethnic Conflict," *Journal of Conflict Resolution* 65, nos. 7–8 (2021): 1278–1307.

[22] Andrei Tsygankov, "Vladimir Putin's Last Stand: The Sources of Russia's Ukraine Policy," *Post-Soviet Affairs* 31, no. 4 (2015): 280.

[23] Rajan Menon and Eugene Rumer, *Conflict in Ukraine: The Unwinding of the Post–Cold War Order* (Cambridge, MA: MIT Press, 2005); Charap and Colton (2017).

[24] John Mearsheimer, "Why the Ukraine Crisis Is the West's Fault: The Liberal Delusions That Provoked Putin," *Foreign Affairs* 93, no. 5 (2014): 77–127.

[25] Tatyana Malyarenko and Stefan Wolff, "The Logic of Competitive Influence-Seeking: Russia, Ukraine, and the Conflict in Donbas," *Post-Soviet Affairs* 34, no. 4 (2018): 191–212. Anderson, "Competitive Intervention, Protracted Conflict, and the Global Prevalence of Civil War" similarly views the Donbas conflict as an example of "competitive intervention" in which third parties (United States and Russia) provide simultaneous assistance to government and rebel forces.

[26] Sambanis, Skaperdas, and Wohlforth, "External Intervention, Identity, and Civil War."

[27] Ibid., 2172.

One common deficiency of the arguments that attribute Russia's intervention to kinship ties or geopolitics is their reliance on Moscow's official rhetoric and documents. Cederman, Rüegger, and Schvitz cite Putin's public statements bemoaning the collapse of the Soviet Union as evidence of his "revisionist worldview."[28] Mearsheimer draws his conclusions that Russia acted defensively in Ukraine from Putin's claims that NATO represented a "direct threat" to Russia.[29] Tsygankov relies on Putin's pronouncements to argue that intervention in Ukraine was "a reflective reaction to what the Kremlin views as neglect of Russia's values and interests and unjust treatment by the West."[30] By taking the official pronouncements of the Russian president as genuine reflections of his views, these authors ignore the manipulations, consistent exaggerations, and outright fabrications evident in Putin's rhetoric. As political scientist Gerard Toal notes, Putin's 2014 Crimean address closely followed a "preexisting script" that intentionally "hyped" the "far-fetched" scenario of a "fascist invasion of Crimea."[31] Yale historian Timothy Snyder called Putin's 2021 essay on Ukraine a "mythical basis" for the Russian invasion.[32] The authors of a comparative study of Russian interventions since 1991 find that protection of coidentity groups, often invoked in Moscow's official pronouncements, "appears to be more of an ex post facto justification."[33] As a result, forecasts of Russia's behavior, based on Moscow's official rhetoric, generally falter. Mearsheimer argued in 2014 that Putin would avoid annexing or conquering Donbas, much less the rest of Ukraine, because he "surely understands that trying to subdue Ukraine would be like swallowing a porcupine."[34] In 2015 Tsygankov suggested that Putin was still concerned with maintaining Ukraine's "cultural and historical ties to Russia"—the very ties that the Russian president irrevocably tore apart by launching a brutal conquest of Ukraine in 2022.[35]

Both geopolitical and identity-based explanations also fail to account for the limited and covert nature of Russia's intervention in Donbas. If Russian

[28] Cederman, Rüegger, and Schvitz, "Redemption through Rebellion," 24.

[29] Mearsheimer, "Why the Ukraine Crisis Is the West's Fault," 3.

[30] Tsygankov, "Vladimir Putin's Last Stand," 297.

[31] Toal, *Near Abroad*.

[32] Timothy Snyder, "Putin's Case for Invading Ukraine Rests on Phony Grievances and Ancient Myths," *Washington Post*, January 28, 2022, https://www.washingtonpost.com/outlook/2022/01/28/putin-russia-ukraine-myths/.

[33] Samuel Charap et al., *Russia's Military Intervention: Patterns, Drivers, and Signposts*, Research Report (Santa Monica, CA: RAND, 2021), 43.

[34] Mearsheimer, "Why the Ukraine Crisis Is the West's Fault," 9.

[35] Tsygankov, "Vladimir Putin's Last Stand," 293.

authorities were interested in organizing a large-scale insurgency campaign to quickly establish control over Donbas, the scale of its initial intervention through proxies like Girkin should have been much larger. As a "signaling mechanism," Girkin's presence in Sloviansk was highly ineffective since it only exposed the ambiguity of the Russian stance and its reluctance to commit a fuller military force to the region. When the conflict in Donbas started escalating in June, the Federation Council revoked the Russian president's authorization to use armed forces in Ukraine. But instead of altogether withdrawing support for the separatists to end the fighting, Putin calibrated a gradual increase in support to fuel the conflict covertly. When Russia deployed its regular troops in August 2014, they were limited to four battalion tactical groups consisting of about four thousand soldiers, twenty tanks, ninety armored vehicles, and thirty artillery pieces—just enough to stop the Ukrainian offensive.[36]

From the perspective of security-based geopolitics, the military advance into eastern Ukraine would have allowed Russia to establish a broader "security belt" on its critically important western flank and buttress its regional power status. Instead, following the defeat of Ukrainian troops near Ilovaisk, Russian troops stopped at the new contact line near Donetsk and Luhansk and in proximity to the Russian border. From the standpoint of ethnic solidarity arguments, Russia's measured response to the rising conflict in Donbas is similarly puzzling. Its restrained strategy put its "kinship group" into greater danger from conflict escalation. It then sought to use the rising violence as leverage over Kyiv to impose a set of institutional changes, the Minsk Accords, with no significance for ethnic Russians or Russian speakers outside Donbas. Only when it became clear that the Minsk Agreements could not be implemented did the Russian leader recognize the independence of the two separatist republics and launch a military offensive against Ukraine.

Interstate Hostility

Russia's deep-rooted resentment of the idea of a sovereign Ukrainian state provides a more compelling explanation of Putin's initial preference for a covert intervention in Donbas and, later, a full-scale assault against the

<hr>

[36] BBC News Ukraina, "Minoborony opublikuvalo analiz boyu pid Ilovaiskom," October 19, 2015. https://www.bbc.com/ukrainian/politics/2015/10/151019_ilovaysk_report_vs.

entire nation.[37] The weakening or overthrowing of a regime perceived as hostile has been identified as one of the main motives behind external support for insurgencies.[38] A prior history of interstate conflict has been shown to substantially increase the probability of an outside intervention to support a rebel group.[39] Although Russia and Ukraine were never engaged in direct military conflict prior to 2014, they had an increasingly conflictual relationship since 1991. The military confrontation between the two states in 2014 became just a new violent phase of the "conflict over Ukraine's status that emerged prior to the breakup of the Soviet Union and never receded."[40] Three primary reasons for Moscow's hostility to Kyiv were (1) its refusal to accept Ukraine's post-1991 borders; (2) its rejection of Ukraine's right to set independent foreign policy goals, such as joining the EU and NATO; and (3) its resentment of Ukraine's nation-building project, particularly in the areas of language policies and memory politics.

Contesting Borders

Moscow's animosity toward Kyiv became particularly visible from during Putin's first term in office, but tensions in bilateral relations had emerged already at the start of Boris Yeltsin's presidency. In response to Ukraine's declaration of independence in August 1991, President Yeltsin issued a statement suggesting the possibility of future border disputes with post-Soviet states. He stressed that Russia "reserves the right to raise the question of revision of borders" in case any newly independent Soviet republic, apart from the Baltics, refused to maintain "allied relations secured by an appropriate treaty."[41] Other Russian officials, including prominent Yeltsin allies like Anatoliy Sobchak, Gavriil Popov, and Aleksandr Rutskoi, even more explicitly commented on the need to contest Ukraine's

---

[37] For a review of the deep historical roots of such hostility, see Eugene Finkel, *Intent to Destroy: Russia's Two-Hundred-Years Quest to Dominate Ukraine* (New York: Basic Books, 2024).

[38] Byman et al. (2001).

[39] One study analyzed 455 rebel groups operating between 1945 and 2010. It found that when states long perceive target countries as hostile they are "almost five times more likely" to stage an intervention compared to states that do not perceive some external threat from a target. See Belgin San-Akca, *States in Disguise: Causes of State Support for Rebel Groups* (Oxford: Oxford University Press, 2016), 91.

[40] D'Anieri, *Ukraine and Russia*, 6.

[41] Vladislav Zubok, *Collapse: The Fall of the Soviet Union* (New Haven, CT: Yale University Press, 2021), 323–324.

borders if it became an independent state. The two regions that drew the particular interest of the revisionists in Yeltsin's camp were Crimea and Donbas.[42]

Over the next two decades territorial claims on parts of Ukraine were issued publicly by various Russian political figures, most prominently by the mayor of Moscow Yuriy Luzhkov. In July 1993, a majority in the Russian Parliament voted in favor of recognizing the city of Sevastopol, the naval base of the Russian Black Sea Fleet, as part of the Russian Federation. Years later numerous members of the Russian Duma from the nationalist and leftist factions argued against ratification of the Russian-Ukrainian Treaty on Friendship, Cooperation and Partnership on the grounds that it would amount to Russia's official recognition of Ukraine's 1991 borders. The notorious leader of the Liberal Democratic Party, Vladimir Zhyrinovskiy, lamented during December 1998 parliamentary hearings that "the ratification of the treaty would mean that Russia has no relationship to Crimea and any other territories [of Ukraine]." He continued, "[T]oday's Ukraine represents anarchy, it's nothing and nowhere, so that means it is ours."[43]

Zhyrinovskiy's views, earlier discounted as the radical fringe position, gradually became part of the mainstream rhetoric during Putin's rule. Less than ten years later, President Putin famously told U.S. president George W. Bush at a behind-the-scenes meeting at the NATO summit in Bucharest that "Ukraine is not even a country."[44] He even made a veiled threat to seize eastern Ukraine because of its ethnic and historic ties to Russia.[45] Putin's successor, Dmitriy Medvedev, adopted similar rhetoric. In August 2009, a little over a year into his presidential term, Medvedev accused the Ukrainian leadership of supplying arms to Georgia, imposing restrictions on use of the Russian language, and distorting Ukraine's shared history with Russia. "Tensions in the relations between Ukraine and Russia are reaching the boiling point," he warned.[46] Medvedev agreed to visit Kyiv to meet the newly elected Ukrainian president, Viktor Yanukovych, in 2010 only once he agreed to sign a

---

[42] Ibid., 324; Steven Pifer, *The Eagle and the Trident: U.S.-Ukraine Relations in Turbulent Times* (Washington, DC: Brookings Institution Press, 2017), 30–31.

[43] Transcript of the meeting is available at RF State Duma, "Stenogramma zasedania 25 dekabria, 1998 goda," December 25, 1998, http://transcript.duma.gov.ru/node/2445/.

[44] *Kommersant*, "Blok NATO razoshelsia na blokpakety," April 7, 2008, https://www.kommersant.ru/doc/877224.

[45] Condoleezza Rice, *No Higher Honor: A Memoir of My Years in Washington* (New York: Crown, 2011), 675-676.

[46] Official Website of the President of the Russian Federation, "Poslanie Prezidentu Ukrainy Viktoru Yushchenko," August 11, 2009, http://www.kremlin.ru/catalog/countries/UA/events/5158.

twenty-five-year extension of the lease on the Sevastopol naval base. Since 2022 Medvedev has become an outspoken advocate of the use of the most brutal tactics in Russia's war against Ukraine.[47]

Contesting Alignments

The second source of bilateral tensions has been Russia's long-standing disapproval of Ukraine's cooperative relations with the West. This first became evident in Russia's opposition to Kyiv's closer ties to NATO. In the Special Charter on a Distinctive Partnership with NATO, signed in July 1997, Ukraine committed itself to increasing "interoperability with the forces of NATO and Partner countries" and cooperation in the areas of military training.[48] Russia opposed the initial wave of NATO enlargement that included three Central European states, but felt particularly resentful about possible NATO membership of the post-Soviet states.[49] Ironically, Ukrainian president Leonid Kuchma first announced the country's intention to join NATO during a bilateral U.S.-Russia summit in Moscow in May 2002.[50] By that time, Kyiv's newly stated objective had already received tacit support from the Bush administration.[51] Ukraine reaffirmed its goal to become a NATO member in the resolution of the National Security and Defense Council adopted in May 2003.[52] The Military Doctrine signed by Kuchma in June 2004 identified NATO membership as the precondition for ensuring Ukraine's security.[53]

In early 2008 President Yushchenko tried to take the next vital step on the path to joining NATO and requested the provision of a Membership Action Plan to Ukraine. Putin's immediate response was to suggest that Russia could "target Ukraine with its offensive rocket system" if Ukrainian territory were

[47] *Newsweek*, "Russia's Medvedev Threatens Ukraine with Pre-emptive Nuclear Strike," May 26, 2023, https://www.newsweek.com/russia-medvedev-ukraine-nuclear-strike-weapons-west-putin-1802829.

[48] North Atlantic Treaty Organization, Charter on a Distinctive Partnership between the North Atlantic Treaty Organization and Ukraine, July 8, 1997, https://www.nato.int/cps/en/natohq/official_texts_25457.htm.

[49] In a May 10, 1995, conversation with the U.S. president Bill Clinton, Yeltsin called it a "new form of encirclement" if NATO "expands right up to the borders of Russia." See National Security Archive, "Summary Report on the One-on-One Meeting between Presidents Clinton and Yeltsin," May 10, 1995, https://nsarchive.gwu.edu/document/16825-document-04-summary-report-one-one.

[50] Pifer, *The Eagle and the Trident*, 223.

[51] Ibid., 222.

[52] Mykola Siruk, "Yevhen Marchuk: Na Shliakhu do NATO," *Den'*, nos. 205–206 (2016), https://day.kyiv.ua/uk/article/den-planety/yevgen-marchuk-na-shlyahu-do-nato.

[53] Liga 360, "Voenna doktryna Ukrainy," approved on June 15, 2004, https://ips.ligazakon.net/document/view/u648_04?an=234&ed=2005_04_21.

used to neutralize Russia's nuclear capabilities.[54] Concerns over Russia's response prevented Western leaders from reaching a consensus on extending a Membership Action Plan to Ukraine during the Bucharest Summit in April 2008.[55] Instead, the Summit Declaration asserted that Ukraine, along with Georgia, would eventually join the alliance without specifying a timetable for the process.[56] This, in the words of RAND political scientist Samuel Charap, represented "the worst of all worlds." Instead of enhancing Ukraine's security, the outcome of the Bucharest Summit "reinforced Moscow's view that NATO was set on incorporating [Ukraine and Georgia]."[57]

The negative repercussions of Ukraine's integration into NATO for Russian-Ukrainian relations were recognized at the time even by some high-ranking U.S. officials. The U.S. ambassador in Russia, William Burns, noted in a January 2008 diplomatic cable, months before the Summit, that Ukraine's integration into NATO represented "an emotional and neuralgic issue" for Moscow tied to "strategic concerns about the impact on Russia's interests in the region."[58] Burns even suggested that Ukraine itself could experience internal conflict over membership in NATO, opening the possibility of Russian intervention. On the eve of the Summit Burns reiterated his earlier argument calling Ukraine's entry into the alliance "the brightest of all redlines for the Russian elite (not just Putin)" and "fertile soil for Russian meddling in Crimea and eastern Ukraine."[59]

In his speech at the Bucharest Summit, the Russian president reaffirmed his opposition to Ukraine's membership in the starkest possible terms. He argued that NATO membership "could put [Ukraine's] statehood in question," while seventeen million ethnic Russians living in Ukraine could become the source of its destabilization.[60] Once elected president in 2010, Yanukovych responded to Russia's security concerns by declaring Ukraine a

---

[54] Official Website of the President of Russian Federation, "Zaiavlenia dlia pressy i otvety na voprosy zhurnalistov po okonchanii peregovorov s Prezidentom Ukrainy Viktorom Yushchenko i vtorogo zasedania Rossiysko-Ukrainskoi mezhgosudarstvennoi komissii," February 12, 2008, http://www.kremlin.ru/events/president/transcripts/24833.

[55] Klaus Wiegrafe, "The Day the War Really Began," *Der Spiegel*, September 25, 2019, https://www.spiegel.de/international/europe/ukraine-how-merkel-prevented-ukraine-s-nato-membership-a-der-spiegel-reconstruction-a-c7f03472-2a21-4e4e-b905-8e45f1fad542.

[56] North Atlantic Treaty Organization, Bucharest Summit Declaration, April 3, 2008, https://www.nato.int/cps/en/natolive/official_texts_8443.htm.

[57] Samuel Charap, "NATO Honesty on Ukraine Could Avert Conflict," *Financial Times*, January 13, 2022, https://www.ft.com/content/74089d46-abb8-4daa-9ee4-e9e9e4c45ab1.

[58] William Burns, "Nyet Means Nyet: Russia's NATO Enlargement Redlines," classified cable, February 1, 2008, cited in William Burns, *The Back Channel: A Memoir of American Diplomacy and the Case for Its Renewal* (New York: Random House, 2019).

[59] Burns, *The Back Channel*, 233.

[60] UNIAN, "Vystuplenie Vladimira Putin na sammite NATO," April 18, 2008, https://www.unian.net/politics/110868-vyistuplenie-vladimira-putina-na-sammite-nato-buharest-4-aprelya-2008-goda.html.

"nonaligned" state. Still, the concept of "nonalignment" (позаблоковість) drew strong criticism from the largest opposition parties, which promised to revive the NATO membership process after regaining power. The lack of genuine elite agreement on Ukraine's foreign policy course indicated that its nonalignment pledge in 2010 was just a temporary fix, not a permanent solution.

Russia sought more than just Ukraine's neutrality. The alternative integration arrangement that Moscow offered to Ukraine was membership in a Russia-led economic union. In September 2003, an embattled President Kuchma endorsed Putin's proposal to form the Common Economic Space with Belarus and Kazakhstan, but Ukraine reversed course following Yushchenko's victory in 2004. Then Russia renewed its push to integrate Ukraine economically after Yanukovych's victory. It offered Ukraine membership in the Customs Union, which was the core of the newly created Eurasian Economic Union. Given Yanukovych's close ties to industrial elites in eastern Ukraine who depended on access to the Russian market, Putin expected a favorable response. Instead, Yanukovych ditched this proposal and concluded long-running talks on the Deep and Comprehensive Free Trade Agreement (DCFTA) with the EU. This was the first tangible step to making Ukraine's EU integration course irreversible. Russia responded in August 2013 by imposing trade sanctions on Ukrainian producers and threatening major economic losses for the Ukrainian economy if the trade agreement went into effect. Ultimately, Yanukovych decided against signing the DCFTA, primarily due to continued disagreement with the EU leaders on the fate of the jailed opposition leader Yulia Tymoshenko. Putin's actions, however, made it clear that he opposed any type of alliance, be it security or economic, between Ukraine and the West.

Contesting Symbols

The third point of contention between Moscow and Kyiv was related to symbols and narratives. The success of Ukraine's nation-building project required reversal of over a century of Russification policies and a critical appraisal of Soviet legacies. Article 10 of Ukraine's 1996 Constitution made Ukrainian the only state language but guaranteed the "free development, use and protection of the Russian, and other national minority languages."[61]

---

[61] Constitution of Ukraine, 2013, https://www.justice.gov/sites/default/files/eoir/legacy/2013/11/08/constitution_14.pdf.

In practice, formal recognition of the Ukrainian language did not preclude the widespread use of Russian as a default language in some regions and in the public domain.[62] Still, Russian elites feared that Ukrainian state policies could lead to the gradual decline of Russian language use. Already in the late 1990s Russian officials complained about "the violations of rights of Russian-speaking people during the so-called Ukrainianization."[63] Article 12 of the Russian-Ukrainian Friendship Treaty had committed Ukraine to providing "opportunities and conditions for learning" the Russian language.[64] But Moscow wanted to see Russian recognized as the second state language to secure its long-term protection. Until then, Russian officials pledged to defend "the interests of the Russians and Russian speakers in the spheres of media, culture, education etc."[65] The confluence of ethnic Russian and Russian-speaking Ukrainians, making up at least half of the Ukrainian population at the time, became a constant feature of Russia's official rhetoric.

Prior to his election, President Yanukovych often made a point of addressing his voters in Russian and campaigned as a protector of the rights of Russian speakers in Ukraine. Once becoming president in 2010 he initiated legislation that would make Russian the "regional language." His draft law, however, avoided a nationwide change in the status of Russian given the likely domestic backlash. Instead, it allowed local councils to elevate the status of the Russian language if at least 10% of a province's population were native Russian speakers. Over the next months, the local councils in thirteen out of twenty-seven administrative units voted to make Russian a regional language. In effect, the adoption of the law "removed state incentives to learn and use Ukrainian."[66]

The new language policy triggered street protests and hunger strikes organized by the opposition parties. The revoking of the law was one of the first decisions adopted by Parliament following Yanukovych's flight into exile in February 2014. The decision, however, backfired by reinforcing the fear of many in the southeastern regions that the new government would remove

---

[62] Dominique Arel, "Language, Status, and State Loyalty in Ukraine," *Harvard Ukrainian Studies* 35, nos. 1–4 (2017–2018): 233.

[63] Remarks of the Russian foreign affairs minister Igor Ivanov at the State Duma hearing: RF State Duma, "Stenogramma zasedania 25 dekabria, 1998 goda," December 25, 1998, http://transcript. duma.gov.ru/node/2445/.

[64] United Nations, "Treaty on Friendship, Cooperation and Partnership between Ukraine and the Russian Federation," signed on May 31, 1997, https://treaties.un.org/Pages/showDetails. aspx?objid=08000002803e6fae.

[65] RF State Duma, "Stenogramma zasedania 25 dekabria, 1998 goda."

[66] Arel, "Language, Status, and State Loyalty in Ukraine," 233.

their rights. And Russia immediately used this issue as evidence that the new government in Kyiv posed a threat to the Russian speakers in Crimea and Donbas. Although the acting president, Oleksandr Turchynov, never signed Parliament's resolution, its polarizing effect created favorable conditions for Russia's destabilization campaign against Ukraine.

Historical memory became another point of contention between Russia and Ukraine in the symbolic domain. Two events that drew intense political disagreements between Kyiv and Moscow were the 1932–1933 famine in Ukraine (known as the Holodomor) and Ukrainian nationalist resistance to Soviet rule during and after World War II.[67] The Ukrainian Parliament's 2006 law recognizing the famine as "genocide of the Ukrainian people" was viewed in Moscow as a veiled attempt to smear Russia as the successor to the USSR.[68] During April 2008 parliamentary hearings a member of the Russian Duma from the ruling United Russia Party, Konstantin Zatulin, insisted that Kyiv's interpretation of the Holodomor was meant to "inflame hostility towards the Russian Federation and the Russian people."[69] Yanukovych, however, stopped short of abolishing the law or removing the now standard interpretation of the famine from history textbooks.

Even greater animosity between Moscow and Kyiv emerged around the legacy of the Ukrainian nationalist movement, represented by its two most prominent organizations—the Organization of Ukrainian Nationalists (OUN) led by Stepan Bandera and the Ukrainian Insurgent Army (UPA) led by Roman Shukhevych. Bandera's support for establishing the Ukrainian state under Nazi Germany's tutelage and his fascist ideological leanings became widely discounted in Ukraine because of his advocacy of Ukrainian independence.[70] Similarly, Shukhevych's role as the commander of UPA in its fight against the Soviet occupation of western Ukraine brought him national recognition despite his earlier service as a deputy commander of the "Ukrainian legion," an auxiliary police battalion created by Abwehr Admiral Wilhelm Canaris in 1941. Both Bandera and Shukhevych were killed by

---

[67] Georgiy Kasianov, *Memory Crash: Politics of History in and around Ukraine, 1980s–2010s* (Budapest: CEU Press, 2022).

[68] Supreme Council of Ukraine, "Zakon Ukrainy pro Holodomor 1932–1933 rokiv v Ukraini," November 28, 2006, https://zakon.rada.gov.ua/laws/show/376-16.

[69] RF State Duma, "Transcript of the Proceedings," April 2, 2008, N16 (989), http://transcript.duma.gov.ru/node/570/.

[70] Timothy Snyder, "A Fascist Hero in Democratic Kiev," *New York Review of Books*, February 24, 2010, https://www.nybooks.com/online/2010/02/24/a-fascist-hero-in-democratic-kiev/.

Soviet security agents, which turned them into martyrs for the Ukrainian nationalist milieu.

Beginning in 2005 there was a notable shift in state policies, from "rehabilitating OUN and UPA to exalting and promoting these organizations."[71] History textbooks depicted them as fighters for Ukrainian independence and part of the "liberation movement," while the government launched various commemorative initiatives in their honor. Russian officials portrayed this shift as a sign of government-sanctioned Russophobia and an affront to the memory of those who fought Nazi Germany. In December 2007 Russia's Foreign Ministry issued a statement protesting "the rise of nationalist, anti-Russian and Russophobic actions in Ukraine," which included "rehabilitation of OUN-UPA."[72] In his public appeal to Yushchenko in August 2009 President Medvedev mentioned "glorification of Nazi collaborators" as one of the main challenges to Russian-Ukrainian relations.[73]

Similar accusations have been constantly repeated and amplified within Ukraine by its largest pro-Russian parties: the Party of Regions (PR) and the Communist Party of Ukraine (KPU). Clashes over historical narratives became a standard element of the election campaigns and deepened the regional cleavage over identity-based issues. They also formed a stereotypical view among some voters in southeastern Ukraine of pro-Western parties as radical nationalist or neo-Nazi forces bent on excluding their opponents from the Ukrainian polity. PR and KPU thus became vital for Moscow as tools of influence over Ukrainian public opinion and advocates of an alternative approach to memory politics. With their defeat following the successful Euromaidan revolution, Moscow could expect from Kyiv only accelerated nation-building and a more concerted pro-Western foreign policy.

From Political Rivalry to Armed Intervention

The inability to resolve any of the top contentious issues in Russian-Ukrainian relations only strengthened the Kremlin's hostility to the Ukrainian state over time. Still, as political scientist Paul D'Anieri notes,

---

[71] Georgiy Kasianov, *Past-Continuous: Istorychna polityka 1980-h–2000-h. Ukraina ta susidy* (Kyiv: Antropos-Logos-Film, 2018), 244.

[72] Russian Ministry of Foreign Affairs, "Zaiavlenie MID Rossii v sviazi s antirossiskimi proiavleniyami na Ukraine," December 14, 2007, https://mid.ru/ru/foreign_policy/news/164 4533/.

[73] *Ukrainska Pravda*, "Medvedev obvinil Yushchenko v antirossiyskom kurse," August 11, 2009, https://www.pravda.com.ua/rus/news/2009/08/11/4498008/.

"Russia was always concerned with regaining control of Ukraine, but whether it was always determined to use force if other means failed is unclear."[74] The decision to intervene militarily required not only resentment of Kyiv but also the perception that the armed intervention was a low-cost alternative. This assessment was based on the obvious effects of the Euromaidan revolution on the Ukrainian state and society. They included (1) a breakdown in the defensive and coercive capacity of the Ukrainian state, (2) cross-regional polarization in response to Euromaidan protests, and (3) low legitimacy of the new post-Maidan government.

Weak State Capacity

The adoption of violent tactics by some Euromaidan protesters in Kyiv triggered diffusion of violent repertoires of contention to the regions.[75] It involved the seizure of municipal buildings in western and central Ukrainian cities, vandalism of municipal property, and assaults on police units by protesters using sticks, chains, and Molotov cocktails. Rather than alienating moderates, violent forms of protest gained broader acceptance within the protest movement.[76]

The increasing reliance on violence by Euromaidan participants challenged the state's monopoly on the legitimate use of force. The attacks on riot police soldiers were framed as a righteous assertion of civic rights; retaliatory police violence against protesters was condemned as an unacceptable transgression. This politicized the fundamental task of policing and led to a split within the ranks of law enforcement. In February police units in several western Ukrainian provinces refused to follow government orders and sided with protesters. Local councils in the West announced that they no longer recognized the authorities in Kyiv and sought to subordinate police units to themselves. Days before Yanukovych fled Kyiv, protesters targeted the security agencies directly. They seized and looted the military base in Lviv and ransacked offices of police and state procuracy in several

---

[74] D'Anieri, *Ukraine and Russia*, 27.

[75] Serhiy Kudelia, "When Numbers Are Not Enough: The Strategic Use of Violence in Ukraine's 2014 Revolution," *Comparative Politics* 50, no. 4 (2018): 501–521.

[76] The share of protesters who expressed willingness to join armed units independent of the state increased from 15% in December 2013 to 50.4% in February 2014. Similarly, the share of those ready to storm and seize buildings as part of protest actions rose from 13.8% to 41% over the same period. Data based on surveys of protesters conducted by the Kyiv International Institute of Sociology in December 2013 and February 2014, https://www.kiis.com.ua/?lang=rus&cat=reports&id=226&page=1&y=2014&m=2.

western Ukrainian towns. These attacks involved destruction of municipal property, burning of government documents, and pilfering of thousands of units of arms and ammunition. Even for a country that had experienced major protest mobilizations before, it was an unprecedented display of civil disobedience enabled by the disarray within the country's main coercive agencies.

After weeks of physical attacks on police forces and condemnations of police conduct, security forces shunned their responsibilities. Many were fearful of being prosecuted for their deployments on Maidan and the use of force against protesters. There was also a complete breakdown of security command structures. Top military and police officials, including the interior and defense ministers and the SBU chief, fled the country. Ukraine's under-funded armed forces lacked the capacity to resist Russian intervention.[77] As the new SBU chief Valentyn Nalyvaichenko admitted on February 28, 2014, days after coming to power, "Our military and security personnel are demoralized. Many of them do not accept the new authorities and are not ready to fulfill orders or even betrayed their oath. . . . The moral and psychological climate among top commanders is extremely poor, if not treacherous."[78]

Regional Polarization

Protests also deepened societal polarization along regional lines and added a clear geopolitical dimension to cross-regional tensions. From the start, Ukrainians were divided in their view of protesters. A month after Euromaidan began, 45.1% expressed support for protest demands, while 35.7% opposed them.[79] By late January the divide was more even, with 47.6% of respondents expressing full or partial support for protests, while 46.1%

[77] According to the released minutes of the meeting of the National Security and Defense Council of Ukraine from February 28, 2014, top Ukrainian officials at the time agreed that Ukraine could not defend Crimea against Russian intervention. Prime Minister Arseniy Yatsenyuk said that Ukraine "was not ready for military operations ... and Russians know it." Deputy Prime Minister Vitaliy Yarema claimed, "Martial law would not help. We do not have the capacity to introduce it in Crimea, we cannot rely on police forces, which do not exist now, and the Security Service of Ukraine, which de facto does not exist. Not to mention the Army." See Iryna Shtohryn, "Chomu ne vtrymaly Krym: Stenohrama RNBO vid 28 lyutoho 2014 roku," *Radio Liberty Ukrainian Service*, February 27, 2019, https://www.radiosvoboda.org/a/29794488.html.

[78] Ibid.

[79] Data based on the survey jointly conducted by the Democratic Initiatives Foundation, named after Ilko Kucheriv, and the Razumkov Center in December 20–24, 2013. See Democratic Initiatives Foundation, "Dva misiatsi protestive v Ukraini: Sho dali?," January 21, 2014, https://dif.org.ua/article/dva-misyatsi-protestiv-v-ukraini-shcho-dali.

expressed full or partial opposition.[80] These views fell along regional lines. When asked to take a side in an early February 2014 survey, an overwhelming majority of western Ukrainians (80.4%) but only a small minority of respondents in eastern Ukraine (7.5%) supported the protesters.[81]

These contrasting views, however, were not conditioned solely by differences in attitudes to Yanukovych.[82] Rather, they were influenced by differences in the perceived goals of the protest actions. Respondents in the Southeast viewed Euromaidan as a Western-led project. Most in eastern (57%) and southern (44%) Ukraine agreed that the protests were influenced by the West seeking to draw Ukraine into its "orbit of political interests." Almost half of eastern Ukrainian respondents (45%) attributed "nationalist sentiments" to the protesters, which exceeded even the share of respondents in Russia with such a view (30.5%). For Ukrainians in western and central regions, by contrast, the protest was primarily a grassroots emotive response to Yanukovych's rule. Most respondents there (67.6% in the West and 54.8% in the Center) viewed it as an expression of people's outrage over the government's corruption.

Contested Government Legitimacy

Views on protest motives also influenced how Ukrainians interpreted the immediate outcome of Euromaidan—the removal of Yanukovych from power. For most respondents in western Ukraine, according to a March 2014 survey, Maidan represented either a revolution (44%) or a movement toward Europe (27%).[83] This meant that the legitimacy of the new Ukrainian

[80] Data based on a survey jointly conducted by KIIS and SOCIC in January 24–February 1, 2014: Kyiv International Institute of Sociology, "Nastroenia Ukrainy—Rezultaty sovmestnogo issledovania KMIS i SOCIS," February 7, 2014, https://www.kiis.com.ua/?lang=rus&cat=reports&id=227&page=1&y=2014&m=2.

[81] Data based on a survey conducted by KIIS and the Levada Center in February 8–18, 2014: Kyiv International Institute of Sociology, "Otnoshenie v Ukraine i Rossii k aktsiyam protesta v Ukraine," February 28, 2014, https://www.kiis.com.ua/?lang=rus&cat=reports&id=231&page=1&y=2014&m=2.

[82] Only about a third of respondents in the South (32.2%) and half in the East (51.9%) sympathized with the president in his confrontation with Euromaidan (ibid.).

[83] Data based on a survey of 1,200 residents of Ukraine conducted in March 14–26, 2014, by Baltic Surveys/The Gallup Organization on behalf of International Republican Institute throughout Ukraine (including Crimea), with a 2.8% error margin. For full results see International Republican Institute, "Public Opinion Survey of Residents of Ukraine," March 14–26, 2014, https://www.iri.org/wp-content/uploads/2014/04/201420April20520IRI20Public20Opinion20Survey20of20Ukraine2C20March2014-262C202014.pdf.

authorities was rooted in the genuine expression of popular will. Most respondents in southeastern Ukraine, by contrast, framed protest outcomes in negative elite-centered terms. For eastern Ukrainians, it largely represented a "coup d'etat" (26%) or a mere "elite conflict" (26%). Most southern Ukrainians similarly tended to view it as a coup (27%) or "chaos" (30%). This framing implied that opposition leaders seized power through intrigues and had dubious legitimacy to run the country. In the two provinces of Donetsk and Luhansk, there was particularly strong reluctance to embrace the new government.[84] Every second respondent in Donetsk and Luhansk oblasts in early April was "confident" that the government of Acting President Turchynov and Prime Minister Yatsenyuk was "illegal."[85] Overall, about two-thirds of respondents in each of the two provinces—significantly more than in any other Ukrainian oblast even in the Southeast—questioned the legality of the post-Maidan authorities.[86]

Never before could Russia expect its covert armed intervention against Kyiv would receive such a welcoming response. Support for joining Russia increased in some regions already during the Euromaidan revolution. In early February, the highest support for the merger between Russia and Ukraine was in Crimea (41%), followed by the Donetsk region (33.2%).[87] When Russia's invasion of Crimea began, the new interior minister of Ukraine Arsen Avakov suggested that "the majority of Crimean residents took a pro-Russian, anti-Ukrainian position."[88] Once Russia announced its annexation of Crimea, the overwhelming majority of respondents in Donetsk (71.8%) and Luhansk (57.8%) regions blamed the new Ukrainian

[84] There are no reliable polling results for the views of residents of Crimea at the time on this question.

[85] Data based on the survey of 3,232 respondents conducted in April 10–15, 2014, by Kyiv International Institute of Sociology. For full results, see Yulia Mostovaya and Sergei Rakhmanin, "Yugo-Vostok: Vetv Dreva Nashego," *ZN*, April 18, 2014, https://zn.ua/internal/yugo-vostok-vetv-dreva-nashego-_.html.

[86] Another survey conducted at the same time corroborated these findings: the majority of respondents in Luhansk (51%) and Donetsk (80%) regions strongly or somewhat disagreed with the legitimacy of Yatsenyuk government. International Foundation for Electoral Systems, "Public Opinion in Ukraine 2014: Findings from the IFES 2014 Survey in Ukraine," 7. Data is based on IFES survey of 2,039 respondents conducted by Kyiv International Institute of Sociology in April 8–15, 2014, with a 2.2% error margin.

[87] Data based on a survey of 2,032 respondents conducted in February 8–18, 2014, by Kyiv International Institute of Sociology and Ilko Kucheriv Democratic Initiatives Foundation, with a 3.4% error margin. Kyiv International Institute of Sociology, "Dynamika Stavlennia Naselennia Ukrainy do Rosii ta Naselennia Rosii do Ukrainy, Yakyh Vidnosyn z Rosieyu Khotily b Ukraintsi," March 4, 2014, https://kiis.com.ua/?lang=ukr&cat=reports&id=236.

[88] Shtohryn, "Chomu ne vtrymaly Krym."

authorities for the loss of the peninsula. Only 8.4% in Donetsk and 15.4% in Luhansk put the blame on Russia.[89] The majority (51%) in the East in early April said that the Ukrainian way of life was most closely associated with "Russian values."[90] And almost half of eastern Ukrainians (46%) in the same time period believed that Ukraine would be better off if it had closer economic and political relations with Russia rather than Europe.[91] The Donetsk and Luhansk regions were also the only ones in Ukraine where Putin remained widely popular even after the Crimean annexation, with the majority of respondents there (66%) expressing an entirely or largely positive view of the Russian president.[92] Thus Crimea and Donbas emerged as the easiest targets for Russia's interventionist strategy.

The Seeds of Conflict

The rivalrous relationship between Russia and Ukraine started at the time of the Soviet collapse and intensified over the following twenty years. The logic of Ukrainian state-building propelled it westward. The traditions of Russia's political class revived the worst anti-Western phobias and desires to dominate its neighbors. Euromaidan protests represented a rejection of the Kremlin's final attempt to keep Ukraine in its fold. While successful in preventing the foreign policy reversal, the Revolution of Dignity (as it is known in Ukraine) left behind a weakened state, a polarized society, and a government with dubious legitimacy. Combined, these effects substantially lowered the costs of Russian military intervention in Ukraine.

While the quick capture of Crimea offered a range of strategic benefits to Putin independent of its implications for Ukraine, covert intervention in Donbas was attractive primarily for its destabilizing effect on the Ukrainian

[89] Data based on the survey of 3,232 respondents conducted in April 10–15, 2014, by Kyiv International Institute of Sociology, "Dumky ta pohliady zhyteliv pivdenno-skhidnykh oblastei Ukrainy: Kviten 2014," April 20, 2014, https://kiis.com.ua/?lang=ukr&cat=reports&id=302&page=1&y=2014&m=4.

[90] Eastern Ukraine in this survey included residents of the Donetsk, Luhansk, and Kharkiv regions. IFES, "Public Opinion in Ukraine 2014," 15.

[91] Another 26% of respondents in eastern Ukraine said that Ukraine would need to have close relations with both Russia and Europe, while 16% preferred closer ties with Europe alone. Ibid., 19.

[92] Putin's favorability in Ukraine at the time stood at 16%. Based on the data from the survey of two thousand respondents conducted by Rating Group, April 15–25, 2014, with a 2.2% error margin. See Rating Group, "Nostalgia za SRSR ta stavlennia do okremyh postatei," May 2014, p. 25, https://ratinggroup.ua/files/ratinggroup/reg_files/rg_historical_ua_052014.pdf.

state.[93] It promised Russia an opportunity to recoup losses associated with Yanukovych's downfall and acquire a new lever of influence over policymakers in Kyiv. The legitimacy crisis and internal chaos caused by the revolutionary events offered Moscow an opening for a fundamental revision of the way the Ukrainian state was organized. For most of its independent history, Ukraine functioned as a highly centralized polity with strict subordination of the executive agencies in the provinces to the centralized executive in Kyiv. Ukraine's democratization progress in the 2000s had little effect on this established hierarchical relationship. But once the legitimacy of the government was in question, a new model with empowered regions suddenly seemed feasible.[94] For Russia, Ukraine's transformation into a federal or decentralized state could prevent the reinstatement of the most contentious nation-building policies in at least some parts of the country. It could also have hampered Ukraine's integration into the EU if some regions promoted trade and other economic relations with Russia independently of Kyiv's policies. Finally, as some scholars at the time suggested, the federal model could have provided a formal or de facto veto power over the government's security policies. This would put an end to Ukraine's NATO aspirations.[95]

Donbas could perfectly serve these goals. Its residents showed a longstanding preference for elevating the status of the Russian language and aversion to nationalist historical narratives. Its industries depended on access to the Russian market and were integrated into Russian supply chains. Public opinion in Donbas consistently disapproved of Ukraine's integration into the EU and NATO. The expanded power of two Donbas provinces thus would allow Moscow to "institutionalize its influence" inside the country.[96] Russia would no longer need to cultivate sympathetic political parties, especially given that their electoral prospects seemed particularly dim with the loss of over one million Crimean voters. Instead, the regional authorities could bargain directly with any new Ukrainian leadership on Russia's behalf. Their exclusive powers over law enforcement, the judiciary, and educational and cultural policies would also turn these autonomous units into "segment

---

[93] On the benefits of Crimea's annexation, see Daniel Treisman, "Why Putin Took Crimea: The Gambler in the Kremlin," *Foreign Affairs* 96, no. 3 (May–June 2016): 47–54.

[94] The proposal for decentralizing power in Ukraine with free elections of region heads was advanced at the time even by some Western political scientists and economists to diffuse the crisis of confidence in the new authorities. See Scott Ghelbach, Roger Myerson, and Tymofiy Mylovanov, "A Way Forward for Ukraine," *New York Times*, March 19, 2014, https://www.nytimes.com/2014/03/20/opinion/a-way-forward-for-ukraine.html.

[95] Oleksandr Sushko, "After the Ukraine-Russia War: Is There a Sustainable Solution?," Policy Memo No. 356 (Washington, DC: PONARS Eurasia, September 2014).

[96] Andrew Bowen, "Coercive Diplomacy and the Donbas: Explaining Russian Strategy in Eastern Ukraine," *Journal of Strategic Studies* 42, nos. 3–4 (2019): 312–343.

states" capable of triggering a new secessionist crisis at any point.[97] Russia would then gain blackmail power over any future Ukrainian leader and threaten an internal uprising for any serious affront to the Kremlin. But the success of this scenario still required a sustained political challenge to Kyiv from within the region. As Moscow quickly realized, such a challenge needed an external push even to get off the ground.

[97] On how "segment states" increase the likelihood of secessionist crisis, see Philip Roeder, *Where Nation-States Come From: Institutional Change in the Age of Nationalism* (Princeton, NJ: Princeton University Press, 2006).

Chapter 3
Imposed Secession

From Crimea to Donbas

The collapse of Yanukovych's regime on February 21, 2014, became a critical juncture that broadened the range of choices for actors both inside and outside Ukraine. For the Ukrainian opposition, it offered a chance to immediately seize political power and claim victory in a lengthy political confrontation. For those tied to the defeated regime, it presented an opportunity to seek new distribution of power between the center and the regions that would guarantee continued access to rents and control over public offices. External actors in the United States and Europe viewed it as a chance to bring Ukraine back to a pro-Western developmental track through the elevation of elite groups favoring a reform agenda.

For Russia, the critical juncture in Kyiv opened at least two possibilities. One was to encourage local elites and the sympathetic public in southeastern Ukraine to advance secessionist demands and disrupt the country's renewed pivot to the West. The presence of influential members of the Russian Duma and Federation Council, Aleksei Pushkov and Mikhail Margelov, at the gathering of administrators from southeastern regions in Kharkiv on February 22 suggested that Moscow considered such a strategy. Its implementation, however, required close coordination of multiple local leaders, whose personal agendas and interests were often at odds. When considering Ukraine's future, one of Russia's prominent neo-imperial polemicists, Aleksandr Prokhanov, argued that "it would all depend on whether left-bank governors could . . . create a Union of left-bank regions or a Federation, which should include Sevastopol and the entire Crimea, and Kharkov, and Lugansk, and Donetsk, and Dnepropetrovsk." It required, as he put it, the emergence of "organizers, people of free will."[1] While Moscow could help with identifying such "organizers," it promised to be a long and tenuous

---

[1] *Rodina*, "Prokhanov ob Ukraine: Na nashyh glazah proiskhodit chudovishnoe deistvie," February 26, 2014, https://rodina.ru/novosti/Proxanov-ob-Ukraine-Na-nashix-glazax-proisxodit-chudovishhnoe-dejstvie.

Seize the City, Undo the State. Serhiy Kudelia, Oxford University Press. © Oxford University Press (2025). DOI: 10.1093/9780197795576.003.0004

process with uncertain results. Given that "critical junctures" are always fleeting moments, waiting for local organizers to act was likely to leave Russia with few if any gains.

The alternative for Moscow was to become such an "organizer," to assist sympathetic local actors and press developments in a favorable direction. This, however, would also require prioritizing those regions of Ukraine where Russia's efforts were more likely to succeed. Of these, Crimea stood out both in its symbolic and strategic significance and in the strength of pro-Russian sympathies there among the public. Most important was its accessibility to the Russian military, which maintained the base in Sevastopol along with about twelve thousand military personnel.[2] The images of the first large rallies under Russian flags in Crimean towns led one Moscow-based nationalist blogger, Yegor Kholmogorov, to describe this mobilization as the "Russian Spring."[3] The label evoked romantic notions of 1848 and its "springtime of nations" that led to major reorganization of states in Europe as well as of 2011 and the "Arab Spring" uprisings that brought down governments in the Middle East. These multiple connotations made it an instantly popular marker for the entire pro-Russian mobilization in Ukraine.

The backing of the movement by the Russian state, however, quickly became the central theme of nationalist writing at the time. Already in early March, Prokhanov recognized that Putin would not be standing on the sidelines of pro-Russian mobilization in Ukraine. Prokhanov's prose suddenly acquired a more confident tone: "In 1991 we experienced a horrific amputation of the juiciest parts of the Russian world. . . . Now Russians in Ukraine have suffered another terrible blow. But today Russia is not being silent. From Smolensk to Yuzhno-Sakhalinsk we hear: 'Crimea! Ukraine! Putin, act!' And Putin acts. Since today's Kremlin hardly resembles the Kremlin of the Yeltsin times."[4] In an article in early April, Kholmogorov already extolled the "Russian Spring" as a "classic, national, ethnic, irredentist revolution" that allowed the "self-fulfillment" of the Russian nation through "external geopolitical action." "Russia does not exist, if it does not attach new territories," he professed.[5] This echoed the observation of Russia's most

---

[2] Kofman et al., *Lessons from Russia's Operations in Crimea and Eastern Ukraine.*

[3] *Live Journal,* "Goroda Geroi—nachalo Russkoi Vesny," February 24, 2014, https://holmogor.livejournal.com/6161827.html.

[4] Aleksandr Prokhanov, "Russkie idut," *Rodina,* March 7, 2014, https://rodina.ru/novosti/Aleksandr-Proxanov-Russkie-idut.

[5] Yegor Kholmogorov, "Vozdukh russkoi vesny," *Vzgliad,* April 10, 2014, https://vz.ru/columns/2014/4/10/681367.html.

prominent conservative thinker, Aleksandr Dugin, two decades earlier: "It will be hard to live through these senseless times. But to give up on our historical mission, on that clear set of actions with which we—stubbornly, with blood and difficulties, but more and more—expand the borders of our land and truth, means to commit a terrible crime—the killing of a national idea is worse than genocide."[6]

Designing a Secessionist Template

The Russian operation to annex Crimea had both military and nonmilitary components. The former started with the deployment around the peninsula of over ten thousand Russian troops and special operation forces without identifying insignia. The latter required simultaneous mobilization of local sympathizers on the public and political levels. Combined, they turned the operation into what Russian defense minister Sergei Shoigu later characterized as a "classic example of hybrid warfare" completed "without firing a single shot."[7]

On the conceptual level, such an operation has long been discussed in specialized Russian military publications. Just several months prior to the invasion the leading Russian security journal, *Military Thought* (*Voennaia Mysl'*), published an article on "new-generation warfare." It emphasized the importance of the nonmilitary phase of the war before the possible start of military engagements.[8] Authored by two retired Russian military officers, it outlined large-scale subversive activities aimed at influencing government officials and military personnel through bribes and coercion. It also described the use of disinformation campaigns to fuel discontent among the local public. Central to the implementation of the strategy were "undercover

---

[6] Aleksandr Dugin, "Rossia mozhet byt ili velikoi, ili nikakoi," in Aleksandr Dugin, *Russkaia Vesh: Ocherki natsional'noi filosofii*, vol. 1 (Moscow: Arktogeia-tsentr, 2001), 103.

[7] Cited in Viktor Baranets, *Spetsoperatsiya Krym 2014* (Moscow: Komsomolskaia Pravda, 2019), 266. Although some Western analysts accepted the "hybrid war" label to characterize Crimean operations, others criticized its use for low analytical utility and weak applicability to Crimea based on its standard definition in Western military thought. From voluminous literature on the term in the context of Russia's operations, see in particular Kent DeBenedektis, *Russian "Hybrid Warfare" and the Annexation of Crimea: The Modern Application of Soviet Political Warfare* (London: I. B. Tauris, 2021); Ofer Fridman, *Russian Hybrid Warfare: Resurgence and Politicisation* (Oxford: Oxford University Press, 2018); Michael Kofman, "Russian Hybrid Warfare and Other Dark Arts," *War on the Rocks*, March 11, 2016, https://warontherocks.com/2016/03/russian-hybrid-warfare-and-other-dark-arts/.

[8] Sergei Chekinov and Sergei Bogdanov, "O kharaktere i soderzhanii voiny novogo pokolenia," *Voennaia Mysl'*, no. 10 (2013): 13–24.

agents" who had to "encourage the discontent to commit unlawful acts, and stoke up chaos, panic, and disobedience."[9] In February 2014 Russia employed undercover agents alongside regular Russian troops in Crimea to accelerate the grassroots mobilization of anti-Kyiv forces.

Crimean "Self-Defense"

Local armed opposition to Kyiv in Crimea was led by a self-defense regiment (*samooborona*), also described as a "people's militia" (*narodnoe opolchenie*). According to its first commander, Mikhail Sheremet, it was officially launched during a rally in Simferopol on February 23, 2014.[10] However, the initial self-defense units had already been formed in Crimea in January in response to the rising violence on Maidan. For the Kremlin they became a critical component of the forthcoming operation in Crimea. The first operational maps prepared by Russia's Ministry of Defense marked the exact locations of militia units with an orange color.[11] Some of these units were later reinforced with Russian paramilitaries.[12] Crimean Cossack units, for example, included close to one thousand Cossacks from the Kuban area. They crossed the Russian-Ukrainian border around Kerch Strait in late February and set up checkpoints along key entry points from mainland Ukraine.[13] There were also "thousands of Russian soldiers dressed as civilians" to ensure sufficient militia size and capacity in each location.[14] Meanwhile, unmarked Russian troops, called "green men," had to act as a backup for the local militia and deter any possible use of force against them.

The visibility of Crimean self-defense units gave the Kremlin "plausible deniability" necessary to frame the operation as a grassroots protest movement organized by the locals.[15] In fact, the movement of militia units was tightly coordinated with the Russian military forces and planned by Russian

---

[9] Ibid., 20.

[10] Mikhail Sheremet. "'Krymskaia vesna': Ka eto bylo. Instina.," TRK Millet, February 19, 2021, https://trkmillet.ru/program-episode/mikhail-sheremet-krimskaya-vesna-kak-ye/.

[11] Baranets, *Spetsoperatsiya Krym 2014*, 202.

[12] Ibid., 187.

[13] *Yuga*, "Kak kazaki v Krymu voevali: Vosmoninania uchastnikov operatsii," March 18, 2015, https://www.yuga.ru/articles/society/7135.html.

[14] Baranets, *Spetsoperatsiya Krym 2014*, 202.

[15] David Ignatius, "What We learned in Crimea," *WashingtonPost*, March 18, 2014, https://www.washingtonpost.com/opinions/david-ignatius-russias-military-delivers-a-striking-lesson-in-crimea/2014/03/18/c1273044-aed7-11e3-9627-c65021d6d572_story.html.

defense officials.[16] Local militia participants often provided critical intelligence to Russian officers regarding possible threats from the Ukrainian troops stationed in Crimea or the actions of pro-Ukrainian civilians. Militia units also had to assist with securing Ukrainian military bases and encourage the defection of Ukrainian military, security forces, and local officials. Rather than surrendering to the foreign army, Ukrainian soldiers had to disarm on demand of the very people they served to defend. Finally, given the uncertainty about public response to the deployment of Russian troops, militia members had to offer reassurance to the locals regarding their safety. By different counts, close to ten thousand people joined Crimean self-defense forces, but the exact share of locals among militia members remains unknown.[17]

The formation of the Crimean militia units was not only encouraged in Moscow but was also led by Russian security specialists. One such specialist was a recently retired FSB officer named Igor Girkin. His emergence in Crimea could be attributed less to his past service in the FSB than to his role as the head of the private security unit of the Russian investment banker Konstantin Malofeyev. Known in Moscow as an "Orthodox oligarch" for his conservative neo-imperialist views, Malofeyev also ran St. Basil Charitable Foundation, which supported Russian Orthodox communities and promoted traditional values.[18] Rather than being a pure philanthropist, however, Malofeyev also had ties to Russia's political establishment. One of his business partners was Sergei Ivanov Jr., son of the head of the presidential administration at the time.[19] His father, a longtime member of Putin's inner circle and a defense minister in 2001–2006, was also one of the architects of the Crimean operation.[20]

Girkin shared Malofeyev's infatuation with Russian imperial heritage. He identified himself as a "monarchist" and considered the power of the Russian tsars "divine."[21] His service to Malofeyev proved far more than just managing his personal security service. In late January 2014 Girkin traveled to Crimea as part of a Malofeyev-sponsored delegation to display the Gifts of the Magi,

---

[16] Baranets, *Spetsoperatsiya Krym 2014*, 202.

[17] Valeriy Kosarev, *Krymskiy Vybor* (Moscow: Algoritm, 2018), 35.

[18] The official website of the foundation lists Malofeyev as founder and his mother, Raisa, as its general director: https://fondsvv.ru/.

[19] *Insider*, "Marashall Malofeyev: Kak rossiyskiy reider zakhavtil Yugo-Vostok Ukrainy," May 27, 2014, https://theins.ru/politika/796.

[20] Baranets, *Spetsoperatsiya Krym 2014*, 177.

[21] Cited in Elena Semyonova, *Dobrovol'tsy: Vek XXI. Bitva za Novorossiyu v portretah eyo geroev* (Moskva: Traditsiya, 2015), 9.

religious relics brought from Jerusalem, to Orthodox believers. Some members of the delegation, however, had a clear political mission. One of them, a member of the Federation Council, Dmitriy Sablin, used the visit to meet top Crimean officials and gauge their views on secession of the peninsula.[22] Upon his return to Moscow, Malofeyev allegedly lobbied the Russian government to capitalize on the chaos unleashed by the Euromaidan revolution and seize parts of Ukraine.[23]

The Crimean trip also brought Girkin in direct contact with Sergei Aksionov, then a member of the Crimean Parliament, whose paramilitary Cossack organization guarded the sacred objects on their tour. Aksionov and Malofeyev first met well before 2014 and found common interests in "monarchy and Orthodoxy."[24] On Malofeyev's recommendation, Aksionov invited Girkin back to Crimea as his "security advisor" and put him in charge of organizing militia units. The official commander of the Crimean militia was Aksionov's close associate Sheremet. But Girkin, who returned to Crimea in late February, was responsible for the operational control of some of the units and their coordination with Russian security officials. Girkin's company unit was also involved in the only direct violent clash with the Ukrainian military, at the cartographic center in Simferopol on March 18, in which a Ukrainian soldier was killed.[25] The battalion's official leader was a local from Crimea, Sergei Turchinenko, who described the altercation as a provocation by the Ukrainians.[26] However, Girkin was the actual commander of the unit later accused of negligence by the Crimean authorities for his role in organizing the violent storming of the base.[27] This resulted in the disarming and dissolution of Girkin's battalion. Still, his Crimean experience proved decisive in his subsequent reinvention as a rebel commander in Donbas. The Girkin-led group that launched a raid into Donbas in April, 2014 consisted mostly of members of his and other Crimean militia units who actively assisted Russia's operation in the peninsula.[28]

---

[22] Aleksina Dorogan, "Razvedka s ikonami: Kak v 2014 Rossiya rabotala v Krymu pod prikrytiem Moskovskogo patriarkhata," *Radio Svoboda*, March 1, 2021, https://ru.krymr.com/a/razvedka-krym-2014-russia-okkupatsiya-pod-prikrytiem-tserkvi/31124680.html.

[23] Aratyunyan, *Hybrid Warriors*, 98.

[24] RBC, "Malofeev rasskazal o svoem uchastii v prisoedinenii Kryma," November 13, 2014, https://www.rbc.ru/politics/13/11/2014/54647847cbb20f11b6a74400.

[25] Andrei Shargorodskiy, "Pogibshye i propavshye: Zhertvy 'beskrovnoi' anneksii Kryma," *Radio Svoboda*, March 18, 2020, https://ru.krymr.com/a/zhertvy-beskrovnoj-anneksii-kryma/30495796.html.

[26] Kosarev, *Krymskiy Vybor*, 83.

[27] Andrei Pinchuk, *Kontur Bezopasnosti* (Moscow: Algoritm, 2017), 182.

[28] Aleksei Zhabin, "Igor Strelkov: 'Voevat ia ne sobiralsia,'" *News*, December 28, 2021, https://news.ru/cis/intervyu-igorem-strelkovym/.

Local Mobilization

Three distinct groups became the recruitment base for "self-defense" companies in Crimea. The first unit was formed from the members of the paramilitary wing of Aksionov's party, Russian Unity (RU), as well as allied pro-Russian organizations such as the Russian Community of Crimea. Sheremet, who became the first militia commander, was, at the time the chair of the Simferopol branch of the party and Aksionov's deputy. Crimean Cossacks provided another pool of recruits. Led by the ataman of the Crimean Cossack district, Vadim Ilovchenko, they successfully negotiated the disarmament of the Ukrainian military base in Bakhchisarai, a town with a sizable Crimean Tartar minority.[29] Given the pro-Ukrainian sympathies of Crimean Tartars, it was significant that many Ukrainian soldiers there took an oath of loyalty to the new Crimean authorities.[30] Less than two months after the launch of the Crimean operation, Ilovchenko led the seizure of the police station in Kramatorsk and became the town's first commandant.

Some militia formations consisted of security professionals, such as members of the riot police unit Berkut, and Afghan war veterans and other retired officers with prior military training. One of them was forty-eight-year-old Afghan war veteran Igor Bezler. A native of Simferopol, he had made a military career in the Russian army and retired at the rank of lieutenant colonel in 1997.[31] Despite being a Russian citizen, he moved to Donbas in the early 2000s to work at the local plant in Horlivka and led the town association of veteran marines. After participating in the annexation of Crimea, where he likely established contact with Russian intelligence operatives, Bezler organized his own militia unit in Horlivka and ruled the city until late 2014.

Pro-Russian civic groups and leaders in Crimea played their own distinct role in the Crimean operation. They were the first to articulate the separatist agenda and mobilize locals around these goals. The leading organization among them was RU, created in December 2009 in a merger of several local pro-Russian groups. Its new leader, Aksionov, positioned RU as an exclusive representative of the Russian community in the peninsula.[32] Still, in

---

[29] *Radio Krym*, "Golosa krymskoi vesny: Vadim Ilovchenko," February 21, 2022, https://crimea-radio.ru/program/golosa-krimskoy-vesni/21-02-2022-vadim-ilovchenko/.

[30] ITV, "Priniali Prisiagu," YouTube, https://t.ly/acnhi, September 13, 2015.

[31] Tsyganok, *Donbass*, 296.

[32] *Novyi Den'*, "'Russkoe edinstvo': Rezultat vyborov v Krymu—eto ne pobeda, no i ne porazhenie," November 16, 2010, https://newdaynews.ru/crimea/309146.html/amp/.

local elections in 2010 the party came in only fifth, with 4% of the votes in the region-wide party list vote. Apart from Aksionov only two other party members won seats in the Crimean legislature. RU fared better in smaller towns. One of its members, Kostiantyn Rubanenko, even won the mayoral race in Bakhchisarai, where the tensions between Crimean Tartars and the Russian community were on the rise. In total 103 RU members became deputies in various local councils in Crimea.[33]

In early 2014, RU capitalized on the disintegration of PR to become the driver of street mobilization across the peninsula. One of its leaders, Sergei Tsekov, made several trips to Moscow along with the chairman of the Crimean Parliament, Vladimir Konstantinov, for meetings with top Russian officials right on the eve of the Russian invasion.[34] Aksionov too held consultations with the Kremlin's representatives in Simferopol in early February, when he likely came into view for the role of a future separatist leader. In several weeks a Russian political strategist and Malofeyev's longtime associate, Aleksandr Borodai, arrived from Moscow to become Aksionov's "Public Relations advisor."[35] Lower-level RU activists later acknowledged that they were independently approached by Russian undercover agents with offers to coordinate pro-Russian actions in their cities.[36] Another major pro-Russian party active only in Sevastopol was the Russian Bloc led by Gennadiy Basov.[37] The party had nine deputies on the city council and received 11.8% of the votes in city council elections in 2010—the third largest share following PR and KPU.[38] Basov cooperated closely with a major local businessman, Aleksei Chalyi, the owner of the local TV channel and online newspaper *ForPost*, known for his pro-Russian views.

The secessionist agenda was publicly articulated in Crimea even before the culmination of Euromaidan protests. On February 4, Tsekov suggested that the Crimean Parliament should appeal to Russia for "support and

---

[33] Author's calculations based on the official results from the Central Electoral Commission of Ukraine, https://www.cvk.gov.ua/pls/vm2010/wp0011.html,

[34] Russkoe Edinstvo, "Etapy stanovlenia Russkoi obshiny Kryma," September 3, 2018, http://www.ruscrimea.ru/etapy-stanovleniya-russkoj-obshhiny-kryma

[35] Ksenia Sobchak, "Interview with Aleksandr Borodai," TV Dozhd, November 12, 2014, https://tvrain.tv/teleshow/sobchak_zhivem/aleksandr_borodaj_strelkov_pytalsja_stat_politiche-378007/.

[36] *Meduza*, "Nikto ne veril, chto eto vserioz," March 27, 2014, https://meduza.io/feature/2017/03/21/nikto-ne-veril-chto-eto-vseriez.

[37] *ForPost*, "Faces of the City: Basov Gennadiy Anatolevich," https://sevastopol.su/faces/basov-gennadiy-anatolevich.

[38] *ForPost*, "Vybory-2010: Offitsialnye rezultaty golosovania po vyboram v Sevastopolskiy gorodskoi sovet," November 5, 2010, https://sevastopol.su/news/vybory-2010-oficialnye-rezultaty-golosovaniya-po-vyboram-v-sevastopolskiy-gorodskoy-sovet.

protection" of its autonomous status.[39] After the violent showdown on Maidan, the chief of the local Cossack union Rus' and a Russian Bloc member in Sevastopol, Viacheslav Bebniov, warned, "[T]he day Yanukovych loses power we would take power here in our hands and city residents would seize SBU and military bases."[40] In three days, on February 23, Chalyi organized the first rally in Sevastopol under Russian national flags. Rally participants declared him the "people's mayor"—a new title meant to give greater legitimacy to separatist leaders over regular officeholders. A similar rally in Simferopol on February 26, organized by Aksionov, ended with clashes between pro-Russian demonstrators and Crimean Tartars, who sought to defend unified Ukraine. Later that evening Aksionov became the new chairman of the Crimean Parliament during a hasty overnight session organized under pressure from Russian special operation forces.[41]

Local councils were then positioned as the only legitimate power center remaining in Ukraine. Using Moscow's condemnations of Euromaidan as a Western-orchestrated coup, pro-Russian activists claimed that the local council deputies were the only remaining legitimate representatives of the people's will. Crimean Parliament and Sevastopol city council deputies used this reasoning to justify subordination of law enforcement to regional executive authority and call for a local referendum on the future of Crimea.

Elite Defection

The new Crimean leadership could maintain the illusion of a locally driven secession only through collaboration of local officials, particularly those in coercive agencies. This required providing them with some security guarantees since Kyiv's reluctance to use force in Crimea was not immediately obvious at the time. The likelihood of a Ukrainian military response was discussed even by pro-Kremlin commentators. Prokhanov warned in early

---

[39] *ForPost*, "Krymskiy deputat nazval Krym 'russkoi avtonomiei' i prosit zashity u Rossii," February 4, 2014, https://sevastopol.su/news/krymskiy-deputat-nazval-krym-russkoy-avtonomiey-i-prosit-zashchity-u-rossii.

[40] *ForPost*, "Kazachiy Ataman Bebniov: Yesli Yanukovich Poteriaet Vlast, My Shturmom Vozmem MVD, SBU, i Voinskie Chasti Ukrainy v Sevastopole," February 20, 2014, https://sevastopol.su/news/kazachiy-ataman-bebnev-esli-yanukovich-poteryaet-vlast-my-shturmom-vozmem-mvd-sbu-i-voinskie.

[41] Prior to the vote, Aksionov received a final vetting from Oleg Belaventsev, a high-ranking Russian officer dispatched to Crimea on February 22 by Defense Minister Shoigu. See Baranets, *Spetsoperatsiya Krym 2014*, 220.

March that if "Kyiv would send their 'freedom trains' along with tanks and armored vehicles to Crimea, there will be clashes and blood will be spilled."[42]

The swiftness and decisiveness of Russian military actions in Crimea served as the best reassurance mechanism for vacillating local elites. Encirclement of Ukrainian military bases and infrastructure by Russian troops, a sharp increase in the number of Russian troops deployed in the peninsula, and transfer of heavy military equipment all added credibility to the Russian threat to use force on behalf of the separatists. The first attempt to blockade the Ukrainian military, the coast guard unit in Sevastopol, was conducted by thirty Russian marines in unmarked uniforms on February 28.[43] That same day Ukraine's National Security and Defense Council (RNBO) held an emergency meeting at which the acting defense minister, Ihor Teniukh, pleaded with Ukrainians to avoid "direct military contact" with the Russian troops. "We are not ready for full-scale war. We have no army today," Teniukh declared. He estimated that out of fifteen thousand Ukrainian troops stationed in Crimea only "1,500–2,000 were ready to follow orders." And they faced a "Russian fighting force of over 20,000," which included newly transferred Russian "special operation forces with experience of fighting in Russia's war zones."[44]

Teniukh's gloomy forecast was reinforced by the head of the foreign intelligence service Viktor Hvozd. He argued, "[W]e cannot throw poorly trained guys in[to] Crimea—there are regular Russian troops there well equipped and in greater numbers—so they will be killed and driven over by tanks."[45] The Ukrainian government also did not expect that the West would provide tangible military assistance to Ukraine in case it resisted. As Prime Minister Yatsenyuk concluded, "I don't think any country, including the signatories of the Budapest Memorandum, are ready to support Ukraine today. . . . [W]e will have to rely only on ourselves."[46] These arguments prevailed; all but one of the council members voted against introducing martial law in Ukraine to stop the Russian intervention. One of the meeting participants, the chief of the State Border Guard Service Mykola Lytyn, later suggested that another

<hr>

[42] Prokhanov, "Russkie Idut."

[43] Lytvyn, *Linia Rozmezhuvannia*, 205.

[44] Iryna Shtohrin, "Chomu ne vtrymaly Krym: Stenohrama RNBO vid 28 lyutoho 2014 roku," *Radio Liberty Ukrainian Service*, February 27, 2019, https://www.radiosvoboda.org/a/29794488.html.

[45] Ibid.

[46] Ibid.

reason for inaction was recognition by the postrevolutionary government that it lacked "influence, authority or contacts with subordinates, particularly those in Crimea."[47]

In addition to weak armed forces, the new authorities in Kyiv quickly realized that they lacked even basic policing capacity on the peninsula. Interior Minister Avakov reported during an RNBO meeting that the police chiefs of Crimea and Sevastopol had resigned. He added, "[I]nterior troops and patrol police are serving, but will not resist Russian troops. . . . [W]e are making contact with police members who did not betray us, but there are very few of them."[48] Some Ukrainian interior troops, including Berkut units from Sevastopol, had already participated in setting up checkpoints on the roads connecting Crimea to mainland Ukraine—near Perekopsk and Armiansk—to prevent movement of Ukrainian troops to the peninsula.[49]

Such defections of Ukrainian security personnel were encouraged by Russian undercover agents. One such group, led by sixty-three-year-old Vladimir Antyufeyev, arrived in Crimea in early March.[50] As a longtime chief of the Security Service of the self-proclaimed Transnistrian Moldovan Republic (PMR) from 1992 to 2011, he had extensive experience with operating security agencies of the secessionist state.[51] Antyufeyev's primary loyalty, however, remained with Russia. "We consider ourselves Russians and we are defending the frontiers of the Slavic state," he asserted in a 1992 interview.[52] According to Prokhanov, who met with Antyufeyev in the 1990s, he wanted Transnistria "to become a symbol for Russia" and assisted with the transfer of Russian volunteers to fight for the self-proclaimed republic.[53] Among those volunteers were Girkin and Borodai, both in their twenties at the time.

Antyufeyev's tasks in Crimea in March 2014 closely resembled what he had accomplished at the start of his career in Transnistria. He had to compel Ukrainian security operatives and border patrol guards to submit to the

---

[47] Lytvyn, *Linia Rozmezhuvannia*, 203.

[48] Shtohrin, "Chomy ne vtrymaly Krym…"

[49] Natasha Vlashenko, *Krazha ili Beloe Solntse Kryma* (Kharkiv: Folio, 2017), 105.

[50] Pinchuk, *Kontur Bezopasnosti*, 175.

[51] *Novosti Pridnestrovia*, "K 70-letiyu Vladimira Antyufeeva MGB vypustilo film o sozdatele organov gosbezopasnosti PMR," February 21, 2021, https://novostipmr.com/ru/news/21-02-21/k-70-letiyu-vladimira-antyufeeva-mgb-vypustilo-film-o-sozdatele.

[52] Anatloiy Kholodyuk, "Imperskiy oskolok na Dnestre: Vospominania soldata," *Proza*, April 5, 2020, https://proza.ru/2020/05/04/1925.

[53] Quoted in the documentary film *Vladimir Antyufeyev: Lichnost zakalennaia zhyznyu*, 2021. See "Russian Actors 2014," Harvard Dataverse, https://doi.org/10.7910/DVN/7DBNNB.

separatist Crimean authorities. Antyufeyev, along with other Transnistrian Security Service operatives, also supervised the formation of the Crimean Security Service, created on March 10. One of Antyufeyev's aides, Andrei Pinchuk, later recalled, "Formally the new head of Crimean SBU was the former deputy head of Sevastopol SBU Petro Zyma, while the real ones were us."[54] The promise of a Russian takeover of the peninsula became their key argument behind the successful conversion of Ukrainian security operatives: "We are promising Russia. Bluffing! . . . We had no certainty about any kind of Russia at the time. But we promised. Bluffing is bluffing. No guarantees."[55] According to Pinchuk, most operatives in the Crimean SBU defected to their side by March 12. As he explained, this "not only prevented possible resistance of SBU operatives and attempts to destabilize the situation through undercover agents, but also compelled them to fulfill our orders."[56] Their most pressing objective at the time—staging the so-called referendum on the status of Crimea—was attained partially through collaboration of defected SBU operatives.

Staged Referendum

Quasi-democratic instruments, such as referendums, have been commonly used by secessionist movements to legitimize their claims on territory. They also became tools for dictators to present their territorial expansion as manifestations of the popular will.[57] In Crimea, and later in Donbas, calling a referendum served both purposes. For the separatist leaders, a referendum allowed them to put responsibility for the illegal power grab on the region's residents. For the Kremlin, it was a way of cloaking their illicit territorial acquisition under the principles of international law.[58] The set of policy recommendations regarding Ukraine offered to the Russian leadership in early February explicitly identified the referendum as a mechanism that would

---

[54] Pinchuk, *Kontur Bezopasnosti*, 177.

[55] Ibid., 178.

[56] Ibid., 183.

[57] On the impact of a plebiscite on Germany's Anschluss of Austria, see Evan Burr Bukey, *Hitler's Austria: Popular Sentiment in the Nazi Era* (Chapel Hill: University of North Carolina Press, 2000), 34.

[58] For an analysis of Russia's annexation of Crimea from the standpoint of international law, see Thomas D. Grant, "Annexation of Crimea," *American Journal of International Law* 109, no. 1 (2015): 68–95.

"allow for self-determination of these regions and possibly further joining the Russian Federation."[59]

Preparing even a staged referendum in a brief time frame, however, required extensive collaboration of lower-level officials, public servants, and law enforcement agencies. In Crimea, the coercive effect of the Russian military presence under the guise of unmarked soldiers proved decisive in bringing this about. The available record shows that the municipal authorities in some Crimean towns were initially reluctant to endorse radical separatist demands. One member of the Crimean Parliament at the time, Valeriy Kosarev, remembered that prior to the referendum his native Yalta "resembled a swamp" due to the passivity of the local authorities: "City council did not adopt any decisions, local militia was in disarray and the Ukrainian flag was still raised over the mayoral building."[60] This changed once the "little green men," as Russian unmarked soldiers came to be known, spread across the peninsula.[61]

Russian authorities thus relied on a variety of different actors and strategies in carrying out the takeover of Crimea. The unmarked troops served to communicate Russian coercive dominance and deter a Ukrainian military response. Local officials articulated the secessionists' demands and campaigned to vote for separation from Ukraine. Local militia units added pressure on the Ukrainian military to disarm and created an impression of grassroots support for the secession. Informal security agents, like Girkin and Antyufeyev, offered technical expertise in organizing the locals to neutralize the Ukrainian coercive apparatus. And a large share of Crimean residents embraced Russia's anti-Kyiv narratives, joined rallies, and enthusiastically participated in a staged referendum, creating a semblance of popular support for the Kremlin's operation to seize Crimea.[62] All of these

[59] Andrei Lipskiy, "Predstavliaetsia pravilnym initsiirovat prisoedinenie vostochnyh oblastei Ukrainy k Rossii," *Novaya Gazeta*, February 25, 2015, https://novayagazeta.ru/articles/2015/02/24/63168-171-predstavlyaetsya-pravilnym-initsiirovat-prisoedinenie-vostochnyh-oblastey-ukrainy-k-rossii-187.

[60] Kosarev, *Krymskiy Vybor*, 77.

[61] The overwhelming presence of the Russian troops in the run-up to and during the voting is, by itself, sufficient to dismiss the validity of its results due to their effect on voting. See Grant, "Annexation of Crimea," 85–86.

[62] The minutes of the RNBO meeting on February 28, 2014, indicate that the Ukrainian political leadership recognized the prevalence of pro-Russian public attitudes in Crimea at the time. For example, the official report of acting SBU chief Valentyn Nalyvaichenko mentioned "mass support among local residents for the actions of the Russian Federation" as one of the main risk factors for Ukraine. See Shtohrin, "Chomy ne vtrymaly Krym…"

elements could now be replicated in other parts of Ukraine targeted by Russian covert operations.[63]

"Making Crimea in Donbas"

Simultaneously with the Crimean operation, Russia started building up pressure along Ukraine's northeastern border. In early March it deployed intelligence and reconnaissance units and stationed artillery batteries in proximity to the Ukrainian territory.[64] The logic behind further Russian intervention was explicated in a special report prepared at the end of March by a group of experts led by Sergei Glaziev, an advisor to the Russian president on Eurasian integration. The report called for support of "pro-Russian regions of Southeastern Ukraine" and for a "unified security belt from Kharkiv to Odesa."[65] Born in Zaporizhzhia, Glaziev personally tried to encourage pro-Russian mobilization in his native city, as well as in Odesa and Kharkiv. In phone calls with local activists, he promised Russian backing and outlined specific steps the activists should take to seize power.[66] In Zaporizhzhia he advised locals to adopt appeals to Putin for assistance, capture oblast state administration, form executive committees, establish control over law enforcement, and rule their towns independently from Kyiv-appointed authorities. In Odesa, Glaziev encouraged protest leaders to force oblast deputies to come to the council building and vote to recognize the new Ukrainian government as illegitimate. "They are people's deputies and should take responsibility for the situation in Odesa oblast. . . . If someone does not understand just take them by their neck and bring them over [to the council building]," Glaziev retorted on March 1. In a conversation with an activist in Zaporizhzhia the same day he stressed that he represented top Russian officials: "I have direct instruction from my superiors to raise people in Ukraine—wherever we can."[67]

---

[63] The policy memo on Ukraine advocated Russian intervention not only in Crimea, but also in other regions of southeastern Ukraine. Lipskiy, "Predstavliaetsia pravilnym initsiirovat prisoedinenie vostochnyh oblastei Ukrainy k Rossii."

[64] Lytvyn, *Linia Rozmezhuvannia*, 212.

[65] Izborskiy Klub, "Ukraina mezhdu Zapadom i Rossiei: Predvaritelnyie itogi ukrainskogo perevorota," April 25, 2014, https://izborsk-club.ru/3069.

[66] Glaziev's intercepted phone conversations were publicized by the Prosecutor General's Office of Ukraine. Ukraine Ofis Heneralnoho prokurora "Dokazy prychetnosti vlady RF do posiahannia na terytorialny tsilisnist Ukrainy," August 23, 2016, https://t.ly/8d62.

[67] Author's translation of intercepted conversations based on audio publicized by Ukraine's Prosecutor General's Office. For original audio and transcript see ibid.

Despite Moscow's efforts, the pro-Russian mobilization across most of Ukraine proved weak or ineffective. As detailed in Chapter 9, pro-Russian activists in Kharkiv and Odesa managed to mobilize thousands of people on the streets but lacked a clear strategy and faced significant internal pushback. The only places where there was little need for Russian prodding to stir the public were the two oblasts of Donbas: Donetsk and Luhansk. Self-mobilization in the region, manifested in the formation of self-defense groups in many urban centers, began immediately after Yanukovych's ouster. Already on March 1, 2014, rallies under Russian flags with demands for "Ukraine's federalization" were held in numerous towns of Donbas. The largest ones—in Donetsk and Luhansk—were spearheaded by new pro-Russian organizations, whose leaders issued radical demands akin to those articulated days earlier in Crimea.

The call for holding a referendum "on the status of our native land" was one of the key demands of thirty-one-year-old Pavel Gubarev. He was a recent history graduate of Donetsk National University and the owner of a small advertising agency that counted local politicians among its clients. Gubarev's own political record, by that point, was rather eclectic. As a student he had participated in gatherings of Russian National Unity, a neo-imperial far-right Russian group, in Donetsk. There Gubarev received, in his words, "manly military patriotic education."[68] Later he ran in city elections in Donetsk as a candidate from the far-left Progressive Socialist Party of Ukraine and won a seat on the raion (district) council. His early political exploits were all driven by his belief that the "region belonged to the larger Russian world."[69] On March 1, Gubarev finally found a large audience receptive to his ideas. Standing on the main square of Donetsk, he addressed tens of thousands of people gathered there for the pro-Russian rally as a leader of "an informal alliance, People's Militia of Donbas (NOD)."[70] On the same day in Luhansk Aleksandr Kharitonov, the leader of another radical pro-Russian group, the Luhansk Guard, read a resolution adopted by the Luhansk oblast council. It questioned the legitimacy of Ukrainian authorities, demanded a referendum on the region's status, and mentioned the possibility of requesting Russia's assistance. Still, local PR leaders in Luhansk, just as in Donetsk, refused to move any further than expressing rhetorical support for protest demands.

---

[68] Pavel Gubarev, *Fakel Novorossii* (Moscow: Piter, 2016), 24.
[69] Ibid., 8.
[70] Ibid., 100.

Compared to Crimea, the local authorities across Donbas showed far less receptivity to radical slogans. The new pro-Russian leaders could not bring the entrenched local elites from the PR to their side. One likely reason for this was the absence of assurances from Moscow to leading local powerbrokers. As Gubarev recalled, PR members "treated us just like Maidan protesters seeking to capture their power."[71] His close ally Sergei Tseplakov characterized some PR deputies as "mobsters with their own bandit groups, chiefs and prior experience with coercion." He quickly realized that "they could not be compelled to vote against Kyiv."[72] By mid-March, SBU had rounded up and arrested the most visible pro-Russian leaders, including the self-proclaimed governors of the two oblasts, Gubarev and Kharitonov. While Crimea was holding its referendum, the pro-Russian movement in Donbas seemed to be devoid of any resources to mount an equally effective challenge on its own. "The non-violent protests already proved senseless and led to a dead end. On the other hand, armed resistance remained a big question due to the lack of manpower and arms," Tseplakov recalled.[73]

The impasse facing the separatist movement in Donbas was clearly felt during the gathering in Lyman on March 29, which attracted only several dozen people.[74] One of its moderators, Natalia Pshenichnaya, was a local activist who, by her own admission, frequently traveled to Donetsk and participated in pro-Russian actions there. She lamented that pro-Russian organizations engaged in mutual recriminations and lacked any coherent goals. Pshenichnaya remembered how they tried to storm the SBU office in Donetsk but could not articulate their demands when they entered the building. "We can always capture a building, but we do not know what to do next. We don't have a program," she concluded. Another Lyman activist, Yuri Yakovlev, agreed that a "revolution under the Russian flag" was impossible. Their best hope, he said, was to expand the movement into other regions of Ukraine and hold a nationwide referendum on their future status.

Despite the waning of the initial pro-Russian mobilization, local activists still sought to replicate the Crimean experience by encouraging more direct involvement of Russian agents. According to Pinchuk, stationed in Simferopol at the time, "visitors from Donbas and other pro-Russian regions

---

[71] Ibid., 102.

[72] Cited in Zhuchkovskiy, *85 dnei Slavianska*, 25.

[73] Ibid., 24.

[74] Author's archived video from Lyman, March 29, 2014. See "Lyman 2014," Harvard Dataverse, https://doi.org/10.7910/DVN/MCQ81K.

came to Crimea asking to 'repeat all that you did here.'"[75] The activists from Gubarev's organization who visited Crimea to "secure arms" in mid-March met with Girkin and received "limited financial assistance."[76] "There is enough support there to make Crimea in Donbas," said Tseplakov following the visit.[77] Borodai received numerous visitors from other Ukrainian regions in Simferopol: "They were, first of all, asking for a supervisor or an organizer. Of course, they asked for arms and medical supplies. But money—almost never."[78]

The future "people's mayor" of Sloviansk, Viacheslav Ponomariov, made a trip to Crimea around the same time with three other town residents. According to his account, he could not establish direct contact with pro-Russian actors in Donetsk, like Oleksandr Khodakovsky or Gubarev, so he went to Crimea in search of further guidance.[79] Aksionov's deputy agreed to meet him but refused to provide any assistance. Ponomariov had an impression that "they already decided on their cooperation partners." So he explained that he only wanted to share information about his activities with the right people: "Since we could not coordinate with anyone in Donetsk, I asked him to inform others that we were planning to seize police stations in five towns in mid-April and gave him my contacts." This brought Ponomariov in touch with Gubarev's wife, Yekaterina, who was directly communicating with Girkin and planning his raid into Donbas.[80] One day before the arrival of Girkin's unit in Donbas she called Ponomariov and told him that "a group was coming for assistance." Ponomariov had to meet them close to the border and lead them into Sloviansk.

Another pro-Russian activist from neighboring Kramatorsk, Pavel Tsveloi, made a similar visit to Crimea in mid-March. He said that by observing the referendum he saw a ready template to be used in Donbas. "We were motivated by the Crimean example—even though it evolved differently. We hoped that the Crimean scenario would happen in Donbas—this was our main expectation," he later recalled.[81] An activist from Mariupol, Dmytro Kuzmenko, mentioned his visit to Crimea and a meeting with Aksionov at

---

[75] Pinchuk, *Kontur Bezopasnosti*, 123.

[76] Gubarev, *Fakel Novorossii*, 158.

[77] Ibid.

[78] Interview with Aleksandr Borodai in Aleksandr Prokhanov, *Novorossia, kroviu umytaya: Peredovitsy* (Moscow: Knigovek, 2016), 273.

[79] Viacheslav Ponomariov, "Narodnyi mer Slavianska o nachale voiny, Girkine i razvedchukakh NATO," WarGonzo, April 2021, https://rutube.ru/video/6909618ed094237021617738f3e88a30/.

[80] Gubarev, *Fakel Novorossii*.

[81] Interview with Pavel Tsveloi, June 28, 2020. After returning from Crimea, however, he failed to mobilize more than a few hundred people to the rallies in late March.

the pro-Russian rallies in the city in late March.[82] A photo of Kuzmenko, an upstart in his early twenties, and Aksionov, posing in a handshake, was later circulated at the pro-Russian rally to explain his nomination as the "people's mayor" of Mariupol.

Multiple uncoordinated visits of diverse activists to Crimea suggest that Russia did not exercise direct control over the spontaneous secessionist movement in Donbas. Rather, local organizers borrowed tactics and protest frames from the Crimean example and applied them creatively in Donbas. In contrast to the Crimean operation, which was closely planned in the Kremlin from the start, protests across Donbas erupted without evident involvement of Russian officials. According to Gubarev, his first direct contact with representatives of Russia, Sergei Glaziev and Konstantin Zatulin, occurred only on March 5—after he had already led the capture of the Donetsk state administration and the treasury building.[83] There is no evidence of meetings between local officials from Donetsk and Luhansk and Russian officials like those that occurred in Crimea in January and February. There is also no record of Moscow's attempts to send high-raking officials, like Oleg Belaventsev, to Donbas to vet its new leaders. The available record suggests the opposite: local political and business actors were confused and disoriented about the true goals and intentions of the Kremlin. As a result, as one pro-Russian activist recalled, "local elites withdrew themselves from the process—some were waiting to see what steps Russia would take and sought hard guarantees, while others took pro-Ukrainian or neutral stances."[84]

Another major difference between Donbas and Crimea was the pattern of militia mobilization. The first Crimean militia units were created by influential public figures, Aksionov and Chalyi, who entrusted their close associates with overall command responsibilities. Their actual organization, training, and unit command were conducted by Russian agents, like Girkin. Their deployment, task assignments, and operational control were exercised in cooperation with Russian military commanders who had to align their actions with Russia's overall military objectives. By contrast, as I detail in subsequent chapters, militia units in Donbas were organized haphazardly and mainly through local town initiatives. While Gubarev called his organization a "people's militia," it was in fact a civic group with no

<hr>

[82] At March 29 rally Kuzmenko announced that he was in "constant contact with Crimea and Russia" to plan a referendum. Author's archived video from Mariupol. See "Mariupol 2014," Harvard Dataverse, https://doi.org/10.7910/DVN/4OBT5H.

[83] Gubarev, *Fakel Novorossii*, 113.

[84] Tsyplakov cited in Zhuchkovskiy, *85 dnei Slavianska*, 25.

militarized branch. The actual armed groups, like Zakharchenko's Oplot, Khodakovskiy's Vostok, and Bolotov's Army of South-East, were present only in Donetsk and Luhansk. They also operated independently from each other.

Smaller self-defense units emerged in towns across Donbas in late February, but their objectives were narrow and limited to those localities. Lacking in manpower and equipment, they could not pose any serious threat to the Ukrainian state. As a pro-Russian activist from Kramatorsk recalled, "There were not enough core activists in any of the towns [of the Kramatorsk agglomeration], a core that could organize everything and ensure the blocking of the towns. We had numerous people who came to us and said that they were ready, but 'ready' meant that they could get a stick and stand with it on a checkpoint—that's all."[85] The fact that, in a matter of days, the Kramatorsk agglomeration turned into the center of separatist resistance could be attributed only to the sudden arrival of a unit ready and capable of using force.

"Little Green Men"—with a Twist

The extent of Russia's involvement in Donbas changed drastically in April. Several militant groups, earlier involved in the Crimean operation, arrived simultaneously in smaller towns of the region with the aim of accelerating the secession of Donbas from Ukraine. This reflected Girkin's view that secessionist efforts could succeed only in case of "the dispersion of protest against Kyiv on the widest possible territory and real seizure of arms."[86] One such group, led by Bezler and overseen by Vasiliy Geranin, an officer in the Main Intelligence Directorate of the Russian Federation (GRU), closely cooperated with the "military wing" of Gubarev's NOD and involved local activists from other towns.[87] Bezler engaged locals to capture the SBU building in Donetsk on April 7.[88] The assault had to give local separatists access to arms and munition. According to Gubarev, the SBU seizure lasted just several hours and yielded an arsenal of forty-seven automatic rifles and fifty-five pistols.[89] Once they acquired the weapons, they quickly withdrew from the SBU building to the seized regional administration building. The arming of

---

[85] Interview with Tsveloi, 2020.

[86] Cited in Gubarev, *Fakel Novorossii*, 159.

[87] Ibid., 163.

[88] Ponomariov, "Narodnyi mer Slavianska o nachale voiny, Girkine i razvedchukakh NATO."

[89] Gubarev, *Fakel Novorossii*, 127.

separatists in Donetsk was one of the factors that prevented a quick clearing operation by Ukraine's special forces and allowed separatists to set up a governing body in the provincial capital.

On April 12 Bezler and Girkin met in Sloviansk to divide the zones of influence.[90] Girkin's unit arrived just a day earlier after crossing the Russian-Ukrainian border in coordination with NOD activists.[91] Together with local militia members, they quickly captured the police station in Sloviansk and Lyman on April 12 and in Kramatorsk on April 13. Meanwhile, Bezler led the capture of the police station in Horlivka on April 14. For the next three months Girkin exercised control over five towns in the Sloviansk-Kramatorsk agglomeration, with a total population close to 300,000. Bezler, meanwhile, maintained a presence in the Horlivka agglomeration, which included the towns of Yenakievo and Toretsk, with a total population of at least 350,000.[92] This marked the launch of the second stage of Russia's covert operation in Ukraine that removed the Ukrainian state presence across most of Donbas.

Girkin's exact reasons for going into Donbas, and the extent to which he was formally subordinate to Russian officials, remain a matter of dispute. By his account, the decision to launch the Donbas raid was reached following conversations with his Crimean boss, Aksionov. After the Russian annexation Aksionov quickly realized that "without Northern Tavria [an area in mainland Ukraine north of Crimea, which includes parts of Kherson, Zaporizhzhia, and Donetsk oblasts that link the peninsula to Russia] Crimea will be a 'black hole' in which one needed to throw as much money as possible just to keep it alive."[93] Meanwhile, the exposed weakness of the Ukrainian defenses revealed an opportunity for Russia to seize other parts of Ukraine. "I was confident that it would be followed by reintegration of Donbas, Kherson, Odessa etc.," Girkin remembered in an interview with a Ukrainian journalist.

The contemporaneous writings of Girkin corroborate that in spring 2014 he saw the Ukrainian state as doomed but was uncertain about Putin's next moves. Posted on an obscure internet forum for antique traders under the nickname "Kotych," they offer a unique glimpse into his reasoning at

---

[90] Ponomariov, "Narodnyi mer Slavianska o nachale voiny, Girkine i razvedchukakh NATO."

[91] Gubarev, *Fakel Novorossii*, 171.

[92] Population data based on Hamilton, *Ukraine – Urbanization Review*, 2013; Pinchuk, *Kontur Bezopasnosti*, 50.

[93] Dmitriy Gordon, "Interview with Igor Girkin," *V Gostiah u Gordona*, May 18, 2020, https://t.ly/41KEE.

the time.[94] On March 23, five days after Putin finalized the annexation of Crimea, Girkin predicted that "by the summer Ukraine would not exist in its current form." He expected to see Ukraine split into two after the south-eastern regions, backed by Russia, declared their independence. Girkin was also very skeptical about Ukraine's capacity to stop the secession of eastern Ukraine. "Like in Crimea, the Ukrainian military will be ready to defend only until the first shot is fired," he wrote on March 22 in response to Yat-senyuk's promise to resist any further Russian intervention. On March 26 Girkin reiterated that he thought the Ukrainian military would only fight "with loud screaming." As a result, he suggested that "one platoon would be enough to go and spread Crimean attitudes."[95]

As to President Putin, Girkin still had lingering doubts. While calling Putin's decisions to annex Crimea "revolutionary," he suggested that the Russian president could stick to this course only if he cleared his circle of people "capable of merely getting their 'cuts' and 'kickbacks.'" In a post on April 1, Girkin named Vladislav Surkov, Konstantin Zatulin, and "Dimon" (a nickname for Dmitry Medvedev) as those whom Putin needed to dismiss. He also adopted an unusually harsh tone in reference to the Russian presi-dent: "Without this radical change among top elites, all our victories will be flushed into the toilet. And if Putin does not understand it, he will be flushed himself." Still, Girkin believed that the logic of personal survival would pre-vent Putin from ending his expansionist policies in Crimea. "If everything is settled, then in a year or two NATO's intercept missiles and fighter jets will be 800 kilometers from Moscow—near Kharkov. Nobody will accept this, at least for security reasons. VVP [Putin's initials] would not want to live with a gun pointed to his head. Well, we will see," Girkin wrote on March 23.

The irreverent and skeptical tone of Girkin's writings defies a simplis-tic characterization of him as Putin's agent or as an obedient soldier under Moscow's command. Instead, the writings point to a complex mix of ideolog-ical and rational calculations behind the incursion. As a longtime believer in the "Russian World," Girkin saw it as a personal mission to return "Russian lands." As a witness to the implosion of the Ukrainian state in Crimea, he also saw an immediate opportunity to carry out his mission. His patrons,

---

[94] Oleg Kashyn, "The Most Dangerous Man in Ukraine Is an Obsessive War Reenactor Play-ing Now with Real Weapons," *The New Republic*, July 22, 2014, https://newrepublic.com/article/118813/igor-strelkov-russian-war-reenactor-fights-real-war-ukraine.

[95] The original internet forum is no longer accessible; the content of Girkin's posts is reproduced based on the records archived by the book's author.

Aksionov and Malofeyev, were ready to bankroll his campaign. At the same time, he felt that without the backing of security professionals like him, the local uprisings would be quickly suppressed. So there was an urgency to act. Finally, he believed that Putin's self-interest should have led him to support further intervention. The arguments in favor of entering Donbas had to look quite compelling.

While Girkin's conflictual resignation from the FSB and his consistent mockery of Putin make it unlikely that he remained part of the security services at the time of his raid, he certainly could have maintained contact with Russian officials through some of his Kremlin-tied associates, like Aksionov or Borodai.[96] At the time, however, Girkin was one of many Russian military adventurers who made their way into Ukraine. Later Girkin claimed that he viewed his role in Donbas as a behind-the-scenes organizer rather than a public symbol of the insurgency: "I wanted to find a charismatic leader and act as an advisor. When I first adopted this role, Ponomariov appeared here and there. And then it all changed when I could not find anyone who could be promoted as a political leader. And then the command from Moscow came."[97] The acknowledgment that he followed orders from Moscow to take a leadership role in the insurgency clearly indicated a degree of coordination with and subordination to the Russian state. This turned him into a proxy actor for the Kremlin—even if he sought to maintain some independence.

The unmasking of Girkin on April 26, just two weeks after his entry in Sloviansk, was an intentional step on the part of his supervisors in Moscow. By that time Ukraine had already launched its ATO. Militants and Ukrainian forces engaged in direct clashes, leading to the first casualties on both sides. It became clear that Ukraine would not yield to the secessionist movement in Donbas without a fight. Girkin's public appearance with the representative of the self-proclaimed DNR government, Denis Pushylin, had to signal Russian military backing for the separatists. Still, some locals around Girkin had already realized that, apart from the Russian mercenaries, there would be no Russian military intervention on the Crimean scale. As a result, they would have to "do everything" themselves.[98]

---

[96] For example, on June 8, 2014, Aksionov called Girkin to report that he was working with unnamed officials in Moscow on providing additional armaments to Girkin's unit. See Politie, "Update on Criminal Investigation of MH17 Disaster," June 19, 2019, https://www.youtube.com/watch?v=Kq-L72slP18&t=1042s&ab_channel=Politie.

[97] Zhuchkovskiy, *85 dnei Slavianska*, 89.

[98] Ponomariov, "Narodnyi mer Slavianska o nachale voiny, Girkine i razvedchukakh NATO."

Russian Militants in Donbas

The militant unit in Sloviansk consisted mainly of locals or Ukrainian citizens from other regions. However, the main commanding positions were held by Russian citizens with prior ties to Girkin. The most influential among them was Sergei Dubinskiy (call sign "Khmuryi"), a retired Russian military intelligence (GRU) colonel originally from Donetsk. He was Girkin's longtime acquaintance, starting with their joint deployment in Chechnya in 2001.[99] In an interview Dubinskiy praised Girkin as "the best operational officer out of about thirty with whom I worked in Chechnya."[100] He recounted that they jointly participated in up to eighty military operations over the course of their three-year service in North Caucasus. By one account, Dubinskiy, who lived in Rostov at the time, arrived in Sloviansk on May 2 and immediately became Girkin's second in command.[101] He was first tasked with organizing the intelligence department, but quickly took on additional responsibilities, including planning of military raids, recruitment, and coordination of militants in nearby towns as well as provision of arms and money transfers from the "mainland" (a code name for Russia). Dubinskiy also became a shadow "commandant" of Kramatorsk, with extended responsibility for neighboring towns. According to his own account, he formed "military garrisons" in Kostiantynivka, Druzhkivka, and Toretsk and maintained ties to Bezler in Horlivka and military battalions in Lysychansk.[102] Dubinskiy made frequent visits to Kostiantynivka and Druzhkivka to oversee militant activities there. When the Zinoviev brothers, militant commanders in Druzhkivka, engaged in looting and failed to organize proper self-defense, Girkin replaced them with his loyalists, who quickly "ended lawlessness" in that town.[103] After the relationship between Bezler and Girkin soured, Dubinskiy served as the intermediary between the two. He traveled "every other day" to Sloviansk and "once a week" to Donetsk and Horlivka.[104] He also claimed that "from May 20 all of the weapon deliveries were conducted through him."[105] In a video filmed in the Kramatorsk city council building in early June Dubinskiy appeared in

---

[99] Zhuchkovskiy, *85 dnei Slavianska*, 182.

[100] Prokhanov, *Novorossia, kroviu umytaya*, 18.

[101] Zhuchkovskiy, *85 dnei Slavianska*.

[102] Ibid.

[103] Aleksandr Barkov, *Novorossia v moem serdtse* (Izdatelskie Reshenia, 2018), 130.

[104] Zhuchkovskiy, *85 dnei Slavianska*, 183.

[105] Ibid.

a camouflage uniform and black balaclava and brandishing a gun. Speaking on behalf of local militia, he expressed gratitude for the assistance provided by various Russian benefactors.[106]

Dubinskiy also admitted participating in direct fighting with Ukrainian troops. He described an attack on a Ukrainian checkpoint on May 23, when a group of militants captured two Ukrainian armored vehicles: "I jumped in one of them, Said in another, and we opened fire at the Ukrainian military camp. . . . [W]e later learned that 35 Ukrainians died in that fight."[107] After Girkin's retreat from Sloviansk, Dubinskiy moved to Donetsk, where he became the head of DNR intelligence service and continued organizing arms deliveries to separatist forces. The investigation into the downing of Malaysia Airlines Flight MH17, which was shot down near Horlivka on July 17, revealed his principal role in ensuring the delivery of the surface-to-air missile system Buk from Russia.[108] This proved that Dubinskiy long maintained direct contact with top defense officials in Moscow and was trusted enough to oversee the supply of the advanced military equipment to Donbas. Dubinskiy also recruited Russian military officers to join the Sloviansk brigade. Girkin's chief of staff, a retired Russian military officer named Eldar Khasanov, came to Sloviansk from Rostov on Dubinskiy's recommendation.[109] Khasanov recalled that Strelkov had single-handed control over the militia but lacked capable staff of career military officers. So his task was to form a "military organization" by seeking out professional military personnel from among the local militants.

Girkin's other close confidante was Evgeniy Skripnik (call sign "Prapor"), a native of Sakhalin. They met in the early 1990s as volunteer fighters during the war in Transnistria. Skripnik viewed the war in Donbas as a "continuation of [the] Transnistrian conflict, in which the fight was for the identity of a Russian man whose ethnicity others wanted to eliminate."[110] Initially Girkin asked Skripnik to secure the main supply route of arms from Russia through Lyman and Yampil. Once Ukrainian troops liberated Yampil, Girkin tasked Skripnik with organizing the defense of Snizhne, an important town

---

[106] Johnny Mnemonic, "Spetsnaz Strelkova," YouTube, June 12, 2014, https://www.youtube.com/watch?v=x1cJGxO414Y.

[107] Zhuchkovskiy, *85 dnei Slavianska*, 183.

[108] Bellingcat, "The Role of Sergey Dubinsky in the Downing of MH17," March 2, 2017, https://www.bellingcat.com/news/uk-and-europe/2017/03/02/the-role-of-sergey-dubinsky-in-the-downing-of-mh17/.

[109] Zhuchkovskiy, *85 dnei Slavianska*, 226.

[110] Elena Semyonova, *Dobrovol'tsy: Vek XXI. Bitva za Novorossiyu v portretah eyo geroev* (Moskva: Traditsiya, 2015), 148.

on the road from Donetsk to the Russian border. Skripnik remembered the difficulty of dealing with apathetic locals who refused to join the separatists: "There was [a] total swamp there. Nobody was willing to fight on principle. And those who wanted were prevented by those who did not. I had to disperse this swamp with fire and sword."[111]

Another group of Russians around Girkin came from the monarchist circles. His participation in reconstruction events as a "white army officer" brought Girkin close to the leaders of the Russian All-Military Union, an emigrant organization founded in 1929 by the White Army general Petr Vrangel. Its longtime leader was Igor Ivanov, who arrived in Sloviansk with three associates on June 22. Ivanov viewed the conflict in civilizational terms, as the war that the West fought against Russia using "a small number of traitors who betrayed the interests of Slavic people." After retreating from Sloviansk Girkin appointed Ivanov as the head of the political department of the newly created DNR army, responsible for the "ideological and educational upbringing of the soldiers." His colleagues recalled that Ivanov started to transform the DNR military according to the traditions of the White Russian Army. As he later claimed, most of the insurgents "fought for the values of the White Army—Orthodox faith, unity of Russia and the Russian language."[112] He also emphasized autonomy and the ideological motives of monarchists in the Donbas militia: "Russian patriots were fighting for Novorossia not 'on orders from or in support of Putin,' as Ukrainian propaganda claimed, and not 'in defiance of Putin,' as others suggested, but driven by patriotic feelings and the need to defend the Russian people and the national interests of Russia."[113]

While elevating Russian citizens to key positions Strelkov sidelined established local activists. Ponomariov, who organized the first self-defense unit in Sloviansk, was arrested on Strelkov's orders and spent several weeks inside the town's SBU building. Local politicians who organized the first separatist rallies, such as the communist Anatoliy Khmelevoi, disappeared from public view after the May 11 referendum. None of the local activists who organized the first anti-Kyiv protests in Sloviansk played any prominent role once Girkin seized the town. Although some of them joined militia units, they performed subsidiary functions under the command of outsiders. Separatist

---

[111] Ibid., 149.

[112] Cited in Semyonova, *Dobrovol'tsy,* 125.

[113] Igor Ivanov, "Belaia idea i voina v Novorosii," in *Na Perednem Kraye: Bitva za Novorossiyu v memuarakh eyo zashitnikov,* ed. E. V. Semionova (Moscow: Traditsiia, 2017), 497.

resistance in Sloviansk was thus fully subordinated to the interests of a small group of Russian citizens acting in coordination with their Moscow chiefs.

Russian Administrators in Donbas

Another influential group of Russian citizens in Donbas in spring and summer of 2014 was organized around Aleksandr Borodai. Its task was to create political and institutional foundations for a new self-declared state in Donetsk and its further de facto integration with Russia. Born in Moscow to the family of a prominent Russian philosopher, Borodai had long espoused nationalist views and, like Girkin, volunteered to fight in Transnistria as a university student. Rather than joining the security service, Borodai initially looked primarily for intellectual ways to advance his vision, first as a journalist in a far-right newspaper, *Zavtra*, and later as a political consultant working on various anti-Western projects on behalf of the Kremlin. The initial tie between Borodai and Girkin was likely based on their ideological affinity and their interest in military adventurism in the name of greater Russia. Both traveled to Chechnya during the second military campaign there in the early 2000s.[114] Borodai, however, was by far better connected of the two. His work for high-level officials in the Kremlin and wealthy businesspeople made him of great use for Girkin. Once he retired from the FSB in 2013, Girkin got a job as Malofeyev's security chief on Borodai's recommendation. Later Borodai continued to exercise patronage over Girkin and, by his own admission, "curated his actions" during the Crimean campaign while both served as advisors to Aksionov.[115] He also played a crucial intermediary role between Girkin and elite actors in Moscow: "I was providing him with funds in Crimea and afterwards when he was in Sloviansk—for all expenditures and 'revolutionary expenses.' I am talking about hundreds of thousands of dollars to support the Strelkov unit and people's militia. These were non-state funds."[116]

One of Borodai's key interlocutors in the Kremlin was Vladislav Surkov. As the deputy chief of the presidential administration between 1999 and 2011,

---

[114] Pinchuk, *Kontur Bezopasnosti*, 133.

[115] Zhuchkovskiy, *85 dnei Slavianska*, 43. Curator in the context of Russia's covert operations in Ukraine is a common reference to an informal handler who guides and monitors actions of agents on the ground on behalf of principals in Russia.

[116] Ibid.

Surkov was responsible for designing the institutional and ideological framework of Putin's political system.[117] This involved, among other elements, reasserting control over key media outlets, preemptive formation of ersatz youth movements to counter pro-democracy activists, simulated opposition-party building, and embracing conservative neo-imperial discourse as a new state ideology. The novelty of Surkov's approach was in consolidating Putin's archaic one-man rule disguised as a modern "sovereign democracy," but one in which every political actor had a scripted role to play.[118] The resulting product resembled the "theater of absurd" with only one sensible lead character.

Despite his focus on domestic politics, Surkov had a long-held interest in Ukraine. Even before his career in the Kremlin he was advocating for the inclusion of Crimea into Russia.[119] Just like Putin, he viewed post-Soviet states as countries "lacking any experience with sovereign statehood."[120] He also ridiculed the desire of Ukraine and other countries to join the EU as merely shifting from "being a province of one country to being a province of another." In contrast was Russia's mission to "be an independent state that influences world politics."[121] In 2013 Surkov became Putin's advisor responsible for dealing with the unrecognized republics of Abkhazia and South Ossetia as well as for designing Russia's policy on Ukraine. In January and February 2014 Surkov visited Kyiv three times for crisis meetings with Yanukovych and served as an intermediary between Ukrainian and Russian leaders.[122] His deep knowledge of the Ukrainian political scene, at least of its pro-Russian actors, made Surkov a natural choice to oversee Moscow's actions both in Crimea and, later, in eastern Ukraine. Eight years later Surkov characterized this period as the "first open geopolitical counterattack by Russia (against the West) and such a decisive one." He admitted feeling "proud" that he was "part of the reconquest."[123] At the time, however, Surkov was more skeptical about the prospects of Russia's interventions

---

[117] Gulnaz Sharafutdinova, *Red Mirror: Putin's Leadership and Russia's Insecure Identity* (Oxford: Oxford University Press, 2020), ch. 6.

[118] Peter Pomerantsev, "The Hidden Author of Putinism: How Vladislav Surkov Invented the New Russia," *The Atlantic*, November 7, 2014, https://www.theatlantic.com/international/archive/2014/11/hidden-author-putinism-russia-vladislav-surkov/382489/.

[119] *Financial Times*, "Vladislav Surkov: An Overdose of Freedom Is Lethal to a State," June 18, 2021, https://www.ft.com/content/1324acbb-f475-47ab-a914-4a96a9d14bac.

[120] Vladislav Surkov, *Teksty 97-07: Stati i vystuplenia* (Moscow: Evropa, 2008), 138.

[121] Ibid.

[122] Natasha Vlashchenko, *Krazha ili Beloe Solntse Kryma* (Folio: Kharkiv, 2017), ch. 3.

[123] *Financial Times*, "Vladislav Surkov."

outside Crimea. According to one of his close associates, Surkov did not believe in the possibility of implementing the "Novorossia project" or the takeover of all of southeastern Ukraine, as advocated by Glaziev.[124] Partly, this was the result of his "pragmatic" approach, rooted in his recognition of resource constraints: "We explored available contacts in Kherson and Mykolaiv, and we realized that we had no one there."[125] According to his advisor, Surkov also questioned the long-term success of the separatist project in Donbas and thus concentrated on the day-to-day management of events there through his proxies.

Borodai became one of the central figures in Surkov's set design in Donbas. Initially, Borodai operated behind the scenes as Moscow's representative to the self-proclaimed government in Donetsk. He remembered that when he arrived in Donetsk, the separatist headquarters in the seized government building resembled "an ants' nest" surrounded by "wild barricades" and filled with "murky individuals." There was a complete lack of coordination, with "different floors of the building literally fighting with each other." He initially saw his task as "bringing these people together, teaching them how to interact, defend, share arms."[126] However, following May 11 referendum, Borodai suddenly entered the public limelight in the role of prime minister, or de facto ruler, of the new self-proclaimed republic. In later interviews Borodai claimed that he became a consensus figure for local separatist leaders due to his outsider status.[127] However, in a phone conversation recorded on May 15, a day prior to the announcement of his new position, Borodai expressed outrage about this role, which he claimed the Kremlin had assigned him: "The city of Moscow created a huge surprise for me. . . . You know who the PM will be—me! Fuck this!"[128]

Through Borodai, Surkov influenced the governance structure and policies of the DNR.[129] In one phone conversation, publicized as part of the Dutch government's investigation into the downing of Flight MH17, Surkov

---

[124] Interview with Anonymous 5, July 23, 2019.

[125] Ibid.

[126] Prokhanov, *Novorossia, kroviu umytaya*, 275.

[127] Interview with Sobchak, 2015.

[128] Politie, "Witness Appeal 11 '19—Possible Russian Influence on Appointments in the DPR," YouTube, November 13, 2019, https://www.youtube.com/watch?v=eahMvdRoC-g&ab_channel=Politie.

[129] According to a November 17, 2022, indictment rendered by the District Court of the Hague in the MH17 criminal case, Borodai and Surkov "had almost daily contact" between June 20 and August 2014. https://uitspraken.rechtspraak.nl/inziendocument?id=ECLI:NL:RBDHA:2022:12216&showbutton=true&keyword=ECLI+NL%3aRBDHA%3a2022%3a12216/.

asked Borodai to prepare a "professional estimate" of the social needs of the region to make sure that "people feel taken care of." He promised that he could process this request quickly and supply the necessary funds to "pay pensions or social assistance." Surkov also provided specific instructions on shaping Borodai's proper image in line with Russia's interests: "You need to have a public meeting on the preparation for winter so that everyone understands that we are there for [a] long [time]."[130] Surkov's email exchange with Denis Pushylin, at the time the chair of the DNR Council, made clear that Russia was funding all expenditures associated with the formation of quasi-state institutions of the self-proclaimed republic. For example, Pushylin emailed Surkov a list of expenses associated with setting up information and culture ministries, including a detailed breakdown of salaries for multiple positions in each agency.[131]

Surkov also proved instrumental in delegating a group of former officials of the self-proclaimed PMR to serve in key ministerial positions in Borodai's own government. On July 3 he informed Borodai that "Antyufeyev (former security chief of PMR) will be traveling to you."[132] He also warned that Antyufeyev's interest in controlling security agencies may clash with that of the local commanderKhodakovskiy. Borodai, however, immediately yielded to Surkov's request: "I think Khodakovskiy would gladly give it up." A week later Antyufeyev, who had just assisted with forming the Crimean security agency out of defected Ukrainians, became Borodai's first deputy in charge of the DNR security bloc. His close associates from the PMR (and Crimean campaign)—Andrei Pinchuk and Oleg Bereza—became the head of the Ministry of State Security of Donetsk People's Republic (MGB) of DNR and the minister of interior, respectively. These appointments, as Surkov predicted, caused lasting friction between them and Khodakovskiy, who also aspired to lead the MGB.[133] In conversation with Surkov, Borodai admitted that there were "problems with Khodakovskiy," but he was full of praise regarding Surkov's candidate: "Antyufeyev has a positive effect and creates a good impression." Even with Moscow's backing, however, Antyufeyev could not subordinate Khodakovskiy's Vostok battalion. Later in August its fighters

---

[130] Politie, "Witness Appeal June 2019: Chain of Responsibility in the Russian Federation 4 (8)," YouTube, June 18, 2019, https://www.youtube.com/watch?v=hPGmFJH2ZO8.

[131] *Medium*, "Breaking Down the Surkov Leaks," October 25, 2016, https://medium.com/dfrlab/breaking-down-the-surkov-leaks-b2feec1423cb.

[132] Politie, "Witness Appeal November 2019—Conversation Surkov and Borodai; Reinforcements from Russia," YouTube, November 13, 2019, https://www.youtube.com/watch?v=RpE0YMivLu0.

[133] Pinchuk, *Kontur Bezopasnosti*, 18.

clashed with armed units of the MGB over the imprisonment of some of their soldiers.[134] Similarly, Bezler maintained full operational independence from Donetsk throughout the summer and refused to follow orders from DNR government.[135] Despite repeated complaints to Surkov about his insubordination and even claims that Bezler plotted to kill him, Borodai failed to remove the militant chief from Horlivka. As Surkov explained in an intercepted phone conversation, Bezler's patron in Moscow, an unnamed top Russian security official, vetoed all requests to replace him with a more loyal commander.[136] As a result, both Girkin and Borodai left the DNR even before Bezler's own departure.

Russia delegated its candidates not only to run the security agencies but also to influence economic policies of the two self-proclaimed republics. Surkov proposed Oleg Sirenko for the DNR, who became Borodai's deputy for financial and economic issues in late July.[137] The new head of the LNR government was another Russian citizen, Marat Bashyrov, who was responsible for government relations and strategic communications in the company owned by the Russian oligarch Viktor Vekselberg. The latter worked closely with then Deputy Prime Minister Surkov on the construction of the new private university Skoltech envisioned as the Russian equivalent of MIT. Another influential figure in the LNR, Pavel Karpov, was sent from Moscow as an advisor to the republic's head Valeriy Bolotov. Earlier Karpov had worked under Surkov in the presidential administration and was also familiar with Borodai.[138] He was widely viewed as the shadow decision-maker in the LNR, while Bolotov served as the frontman.[139]

Indicative of Russia's role in Donbas, all Moscow-delegated candidates with no prior ties to the region took precedence for Borodai over locals who participated in the initial stage of the separatist uprising. Just like Khodakovskiy lost his bid to control the MGB, another local commander and future DNR head, Aleksandr Zakharchenko, had to recognize the authority of Bereza, a Russian newcomer to Donbas, and take the position of his deputy in the newly created interior ministry.[140] A local activist from

[134] Pinchuk, *Kontur Bezopasnosti,* 19.

[135] Politie, "Witness Appeal November 2019."

[136] Ibid.

[137] Ibid.

[138] Aleksei Dobrov, "Chelovek Surkova u istokov DNR," *Realna Gazeta,* July 30, 2015, https://realgazeta.com.ua/chelovek-surkova-v-lnr/.

[139] Yulia Polukhina, "Vsyo poshlo po klanu," *Novaya Gazeta,* October 5, 2015.

[140] Pinchuk, *Kontur Bezopasnosti,* 77.

Makeevka, Leonid Baranov, who initially headed a DNR special committee that was a precursor to the MGB, had to subordinate himself to Pinchuk, a Russian citizen. Gubarev complained that Borodai ignored all of his proposals to put banking institutions under the government's control. Antyufeyev's appointee from Crimea in charge of finances similarly dismissed Gubarev's ideas.[141] Even the first prosecutor general of the DNR, Ravil Khalikov, came to Donetsk from Moscow in late May after a long career working in various Russian state agencies and prior war experience in Afghanistan and Chechnya.[142] In conversation with Surkov, Borodai mentioned Khalikov as one of three individuals who could take over for him in Donetsk in his absence, the other two being Khodakovskiy and Zakharchenko.[143] According to Pinchuk, who witnessed these conflicts firsthand, the sidelining of locals created tensions that could be resolved only with Moscow's help.[144] Usually, solutions came at the locals' expense, and some, like Baranov, had to leave the DNR for good.

Russian actors were also behind the fundraising and recruitment campaigns conducted through a variety of nationalist and neo-imperial organizations. The most prominent among them were the Imperial Movement; the Interbrigada of the writer-turned-politician Eduard Limonov; the Eurasian Youth Movement, affiliated with the nationalist conservate ideologue Aleksandr Dugin; and private military companies, such as the Wagner Group. The supply of mercenaries from Russia increased in June once newly elected president Petro Poroshenko resumed ATO and violence across Donbas intensified. In his June 4 article Prokhanov hailed the assistance to their "Donetsk brothers" coming from Russia: "Volunteers are moving there by themselves, in small streams or large flows. They break through the border, get ambushed and die. They reach Sloviansk and Kramatorsk, replace insurgents killed on the checkpoints. They are Cossacks, members of military-sports clubs. There are veterans of wars in Afghanistan and Chechnya. They are young and old."[145] Even if the Russian state was not directly involved in recruitment efforts, it was interested in supporting them. One clear sign of this was the organization of training camps for Russian volunteers near Rostov and assistance of the Russian border patrol service with their transfer

[141] Gubarev, *Fakel Novorossii*, 228.
[142] Pinchuk, *Kontur Bezopasnosti*, 99.
[143] Politie, "Witness Appeal November 2019."
[144] Pinchuk, *Kontur Bezopasnosti*, 11.
[145] Aleksandr Prokhanov, "Oruzhie! Daite Oruzhie!," *Zavtra*, June 5, 2014, https://pub.wikireading.ru/156241.

into Ukraine. The supply of mercenaries strengthened the capacity of rebel groups since some of them, by one estimate about 20%, were retired military officers.[146] There was also a considerable fundraising effort launched to provide for the military and humanitarian needs of Donbas. According to a source involved in these efforts, about sixty million rubles (close to two million U.S. dollars at the time) was raised in the spring and summer of 2014.[147]

This concentration of Russian citizens at the top of the separatist republics interfered with Moscow's efforts to position itself as an impartial mediator in the talks on Donbas. In a later interview Borodai admitted that Western leaders viewed the composition of the DNR government as a clear indication of the Kremlin's direct involvement in the conflict: "The prime minister was a Russian from Moscow, the first deputy PM, Antyufeyev, was similarly from Moscow, the minister of state security had the same background, the minister of interior affairs had the same background, the minister of defense exactly the same, the prosecutor general was similarly from Moscow.... For international talks in which Russia was already involved this government looked outrageous.... So I had to find someone born in Donbas to take my place."[148]

Russia's Informal Patronage

Apart from the visible presence of Russia-led groups directly engaged in the military and political takeover of Donbas, there were informal ties that Russian agents established with local actors in various parts of the region. A prominent example was in the city of Mariupol. One high-ranking Russian official involved in the Crimean operation, Dmitriy Sablin, was a native of the city. He had made a successful political career in Moscow as an advisor to Moscow oblast governor Boris Gromov and then a member of the Russian State Duma and a senior functionary of the ruling party United Russia. In 2013, he became a member of the Federation Council, the upper chamber of the Russian Parliament, where he served on the Security and Defense Committee. Sablin also maintained political and business ties to Mariupol, where his parents still resided. In October 2012 he organized the

---

[146] Zhuchkovskiy, *85 dnei Slavianska*, 167.

[147] Ibid., 160.

[148] Gennadiy Dubovoi, "Legendarnye podrazdelenia ot Gennadia Dubovogo," YouTube, March 15, 2019, https://t.ly/RIcn.

Interparliamentary Orthodox Assembly in Mariupol, which brought legislators from Russia, Ukraine, and other countries to tackle "globalization problems" from the standpoint of "Christian morals." He invested personal funds in the city's reconstruction, which earned him the title of "honorary resident" from municipal authorities.[149] And he maintained influence over local politics through his business partner Petr Ivanov, who became the head of the PR faction on the city council. The two leading pro-Russian activists in Mariupol in spring 2014, Dmytro and Denis Kuzmenko, were also the organizers of the local boxing club TOR, which allegedly provided protection services to Ivanov's and Sablin's businesses in Mariupol. Given the absence of any record of political activism prior to 2014, the two brothers, who suddenly became strong proponents of union with Russia, were likely acting as proxies for Sablin's plans for the city.[150]

Russian security services had long cultivated ties to pro-Russian activists and organizations in Mariupol. One of them was Stanislav Shydlovskiy, sixty-two years old and a founder of the Russian Union of Donbas, created after the Orange Revolution in 2006.[151] This group became one of the early formal organizers of the pro-Russian rallies in the city. Speaking at one such rally Shydlovskiy advocated for the separation of Novorossia from Ukraine.[152] Later that spring, according to the account of a Ukrainian SBU officer, Shydlovskiy visited Rostov for a meeting with the Russian FSB operative there. He received funds and technical equipment for launching a subversive cell in Mariupol.[153] Another target was Oleg Butskoi, who introduced himself as a veteran of Ukrainian intelligence services but was allegedly run by Russia's military intelligence.[154] There was also a local leader of Don Cossacks, Vadim Belobrod (call sign "Ataman"), who organized a self-defense unit in one of the city's districts and later visited a training base in Russia.[155] A forty-year-old named Petr Kassai, was a local Communist Party organizer paid by Moscow to conduct pro-Russian propaganda activities among local youth.[156] Yet another local, Igor Lyutikov, admitted during one of the rallies that he had gone to Taganrog, a neighboring Russian

---

[149] Interview with Yuri Khotlubei, November 20, 2018. Sablin also invested in the city's real estate through a company, which Ivanov helped to manage.

[150] The Kuzmenko brothers also had prior criminal convictions and were viewed as "smal-time thugs" by law-enforcement. Interview with Ivan Bohdan, November 19, 2018.

[151] Ivan Bohdan, *Patriotv'yazni* (Mariupol: KIT, 2018), 231.

[152] Author's archived video from Mariupol, March 5, 2014. See "Mariupol 2014," Harvard Dataverse, https://doi.org/10.7910/DVN/4OBT5H.

[153] Bohdan, *Patriotv'yazni*, 237.

[154] Ivan Bohdan, *Mariupol 2014* (Mariupol: KIT, 2016), 31.

[155] Bohdan, *Patriotv'yazni*, 223.

[156] Ibid., 183.

town, to meet with a Cossack ataman. "Don Cossacks told me that they would be supporting Mariupol just as they supported Crimea," Lyutikov proclaimed. "At the highest levels of power Russia will not forget us. It will never give up on Russian speakers."[157]

The most lethal violent incident that Mariupol witnessed in spring of 2014 resulted from an operation organized with Russia's involvement. On the morning of May 9, a national holiday commemorating the victory in World War II, a group of about fifteen armed separatists entered the police station and tried to capture it by force. They had received preliminary training and firearms at the Vostok battalion base in Donetsk and, by one account, at the Russian military base in Taganrog.[158] The organizer of the assault was a fifty-six-year-old retired Ukrainian police officer, Oleg Nedavniy (call sign "Mongoose"), who, according to an SBU officer, coordinated his activities with Russian military intelligence and had met with Strelkov in Sloviansk.[159] At least eleven people were killed as a result of the attack, among them six Ukrainian police and military personnel, including the head of the city's patrol police.

Russia not only recruited and trained militant leaders in Mariupol but also provided them with arms. Several criminal cases investigated by Ukrainian law enforcement shed light on the supply of weapons to militants in the city by Russian intelligence operatives.[160] At the end of May Russian agents organized arms deliveries from Crimea to Berdiansk meant to be transferred further on to Mariupol. The total cache consisted of seventy-three boxes, which included eighty-eight Kalashnikov rifles (AK-74), eight machine guns, twenty-four grenade throwers, 918 grenades, and over twenty thousand bullets. According to evidence from the same criminal case, town militants also traveled to the Russian city Rostov-on-Don to receive instructions from FSB operatives and cash in the amount of twenty thousand dollars.

Another group of Russian actors who played a significant role in the Luhansk oblast was linked to the organization of the Don Cossack Army. The adoption of a 2005 law on State Service of Russian Cossacks allowed Cossack organizations to fulfill law enforcement functions and provide

---

[157] Author's archived video from Mariupol, March 29, 2014. See "Mariupol 2014," Harvard Dataverse, https://doi.org/10.7910/DVN/4OBT5H.

[158] Bohdan, *Mariupol 2014*, 116.

[159] Ibid., 115.

[160] Case No. 310/6513/14-K, April 6, 2015, http://www.reyestr.court.gov.ua/Review/43467650.

other auxiliary services to the Russian military, including border protection, counterterrorism, and territorial defense.[161] Cossacks also received access to state funds to finance their activities, including military training and classes in patriotism for youth.[162] Russian municipal authorities could establish contractual relations with the Cossack militia to patrol the streets along with the regular police officers.

The Don Cossack Army has been long led by ataman Nikolai Kozitsyn. Born in Dzerzhynsk (now Toretsk), Donetsk oblast, and a graduate of the police academy in Kharkiv, he later moved to Novocherkassk, a historical center of Don Cossacks. In the early 1990s Kozitsyn participated in the revival of the Don Cossack movement that had been suppressed under Soviet rule. Along with other Cossack activists he traveled to Transnistria in 1992 to fight on the side of the secessionist republic. Elected in 1994 as the chieftain of the International Union of Civic Organizations "Don Cossacks," Kozitsyn sought to integrate Cossack organizations in areas that he viewed as their "historical lands." For this purpose, he established Donetsk and Luhansk districts of Don Cossacks which encompassed towns in the southern part of Luhansk oblast and the eastern part of Donetsk oblast.

On April 9, two days after the capture of government buildings in Luhansk and Donetsk, Kozitsyn issued an order to form a Cossack National Guard in Ukraine and appointed three Ukrainian citizens as chiefs of its individual units. He also made Mykola Tarasenko, a Luhansk local who days earlier had participated in the storming of the SBU building, head of the security service of the new national guard. This signified the start of the formal involvement of Don Cossacks in the separatist uprising in Donbas. Kozitsyn later claimed that he crossed the border into Donbas on May 3 with about 250 people under his command.[163] He established his base in Antratsyt, a town of about fifty thousand people in Luhansk oblast located about sixty kilometers from the Russian border. The head of the Ukraine-appointed Antrasyt raion state administration Oleksandr Tymoshenko earlier stated that he agreed to transfer the local government building to Russian Cossacks.[164] One of Kozitsyn's appointed chiefs, a Ukrainian from Donetsk

[161] Federalnyi zakon ot 5.12.2005 N145-ФЗ, "O gosudarstvennoi sluzhbe rossiiskogo kazachestva," https://legalacts.ru/doc/federalnyi-zakon-ot-05122005-n-154-fz-o/.

[162] Interview with Aleksei Bredikhin, July 22, 2019.

[163] Aleksandr Prokhanov, "Beseda Aleksandra Prokhanova s Nikolaem Kozitsynym," *Zavtra* December 11, 2014, https://ru-prokhanov.livejournal.com/333947.html.

[164] Dinara Setdikova, "Vezhlivye kazaki pribyli v Antratsyt," *Radio Svoboda*, May 6, 2014, https://www.svoboda.org/a/25374732.html.

oblast named Serhiy Grashchenko, moved into Lyman in May and became its commander. Another loyalist, Pavel Driomov, seized Stakhanov and later became the commandant in Sieverodonetsk. By the summer, Don Cossacks had quickly become the largest armed group in the Luhansk region, with up to four thousand fighters in Lysychansk, Khrustalnyi (then Krasnyi Luch), Dovzhansk (then Sverdlovsk), and Alchevsk.[165] Although direct control of the Cossacks from Moscow was hard to establish, Kozitsyn sought to emphasize his loyalties to Russian leadership by hanging two photos in his office in Antratsyt—one of Putin and one of Surkov.[166]

Russia also exercised indirect influence over militia mobilization in the Luhansk oblast by assisting local activists committed to the secessionist cause. One was thirty-nine-year-old Oleksiy Mozgovoi, a native of the Luhansk region. In early March he met with Valeriy Bolotov and other members of a Luhansk-based underground resistance cell and agreed to become one of the public faces of the anti-Kyiv movement.[167] He set up several tents near the Luhansk state administration building and launched a public advocacy campaign for joining Russia. On March 16, the day of the Crimean referendum, Mozgovoi declared that he would like to see "the East of Ukraine reunited with Russia."[168] In April Mozgovoi visited Moscow, where he participated in talk shows on Russian state television and met with the heads of two Duma party factions, Vladimir Zhyrinovskiy and Sergei Mironov. Shortly afterward, Mozgovoi returned to Donbas and organized his own militant group, with a training camp in Dovzhansk just fifteen miles from the Russian border.

In May Russian military instructors started providing tactical training and arming of local militia in the border area stretching from Dovzhansk in the Luhansk oblast to Shakhtarsk in the Donetsk oblast.[169] Ukrainian border checkpoints in the area, meanwhile, came under pressure from groups of locals who obstructed their operation and demanded their subordination to separatist authorities. As a result, the checkpoints could no longer stop the movement of separatist activists across the border or even armored vehicles

---

[165] Tsyganok, *Donbass*, 304.

[166] *Censor*, "Putin, Bog, i Surkov—sviataia troitsa glavaria terroristov atamana Kozitsyna," November 13, 2014, https://censor.net/ru/video_news/311820/putin_bog_i_surkov_svyataya_troi tsa_glavarya_terroristov_atamana_kozitsyna_video.

[167] Aleksandr Zhuchkovskiy, *Mozgovoi* (Nizhniy Novgorod: Chernaya Sotnia, 2020), 20.

[168] Luganskij, "Miting v Luganske v podderzhku narodnogo referenduma: Vystuplenie Alekseia Mozgovogo," YouTube, February 16, 2015, https://www.youtube.com/watch?v=dZP-p5OL yVE&t=7s&ab_channel=Luganskij.

[169] Lytvyn, *Linia Rozmezhuvannia*, 228.

supplied from Russia.[170] Two attempts by the border patrol to detain separatist leaders Pushylin and Bolotov as they crossed over from Russia in May failed due to pressure from mobilized local civilians and militia members who accompanied them.[171]

Beginning in mid-May, Ukrainian border checkpoints in Donbas became targets of militants' armed assaults. Unable to hold many of the key Ukrainian border stations, separatist militia received fire support from Russian troops, who shelled Ukrainian border patrol units with mortars, multiple-launch rocket systems, and artillery. The shelling, especially intense in July, was often coordinated with militants' assault operations. According to Mykola Lytvyn, the chief of Ukraine's State Border Patrol Service at the time, "border guards had to defend themselves from the attacks on the two sides."[172] This indicates the significance that Russia attributed to establishing control over entry points to Donbas, essential for maintaining the flow of arms and equipment to the separatist militia.

Sliding into Violence

Russia operated in Donbas through private agents and a broad network of local actors. At the *mobilization stage* Moscow provided strategic advice and financial support to local actors willing to impose the secessionist agenda on local authorities. At the *militarization stage* Russian actors led armed seizures of government buildings and empowered locals to take similar actions in other towns. They also turned self-defense units into proto-military groups, established hierarchical and operational control over them, led recruitment efforts, and coordinated provision and distribution of arms from Russia. At the *conflict stage* Russian actors organized defense planning and coordination of disparate units, recruited foreign volunteer fighters, ensured provision of heavy military equipment, and led efforts to build the institutions of two quasi-states. The Russian government also used its state-controlled media to launch a disinformation campaign against

[170] Ibid., 231.

[171] One border patrol officer recounts the arrival of over two hundred civilians, including children, from nearby villages shortly after Bolotov was detained at the Dovzhansky border checkpoint on May 17, 2014. After several hours of protests Bolotov was released. See Mikhail Zhyrohov, *Bitva za Lugansk* (Kiev: Patriot Book, 2019), 49.

[172] Lytvyn, *Linia Rozmezhuvannia*, 280.

Ukrainian leadership and in support of Donbas separatists, conducted large-scale military exercises near the Ukrainian border to raise the likelihood of its military intervention, provided fire cover for insurgents, and backed separatist demands for autonomy in high-level diplomatic talks.

In Donbas Russia made several important adjustments to the secessionist strategy adopted earlier in Crimea. First, it did not deploy regular troops or special operation forces to back local militia units at the start of the conflict. Instead, it relied on retired security officers, adventurists, and ideological zealots to turn local militia into capable fighting units. As Girkin explained, "We counted on bringing a core into a loose mass of locals which would become the center of crystallization. And this is exactly what happened. Maybe not at the scale that I expected, but out of these 50 people [a Girkin-led unit from Crimea] emerged the entire *opolchenie* [militia]."[173] Only in July, once it became clear that local militia were on the verge of defeat, did Russian military command start sending professional soldiers and, later, entire battalion-tactical groups to engage Ukrainian troops directly.

Second, Russia was no longer hiding behind local public figures to preserve an impression of legality for the secession process. Instead, key public figures in the DNR were Russian citizens with ties to Russian security services or government officials. Putin's refusal to recognize the independence of the DNR and LNR also suggested that, in contrast to Crimea, the Kremlin viewed separatist republics at the time primarily as a lever of influence over the new Ukrainian government. As a result, Moscow prioritized the buildup of the statelets' institutional capacity, while the role of civilian overseers in Donbas, such as Surkov, became as substantial as that of security professionals.

Third, in contrast to the nonviolent takeover of Crimea, in Donbas Moscow intentionally fostered violence, depicted as a manifestation of the internal armed conflict. It was used to consolidate anti-Ukrainian sentiment among the region's residents and mobilize resentment toward the Ukrainian political leadership within Russian society. Violence also became a vital element of the new separatist ideology built on the sense of victimhood and gratitude to Russia as a protector of the "Donbas people." Russian propaganda used claims about civil war in Donbas as the prima facie evidence of state failure in Ukraine and the price Ukrainians paid for the success of their antigovernment uprising.

---

[173] Zhabin, "Igor Strelkov."

Still, Russia's efforts to trigger a broader insurrection in the region and consolidate separatist rule were hardly certain to succeed. Girkin's unit included just a dozen militants with the rank of officer or prior military experience; the majority were novices who had volunteered to join the Crimean militia weeks earlier.[174] Girkin later explained, "If we had access to the full resources of the Russian state, we would have had at least ten times more people in my unit and we would have been armed with more than just guns and assault rifles."[175] Hence, successful capture of Donbas required much greater local involvement than in Crimea. As Borodai admitted, however, even before the raid he doubted sufficient local mobilization was likely: "I had a low opinion of the people representing different protest groups in Donbas. I realized that the level of support was not as high as in Crimea."[176] Aware of their limited coercive resources, Girkin and Borodai counted on the swift deployment of Russian troops. Girkin later admitted that he was "not planning to fight." Instead, he was "planning to stage coercive actions, form a militia, ensure the holding of the referendum, after which Russia had to send its peacekeepers." His decision to enter Donbas was thus premised on the belief that "there should have been another Crimean scenario without armed conflict." As he quickly saw, however, "Moscow decided differently."[177]

Ukrainian security professionals involved in the conflict from the start confirmed that the number of militants at the outset was exceedingly small. "Initially they had barely 300 people. It was all a bubble," recalled Ukrainian intelligence operative Valeriy Kulish, who worked in Sloviansk at the time.[178] Cognizant of the Kremlin's unwillingness to send regular troops, one of Girkin's early backers, Sergei Aksionov, advised him to leave Donbas along with his unit already in mid-May.[179] Dubinskiy similarly recounted that following the capture of Karachun Hill overlooking Sloviansk by Ukrainian troops in early May, "senior comrades" believed that resistance could be "quickly suppressed," and instructed Girkin to withdraw.[180] Instead, Girkin continued bluffing. By the third week of May all major towns in Donbas

---

[174] Gordon, "Interview with Igor Girkin."

[175] Interview with Andrei Karaulov, 2020, archived video. See "Russian Actors 2014," Harvard Dataverse, https://doi.org/10.7910/DVN/7DBNNB.

[176] Cited in Zhuchkovskiy, *85 dnei Slavianska*, 45.

[177] Zhabin, "Igor Strelkov."

[178] Cited in Artem Shevchenko, *Sloviansk: Pochatok Viyny* (Kharkiv: Folio, 2020), 262.

[179] Zhuchkovskiy, *85 dnei Slavianska*, 139.

[180] Ibid., 338.

on the government-issued map of the Ukrainian counterterrorism operation were identified as being under full or partial "terrorist control."[181] The Ukrainian authorities thus acknowledged the loss of over twenty-six of thirty-six districts (raions) of the Donetsk and Luhansk regions.

If Girkin's unit was so small and concentrated in just several midsize towns, what explains the quick and successful diffusion of separatist presence throughout most of the region? To answer this question, I will now focus on factors internal to Donbas. As I show in Chapter 4, prior pro-Russian mobilization across Donbas tied to regional identity appeals predisposed many residents to embrace separatist demands and welcome the appearance of militants in their towns. The formation of self-defense groups in Donbas prior to Girkin's arrival, as detailed in Chapter 5, produced a network of like-minded activists capable of using force. Most of them later joined the ranks of separatist militias and started wielding power in their towns. Chapters 6 and 7 discuss the response of the municipal authorities and law enforcement to the separatist challenge. In most cases, they provided crucial administrative support that allowed militants to combine fighting with governing.

---

[181] The official map of ATO with areas designated as under separatist control as of May 20, 2014, is available at https://media.slovoidilo.ua/maps/nsdc/2014/05/large/map-nsdc-2014-05-20-uk-w3000.jpg.

Chapter 4
The "Russian Spring" and Its Discontents

On February 22, the day the Ukrainian Parliament voted to remove Yanukovych from the presidency, two competing rallies gathered in the center of Kramatorsk.[1] The first one was staged near the Stalin-era building of the Culture Palace, adorned with tall white columns and located on the city's main square. It was haphazardly organized, with no microphones for the speakers or moderators and no flags or other political symbols displayed. The meeting's purpose, however, became immediately clear. Several young men in their twenties wearing orange and black ribbons introduced themselves as activists of a new organization, the Donbas People's Militia. Speaking in short emotional outbursts, they announced the formation of the town's self-defense unit. The crowd of several hundred people responded with an equally passionate cheer: "Donbas is strong!"

The town police chief, Serhiy Zabor, dressed in a long black civilian coat, stood in the crowd, and carefully listened to the speakers. At one point he ascended the steps of the building and tried to assure everyone that the police and other public services were operating as normal. "We have checkpoints around the city and can ensure order. . . . The only problem is the constant spread of panic that Banderovites are coming here—this is unnecessary," Zabor pleaded. His appeals went unheeded. Minutes later, a man, introduced as a factory worker, reiterated the need to form a town militia to protect the city "from Western Ukrainian fascists" who were, he insisted, "seizing public buildings and murdering policemen." A young man in his twenties claimed to have visited Maidan days earlier and concluded, "They [Maidan protesters] cannot be treated as human beings . . . whether or not they win—they will never work again or live a peaceful life. . . . These beasts already tasted blood, and unless they are destroyed, they won't stop."

One did not have to travel to Kyiv, however, to find Maidan supporters. Some of them gathered right across the street from anti-Maidan rally near

[1] The following description is based on the author's archived videos from Kramatorsk, February 22, 2014. See "Kramatorsk 2014," Harvard Dataverse, https://doi.org/10.7910/DVN/PAVEVZ

Seize the City, Undo the State. Serhiy Kudelia, Oxford University Press. © Oxford University Press (2025).
DOI: 10.1093/9780197795576.003.0005

the monument to the nineteenth-century Ukrainian poet Taras Shevchenko. They wanted to commemorate a Maidan protester from Kramatorsk, Serhiy Bondarev, killed during the recent clashes with riot police in Kyiv. Instead, they became an instant target for their opponents, who approached shouting angry obscenities. A few dozen policemen lined the street to separate the groups. Meanwhile, the police chief now turned to the Maidan supporters and apologized for "not having sufficient forces to disperse the other side." As the anti-Maidan chanting grew louder and more aggressive, he attempted to persuade the Maidan activists to walk away. "You are the sensible ones, and those guys cannot be managed," he said, pointing to the anti-Maidan crowd. After some angry exchanges, the pro-Maidan demonstrators withdrew from the square to the loud applause of their foes.

Over the next weeks, similar confrontations occurred in towns across Donbas. In all of them anti-Maidan activists far outnumbered Maidan supporters and acted out their aggression by yelling and fighting. As Maidan protests in Kyiv and other towns subsided, their opponents in Donbas launched a protest wave unprecedented for the region. Even with the experience of large-scale miner strikes in the 1990s, the region never before saw simultaneous and repeated contention in all major towns. Despite the relatively small rally size, usually limited to several hundred people, they put local authorities, unaccustomed to such protests, on the defensive. Out of this anti-Maidan movement the core of separatist activists crystallized. They further used rallies to expand a pro-Russian activist network and build new ties. Many town militants, who later took up arms against Ukraine, started as rally organizers or participants. In a poll of militants, almost half of respondents indicated that they participated in such rallies at least several times a month (15.2%) or weekly (32.6%) prior to joining militia units.[2] Only 12.2% said that they did not attend any political gatherings prior to January 2014. Thus, the Euromaidan revolution led to the rise of political activism not only among its supporters but also among its antagonists.

This chapter traces anti-Kyiv mobilization across Donbas in March–May 2014, with a focus on how demands were framed and communicated.

---

[2] Based on author's online poll, conducted April 30 to May 15, 2015. The survey participants were a sample selected from profiles on social networks listed in the database "Myrotvorets" created with the assistance of the Security Service and the Interior Ministry of Ukraine (https://psb4ukr. org/criminal/). Invitations to participate in the survey were sent to 204 militia members, of whom 55 responded. Before the outbreak of hostilities 65.3% of respondents lived in the Donetsk region and 28.5% in the Luhansk region. At the time of the survey, most participants (86.1%) were over forty years old.

The initial protest stage in February and March was characterized by repeated expressions of outrage over the violent tactics of protesters on Maidan, resentment over the capture of power by force, and fear of violence spillover into Donbas. Starting in April, rallies became increasingly focused on expressions of indignation over Ukraine's military response and the rise of civilian victimization. The use of regional identity frames was prevalent at both stages and served as a coordinating device for the leaders. Still, the chapter also demonstrates that the communities in the region were far from unified in their response, as some locals sought to organize rallies in support of a united Ukraine. These attempts at countermobilization by smaller groups of pro-Ukrainian activists, however, were violently suppressed by the pro-Russian side. Their clashes on the streets in March and April became a backdrop for the escalation of civil confrontation to the level of armed conflict in May.

Mobilization Frames

The first instances of grassroots public mobilization across Donbas occurred in late February, immediately after Yanukovych fled Kyiv. Some were triggered by rumors about the intended removal of monuments to the founder of the Soviet state, Vladimir Lenin, standing in every town of the region. In anticipation of Maidan supporters, local activists set up tents around the monuments and organized town patrols. One of the separatist leaders, Andrei Purgin, recalled that this early mobilization phase brought together activists from the left and the right: "Leftists wanted to protect Lenin, right-wingers asserted the right to remove it themselves, and not to allow outsiders do this. So, some were standing there with red armbands, while others were standing with Russian imperial tricolors."[3]

The expectation of an assault by nationalist paramilitaries from Kyiv also served as justification for the initial arming of anti-Maidan activists. On the evening of February 23, Lysychansk residents saw news reports that the Lenin monument had been pulled down near the town's glass plant by undercover members of Right Sector (RS), an ultra-nationalist group, which emerged during Euromaidan and practiced violent resistance. In a few hours dozens of residents had gathered near another Lenin monument in the

[3] Cited in Prokhanov, *Novorossia, kroviu umytaya*, 242.

city center. As one of the witnesses recalled, "People started arming themselves with clubs and sticks already on Lenin Square."[4] Although the first attack turned out to be the prank of a drunken local, it reinforced the perception of an external threat and provoked new rumors about the arrival of armed outsiders. This started a wave of defensive mobilization: "It all began with men in their thirties, and then men in their fifties followed. At a later stage about a fifth in the self-defense groups were in their early twenties."[5] A local journalist and oblast council deputy, Andriy Shapovalov, believed that violent protest tactics used during Euromaidan lifted any constraints on similar mobilization in Donbas: "They reasoned that if those protesters on Maidan could do this, why should not they do the same?"[6]

Ideological Antagonism

The initial framing of mobilization in Donbas was based on three distinct ideas, two of which have been deeply engrained in the political discourse and popular narratives prevalent in the region. The first used the common trope of fascism to reject the new authorities as ideologically alien to the prevailing internationalist values of the region. The use of this trope dated back to the 2004 presidential election, when the opposition candidate, Viktor Yushchenko, was greeted in Donetsk with posters depicting him in a Nazi uniform. His supporters were often referred to as *nashysty*—a play on words that distorted the name of his party, Nasha Ukraina (Our Ukraine), to create an association with fascism. In 2013, months prior to the Euromaidan revolution, PR organized a series of rallies in all major cities of Ukraine under the slogan "To Europe—without Fascism." Opposition leaders again were portrayed as fascists seeking minority exclusion and ready to use violence. Later, references to all Euromaidan protesters as neo-Nazis became ubiquitous in pro-government and Russian media coverage. The prominence of far-right groups in launching the violent phase of Euromaidan protests in January 2014 was used to discredit the entire movement.[7]

---

[4] Interview with Apryshkin, 2021.
[5] Ibid.
[6] Interview with Shapovalov, 2019.
[7] Lucan Way, *Pluralism by Default: Weak Autocrats and the Rise of Competitive Politics* (Baltimore: Johns Hopkins University Press, 2015), 86.

Separatist activists in Donbas seized on antifascist rhetoric to mobilize support and fuel resentment of the new government in Kyiv. Flyers distributed in Sloviansk inviting people to the first major rally on March 1 featured an appeal to "say no to neo-fascism."[8] In Lyman one of the rally speakers, Kostiantyn Burlaka, characterized the new Ukrainian authorities as fascist and insisted that they would continue posing a threat to Donbas even if the region seceded.[9] In Mariupol protesters decided to form an antifascist committee to stop the alleged spread of the ideology. This framing was especially effective in Donbas, where 79% of residents viewed Stepan Bandera, the ultranationalist ideologue, in negative terms.[10] "Bandera will not pass!" became the rallying cry of protesters in Kramatorsk on March 1 when they faced Maidan activists.

Security Threat

The ideological antagonism was inextricably linked to warnings about a threat to the physical safety of the region's residents. "Today we all feel fear for our friends and relatives everywhere!" – the secretary of Kostiantynivka city council Yuri Rozumnyi proclaimed at the town rally on March 1.[11] The use of violent tactics by far-right groups during Euromaidan and the shooting of police in the final days of the revolution added credibility to such claims.[12] The official recognition of the RS leader Dmytro Yarosh as an advisor to the new SBU chief Valentyn Nalyvaichenko and the appointment of Andriy Parubiy, once a leader of a far-right party, as National Security and Defense Council secretary might have suggested that nationalists' violent tactics could become part of the government's policies. In an April 2014 survey, 73% of respondents in Donetsk oblast and 63% of respondents in Luhansk oblast agreed that the RS was a "major military formation with

[8] *Slavgord*, "V sotsialnyh setia slaviantsev prizyvayut," February 27, 2014, https://slavgorod.com.ua/news/article/447/.

[9] Author's archived video from Lyman, March 1, 2014. See "Lyman 2014," Harvard Dataverse, https://doi.org/10.7910/DVN/MCQ81K

[10] The intensity of negative attitudes was markedly stronger there than in any other oblast of the Southeast. Data based on the survey by Rating Group of two thousand respondents conducted April 15–25, 2014, with 2.2% error margin: https://ratinggroup.ua/research/ukraine/nostalgiya_po_sssr_i_otnoshenie_k_otdelnym_lichnostyam.html.

[11] Author's archived video from Kostiantynivka, March 1, 2014. See "Kostiantynivka 2014," Harvard Dataverse, https://doi.org/10.7910/DVN/GMJEVH.

[12] Kudelia, "When Numbers Are Not Enough."

influence over government that threatened citizens and the unity of the country."[13] This was substantially higher than in any other province of southeastern Ukraine.[14] The use of RS as a moniker was thus an effective way of fostering the sense of threat among Donbas residents and emphasizing the need for self-defense.

Local elites in Donbas started invoking the imminence of civil war already in January as protests in Kyiv turned violent. City councils across the region adopted similar appeals to town residents, warning that violence in Kyiv could spill over into other parts of Ukraine. "The events that are now described as a revolution in reality lead to civil war. . . . It will also lead to bloodshed and violence, looting and chaos," alerted a Lysychansk City Council resolution.[15] "There will be no winners in the forthcoming civil war," cautioned the Bakhmut City Council.[16] Illia Kononov, a sociologist from Luhansk National University, recalled that these alarmist statements generated wider public fears: "People became really afraid that it would lead to war—we already felt that in January."[17]

Kostiantyn Savinov, who served as deputy mayor of Donetsk at the time, recalled a sense of threat when he observed violent attacks on government buildings by Maidan protesters.[18] But local elites amplified these fears by spreading unsubstantiated rumors about the actions of the radicals. Savinov's colleague, secretary of Donetsk City Council Sergiy Bogachev, posted a message on his Facebook page in late January declaring that "700 Maidan militants are coming on several buses and cars to Donetsk oblast in order to stage mass disturbances, including the storming of government buildings."[19] During a public meeting in Toretsk in early February 2014, the town's representative in Parliament, Ihor Shkiria, warned that Maidan's victory would have direct repercussions for locals: "Guys with sticks or firearms

[13] Data based on a survey by Kyiv International Institute of Sociology of 3,232 respondents conducted April 10–15, 2014, with .95% error margin. For full results, see Yulia Mostovaya and Sergei Rakhmanin, "Yugo-Vostok: Vetv Dreva Nashego," *ZN*, April 18, 2014, https://zn.ua/internal/yugo-vostok-vetv-dreva-nashego-_.html.

[14] Ibid. The greatest support for this statement outside Donbas was in Kherson, with 55% in agreement. In the rest of the provinces of the region, fewer than half agreed with this view.

[15] *Novyi Put*, "Resolution of Lysychank City Council," January 29, 2014.

[16] *Vecherniy Bakhmut*, "Trebuem zhestkih i reshytelnyh deistviy," January 30, 2014, https://bahmut.com.ua/news/politics/1344-trebuem-zhestkih-i-reshitelnyh-mer-artemovskie-deputaty-prinyali-obraschenie-k-prezidentu.html.

[17] Interview with Illia Kononov, August 3, 2019.

[18] Interview with Savinov, 2019.

[19] *Ostrov*, "Vyshedshyi iz podvala DNR eks-sekretar Donetskogo gorsoveta Bogachev," October 29, 2018, https://www.ostro.org/general/politics/news/557491/.

will come in our towns and our factories and act like criminal brigades from the 1990s."[20] "The enemy is at the gates," – cautioned another town official during March 1 rally in Kostiantynivka.[21]

The initiative of the local authorities to create town militias became a defensive response to such perceived threats. "Some of our public organizations will be providing public safety to protect from crusading radicals," declared the city council in Lysychansk in late January. "We fully support this initiative of Ukrainian and Don Cossacks, police, and Afghan veterans. We are giving them the mandate of trust to protect residents of our region from extremism." In a statement published in the local press, council members even called on town residents to "join militia units to push back the provocateurs who are endangering the lives of our children and parents."[22]

The day after the final violent showdown on Maidan on February 20, hundreds of men with sticks gathered in Luhansk's central square to protest the "armed coup" in Kyiv. Although the rally was ostensibly organized by Afghan war veterans, the actual organizers were the province authorities. The show of force had to signal their own defensive capacity in case of any outside incursion. Many locals who participated in the rally were directed by "specially trained groups that would order them to move in a certain direction."[23] However, after interviewing some of them Kononov also found that many young people "sincerely felt that there was a need for such action." Even visually, he argued, the local authorities sought to communicate the rising risks to the locals: "The windows of the government building were stacked with sandbags as if they were preparing for some kind of a siege."[24]

The authorities of Donetsk province, led by Andriy Shyshatskiy, were behind the protest actions in their capital city on February 24. Under the guise of the civic groups Defense of Donbas and Civic Front, which set up tents on the central square, they encouraged recruitment of locals into the militia.[25] Municipal administrations hence became focal points for defensive coordination and served to strengthen people's confidence in their capacity to resist. Local authorities initiated the construction of checkpoints,

---

[20] *Dzerzhynskiy Shakhtior*, "My khotim zhyt', sozidat', trudit'sia bez revoliutsiy i kataklizmov," February 18, 2014, 1.

[21] Author's archived video from Kostiantynivka, March 1, 2014. See "Kostiantynivka 2014," Harvard Dataverse, https://doi.org/10.7910/DVN/GMJEVH.

[22] *Novyi Put*, January 29, 2014.

[23] Interview with Kononov, 2019.

[24] Ibid.

[25] Kazansky and Vorotyntseva (*Yak Ukraina Vtrachala Donbas*, 2020): 191.

encouraged joint patrols with the police, and recruited individuals into self-defense groups from factories and civic organizations.

Attempts to leverage the mobilizing effect of fear were clear from the rhetoric used at many anti-Kyiv rallies in Donbas at the time. In Lyman, rally speakers called people to join self-defense groups as a preemptive action. "If we do nothing, they will start attacking us!" one pleaded.[26] In Toretsk, the threat of the RS was mentioned as the reason to start arming. "They will bring arms from Lviv here and we are not ready—we have nothing!" a rally participant there despaired.[27] Another speaker, who introduced himself as a miner, warned that there could be a "heavenly thousand or tens of thousands" if outsiders attempted to enter the city. When Bakhmut mayor Oleksiy Reva arrived at the checkpoint set up to block the Ukrainian arms storage he met local activists who refused to move. "We want to prevent the transfer of arms to Western Ukraine and prevent the armament of RS. We are fearful that they will be shooting our families and put Donbas on its knees," – one of the men at the checkpoint asserted.[28] The risk of an attack from other regions of Ukraine was similarly mentioned by the moderator of the rally in Rubizhne, Nellia Zadiraka, on March 1: "They will come with machine guns here—they can shoot us here . . . but believe me—we are here and let them kill me if they want. . . . Hundreds of young guys will rise up instead of me. . . . If the time comes, we will find arms."[29]

Regional Identity

The mobilizing effect of fear encourages resistance over surrender if group members have confidence in their capacity to act collectively. This requires a particularly strong in-group sense of solidarity and an agreement over what constitutes an out-group.[30] The underlying basis for group action is

[26] Based on the author's archived video of the rally in Lyman. See "Lyman 2014," Harvard Dataverse, https://doi.org/10.7910/DVN/MCQ81K.

[27] Based on the author's archived video of the rally in Toretsk. See "Toretsk 2014," Harvard Dataverse, https://doi.org/10.7910/DVN/OSQ1SE.

[28] Based on the author's archived video from Bakhmut, March 19, 2014. See "Bakhmut 2014," Harvard Dataverse, https://doi.org/10.7910/DVN/JU9DSN.

[29] Based on the author's archived video of the rally in Rubizhne. See "Rubizhne 2014," Harvard Dataverse, https://doi.org/10.7910/DVN/ONLPT3.

[30] Roger Petersen, *Western Intervention in the Balkans: The Strategic Use of Emotion in Conflict* (Cambridge: Cambridge University Press, 2011).

formed out of "broadly accepted cultural or organizational procedures."[31] In Donbas, the in-group cohesiveness rested on its regional identity that long set it apart from other Ukrainian regions.[32] It subsumed various ethnic identifications, turning the region into an "urban melting-pot."[33] Donbas identity was based on a shared sense of belonging to what the Luhansk-based sociologist Kononov described as a "unique community of people with roots both in Ukraine and Russia." He concluded that "in a sociocultural sense the people in the two provinces are essentially the same."[34] Donetsk-born writer Volodymyr Rafeienko attributed the "marginalization" of national identity in Donbas to the "ethos of [an] industrial region" in which the Soviet state sought to "denationalize the cities." Instead, it created a "myth of miners and metallurgy workers as a special human race" that became the foundation of the unique regional pride.[35]

The PR, founded by Donbas business and political elites, used this local pride in several earlier crisis points in the country's history.[36] During the 2004 presidential election, references to the "Donbas character" became a staple of PR leader Viktor Yanukovych's campaign.[37] Throughout the 2000s the "Donetsk identity" was most frequently mentioned in regional newspapers controlled by PR officials.[38] It resonated with a large majority of the region's residents and turned Donbas into a "political ghetto of the Party of Regions."[39] Used to counter the nation-building agenda of center-right

---

[31] Nelson Kasfir, "Domestic Anarchy, Security Dilemmas, and Violent Predation: Cases of Failure," in *When States Fail: Causes and Consequences*, ed. Robert I. Rotberg (Princeton, NJ: Princeton University Press, 2004), 71.

[32] The strength of regional identity in Donbas is widely acknowledged by various earlier scholars of the region. See, for example, Hiroaki Kuromiya, *Freedom and Terror in the Donbas: A Ukrainian-Russian Borderland, 1870s–1990s* (Cambridge: Cambridge University Press, 1998); Illia Kononov, "Donbas v Etnokulturnyh Koordynatah Ukrainy (Sociological Analysis)" (PhD dissertation, Taras Shevchenko Luhansk National Pedagogical University, 2005); Ararat Osipian and Alexandr Osipian, "Why Donbas Votes for Yanukovych: Confronting the Ukrainian Orange Revolution," *Demokratizatsiya: The Journal of Post-Soviet Democratization* 14, no. 4 (2006): 495–517; Kerstin Zimmer, "Trapped in the Past Glory: Self-Identification and Self-Symbolisation in the Donbas," in *Re-constructing the Post-Soviet Industrial Region: The Donbass in Transition*, ed. Adam Swain (London: Routledge, 2007): 97–122; Kuzio, *Putin's War against Ukraine*.

[33] Andrew Wilson, "Elements of a Theory of Ukrainian Ethno-national Identities," *Nations and Nationalism* 8, no. 1 (2002): 42.

[34] Kononov, "Donbas v Etnokulturnyh Koordynatah Ukrainy."

[35] Cited in Oleksandr Mykhed, *"Ya zmishayu tvoyu krov iz vuhilliam": Zrozumity ukrainskyi Skhid* (Kyiv: Nash Format, 2021), 317.

[36] Interview with Yevhen Kopatko, December 16, 2014.

[37] Osipian and Osipian, "Why Donbas Votes for Yanukovych."

[38] Viktor Kotyhorenko et al., eds., *Donbas v ethnopolitychnomu vymiri* (Kyiv: Kuras Institute of Political and Ethnonational Studies, 2014), 460.

[39] Interview with Hryhoriy Nemyria, December 2014.

parties, regional identification also became an obstacle to the development of a civic attachment to the Ukrainian state. In August 2013, Donbas was the only region in Ukraine where a majority (57%) indicated that they were still fully or largely against Ukraine's independent statehood.[40]

Separatist organizations such as Donetsk Republic, established in 2005, also sought to capitalize on the identity cleavage. Its founder, Andrei Purgin, described Donbas as the "territory of lost ethnicity." He wanted to turn "strong regional patriotism" into "regional ethnicity under the cover of the Russian world." Purgin imagined his homeland as the house that had economic resources as its foundation, "regional patriotism" as its "walls and windows," and the "Russian world" as its roof. In his view, this construction had to "protect from the aggressive Ukrainian ethnicity."[41]

Regional identity gained special salience in the wake of the Euromaidan revolution. Local elites sought to accentuate the differences between Donbas residents and Maidan supporters along ethical and ideological dimensions. On the one hand, they stressed the sacrifice of the industrial workers of Donbas that sustained the economy of the entire country. On the other hand, some of the nationalist slogans of Maidan protesters served as a contrast to the internationalist ethos of the region. A miner speaking at a rally in Toretsk on May 29 summed up both of these dimensions as follows: "When they were dancing on Maidan, burning things in Kiev, forming a government—we were working. But now when blood flows in our land—this is fascism." These sentiments further reinforced the image of Donbas as a unique region in Ukraine. When the armed conflict began in the spring of 2014 the share of those in Donetsk and Luhansk oblasts who defined themselves through their regional belonging or their native town was almost double the number of those for whom Ukrainian citizenship was an indispensable identity (51.3% vs. 28.1%).[42]

Another feature of all early rallies across Donbas was appealing to Russia for assistance. Rather than an expression of long-held irridentist desires, this was a response to a highly volatile and uncertain security situation on

---

[40] Data based on a survey of two thousand respondents conducted by Rating Group, August 9–18, 2013, https://ratinggroup.ua/research/ukraine/dinamika_patrioticheskih_nastroeniy _avgust_2013.html.

[41] Prokhanov, *Novorossia, kroviu umytaya*, 242.

[42] By contrast, in two Western Ukrainian regions (Lviv and Ivano-Frankivsk) almost half of all respondents (49.7%) identified Ukrainian citizenship as indispensable for their identity. See Illia Kononov and Svitlana Khobta, *Zvit za Resul'tatamy Doslidzhennia Zhyttevi Svity Skhodu i Zahodu Ukrainy* (Luhansk: Taras Shevchenko Luhansk National Pedagogical University, 2014).

the ground. In Sloviansk, the rally on March 1 was accompanied by frequent chanting of "Russia!" and ended with the adoption of a resolution asking Putin for support.[43] During the rally in neighboring Toretsk on the same day, most of the speakers also made references to Russia as their potential defender. One woman insisted, "Russia won't appear here by itself—we need to tell it that we need protection." A man cited a Russian news anchor who suggested that "if we rise up Russia will help us."[44] A similar view was articulated during a March 1 rally in Rubizhne by the local Communist Party chief Nellia Zadiraka: "Russia said that if you do not appeal to us then we cannot come and support or save you."[45]

Autonomous Status

Despite the explicit pro-Russian rhetoric of the rallies, even their most radical speakers did not initially question the future of Donbas as an integral part of Ukraine. Rather, their stated objective was an autonomy that would provide authorities in Donetsk and Luhansk with new powers. Of particular significance were control over law enforcement, protection of Russian-language rights in educational and cultural spheres, and retaining most of the revenues collected locally. Ukraine's transformation into a de jure federal state, a related demand, would codify the region's expanded powers in the Constitution. At a rally in Lyman Burlaka suggested that the Donetsk oblast should have the powers of any U.S. state so that it "could live by its own rules."[46] The resolution of the March 5 rally in Severodonetsk called for economic autonomy of the region: "We demand the protection of economic rights of Donbas residents. Those funds that we earned with our own hands need to be spent on the development of our cities. We insist on financial federalism!"[47] At a rally in Dobropillia on April 19 Lyudmila Vinogradskaia, who introduced herself as a DNR deputy, stressed the need for

---

[43] Author's archived video from Sloviansk, March 1, 2014. See "Sloviansk 2014," Harvard Dataverse, https://doi.org/10.7910/DVN/JU50BB.

[44] Author's archived video from Toretsk, March 1, 2014. See "Toretsk 2014," Harvard Dataverse, https://doi.org/10.7910/DVN/OSQ1SE.

[45] Author's archived video from Rubizhne, March 1, 2014. See "Rubizhne 2014," Harvard Dataverse, https://doi.org/10.7910/DVN/ONLPT3.

[46] Based on the author's archived video of the rally in Lyman. See "Lyman 2014," Harvard Dataverse, https://doi.org/10.7910/DVN/MCQ81K

[47] Based on the author's archived video of the rally in Sieverodonetsk, March 5, 2014. See "Sieverodonetsk 2014," Harvard Dataverse, https://doi.org/10.7910/DVN/1KHPZE.

Donbas to receive "budget independence" since "Ukraine can survive only as a federal state."[48]

These demands for a change in the administrative status of the region were not new. One of the first region-based civic organizations in Ukraine, the International Movement of Donbas, formed in the final years of the USSR, advocated for the region's "self-governing" status within a "federal Ukraine."[49] Calls for regional autonomy were also voiced during the miners' strikes in July 1993. A year later a special plebiscite was held in Donetsk and Luhansk oblasts in which over two-thirds of voters supported turning Ukraine into a federal state and making Russian the second state language. For Purgin, the success of the plebiscite made 1994 "the birth year of Donetsk separatism."[50] On the elite level, however, these ideas were publicly embraced only a decade later, when some of the key figures of the newly established PR, including Yanukovych, started promoting a federalist structure for Ukraine.[51] Federalism was an opportunistic demand for Donbas elites who hoped to receive "complete hegemony" in regions where they were popular.[52] Once elected president, Yanukovych dismissed federal ideas and asserted that Ukraine would remain "a unitary state."[53] Four years later, faced with a new challenge to their authority, some key party figures sought to bring federalization back onto the political agenda. On February 18, 2014, the leadership of the Luhansk oblast council expressed support for holding a referendum on making Ukraine a federal state as "the only way to preserve the state and protect the right of our people to decide how they should live."[54]

The residents of Donbas also showed a predisposition to greater autonomy for the region within Ukraine or even complete separation. A survey conducted in late April and early May demonstrated strong majority support (80%) among respondents in Donbas for a change in the region's status.[55] Only 9% favored maintaining the status quo. By contrast, almost

[48] Based on the author's archived video of the rally in Dobropillia. See "Dobropillia 2014," Harvard Dataverse, https://doi.org/10.7910/DVN/MU1NF6.

[49] Novorossia TV, "Internatstional'noe dvizhenie Donbassa: u istokov politicheskoi sub'ektnosti regiona," November 19, 2019, https://t.ly/kzSx.

[50] Marina Tretiakova, "Referendum o federalizatsii Donbassa: 20 let bor'by," *Aktualnye Kommentarii*, December 9, 2014, https://actualcomment.ru/referendum-o-federalizatsii-donbassa-20-let-borby.html.

[51] Kazansky and Vorotyntseva, *Yak Ukraina Vtrachala Donbas*, 109.

[52] Ibid., 117.

[53] Ibid., 118.

[54] *Vostochnyi Variant*, "Preizidium oblsoveta obratilsia k Yanukovichu," February 18, 2014, https://v-variant.com.ua/ru/prezydyum-oblsoveta-obratylsia-k-yanukovychu-prosiat-vvesty-chp-a-takzhe-zahovoryly-o-federalyzatsyy-ukrayn-obnovleno/.

[55] Survey results cited in Katchanovski, "The Separatist War in Donbas," 484.

a quarter (23%) wanted to see the region gaining autonomy within federal Ukraine. Nowhere else in the country did the acquisition of autonomy for a region receive more than 10% support. Notable was public endorsement of more radical alternatives—about a third of respondents (31%) backed the region's secession, resulting either in an independent state (8%) or ascension to Russia (23%). While in other regions majorities of over two-thirds were in favor of keeping Ukraine as a unitary state, it was a preference of just 35% of Donbas residents. These differences in the vision of the region's future in spring 2014 explain the greater receptivity of Donbas to separatist appeals.

Countering Separatism, Enduring Violence

Despite being substantially outnumbered, supporters of a unitary state in Donbas sought to counter separatist mobilization with their own actions. Many of them were earlier Maidan backers who either traveled to Kyiv during protests or staged protests in their towns. Even where they had to yield to separatist dominance, their public acts of defiance undercut the impression of a unified embrace of separatist narratives. Donetsk and Luhansk witnessed the first pro-Ukrainian rallies already in early March. To encourage wider participation, rally organizers in Donetsk avoided any references to Euromaidan and positioned them as gatherings in support of a unified Ukraine.[56] "We sought to avoid political flags or slogans. The only political slogan we accepted was that Donetsk belonged to Ukraine," recalled one of the organizers, Bohdan Chaban, who managed a local pub at the time.[57] Organized by civic activists, these rallies attracted thousands of residents but featured no local authorities. They also instantly became targets of physical assaults staged by their opponents.

The first sizable pro-Ukrainian rally in Donetsk, on March 5, was surrounded by an aggressive pro-Russian crowd. Only the narrow police line separating them managed to prevent escalation. Eight days later, however, the police appeared helpless. The two large gatherings, one under the Ukrainian flag and the other under the Russian, faced off again on Lenin Square in Donetsk. The police retreated during the first

[56] Interview with Enrique Menendez, July 5, 2019.
[57] Cited in *Hromadske*, "Yuzivska Vesna: Yak my borylysia za Donetsk," April 28, 2016, https://t.ly/IRqS.

attempts by pro-Russian participants to break through to their opponents. As one pro-Russian demonstrator later admitted, some of the police had just returned from Maidan and sympathized with the pro-Russian side: "We agreed with the police that we would pressure them a bit and they would disperse. From the outside it seemed as if a dozen demonstrators attacked police, and they could not withstand the assault. In reality, police just did not resist."[58] The advisor to Donetsk's governor at the time, Kostiantyn Batozskyi, also attributed police inaction to their earlier experience countering protests in Kyiv: "Eighteen thousand policemen in Donetsk oblast all went through rotations on Maidan and returned feeling no loyalty to the new authorities. They did not understand why the government should be defended."[59]

Armed with metal sticks and chains, firecrackers and pepper spray, pro-Russian radicals chased pro-Ukrainian demonstrators from the square. They also smashed the windows of the bus used to evacuate pro-Ukrainian rally participants. In the ensuing fighting one of the pro-Ukrainian activists, Dmytro Cherniavskyi, was stabbed to death. Cherniavskyi, a twenty-two-year-old member of the nationalist party Svoboda, was a native of the Donetsk oblast. Earlier he had volunteered for the local self-defense group meant to protect pro-Ukrainian gatherings in Donetsk. Cherniavskyi became the first fatality of the rising confrontation in Donbas. Enrique Menendez, a local civic activist with Spanish roots, remembered that his killing produced a split within the pro-Ukrainian group. Some, like Menendez, argued that there should be no new rallies for as long as the local authorities could not guarantee the safety of their participants.[60] Others advocated for a more forceful response that would mirror the violent tactics used by the pro-Russian side. Most of the pro-Maidan activists in Donetsk, however, sought to avoid escalation and rejected calls to arms.[61] As a result, the pro-Ukrainian self-defense unit in Donetsk numbered just about forty people.

Only two more pro-Ukrainian rallies were held in Donetsk in April. The gathering of several thousand on April 17 had already been scheduled to take place outside the city center due to security concerns. Meanwhile,

---

[58] Kristina Melnikova, "Desiat' let my gotovilis i verili: Kak nachinalas Russkaia vesna na Donbasse," *Eurasia Daily*, July 4, 2016, https://eadaily.com/ru/news/2016/07/04/desyat-let-my-gotovilis-i-verili-kak-nachinalas-russkaya-vesna-na-donbasse.

[59] Interview with Kostiantyn Batozskyi, December 2014.

[60] Interview with Menendez, 2019.

[61] Interview with Yegor Firsov, December 2014.

Donetsk police appealed to avoid attending any mass gatherings.[62] On the same day, several hundred people attended a pro-Ukrainian rally in Kramatorsk, earlier seized by Girkin's militants, and unfolded a forty-meter-long national flag.[63] "We still naïvely believed that if we come out and express a different viewpoint we would be heard," one rally participant from Kramatorsk recalled.[64] The final rally in support of Ukraine in Donetsk, on April 28, ended with renewed clashes and beatings of pro-Ukrainian protesters chased by masked thugs with sticks and petards. The street violence in the absence of a police response made the costs of further pro-Ukrainian organizing in Donetsk far too excessive.

In Luhansk, the pro-Ukrainian mobilization was just as short-lived. On March 5 Luhansk witnessed its largest pro-Ukrainian rally under the unifying slogan "Luhansk against the War!"[65] It was held simultaneously with the one in Donetsk but faced no serious obstruction from the pro-Russian side. That changed five days later, when another pro-Ukrainian rally gathered near the Shevchenko monument, while pro-Russian demonstrators held their rally across the street at a World War II memorial. The juxtaposition of the two rallies with conflicting agendas set the stage for their direct confrontation. A large group of men from the pro-Russian rally, some in masks and holding Russian flags, marched over to the pro-Ukrainian demonstrators and tried to push them out of the square. Just like in Donetsk, instead of stopping them Luhansk police quickly dispersed. A pro-Ukrainian participant recalled the details of the assault: "They knocked people off the monument's pedestal. They shouted 'Fascists!' and started beating us. I just could not understand what was happening."[66] Only the next day one of the pro-Russian organizers, Arseniy Klinchaev, was arrested. This was followed by the arrest of Luhansk Guard leader Aleksandr Kharitonov and the removal of the organization's tents from the town square. Still, the capture of the SBU building in Luhansk on April 6 gave the pro-Russian side a new momentum. One member of the local soccer ultras, who sided with pro-Ukrainian demonstrators, remembered that the team realized they were now

---

[62] *Ukrains'ka Pravda*, "Militsia prosyt' ne ity na mitynhy v Donetsku cherez 'radykaliv,'" April 17, 2014: https://www.pravda.com.ua/news/2014/04/17/7022751/.

[63] Donets'ka oblasna derzhavna administratsiia, "17 kvitnia—Den' vilnyh lyudei u Kramatorsku," April 17, 2022, https://dn.gov.ua/news/17-kvitnya-2014-roku-den-vilnih-lyudej-u-kramatorsku.

[64] *Suspilne Donbas*, "Povernuty Donbas: Kramatorsk," YouTube, July 5, 2019, https://youtu.be/CB4lbYgBk6Y.

[65] Sergei Sakadynskiy, *Luganskiy Razlom* (Moscow: Izdatelskie Reshenia, 2016).

[66] Cited in Serhiy Hlotov et al., eds., *U vohnianomu kiltsi: Oborona Luhanskoho aeroportu* (Kharkiv: Folio, 2018), 35.

"out of the game." He recognized that the coercive advantage was on the pro-Russian side: "They already had weapons and we had none. And none of the security agencies came to our assistance."[67]

In contrast to Donetsk, where pro-Ukrainian demonstrators faced violence, subsequent pro-Ukrainian rallies in Luhansk in April were ignored by separatist leaders. The last one, on April 28, coincided with the declaration of the Luhansk People's Republic. The rally ended with a march to the regional police office to demand that police restrain the rising separatist tide. However, these appeals had no effect. The next day, pro-Russian activists completed their symbolic takeover of power by raising Russian flags over key government buildings, including that of the regional state administration and the prosecutor's office and the court building. At the gathering of pro-Ukrainian activists later that day many decided to leave the city. Those who remained switched to providing covert assistance to the Ukrainian soldiers still stationed at the city airport.[68]

The pro-Ukrainian demonstrations in most other towns in Donbas followed the same trajectories—from enthusiasm and defiance to intimidation and, ultimately, withdrawal. Mariupol witnessed some of the largest and most frequent pro-Ukrainian rallies of any town in the region apart from Donetsk. While the first rally in March attracted just a few dozen participants, the next one, on March 5, gathered around two thousand people. It was organized with the support of local authorities and staged on the steps of the city council building. Apart from civil society representatives, its speakers included the mayor, Yuriy Khotlubei, and Ukrainian Parliament member Oleksiy Belyi. Their repeated message was the need for peaceful reconciliation. A student from the town's Priazov University called for peace on behalf of all others studying in Mariupol. The local priest of the Ukrainian Orthodox Church of Kyiv Patriarchate preached for unity of the country as a way of "defeating the devil." When a pro-Russian activist got to the microphone to warn about "fascists," the crowd responded with a single chant: "We want peace!" In his final remarks, Mariupol's mayor Khotlubei praised the rally participants as "true patriots" trying to "defend our beautiful city from extremism."[69]

Countermobilization for Ukraine in most other towns was much weaker and organized by only a few local activists. In Selydove, a pro-Ukrainian

<hr>

[67] Ibid., 50.
[68] Ibid., 90.
[69] Based on the author's archived video from Mariupol, March 5, 2014. See "Mariupol 2014," Harvard Dataverse, https://doi.org/10.7910/DVN/4OBT5H.

demonstration consisted of just two participants—a father and son. Volodymyr Kruzhko was a small entrepreneur and Svoboda member, while his son, twenty-year-old Bohdan, spent weeks on Maidan in support of anti-Yanukovych protests. They appeared on the town's square with a Ukrainian banner during the pro-Russian rally there on March 22.[70] The moment they unfolded the flag they were surrounded and insulted by dozens of angry rally participants. Although police quickly moved them out of the crowd, local separatists viewed their very appearance as a veiled threat. The following day a group of young men, ostensibly from the new militia unit Patriotic Forces of Donbas, arrived in Selydove to meet with Kruzhko personally. Their street encounters attracted town residents. "We don't want any demonstrations here," one of the visitors told the younger Kruzhko. "They are just holding a flag of their country. What do you want from them?" a woman interfered. "We want them to promise that they won't be insulting older people," a visitor from Donetsk responded. Faced with sudden pushback from the locals, the visitors cut the conversation short. "There is no one to talk to here, so we will be leaving. . . . Just please do not touch them since they are just youngsters," one of them said before they jumped in their cars and drove away.[71]

A more numerous Ukrainian counteraction happened in Starobilsk on April 24. It was staged next to a pro-Russian rally of about one hundred people in front of the town's Culture Palace.[72] Despite lacking in numbers, the pro-Ukrainian side was far more vocal and energetic, yelling, "Stop lying! Kolorady [a derogatory term for Russia sympathizers] get out of here! Putin is a fascist!" Some were local Euromaidan activists who intentionally replicated obstruction tactics used by anti-Maidan agitators weeks earlier.[73] The report in the local newspaper proved that the counter-rally served its purpose. It noted the presence of the two opposing camps and concluded that there was "no end in sight to ideological confrontation" in Starobilsk.[74]

A similar tactic of staging pro-Ukrainian counter-rallies was used in other towns. On April 19 about a dozen people gathered under Ukrainian flags across the street from a pro-Russian crowd of several hundred on the

---

[70] Interview with Bohdan Kruzhko, October 18, 2018.

[71] Based on author's archived video from Selydove. See "Selydove 2014," Harvard Dataverse, https://doi.org/10.7910/DVN/1U1EAM.

[72] Based on the author's archived from Starobilsk. See "Starobilsk 2014," Harvard Dataverse, https://doi.org/10.7910/DVN/LSPYTI.

[73] Interview with Volodymyr Hryhorenko, July 8, 2019.

[74] N. Bondar, "Davaite Zhyty Myrno," *Visnyk Starobilshyny*, Nos. 35–36, May 2, 2014.

central square of Toretsk. Although they immediately became targets of verbal attacks, there was no attempt to engage in physical confrontation. In the miners' town of Novohrodivka the organizers of a counter-rally went even further. One pro-Ukrainian activist and council member, Kostiantyn Museiko, and a local entrepreneur, Oleksandr Balinov, publicly defied the separatists by taking down the DNR flag from the city council building. "If the municipal authorities are not willing to follow the law on the state flag, mandating its display on government buildings, then we as deputies of the city council will be fulfilling this law and removing this flag of an unknown republic," said Balinov, looking straight into the camera. Minutes later a man climbed up the ladder and took the DNR flag out of the flag post. "This will be our material evidence of a crime which will be presented to the police," Balinov continued, rolling up the banner and putting it away.[75] The footage was shown on the local KAPRI television channel and received wide publicity. This was a daring act, but Balinov was oblivious to the risks.[76] Days earlier, he had attended a pro-Ukrainian rally in Donetsk whose relatively large size had a reassuring effect.

For many pro-Ukrainian activists living closer to Sloviansk any public expression of support for Ukraine was impossible after Girkin's arrival there. In Druzhkivka, a town in the Sloviansk agglomeration, the last pro-Ukrainian rally before the town's liberation was held on April 17. It attracted about one thousand people, but no representatives of the local government attended. According to a local party activist, the presence of armed men had an intimidating effect and prevented further actions.[77] Bakhmut offers another example of a pro-Ukrainian group that went underground due to perceived risks. In early March, local pro-Ukrainian activists organized the People's Council, which intended to counterbalance the pro-Russian activists in the city.[78] According to a group member, they tried to engage in an information campaign using the mailing list "Ukrainian Bakhmut."[79] However, public actions were no longer possible since locals reacted in a very aggressive manner to pro-Kyiv appeals.[80] As a result, a local pro-Ukrainian activist said he "could not find any person who would

---

[75] Based on the author's archived video from Novohrodivka. See "Novohrodivka 2014," Harvard Dataverse, https://doi.org/10.7910/DVN/B8UUQL.

[76] Interview with Oleksandr Balinov, October 18, 2018.

[77] Interview with Tetyana Bukharkova, September 11, 2018.

[78] Interview with Stanislav Tremasov, September 20, 2018.

[79] Interview with Gayene Avakian, November 4, 2018.

[80] Interview with Dmytro Kononets, September 17, 2018. By one estimate, about two-thirds of town residents supported DNR. Interview with Kostiantyn Mateichenko, November 2018.

support armed resistance" against the DNR. "Some were just fearful that they would be denounced," he recalled.

The risk of reprisal for pro-Ukrainian activism increased appreciably in April as threats and verbal assaults escalated to beatings and killings. On April 6 pro-Ukrainian activists of Sieverodonetsk organized a flash mob they called "With Ukraine at Heart" on the town's main square. Several dozen people with Ukrainian flags and balloons turned into an instant target for anti-Kyiv demonstrators arriving with sticks and empty bottles. People holding national symbols were quickly pushed to the other side of the street and chased away once they unfurled a large Ukrainian banner.[81] In the absence of a police response, this created for many a lasting sense of vulnerability and defenselessness.[82] Still, this attack did not stop pro-Ukrainian activists in the nearby town of Rubizhne from holding their own rally on the central square on April 21. Their appearance refuted standard claims about there being just a handful of Ukraine supporters in town and defied their depiction as extreme nationalists. They recited Ukrainian poems and called for reconciliation. Many of them addressed the gathering in Russian, like a young man, Dmytro Ryzhkov, who proclaimed, "We are here to show that we live in Ukraine, and I am Ukrainian."[83] The rally, however, was interrupted by a large group of men, most dressed in black, who ran onto the city council steps, tore Ukrainian flags away from the demonstrators, and assaulted those who resisted. Their coordinator, the head of the town's Afghan war veteran organization Volodymyr Shcherbak, observed the assault from the outside. Many pro-Ukrainian activists sustained injuries, and a local folk musician, Vasyl Lyutyi, was tied to a tree and badly beaten. "They wanted to tear him apart," a local journalist recalled.[84] Instead of going after his attackers, the police detained the musician.[85]

The following day members of political parties and local government officials gathered at the city council building to condemn the violent clashes. Acting mayor Oleksandr Khomenko and local police chief Dmytro Shpak blamed outsiders for initiating the violence. Shpak explained, "Most of them

---

[81] Interview with Oleksiy Svetikov, June 11, 2019.

[82] Interview with Olena Nizhelska, June 14, 2019.

[83] Author's archived video from Rubizhne, April 2014. See "Rubizhne 2014," Harvard Dataverse, https://doi.org/10.7910/DVN/ONLPT3.

[84] Interview with Oleksiy Artyukh, 2019.

[85] *Severodonetsk.Info*, "Ukrainskogo muzykanta iz Rubezhnogo, kotorogo priviazali k derevu, mogut eshe posadit na 5 let," April 22, 2014, http://sever.lg.ua/2014-04-22-ukrainskogo-muzykanta-iz-rubezhnogo-kotorogo-privyazyvali-k-derevu-mogut-eshche-i-posadit.

were former convicts from Lysychansk, Severodonetsk and Kremennaia. They were drunk and possessed tools for violence and sought to destabilize the situation."[86] In response, the organizer of the rally, the head of the Batkivshyna Party office, questioned the actions of the police which allowed buses with men into town. In the end all meeting participants signed a pledge to avoid violence and participate only in events for "peace and unity." The only one who refused to sign the memorandum was the local KPU office head Zadiraka—the main speaker at all the pro-Russian rallies in town.

Fighting Militants, Facing Outrage

By early April the separatist movement in Donbas was losing momentum. The rallies under Russian flags, earlier attended by thousands, could now bring out barely several hundred people. The reasons for demobilization ranged from the sense of futility of further protests to poor organization and lack of clarity regarding the tactics and the cause of the movement. In Lysychansk, for example, even KPU sympathizers admitted that their organization was like a "circus and mayhem."[87] During the rally in Toretsk on April 5 a woman guarding a checkpoint at the Volodarska mine near Bakhmut could not contain her frustration at the small numbers. She scolded town residents for being too passive compared to other cities. "I am ashamed of my own town!" she exclaimed. Another speaker at the rally similarly despaired: "There are fewer and fewer people coming to these rallies. We invite miners but they are silent. We have four thousand miners here at least—why are they not here? Are they cowards? Are they threatening to fire you? Then write hundreds of resignations! You are just indifferent people. You will be ashamed to look your kids in the eye."[88]

Ukraine's launch of ATO in mid-April gave new impetus to the waning movement. The fears of nationalist assaults were superseded by anxieties over possible violent crackdowns by Ukrainian troops and volunteer brigades.[89] Local activists blocked several arms storage sites in Donbas to prevent the transfer of arms to the Ukrainian military. One such checkpoint was set up already in March near the entrance to the Volodarskoho

---

[86] "Novyny mista," *Rubizhanski Novyny*, May 2, 2014, 1.

[87] Interview with Apryshkin, 2021.

[88] Based on the author's archived video from Toretsk, April 5, 2014. See "Toretsk 2014," Harvard Dataverse, https://doi.org/10.7910/DVN/OSQ1SE.

[89] Interview with Marina Romantsova, September 2018.

mine in the vicinity of Bakhmut.[90] It was the location of Soviet-era munitions, which was rumored to have one of the largest arsenals of weapons in Ukraine. Once the first Ukrainian troops appeared in towns of the Sloviansk agglomeration local civilians mobilized to block their movement. On April 15, just two days into ATO, a large crowd of locals in Kramatorsk stopped six infantry fighting vehicles and several armored personnel carriers of the 25th Airborne brigade from Dnipropetrovsk with sixty soldiers and five officers.[91] Faced with angry locals, the commander of the unit ordered the soldiers to surrender over fifty assault rifles, several antitank guns, all six vehicles, and a self-propelled gun-mortar. Two soldiers and one officer, all natives of Donbas, joined the militia, while the rest returned to Ukraine. This episode became the first major blow to the ATO and a clear indication of the hostility spreading among locals.

That same day the head of Ukraine's antiterrorist operation, Lieutenant General Vasyl Krutov, personally arrived in Kramatorsk to inspect the military airfield there. He found it surrounded with tires and scrap metal used by locals as a pressure tactic. When Krutov exited the base, he faced hundreds of angry civilians who accused him of planning to kill town residents. Some of them even grabbed the general's collar and dragged him into the crowd. "We are peaceful people! We have the right to choose! Get your troops out of here!" protesters shouted as they pushed him around. A reporter accompanying Krutov observed, "An hour ago we were at the border between Donetsk and Kharkiv regions and the general was pontificating about this big counter-terrorist operation. Now, he was almost torn to pieces by the crowd here and barely got back into his own base."[92]

An altercation between Ukrainian military and civilians near Kramatorsk resulted in the first civilian deaths. On May 3 Ukrainian special operation forces Alfa tried to enter the city on several armored personnel vehicles. They were stopped by the crowd shouting "Fascists!" and demanding they leave. When some of the retreating vehicles stormed the separatist checkpoint, shooting erupted. At least on civilian present at the checkpoint, a twenty-one-year-old nurse, Yulia Izotova, died of gunshot wounds. Another fifteen people were reported wounded. Izotova's burial on May 5 turned into

<hr>

[90] Based on the author's archived video. See "Bakhmut 2014," Harvard Dataverse, https://doi.org/10.7910/DVN/JU9DSN.

[91] Daria Bura and Oleksandr Krasovytskyi, *Khronika Viyny 2014–2020: Vid Maidanu do Ilovaisku* (Kharkiv: Folio, 2020), 84.

[92] Simon Ostrovsky, "Pro-Russian Protesters Attempt to Seize Airfield: Russian Roulette. Dispatch 27," *Vice*, April 18, 2014, https://www.youtube.com/watch?v=8mywTyAhlJM.

a one-thousand-strong march, which gave way to expressions of indignation at the Ukrainian government.[93] Local residents remembered this episode as a turning point which shifted the attitudes of the locals decisively against Ukraine.[94]

Episodes of arbitrary violence against civilians blamed on Ukrainian troops occurred in multiple towns of Donbas in early May. The indignation they produced commonly arises out of a sense of perceived injustice, often committed against a weaker side.[95] Its effect is to "expand one's sense of identity and heighten attention to slights to that identity."[96] In contrast to fear, which may have a demobilizing effect, indignation emboldens individuals to seek to rectify the committed injustice. When it emerges in the context of confrontation with authorities, it "increases an individual's likelihood of political resistance, even if it jeopardizes security."[97] Just like the brutal beatings of students by riot police triggered mass mobilization and launched the Revolution of Dignity in Kyiv, the scenes of wounded and killed civilians in altercations with Ukrainian military reignited mobilization behind the separatist cause in Donbas.

The emboldening effect of indignation is clear in several instances of civilian victimization at the outset of the Donbas conflict. On May 3, several armored Ukrainian vehicles entered Kostiantynivka and engaged in sporadic clashes with the militants. But when they came under militant fire they quickly withdrew. Vladimir Averin, a native of Kostiantynivka who lived in Donetsk at the time, said that reports of these clashes persuaded him to return to his hometown and join the separatist side.[98] He immediately drew parallels with the shocking violence in Odesa that happened a day earlier. Six people were killed there following a violent confrontation between pro-Ukrainian and pro-Russian demonstrators on the city streets. Later that day another forty-two people, including thirty-four men, seven women, and one teenage boy, died in or near the trade union building, the site of the pro-Russian camp in Odesa.[99] It caught fire and burned down

---

[93] Interview with Oleksiy Ladyka, September 2018.

[94] Interview with Oleksandr Yermolchenko, September 10, 2018.

[95] Stefano Costalli and Andrea Ruggeri, "Emotions, Ideologies, and Violent Political Mobilization," *PS: Political Science & Politics* 50, no. 4 (October 2017): 923–927.

[96] Wendy Pearlman, "Emotions and the Microfoundations of the Arab Uprisings," *Perspectives on Politics* 11, no. 2 (June 2013): 392.

[97] Ibid.

[98] Interview with Vladimir Averin, May 28, 2020.

[99] Matilda Bogner, "7 Years with No Answers: What Is Lacking in the Investigations of the Events in Odesa on 2 May 2014?," UN OHCHR, April 30, 2021, https://ukraine.un.org/en/126054-7-years-no-answers-what-lacking-investigations-events-odesa-2-may-2014.

following the retaliatory assault of pro-Ukrainian demonstrators. Given the prevalence of pro-Russian demonstrators among the victims of these Odesa clashes, they came to be viewed in Donbas as a prelude to similar attacks elsewhere. Hence, Odesa became an important mobilizing tool and a constant point of reference during the rallies. One activist from Sieverodonetsk, for example, acknowledged its decisive effect on persuading people to come to the separatist referendum nine days later: "It was a huge catalyst of the entire process. Without the events of May 2 in Odesa, there would have been no referendum."[100]

In Toretsk the local authorities organized a rally two days after the violence in Odesa. It equaled in size the protests from early March. The town mayor Volodymyr Sleptsov opened the rally condemning violent attacks against civilians: "In almost all towns of Donetsk oblast there is violence and unarmed people are shot for expressing divergent opinion—this is bigotry. . . . Government cannot use military against its own people—they need to defend our borders. So today one of our main demands is that armed forces should stop violence against the people." Another speaker, Svetlana Pozniakova, evoked the example of Odesa in a speech full of indignation: "Remember Odesa. . . . This is fascism that all countries have been fighting. If you think we will avoid their fate—think again. Neighboring towns Kostiantynivka and Druzhkivka—they thought the same. But they [Ukrainian forces] came and started shooting them. I feel pain about it. . . . All the responsibility for deaths lies on this junta [the Ukrainian government]. . . . They should be punished by death. Even Hitler did not fight his own people. They know they are supported by the U.S. and NATO. They are killers. Be damned, rascals!"[101]

The spread of rumors about civilian victimization in neighboring towns of Donbas became common during the rallies held throughout May. At a rally in Toretsk on May 24 one woman pleaded, "Sloviansk downtown is being bombed and all houses are ruined. Women are sent to monasteries. . . . They [Ukrainian forces] are shooting at the buses evacuating people from there."[102] Five days later the town witnessed its largest gathering since the start of protests. It began with a moment of silence

---

[100] Aleksandr Bovdunov, "Kogda my horonim nashyh rebiat, groby nakryvaem trikolorom," *Voennoe Obozrenie*, August 26, 2014, https://topwar.ru/56789-kogda-my-horonim-nashih-rebyat-groby-nakryvaem-trikolorom.html.

[101] Based on the author's archived video from Toretsk, May 5, 2014. See "Toretsk 2014," Harvard Dataverse, https://doi.org/10.7910/DVN/OSQ1SE.

[102] Based on the author's archived video from Toretsk, May 24, 2014. See "Toretsk 2014," Harvard Dataverse, https://doi.org/10.7910/DVN/OSQ1SE.

for two residents—Lyudmyla Pohrebnyak and Olga Prokhorenko—killed in the preceding days during the bombings of Sloviansk and Donetsk. Prokhorenko's son Rodion appeared on stage visibly shaken and covered with wounds. His short speech ended with an emotional appeal to "kill all of this scum, these Kievites." Deputy Mayor Serhiy Kulikov followed by stressing that both victims were civilians: "One was an entrepreneur and another one a teacher. They did not do anything. They are those chips that fly when wood is chopped. Because that's what the Ukrainian government thinks—we cannot do it without civilian victims, so they throw bombs on Donetsk.... Nobody is sure that our city won't be bombed by planes tomorrow."[103]

Some of the subsequent attacks on civilians in Donbas were documented in video footage. In Mariupol, the Ukrainian military and volunteer forces arrived at the city police station on May 9 to stop the separatist assault. The ensuing violence, however, led to many civilian casualties. The videos from that day showed civilians lying in blood next to the coffee shop and trying to dodge bullets sprayed randomly by retreating Ukrainian soldiers.[104] Filmed from multiple angles, the videos were widely shared across social media platforms and on Russian television. Many in the city interpreted these actions as reprisals by Ukrainian forces. The front-page headline of the city newspaper *Priazovskiy Rabochiy*, which earlier advocated for a united Ukraine, was clear in its attribution of blame: "On Victory Day the army destroyed the police department with guns and rifles and was shooting at unarmed city residents."[105]

Violence against civilians triggered riots that targeted the Ukrainian military base in Mariupol. On May 10 the base was stormed and set on fire, while rioters rode away on a remaining armored vehicle. There was also an outpouring of support for the separatist side. On May 11, the day of the separatist referendum, local media reported long lines at the polling stations, the turnout higher than during any previous presidential elections.[106] The city's main newspaper reported that people were standing in line "for three

---

[103] Based on the author's archived video from Toretsk, May 29, 2014. See "Toretsk 2014," Harvard Dataverse, https://doi.org/10.7910/DVN/OSQ1SE.

[104] Author's archived video from Mariupol, May 9, 2014. See "Mariupol 2014," Harvard Dataverse, https://doi.org/10.7910/DVN/4OBT5H.

[105] Lyudmila Ermishyna and Aleksandr Pankov, "Na den pobedy armia unichtozhyla iz pushek i avtomatov gosupravlenie militsii i streliala po bezoruzhnym gorozhanam," *Priazovskiy Rabochiy*, No. 67, May 13, 2014, https://issuu.com/priazrab/docs/67___2014

[106] *Mariupol News*, "V Mariupol prokhodit referendum," May 11, 2014, https://web.archive.org /web/20200812142553/http://mariupolnews.com.ua/news/view/v-mariupole-prohodit-referen dum.

or more hours" to get a chance to vote at one of the four open polling stations.[107] For turnout numbers, it cited separatist sources writing that 43% of city residents voted and 92.9% of them supported DNR. Its editor-in-chief, Mykola Tokarskyi, observed in his opinion column that "after the shooting and the killing of people on May 9 many of those who a day earlier hesitated, unequivocally decided to participate in voting [in the referendum]."[108]

Who is to Blame?

Once the armed conflict intensified and violence spread to more towns, the number of civilians killed rose as well. At the end of July 2014, the World Health Organization estimated the number of casualties at 1,129 killed and 3,442 wounded.[109] Although the exact share of civilians among them remains unclear, UN reports listed numerous examples of civilians murdered in June and July, suggesting hundreds of victims. Close to 90% of civilian deaths were the result of shelling of residential areas by "mortars, canons, howitzers, tanks and multiple launch rocket systems."[110]

In a survey conducted in eight towns of Ukraine-controlled areas of Donbas in May and June 2015, I asked locals about their perception of responsibility for the civilian victimization in the first months of the conflict.[111] Only 17% of respondents said they personally knew someone who was harmed by the militants, while almost twice as many—32%—said that they were personally familiar with people affected by the shelling by the Ukrainian army. Overall, most respondents (52%) indicated some degree of direct or indirect knowledge about the instances of civilian harm caused by the Ukrainian troops. A smaller share, 44%, said they were aware of civilian victimization by the militant side. These findings are particularly striking

[107] Lyudmila Ermishyna, Ekaterina Svistun, "Na referendume v Mariupole vystraivalis' mnogotysichanye ocheredi," *Priazovskiy Rabochiy*, No. 67, May 13, 2014, 2.

[108] Nikolai Tokarskiy, "Referendum proshel. Chto dalshe?", *Priazovskiy Rabochiy*, No. 68, May 14, 2014, 2

[109] Office of the United Nations High Commissioner for Human Rights, "Report on the Human Rights Situation in Ukraine, July 15, 2014," July 28, 2014, https://www.ohchr.org/sites/default/files/Documents/Countries/UA/HRMMUReport15June2014.pdf.

[110] Office of the United Nations High Commissioner for Human Rights, "Accountability for Killings in Ukraine from January 2014 to May 2016," 2016, 11, https://www.ohchr.org/sites/default/files/Documents/Countries/UA/OHCHRThematicReportUkraineJan2014-May2016_EN.pdf.

[111] The survey was conducted through face-to-face interviews with the final sample of 222 respondents. For further details about the survey, see Serhiy Kudelia and Johanna van Zyl, "In My Name: The Impact of Regional Identity on Civilian Attitudes in the Armed Conflict in Donbas," *Nationalities Papers* 47, no. 5 (2019): 807–808.

given that the survey was conducted in towns under Ukraine's control at the time, which should have given respondents incentive to blame the militants more. One of the main predictors of blame attribution was a respondent's self-ascribed identity. Individuals who identified themselves as residents of Donbas or of their town (localized identity) and viewed their region as "unique" were much less likely to report instances of civilian victimization by insurgents.[112]

Regional attachment thus became a crucial mechanism in leading people to choose anti-Kyiv side in the unfolding conflict. It produced an in-group cohesion among regional residents as they observed violence by out-group actors during protests in the Ukrainian capital and other cities of Ukraine. The widespread belief in the stand-alone position of Donbas on economic and cultural map of Ukraine also encouraged support for autonomy or even secessionist demands. At a later stage, the sense of regional solidarity diverted the blame for conflict outbreak from local militants, perceived as members of an in-group, to the Ukrainian security personnel. As the next chapter shows, the organization of militia groups across Donbas occurred in response to rising public demands for security and self-sufficiency of the region.

---

[112] The odds of possessing knowledge of insurgent victimization for those identifying themselves as Ukrainian were 3.17 times greater than those identifying with Donbas or the local city. One measure that shows the significance of local identity in shaping the views of militants was the respondent's perception of Donbas as a "unique region." The odds of knowledge of insurgent victimization decreased by 65% for those identifying Donbas as "unique" compared to other regions of Ukraine. See Kudelia and van Zyl, "In My Name."

Chapter 5
The Rise of Town Militias

On the evening of April 12, 2014, after Girkin's unit seized Sloviansk, two DNR flags were raised on the main square and over the city council building in another town of the Donetsk oblast: Bakhmut. Located just forty-five kilometers apart, the two cities were strikingly different. Sloviansk, located amid the picturesque landscape on the edge of Donbas, was more famous as a quaint resort area than as a modern industrial hub. Bakhmut developed as the center of the salt mining industry and even functioned as the capital of the newly formed Donetsk governorship in the 1920s. Several rounded neoclassical buildings from the Stalinist era faced the town's main square, location of the first major pro-Russian rally on March 1.

As the rumors about the arrival of "green men" in Sloviansk spread, a few hundred people gathered on the square next to Bakhmut city council building, still draped in national blue and yellow colors. The primary concern for the rally speakers was how to respond to the sudden militarization of everyday life in the region. "I tried to go to Sloviansk and could not reach it—I saw armored vehicles at different points on the road and well-trained armed men," a female participant explained.[1] The deployment of Ukrainian troops near Sloviansk did not produce accommodating rhetoric from rally speakers. In fact, some interpreted the rally as a call for action on behalf of the militants: "Our guys just started this . . . and we need to unite and help them. We are defending our children!"[2] As the news report from the rally broadcast on the local TV station Zakaz observed, "The slogan 'Artemovsk [the previous name of Bakhmut], rise up!' became the most frequent refrain of the rally."[3] The town militia had already formed in Bakhmut in early March, but it consisted of just a dozen activists. One of their leaders was Maksim Zhyznevskiy, a tall man in his late twenties, a small business entrepreneur and Bakhmut native. He established ties with Girkin during

---

[1] Author's archived video from Bakhmut, April 12, 2014. See "Bakhmut 2014," Harvard Dataverse, https://doi.org/10.7910/DVN/JU9DSN.

[2] Ibid.

[3] Ibid.

Seize the City, Undo the State. Serhiy Kudelia, Oxford University Press. © Oxford University Press (2025). DOI: 10.1093/9780197795576.003.0006

his trip to Crimea in March.[4] Similar militia units had been formed in other towns of the region, but most of them received arms and engaged in visible public actions only after Girkin's arrival in Sloviansk.

In this chapter I trace the evolution of self-defense units in Donbas from their formation as public safety patrols in January 2014 to their conversion into irregular armed units under the command of Russian and local actors. Local elites spearheaded their formation by creating the legal framework for their functioning. They justified the units to the public as a proper response to the rising nationalist threat. This top-down elite initiative helped to create the first micro-networks of pro-Russian activists that would later form the basis for town-based militia units. Until April they remained fragmented, often operated under the patronage of local authorities, and lacked cross-town coordination and a common agenda. They were also largely unarmed and, apart from the tactics used in Donetsk and Luhansk, did not engage in violent confrontation with town officials. The incursion of the armed unit under Girkin's command led to a radical change in militia dynamics. His capture of Sloviansk lifted constraints on the use of force and led to the coercive takeover of several neighboring towns through joint actions of local and outside actors. It also created a new command center for disjointed militia groups, offered them a ready template for action, and escalated violence across the region.

Local Elite Patronage

The formation of paramilitary groups in Donbas began with the resolutions of the oblast councils in Donetsk and Luhansk authorizing the creation of "voluntary people's *druzhyny* [patrols]" (DND) in late January 2014.[5] The name signaled an attempt to replicate the Soviet experience with the involvement of citizens in everyday policing of public life. The DND was first instituted in 1959 to engage the public in assisting law enforcement with fighting petty crimes. By the mid-1980s, DND units became a mass

---

[4] The official website of Girkin's movement lists Zhyznevskiy as the founder of a "people's militia" in Bakhmut and a "commander of resistance" beginning on April 19, 2014. It also states that Zhyznevskiy was "fulfilling special tasks of Igor Strelkov [Girkin]." See "Nagrazhdenie zashitnikov Novorossii," October 13, 2015, at http://web.archive.org/web/20190314000511/http://novorossia. pro/news/odnovorossia/1242-nagrazhdenie-zaschitnikov-novorossii.html.

[5] "People's patrol" groups were also formed under the supervision of municipal authorities in Crimea. In Sevastopol members of DND Rubezh, established in late January, assisted Russian troops in blocking Ukrainian military bases in March. See Vasiliy Sakharov, *Zapiski Dobrovoltsa*, last edited online July 5, 2018: http://samlib.ru/s/saharow_w_i/zapiskidobrowolxca.shtml.

phenomenon, with millions of people involved in patrolling the streets or guarding state assets across the country.

The newly formed DND units in Donbas particularly drew members of the Cossack organizations, Afghan war veterans, and retired security officers, and they received immediate support from local officials. On January 27 the Luhansk oblast council adopted a special resolution endorsing the DND to "protect our compatriots from radicals engaged in lawless actions." One of the few council deputies who disagreed with the resolution was Andriy Shapovalov, who also worked as a local TV reporter. "Why would we need to legalize these drunk marginals?," he later remembered asking the regional police chief.[6] But the chief, Yevhen Polskoi, insisted it was a necessary measure to buttress local policing capacity. Similarly, the Donetsk PR office claimed that a DND would help to "fight provocateurs who could arrive from Western oblasts."[7]

On January 30, the head of the Luhansk oblast state administration, Volodymyr Pristiuk, announced that over eight thousand people had joined the voluntary patrol groups across Luhansk oblast. Three weeks later, after the ouster of Yanukovych, city and oblast council deputies in Luhansk issued another joint statement with a public call to start forming militia-like units. In Donetsk, the chairman of the oblast state administration Andriy Shyshatskiy gathered town mayors and instructed them to set up "self-defense units" in each of their towns. Citing the threat of Right Sector activists, he advised the mayors to "gather all men with hunting rifles into town self-defense units to fight them back."[8] While some of the mayors, like Henadiy Kostyukov from Kramatorsk and Yuriy Khotlubei from Mariupol, objected, the head of the oblast police Roman Romanov insisted that they had to "report to him" when they had fulfilled this request.

Some of the militia groups formed in January emerged without any top-down commands. In Druzhkivka, Afghan war veterans, Cossacks, and sports club members were organized as the self-defense group Shchyt (Shield), headed by Afghan war veteran Anatoliy Podoprigora.[9] His brother Vitaliy was the city council deputy and a PR member. The local authorities

    [6] Interview with Andriy Shapovalov, July 14, 2019.

    [7] BBC Ukraina, "Regiony ukrepliayutsia i gotoviatsia k provokatsiyam," January 28, 2014, https://www.bbc.com/ukrainian/ukraine_in_russian/2014/01/140128_ru_s_regional_protests.

    [8] Evgeniy Plinskiy, "Nellia Shtepa: 'Ia vyshyla na lifchike imia i datu rozhdeniya—chtoby opoznali telo, esli menia vyrbosiat kuda-to mertvoi," LB, October 29, 2015, https://rus.lb.ua/society/2015/10/29/319648_nelya_shtepa_ya_vishila_lifchike_imya.html.

    [9] *Druzhkovskiy Rabochiy*, "Kliuchevoi moment," February 27, 2014, 3, https://issuu.com/dzhulianochka/docs/09_fe8940fe2c27dd.

provided the organization with an office in the town's cultural center. In an interview with the town newspaper Podoprigora explained that the goal of the group was to "assist law enforcement in maintaining order in the city."[10] He also appealed to residents to provide "financial assistance" to the group at this "key moment" in Druzhkivka's history. Shchyt received explicit backing from the town mayor, Valeriy Gnatenko, even after the fall of the Yanukovych regime. During the press conference on February 27 Gnatenko expressed confidence that the self-defense group could help with ensuring order and protect communal property.[11] According to the town's police chief, Serhiy Novikov, police units patrolled streets with Don Cossacks, workers from the town's machine-building company, and other "volunteers."[12] In a few weeks, members of Shchyt participated in the capture of the SBU building in Donetsk. On April 11, led by another Afghan war veteran, Yuriy Protsenko (call sign "Dushman"), they joined Girkin in Sloviansk and participated in the subsequent seizure of the police station there.[13]

In neighboring Kostiantynivka a similar quasi-militant organization, Pravoporiadok (Legal Order), emerged in January. Its organizers were Afghan war veterans who later played the main role in the town's insurgency mobilization.[14] As in Druzhkivka, the organization was given an office in the municipal government building and started regular street patrols with the police.[15] The head of the town police, Volodymyr Goncharov, claimed in an interview with the town newspaper that new members received screening for prior convictions.[16] He also indicated that Pravoporiadok provided protection services for the municipal authorities. When members of pro-Maidan parties tried to hold talks with the city council secretary on forming a joint consultative council in late February, they faced Pravoporiadok members who presented themselves as their informal guards. On April 7,

---

[10] Ibid.

[11] Vasiliy Ramishvili, "Istoria vershytsia na glazah," *Druzhkovskiy Rabochiy*, March 6, 2014, 2, https://issuu.com/dzhulianochka/docs/10.

[12] Tatiana Volynets, "Sergei Novikov: 'Spokoistvie Druzhkovchan—pod pristalnym kontrolem,'" *Druzhkovka na Ladoniah plius*, March 26, 2014, 7, https://issuu.com/dnl_plus/docs/287_13.

[13] Protsenko was later captured by the Ukrainian forces and exchanged for a Ukrainian officer. He then moved to Donetsk and became the deputy commander of the Vostok battalion. Elena Gromova, "Dushman: Moi dom nahoditsia na okkupirovanoi territorii," *Voennoe Obozrenie*, July 14, 2015, https://topwar.ru/78732-dushman-moy-dom-nahoditsya-na-okkupirovannoy-territorii.html.

[14] Interview with Volodymyr Berezin, September 13, 2018.

[15] Interview with Yaroslav Malanchuk, September 13, 2018.

[16] *Provintsiya*, "V Konstantinovke novyi nachalnik militsii," March 28, 2014, https://www.konstantinovka.com.ua/newspaper/sluzhba-103-soobschaet/v-konstantinovke-novyy-nachalnik-milicii.

following the separatist capture of the regional administration building in Donetsk, Pravoporiadok members set up the first checkpoints on the entrances to Kostiantynivka and guarded them alongside the police.

Later in April three organizers of Pravoporiadok in Kostinantynivka joined Girkin-led insurgent units in Sloviansk. One of them, Sergiy Zhatko, the head of the local Afghan veteran organization, became the commander of one of the militia units there, while his deputy, Sergiy Tatarin, was killed fighting Ukrainian forces in May. In an interview with the town newspaper, Tatarin's widow showed no remorse for his involvement in the militia and said that his example inspired her to "fight the fascist junta" until victory. Another Pravoporiadok organizer, Sergiy Smirnov, explained in the same newspaper that Tatarin was moved by his belief in Novorossia as "a project for the renewal of humanity . . . in which all material, including human life, was secondary."[17]

The organization of a self-defense unit in another town of the Sloviansk agglomeration, Lyman, started immediately after Yanukovych's fall. The first proposals came from several members of the city council during its meeting on February 24. One of them, Oleksandr Sydorenko, a sixty-year-old retired railway worker, said that the newly formed self-defense group Oplot Krasnolimanshiny (The Guard of Lyman) should be empowered to protect the town "from vandals and nationalists." Another council member, Ivan Yerdakiy, once a communist candidate for mayor, even suggested that local factory directors should delegate some of their workers to this group.[18] Both Mayor Perebyinis and Police Chief Borys Lukianov quickly embraced these proposals. The chief organizer of the Lyman militia was Kostiantyn Burlaka, the head of the Afghan war veterans organization. During the rally on March 1 Burlaka announced that around one hundred volunteer Cossacks and Afghan veterans were ready to "meet outsiders with Molotov cocktails." "We will welcome them very peacefully," Burlaka said with a smirk, but "if they start shooting at us, we will shoot back."[19]

In Toretsk on February 24, the city council adopted a special resolution to form a self-defense group. In an appeal published in the town newspaper Mayor Volodymyr Sleptsov announced the formation of "people's patrols in

---

[17] *Narodnaia Gazeta*, "Pogib nash drug. Pogib, zashishaya rodnoi gorod," June 4, 2014, 3.

[18] Author's archived video from Lyman, February 24, 2014. See "Lyman 2014," Harvard Dataverse, https://doi.org/10.7910/DVN/MCQ81K

[19] Author's archived video from Lyman, March 1, 2014. See "Lyman 2014," Harvard Dataverse, https://doi.org/10.7910/DVN/MCQ81K

factories and public organizations."[20] He designated the city council building as the headquarters for all patrol units and assigned their coordination to the city council secretary, Yuriy Yevsikov. As Yevsikov later recounted, militia formation was spurred by a genuine feeling that Maidan activists could pose a threat to the local communities.[21] The joint patrols, however, did not last long. According to Yevsikov, "there was just no one to fight with."[22] Yet self-defense members continued their own cooperation independent of the authorities.

In mid-March, men in camouflage uniforms from the Toretsk patrol began to set up checkpoints and started addressing local pro-Russian rallies. Volodymyr Stelmakh (call sign "Batia," or "Dad"), a heavily built fifty-eight-year-old and the town's future militia commander, first spoke at the April 5 rally. He had already become a fixture in late February, when he encamped on the main square next to the Lenin monument. The deputy mayor of the town remembered seeing him there dressed in a military uniform adorned with medals and wearing a marine beret.[23] Stelmakh worked on a farm in a nearby village and served as deputy head of the city's Afghan veterans group. He even claimed to have participated in military operations in Yugoslavia and Chechnya.[24] Speaking at the rally, Stelmakh admonished those locals who "just sit and wait until Banderlogi [Bandera followers] come here." The number of militants in Toretsk was still small and, as Stelmakh later admitted, reached one hundred only by the end of July.[25] According to Yevsikov, they were barely seen on the streets and possessed no visible firearms until June.

In Novohrodivka, a town in Pokrovsk agglomeration, its mayor Oleksandr Antonenko announced the launch of joint patrols at the city council session on February 26.[26] They included members of the local Afghan veterans organization Shuravi (an Afghan name for Soviet citizens) and town

---

[20] *Dzerzhynskiy Shakhtior,* "Obrashenie k gromade goroda Dzerzhynska," February 25, 2014, 1.

[21] Interview with Yuri Yevsikov, November 8, 2018.

[22] Ibid.

[23] Ibid.

[24] Stelmakh was also the first known militant who spotted Flight MH17 on July 17, 2014, and reported its movement to Bezler two minutes before the plane was shot down by a Buk missile. See Bellingcat, "'A Birdie Is Flying towards You': Identifying the Separatists Linked to Downing of MH17," June 2019, https://www.bellingcat.com/app/uploads/2019/06/a-birdie-is-flying-towards-you.pdf.

[25] Author's archived video of Stelmakh. See "Toretsk 2014," Harvard Dataverse, https://doi.org/10.7910/DVN/OSQ1SE.

[26] *Regionalnye Vesti,* "Obrashenie Novogrodovskogo gorodskogo golovy A. V. Antonenko k zhyteliam Novogrodovki," February 28, 2014, 1.

Cossacks. In an interview with the local press, the chairman of the organization, Volodymyr Vostrukhov, said that he coordinated joint patrols with the mayor, Police Chief Oleksandr Ananiev, and the local Cossack leader Yuriy Volkov. "Our guys—Afghans—conduct patrols at night, while Cossacks patrol the streets during the day. Afghans want to maintain order in the city," stressed Vostrukhov.[27] Later he started using separatist symbols on social media, while members of Shuravi turned into the de facto enforcement arm of the DNR. Their leader, Volodymyr Mirutenko, made "Shuravi" his call-sign after joining DNR militia. In December 2014 he was detained by the SBU on charges of planning subversive activities in other Ukrainian cities on behalf of the DNR. In addition to former Afghan war veterans and Cossacks, pro-DNR militants in Novohrodivka included representatives of the criminal underworld. Chief among them was Vasyl Boziavkin, a local mobster who had spent eight years in jail on criminal charges. He acted together with his older brother, Gennadiy, also a convicted criminal.[28] In recognition of his role in organizing Novohrodivka's militia, Vasyl Boziavkin became deputy of the DNR People's Council in November 2014.[29]

The Afghan war veterans also formed the backbone of a self-defense group in Rubizhne in Luhansk province. The town's acting mayor, Khomenko, announced its formation at a rally on March 1: "We have organized people's patrols—these young people are legal. They are going through background checks and patrol the streets with the police."[30] Khomenko even agreed to provide them with badges identifying them as DND members. The key leaders of the town militia emerged from a "military-patriotic" organization called Rubezh, which was run by Afghan war veterans. In preceding years it had organized commemorative events, provided basic military training to high school students, and staged combat reenactments with the participation of local youth.[31] At least three of the organization's founders—Andriy Timokhin, Gennadiy Moralishvili, and Sergiy Chub—participated in the storming of the SBU building in Luhansk in April and joined separatist militia there. Central among them was fifty-one-year-old Timokhin, a member of the city council and a physical education instructor at a local college.[32]

[27] *Regionalnye Vesti*, "Volna Mitingov i Protestov," March 7, 2014, 2.
[28] Interview with Anton Kuhliev, October 17, 2018.
[29] The list of DNR People's Council deputies of the first convocation is at https://t.ly/rW91.
[30] Author's archived video from Rubizhne, March 1, 2014. See "Rubizhne 2014," Harvard Dataverse, https://doi.org/10.7910/DVN/ONLPT3.
[31] Neofitsialnyi sait veteranov Afghanistana goroda Rubezhnoe, https://rubezh.at.ua/.
[32] Interview with Mykhailo Barabash, June 13, 2019.

Through his ties to the college and veteran organizations Timokhin actively recruited youth into the self-defense unit.[33] Another source of recruits was a local bikers pub, Ice Beer, a popular gathering spot for the town's rock music fans. In the view of a journalist familiar with the scene, the imperialist lyrics of some Russian rock bands might have ideologically predisposed pub regulars to separatist appeals.[34] However, the success of these recruitment efforts was still very limited. Based on police estimates, the number of local militants never exceeded seventy.[35]

Although patrols started turning into armed militias in late April, the calls to take up arms were voiced immediately after Yanukovych's fall. At a March 1 rally in Sieverodonetsk one participant proclaimed, "What if they decide to come here from Maidan? We need to use force to fight back, so these volunteers need to have weapons—at least the same that nationalists have."[36] By then, Sieverodonetsk already had a self-defense group formed by the city council deputy and the chair of the local Afghan veterans group, Oleksandr Bondarenko. Mayor Valentyn Kazakov reiterated his support for the group during a rally on March 5: "I share your concerns about our country and the city. We created people's militia units who patrol the streets along with police."[37] Still, as a local separatist activist, Andrei Lavin, admitted, the town's contingent of militants had only seven firearms and a handful of members. As Lavin later observed, "Frankly, if our opponents immediately used against us the kinds of resources they deployed later we would be swept away in a matter of hours."[38] This changed with the arrival of dozens of militants from other towns of Luhansk province on May 7.[39] They brought a truck full of firearms, which they allegedly hid in either the local KPU office or the storage facilities of the city's food market. That same day militants stormed the building of the city procuracy and attacked the company office of a local Euromaidan activist. Most of the newly arrived militants settled in the city's largest hotel, Mir (Peace), owned by a Member of Parliament Oleksiy Kunchenko.

One of the goals of the militants was to help local separatists stage a referendum on May 11. Dressed in black uniforms, they set up checkpoints

---

[33] Interview with Artyukh, 2019.

[34] Ibid.

[35] Cited in *Suspilne Donbas*, "Povernuty Donbas: Rubizhne," YouTube, July 21, 2019, https://youtu.be/LNPayf18vbA.

[36] Author's archived video from Sieverodonetsk, March 1, 2014. See "Sieverodonetsk 2014," Harvard Dataverse, https://doi.org/10.7910/DVN/1KHPZE.

[37] Author's archived video from Sieverodonetsk, March 5, 2014. See "Sieverodonetsk 2014," Harvard Dataverse, https://doi.org/10.7910/DVN/1KHPZE.

[38] Bovdunov, "Kogda my horonim nashyh rebiat, groby nakryvaem trikolorom," 1.

[39] Interview with Olga Lishyk, June 12, 2019.

throughout the city, guarded polling stations, and moved between several captured buildings. Their main base was outside the city center in a high-rise building that housed the State Institute of the Nitrogen Industry.[40] The first nominal commander of Sieverodonetsk militia was Sergiy Pak, a fifty-one-year-old local entrepreneur with alleged ties to the city's criminal underworld.[41] Some of his closest associates were similarly locals with entrepreneurial experience.[42] Pak represented the LNR during a roundtable with local businessmen on May 13 which included other top city and law enforcement officials.[43] By that time many entrepreneurs had started hiring additional security guards to protect their companies from possible looting.[44] They also raised around ten thousand dollars, which they donated to the local police to ensure their proper operation.[45] During the meeting, armed militants insisted on making similar donations to the separatist organization. Pak then approached individual businessmen with requests to finance specific expenses of the militants, such as bulletproof vests.[46] However, he lacked sufficient authority with the militant units, composed largely of Cossacks from the nearby towns of Kadiivka (then Stakhanov), Rovenky, and Antratsyt. Charged with conducting illicit activities, he was quickly purged from the town militia. His replacement was Pavel Driomov, a thirty-seven-year-old Kadiivka native whose Cossack background made him a more natural leader of the militants.[47] He had participated in the storming of the SBU building in Luhansk on April 6 which paved the path to the formation of the LNR.

Driomov's sudden rise to a leadership position in Sieverodonetsk, despite his outsider status, was another sign that few locals from the town itself were willing to join the DND. In the view of a local resident later abducted by militants, it also marked a shift from haphazard self-defense forces to a more professionalized militia.[48] Driomov sought to unify disparate militant units in the city into a joint regiment and make it part of Kozitsyn's Don Cossack Army. He also maintained contacts with another militia leader, Oleksiy Mozgovoi, in Lysychansk and coordinated his actions with

<hr>

[40] Interview with Svetikov, 2019.

[41] Interview with Anonymous 2, June 10, 2021.

[42] Ibid.

[43] Aleksandr Vasiliev, "Predstaviteli LNR zaiavili o sebe v biznes-klube 'Evropeiskiy vybor' v Severodonetske," *Severodonetsk.Info*, May 14, 2014, http://sever.lg.ua/2014-05-14-predstaviteli-lnr-zayavili-o-sebe-v-biznes-klube-evropeiskii-vybor-v-severodonetske.

[44] Interview with Anonymous 2, 2021.

[45] Ibid.

[46] Ibid.

[47] Bovdunov, "Kogda my horonim nashyh rebiat, groby nakryvaem trikolorom."

[48] Interview with Anonymous No. 2, 2021.

Strelkov.[49] One of the youngest members of Driomov's unit was sixteen-year-old Mark Vorzhev, who continued fighting on the separatist side for the next eight years. In June 2022, after Russian troops occupied Sieverodonetsk, Vorzhev became the first acting head of city administration under LNR control.[50]

In Lysychansk, just as in Sieverodonetsk, the sizable militia group appeared only with the arrival of out-of-towners from other parts of Luhansk province. Despite earlier calls from the city council to join militia units, the town's separatists failed to form any.[51] This could be partially attributed to opposition from the town's most influential businessman and former mayor, Serhiy Dunaev. Despite his earlier anti-Maidan rhetoric, Dunaev hoped to maintain his political influence and assets in the city even under the new government. In late February he met with dozens of young PR activists at the stadium and pleaded with them "not to follow provocateurs" in joining self-defense units because it would be "difficult to stop the bloodshed later."[52] The power balance in the city shifted in favor of the separatists only in the second half of May. Dozens of militants led by Luhansk oblast native Mozgovoi entered the town's glass-producing factory and asked all workers to vacate its premises. From May 20 until their retreat from the city in July the plant served as the training base for Mozgovoi's Prizrak (Ghost) battalion. It was first composed of militants from other parts of Luhansk oblast but quickly attracted "local elements." Their arrival became the turning point to full militant control over Lysychansk.[53] The choice of the base was also significant since it belonged to Dunaev. Its capture put him at the behest of the militants and showed who was really in charge. Mozgovoi's shrewd tactical choices were made on the advice of town locals who once held "high-level administrative positions."[54]

Russian Patronage

Despite the proliferation of militia groups, the ones that represented a relatively capable fighting force from the start were all under the command

---

[49] Zhuchkovskiy, *Mozgovoi*, 322.

[50] *Vchasno*, "Deviat klasiv osvity ta lyubov do radianshyny," June 25, 2022, https://vchasnoua. com/donbass/72867-deviat-klasiv-osvity-ta-liubov-do-radianshchyny-u-sievierodonetsku-okupan tamy-pryznacheno-mera.

[51] Interview with Apryshkin, 2021.

[52] Author's archived video from Lysychansk, February 24, 2014. See "Lysychansk 2014," Harvard Dataverse, https://doi.org/10.7910/DVN/R6HS13.

[53] Interview with Apryshkin, 2021. In addition to Mozgovoi's battalion, there were also Cossack units in Lysychansk. They seized the buildings of SBU and Prosecutor General's Office.

[54] Ibid.

of Russian actors.[55] The largest militant contingent outside Sloviansk was formed in nearby Kramatorsk. Its first commandant was Vadim Ilovchenko (also known as Ilovaiskiy), a Crimean Cossack who arrived in Donbas together with Girkin. A native of Crimea, he actively aided the Russian annexation of the peninsula with his contingent of about seventy people. Ilovchenko met Strelkov in Bakhchisarai in March 2014 and agreed to join his force as a platoon commander. After the seizure of Sloviansk, Strelkov ordered Ilovchenko to lead a group of militants called Wolf's Hundred into Kramatorsk.[56] Initially the group consisted of Russian and Crimean mercenaries, but later had to rely more on locals and new Russian volunteers.[57]

The widespread separatist sympathies of people in Kramatorsk did not produce mass recruitment into militias. "If at least one percent of town residents joined us at the time, the city would have been protected much better," Ilovchenko recalled.[58] As a result, they had to turn to neighboring villages for recruits. They also attracted petty criminals, who, tasked with serving on checkpoints, sought extortion opportunities.[59] At the end of May, the size of the insurgent force in Kramatorsk was about three hundred—a minuscule number for a city of about 200,000 and well below what militant leaders expected.[60] By then Girkin had transferred full authority over the city to a retired Russian military intelligence officer Sergei Dubinskiy, who remained in charge until their withdrawal in early July.

In Kostiantynivka, twenty miles to the south, the local militia was led by Leonid Kharchenko (call sign "Mole), a forty-two-year-old native of the town and, by some accounts, a member of the criminal underworld. According to the SBU, he was convicted of gang rape at the age of fifteen and spent three years in juvenile prison.[61] The circumstances of Kharchenko's rise within the town militia remain unknown, but in a 2015 interview he

---

[55] This aligns with the finding that anticipation of external foreign support by the opposition within a country raises the probability of a civil conflict and the use of violence during the uprising. See Jaime Jackson, Belgin San-Akca, and Zeev Maoz, "International Support Networks and the Calculus of Uprising," *Journal of Peace Research* 57, no. 5 (2020): 632–647.

[56] ICORPUS, "Interview with Vadim Ilovchenko," YouTube, October 31, 2014, https://www.youtube.com/watch?v=mlzqSiDqU-M&ab_channel=ICORPUS.

[57] Vasiliy Sakharov, *Zapiski Dobrovoltsa-2*, last edited online August 31, 2015, http://samlib.ru/s/saharow_w_i/zapiski-2.shtml.

[58] ICORPUS, "Interview with Vadim Ilovchenko."

[59] Interview with Maryna Romantsova, September 10, 2018.

[60] ICORPUS, "Interview with Vadim Ilovchenko."

[61] Bellingcat, "JIT Indictments and Reactions: Analyzing New Evidence Linking Separatists and Russian Officials to MH17," July 17, 2019, https://www.bellingcat.com/news/uk-and-europe/2019/07/17/jit-indictments-and-reactions-analyzing-new-evidence-linking-separatists-and-russian-offi cials-to-mh17/.

acknowledged acting under Dubinskiy's command.[62] Their relationship was further documented in the investigation of the downing of Flight MH17 and the indictment by the Hague District Court.[63] In less than two weeks after the takeover of Kostiantynivka by Ukrainian troops, Kharchenko reported to Dubinskiy in his new position as commander of a reconnaissance battalion and informed him about the shooting down of Ukrainian military aircraft.[64] Kharchenko later joined the counterintelligence service of the DNR guard.

The self-defense group in another town of the agglomeration, Lyman, was also, initially, under Girkin's command. Several members of his unit arrived there on April 12 to help the Lyman DND take over the police station. When some town militants later turned to looting, Girkin sent a group of his fighters from Sloviansk to impose order. In a brief operation, they surrounded the city council building with militants inside and arrested some of them.[65] Shortly afterward the contingent in Lyman received a new and supposedly more professional commander, Serhiy Grashchenko.[66] In his early forties with a thick moustache and a boisterous demeanor, he was trained in the Soviet military and fought as part of Cossack units in Abkhazia and Chechnya. In 2007 he became a chief from the Donetsk Cossack district in the Great Don Army, a civic organization based in the Russian city of Novocherkassk and led by Nikolai Kozitsyn. When Ukrainian forces liberated Lyman in early June, Girkin quickly blamed the defeat on the incompetence of its Cossack commanders.

Bakhmut came under the influence of competing Russian actors. The militant wing of the separatist movement in town in April through June 2014 was led by Serhiy Iochkov ("Veles") who received Girkin's backing. Earlier he had worked in the town's Prosecutor General's Office as the head of an anticorruption department.[67] Iochkov's mother taught Russian in the

---

[62] ICORPUS, "Interview with the Head of the 2nd Department of GRU DNR Leonid Kharchenko," YouTube, April 11, 2015, https://www.youtube.com/watch?v=7a2WJGvADP Y&ab_channel=ICORPUS.

[63] Politie, "Update on Criminal Investigation of MH17 Disaster," YouTube, June 19, 2019, https://www.youtube.com/watch?v=Kq-L72slP18&t=1042s&ab_channel=Politie.

[64] This suggests that militants likely took the passenger airplane MH17 flying from Amsterdam to Kuala Lumpur for a Ukrainian military aircraft. Court of the Hague, "Judgement against Leonid Volodymyrovych Kharchenko," November 17, 2022, https://uitspraken.rechtspraak.nl/inziendo cument?id=ECLI:NL:RBDHA:2022:12218&showbutton=true&keyword=ECLI%3aNL%3aR BDHA%3a2022%3a12218/.

[65] Interview with Oleksandr Lomako, November 7, 2018.

[66] Interview with Roman Punin, November 6, 2018.

[67] Interview with Volodymyr Sutkovoi, September 18, 2018.

Bakhmut high school he attended.[68] His teacher remembered him as a smart and idealistic student with a passion for justice.[69] Iochkov came into prominence when his group seized the building housing the Prosecutor General's Office, his prior workplace, which became the main militant base. It was also the site of illegal detentions and torture of residents suspected of pro-Ukrainian sympathies.[70] Without external backing, however, the militant group would not have represented a major force. By the end of June there were only about forty militants in Bakhmut and fewer than half of them had firearms.[71]

Iochkov made his first and only public address during the city council session on June 2. He introduced himself as Girkin's subordinate charged with protecting the city "so that our residents do not have to experience what Sloviansk is going through."[72] Five days later Iochkov was killed in an ambush organized by the Ukrainian special operations unit. His death resulted in disarray among the militant ranks and put the town outside Girkin's control. As Girkin later explained, he lost any influence over the city due to the difficulty of accessing Bakhmut from Sloviansk: "I could not send people with armored vehicles there, especially since I had no tanks until the last moment. They would have to cover 100 kilometers along the highway, while Ukrainians set up their base in Malinovka, halfway between Sloviansk and Artiomovsk (Bakhmut). I also could not send armored vehicles outside Sloviansk since Ukrainians also had airpower dominance."[73] The remaining militants in Bakhmut instead came under the command of Bezler, who was stationed in nearby Horlivka, about twenty miles away.[74]

Another town under Bezler's control was Toretsk, a part of Horlivka's urban agglomeration. According to the town's deputy mayor, town leaders recognized that the militant commander Stelmakh was "not the driver of the events" but Bezler's subordinate.[75] Stelmakh alluded to Bezler's

---

[68] Interview with Avakyan, 2018.

[69] Interview with Sutkovoi, 2018.

[70] Artemivsk City Court, Verdict in the Case No. 219/2036/15-K, December 8, 2017, http://www.reyestr.court.gov.ua/Review/71619389.

[71] Interview with Kostiantyn Mateichenko, November 2018; Zhuchkovskiy, *85 dnei Slavianska*, 327.

[72] Author's archived video from Bakhmut, June 2, 2014. See "Bakhmut 2014," Harvard Dataverse, https://doi.org/10.7910/DVN/JU9DSN.

[73] Zhuchkovskiy, *85 dnei Slavianska*, 327.

[74] Interview with Oleksandr Shynkarenko, September 18, 2018.

[75] Interview with S. Vynnyk, 2018. This has been further corroborated in the Bellingat investigation of the MH17 downing, which released the recording of a phone conversation of Stelmakh

patronage while speaking during a May 20 rally in Toretsk. He promised that if Ukrainian troops advanced on their town, "Gorlovka will send reinforcements—at least two thousand will be here." Meanwhile, he admitted that about "thirty men went to Gorlovka (Horlivka) for training," but access to more arms depended on successful shipments from Russia.[76] The actual number of militants in Toretsk, however, remained small for the entire duration of their presence. When a Ukrainian special forces unit with thirty-three men entered Toretsk in the early hours of July 21 and seized the city council building, there were only twenty-seven militants inside.[77] Bezler indeed sent reinforcements, which included two trucks full of militants, two armored personnel carriers, and a tank. They could sustain the fighting for only about seven hours before retreating to Horlivka.[78]

Gaining Coercive Dominance

The separatist capture of the oblast state administration in Donetsk and seizure of the SBU office in Luhansk on April 6 symbolized the takeover of the main centers of political and coercive power in the region. The new government urgently dispatched its representatives to deal with the militants in the seized buildings. However, Deputy Prime Minister Vitaly Yarema in Donetsk and National Security and Defense Council Secretary Andriy Parubiy in Luhansk could not organize a quick removal of separatists from the two cities. Neither of them had sufficient authority to make decisions regarding the use of force. The interior troops in Luhansk, tasked with surrounding the SBU building to allow for the entry of special operation forces, refused to follow orders. The backup forces dispatched to Luhansk from other regions did not have the necessary arms and equipment.[79] Local elite actors insisted on the need to negotiate with separatists rather than use force against them. In Donetsk, Akhmetov appealed to the Ukrainian authorities to "let the steam out" before applying coercion.[80] There was also a concern that any

reporting to Bezler minutes before the airplane was shot down: Bellingcat, "Identifying the Separatists Linked to the Downing of MH17," June 19, 2019, https://www.bellingcat.com/news/uk-and-europe/2019/06/19/identifying-the-separatists-linked-to-the-downing-of-mh17/.

[76] Author's archived video from Toretsk, May 20, 2014. See "Toretsk 2014," Harvard Dataverse, https://doi.org/10.7910/DVN/OSQ1SE.

[77] Author's archived video of Stelmakh. See "Toretsk 2014," Harvard Dataverse, https://doi.org/10.7910/DVN/OSQ1SE.

[78] Serhiy Horbatenko, "8 chasov v zdanii, po kotoromu biot tank: Kak VSU osvobozhdali Toretsk," *Radio Svoboda*, November 11, 2019: https://www.radiosvoboda.org/a/30261723.html.

[79] Kazansky and Vorotyntseva, *Yak Ukraina vtrachala Donbas*, 258–259.

[80] Interview with Nemyria, 2014.

bloodshed during the storming of government buildings might provoke a public backlash and strengthen local resistance to Kyiv.

Separatist control in early April, however, was still limited to the two buildings in the regional capitals. The crumbling of the state's monopoly on the use of force in the rest of the region started only with the storming of the police stations and SBU office in Sloviansk by Girkin's unit. These tactics were repeated in other towns. In Kramatorsk, the armed unit of twenty-eight militants surrounded the town's police station on the evening of April 12. The next day they also took over the city council building and raised the DNR flag. Full coercive control over Kramatorsk was established on April 21, when militants from Sloviansk escorted the police chief, Vitaliy Kolupai, out of the police station.[81] The militant commandant at the time later described how he met with the city's entire police department and announced that they would now be working for him.[82] He selected a new police chief from within their ranks, twenty-nine-year-old police lieutenant Denis Besproskurnyi, who appointed his own deputies and started offering "active assistance" to the separatists.

Days earlier Bezler held a similar public meeting with police personnel after seizing the police station in Horlivka.[83] He presented himself as a "lieutenant colonel of the Russian army" and introduced a new police chairman, Oleksandr Shulzhenko, a former patrol police chief from Horlivka. He also demanded that they wear St. George's ribbons, a black-and-orange decoration tied to pro-Russian stance, to distinguish them from "other policemen who have not joined the people yet." Shulzhenko's agreement to serve as the new police chief under Bezler allowed him to recruit several traffic policemen and Berkut soldiers.[84] The police station became the main militant base and detention facility, where Bezler personally assaulted and interrogated detainees.

In most towns, however, local separatists, still limited in number, abstained from taking police stations by force. Instead, they held talks with police chiefs, asking them to pledge their loyalty "to the people" publicly.

[81] Author's archived video from Kramatorsk, April 21, 2014. See "Kramatorsk 2014," Harvard Dataverse, https://doi.org/10.7910/DVN/PAVEVZ.

[82] ICORPUS, "Interview with Vadim Ilovchenko."

[83] Aleksei Gonacharenko, "Gorlovskaia militsia perehodit pod okkupantov," YouTube, April 14, 2014: https://t.ly/Xk-c.

[84] Justice for Peace in Donbas, "Prisons and Torture Houses of Horlivka: The MoI Basement," April 14, 2016, https://www.jfp.org.ua/rights/porushennia/violation_categories/nezakonni-mistsia-nesvobody/rights_violations/tiurmy-ta-kativni-horlivky-pidval-mu-hu-mvs?locale=en.

In Bakhmut, local militant leader Iochkov negotiated with the town's chief policeman, Serhiy Bratkov, following a rally on April 13. After the talks Bratkov promised the demonstrators that "they [the police] would stand shoulder to shoulder and defend the city."[85] In Mariupol separatists proved similarly effective in compelling the local police to yield to their demands. After capturing the city council building on April 13, they removed Ukrainian flags from the building and blocked it with sandbags, tires, and barbed wire. The new de facto leader of the separatist movement there, Denys Kuzmenko, negotiated with Deputy Police Chief Serhiy Skliarov inside the building and even requested police reinforcement for the militants' protection.[86]

The Ukrainian military bases in several towns of Donbas became the only visible power centers outside militants' control. In contrast to Crimea, where soldiers quickly lay down their arms and surrendered, the Ukrainian military stationed in the towns of Donbas held on and fought back. In Kramatorsk militants made repeated attempts to capture its military airfield. The initial attack on the airport on April 14 was successfully repelled with the help of special operations unit Alfa.[87] Despite continued pressure and new storming attempts over the following weeks, the base remained under Ukrainian military control. The military base in Bakhmut provided maintenance and repair services for Ukrainian military vehicles and equipment. In spring 2014 there were at least 260 tanks and over 300 armored personnel carriers and infantry fighting vehicles stored there.[88] Following the first attempt to storm the base by a militant group from Sloviansk on April 23, Kyiv reinforced its defense with the special forces regiment. All further assaults, including by the militants under Bezler's command, proved futile.[89] A Ukrainian military base in Mariupol was attacked on April 16, three days after the capture of the city council building. Earlier, separatist leaders had approached the base commanders with requests to subordinate themselves to the DNR.[90] When the Ukrainian officers refused to surrender, the separatists decided to take the base by force. Several dozen men in camouflage

<hr>

[85] Author's archived video from Bakhmut, April 13, 2014. See "Bakhmut 2014," Harvard Dataverse, https://doi.org/10.7910/DVN/JU9DSN.

[86] 0629, "V Mariupole zahvacheno zdanie gorodskogo soveta," April 13, 2014, https://www.0629.com.ua/news/514955/v-mariupole-zahvaceno-zdanie-gorodskogo-soveta-obnovlaetsafoto.

[87] Zhuchkovskiy, *85 dnei Slavianska*, 60.

[88] Mikhail Zhyrokhov, "Piat' shtrumov artemovskoi bazy," Liga, https://project.liga.net/projects/shturm_artemovska/.

[89] Ibid.

[90] Mariupol, *Posledniy Forpost* (Mariupol: Poligraf UA, 2018), 79–80.

broke through the gates and started throwing Molotov cocktails. In response, the soldiers opened fire. The ensuing skirmishes lasted deep into the night. Three attackers ended up being killed and at least thirteen were wounded, but the base remained under Ukrainian control until May 9.

Exercising Coercive Control

The removal of the physical or symbolic presence of the Ukrainian state was only the first step for the militants. To sustain their dominance, they had to apply coercion consistently while enforcing their rules and cracking down on suspected pro-Ukrainian actors. In Sloviansk, Girkin put the town's mayor, Shtepa, under arrest and kept her locked up until the militants withdrew. Numerous town residents suspected of cooperating with the Ukrainian side were detained, interrogated, and thrown into the basement of the SBU. Some were executed.[91] Among the most notorious early examples of repression was the abduction on April 17 of the prominent Horlivka politician Volodymyr Rybak. He was the only council member who resisted the removal of the Ukrainian flag from the municipal building.[92] Bezler gave a direct order to one of the militants to capture Rybak and take him "far outside the town."[93] Days later Rybak's body was found in the river Torets. Bezler and Girkin were also responsible for the murders of two young Maidan activists, eighteen-year-old Yuriy Popravka and twenty-five-year-old Yuriy Diakovskyi, whom they charged with attacking a militant checkpoint. Another example of militant violence was the murder of four members of the Church of the Transfiguration in Sloviansk, two Protestant deacons, Viktor Brodarsky and Volodymyr Velychko, and the two sons of the church priest, Ruvim and Albert Pavenko. They were abducted by militants in June and their bodies were later found in a mass grave.[94] Another Protestant pastor from Sloviansk recalled that his church, Christian Center of the Good News, was occupied by the separatists, who distrusted non-Orthodox

[91] Zhuchkovskiy, *85 dnei Slavianska*, 51.

[92] Halya Coynash, "Tortured to Death for Defending Ukraine: The First War Crimes Russia Brought to Donbas," Kharkiv Human Rights Protection Group, April 17, 2019, https://khpg.org/en/1555269923.

[93] Based on intercepted phone conversations released by the SBU. Serhiy Horbatenko, "Kontroliruemyi ad Bezlera: Ukraina, nakonets, gotova sudit rossiyskogo ofitsera za pytki," *Radio Svoboda*, August 4, 2021, https://www.radiosvoboda.org/a/bezler-bes-sud/31391687.html

[94] Scott Petersen, "A Ukrainian Murder Mystery Ensnares a Church in Former Rebel Stronghold," *Christian Science Monitor*, August 12, 2014, https://www.csmonitor.com/World/Europe/2014/0812/A-Ukrainian-murder-mystery-ensnares-a-church-in-former-rebel-stronghold.

churches due to their perceived ties to the West. Several dozen militants turned the premises of the Protestant church into their barracks. To the pastor's surprise, even some parishioners joined the militants during the church takeover.[95] These early public examples of violence signaled that militants effectively replaced Ukraine's law enforcement as exclusive wielders of force.

Coercion was used to punish not only politically suspect residents but also petty criminals. Militant tribunals decided on the punishment of those accused of theft and other misdemeanors. Wartime justice was sometimes exercised based solely on Girkin's orders. One such order referenced the USSR Supreme Soviet June 1941 decree "on martial law." It sentenced Sloviansk resident Oleksiy Pichko to execution by firing squad for marauding.[96] The order emphasized that "DNR militant command will . . . inescapably punish anyone irrespective of their status or prior merits." In a show of impartiality, Girkin even arrested his own hand-picked mayor Ponomariov on suspicions of looting. Over three months of his rule in Sloviansk, Girkin held four "military tribunals" and issued death sentences to at least four men. Two of them were militant commanders from Girkin's own unit, one was a local civilian, and the fourth was a young Right Sector activist accused of killing a militant at a checkpoint.[97]

In other towns militants emulated Girkin and Bezler and engaged in similar acts of selective violence against local civilians suspected of pro-Ukrainian sympathies. In Kramatorsk, the head of the public transportation department, Sergei Shatskiy, was abducted by militants on May 4 after he refused to authorize provision of trolleys for building the barricades. Six days later militants arrested the director of the Kramatorsk airfield, Dmitry Podushkin.[98] Podushkin was released two months later, but Shatskiy disappeared without a trace. Militants in Kramatorsk also targeted local civilians accused of aiding Ukrainian military units outside the city. A group of women who covertly delivered food and other supplies to Ukrainian checkpoints were stopped, interrogated, and detained for several days. Their release became possible only after the intervention of a deputy mayor.[99]

---

[95] Interview with Peter Dudnyk, December 10, 2014.

[96] Max Seddon, "Documents Show Rebel Justice in East Ukraine Was Bureaucratic, Swift and Merciless," *BuzzFeed News*, July 10, 2014, https://www.buzzfeednews.com/article/maxseddon/documents-show-rebel-justice-in-east-ukraine-was-bureaucrati.

[97] Zhuchkovskiy, *85 dnei Slavianska*, 185.

[98] Aleksei Ladyka, "V Kramatorske do sih por ishut lyudei, propavshyh eshe vnachale konflikta," *Radio Svoboda*, May 26, 2016, https://www.radiosvoboda.org/a/27747739.html.

[99] Interview with Romantsova, 2018.

When police witnessed militants coercing civilians, they did not interfere. In Druzhkivka, sixty-four-year-old resident Anatoliy Vodolazskyi staged a solo picket on the town's main square on the morning of May 22 with a Ukrainian flag attached to a long fishing rod. He sought to counter the raising of the Russian and separatist flags on the town's administrative buildings. Aware of the risks, Vodolazskyi notified the police and journalists of the time of his picket.[100] Despite a police presence, he managed to stand there for just a few minutes.[101] Three masked men in camouflage and machine guns jumped out of a parked car, briefly talked to the policemen, and ran to Vodolazskyi. One of them pointed a gun directly at him, while another seized the fishing rod and detached the flag. As they escorted him to their car, one of the policemen reached out to Vodolazskyi to shake his hand but appeared powerless to stop the abduction. He was then taken to the basement of the city council building in neighboring Kramatorsk, which had become an unofficial prison with numerous detainees.[102] Vodolazskyi was ultimately released, supposedly on the orders of someone he believed was a Russian military officer. However, his transfer to Kramatorsk for interrogation indicated close coordination of local militants in Druzhkivka with the Russian commanders in Kramatorsk.

In some cases, local law enforcement not only abetted the militants but even joined their ranks. Rubizhne's city councilman Valeriy Kharchuk was abducted in early May after speaking against the separatist referendum on local TV. On the way to militant headquarters in Luhansk for interrogation, the car containing Kharchuk was stopped by a traffic policeman. When the policeman saw him tied up in the backseat of the car, he asked who the captured man was. "They explained that I was 'Pravosek' [a Right Sector member] and the policeman said 'Good job!' and told them to move along," Kharchuk recalled. Once at the separatist-controlled Luhansk SBU, Kharchuk recognized a former policeman fired for bribery. The ex-cop, now one of the militants, offered him unexpected assistance: "He interfered on my behalf and vouched that I was not from the Right Sector."[103]

In Kostiantynivka militants targeted members of the nationalist party Svoboda. Local Svoboda activist Yaroslav Malanchuk, a tall man with a

<hr>

[100] Interview with Anatoliy Vodolazskyi, September 20, 2018.

[101] Author's archived video from Druzhkivka. See "Druzhkivka 2014," Harvard Dataverse, https://doi.org/10.7910/DVN/ZURDUZ.

[102] Interview with Vodolazskyi, 2018.

[103] Interview with Valeriy Kharchuk, June 13, 2019.

strong western Ukrainian accent revealing his origins, was detained on April 29 and accused of planning resistance. Malanchuk recalled that his interrogators were locals but referred to several mercenaries from Russia as *spetsy* (profis).[104] The head of the town's Svoboda organization, Artem Popik, was detained the next day. Many of those detained by militants in Kostiantynivka were kept in the basement of the city council building while local officials continued working on its upper floors. According to the town's police chief, Volodymyr Honcharov, who spent two days there as a detainee, the basement was "an abandoned area with broken glass, construction junk and no access to water."[105]

Coercive pressure in Kostiantynivka was also directed at the town's opposition newspaper, *Provintsia*, which openly advocated for Ukrainian unity. The town's alleged militant commandant, Roman Usatyuk, approached the paper's owners, Galina and Mikhail Razputko, demanding they give the DNR more favorable coverage.[106] After their refusal, they received a call from Vitaliy Demenkov, a former Afghan veteran and one of the organizers of the local self-defense group. He threatened to burn down the newspaper office unless its current owners transferred control of the newspaper to DNR loyalist Vladimir Averin. One of the newspaper's founders, Averin had arrived in Kostiantynivka from Donetsk in early May. In the 1990s he lived for several years in St. Petersburg, where he joined the Russian Party—one of the first ethnic nationalist parties in Russia with an openly imperial worldview.[107] When he returned to Donetsk, he was convinced that Russia should reclaim its historical territories from Ukraine. The separatist insurgency in the region presented exactly this opportunity.

On May 10 Averin took over the newspaper and made the local militant commandant his deputy editor in charge of security. He raised the Russian flag in front of the newspaper office and renamed it *Narodnaia Gazeta* (People's Newspaper) to distance the publication from its old brand. According to Averin, the residents of Kostiantynivka were overwhelmingly on the side of the DNR and "hated" the pro-Ukrainian stance of the Razputkos' publication. To leave no doubt about its loyalties, the newspaper adopted a new

[104] Interview with Malanchuk, 2018.

[105] V. Danko,"Vladimir Goncharov: Chest pod formoi menta," *Provintsia*, July 16, 2014, https://www.konstantinovka.com.ua/newspaper/chelovek-i-zakon/vladimir-goncharov-chest-pod-formoy-menta.

[106] Interview with Mykhailo Razputko, September 13, 2018.

[107] Interview with Vladimir Averin, May 28, 2020.

design, with the DNR flag in the top left corner of the front page. From a media outlet famous for questioning the authorities, the newspaper turned into a propaganda tool for militants engaged in recruitment and fundraising on their behalf.

Similar pressure on media outlets occurred in other towns. In Bakhmut, DNR representatives entered the office of a private newspaper, *Sobytia*, demanding publication of separatist materials. Shortly afterward, its editor-in-chief, Vadym Mardian, was detained and pressured to change the tone of the newspaper's articles.[108] Intimidated, newspaper personnel who refused to cooperate had to work from home or go into hiding. In Sieverodonetsk the communist city councilman Pavel Korchagin demanded favorable coverage of the separatists from editors of several online media. One of them, Oleksiy Svetikov, decided to flee to Kyiv after receiving direct threats from Korchagin.[109] An editor of another outlet critical of the militants, Serhiy Samarskyi, was detained and transferred to Lugansk for interrogation.[110] Apart from being a journalist, Samarskyi was also a city council deputy from the opposition party. He spent about a week in separatist detainment and was interrogated about the "underground resistance movement."[111]

Coercion turned deadly in several smaller towns, including Lyman. Valeriy Salo's case is illustrative of the ruthlessness with which residents suddenly turned on each other.[112] Salo was a farmer and a deputy of the village council in Shandryholove, located ten miles from Lyman. During a village council meeting he spoke against the separatist referendum and advocated assisting Ukrainian army units stationed in Izyum on the border with Donetsk oblast. As a result, he and his family members were branded Right Sector activists. On the evening of May 7 Salo was abducted by four militants in camouflage uniform. Among them witnesses recognized known separatist leaders from Lyman—Mikulin, Sydorenko, and Burlaka.[113] They forced Salo into his own car and drove away. His burned body was found the next day in a forest about twenty miles from the village.

---

[108] Interview with Vadym Mardian, September 18, 2018.
[109] Interview with Svetikov, 2019.
[110] Interview with Serhiy Samarskyi, June 3, 2015.
[111] Ibid.
[112] Interview with Viktor Zaitsev, November 6, 2018.
[113] Police interrogation report, Olena Salo, September 13, 2014. For a copy see "Lyman 2014," Harvard Dataverse, https://doi.org/10.7910/DVN/MCQ81K.

An attack against pro-Ukrainian activists Viktor and Natalia Zaitsev occurred the very next day in the village of Novoselivka. Viktor worked in the railway guard unit in Lyman, while Natalia taught Ukrainian language and literature in the village school. Earlier Natalia had had a violent altercation with the father of one of her students after she disparaged militants in front of the class. He physically assaulted her and threatened to rape her unless she stopped badmouthing the separatists. On the afternoon of May 8, several armed militants in masks broke into the Zaitsevs' house, fired random shots, and beat Viktor, Natalia, and their son. They warned the three "not to say a word about Ukraine" or they would suffer Salo's fate. Among the attackers Zaitsev recognized her student's father and a local militant organizer Yuriy Mikulin. The next day they fled their village to a Ukraine-controlled area.[114]

In Soledar, a town near Bakhmut, Ivan Reznichenko, a city council member and a member of the opposition party Batkivschyna, was abducted on June 21 by two pro-DNR locals.[115] Reznichenko was a well-known city activist and a leader of the independent trade union at the salt-producing factory Artemsil. Earlier he had removed a DNR flag raised over the city council building and condemned separatist authorities during a city council session. His body was discovered later in one of the mine pits following the confession of the arrested perpetrator.[116]

When militants were lacking number, they sought assistance from key strongholds, such as Donetsk. In the town of Novohrodivka the local opposition activist and former mayoral candidate Kostiantyn Museiko; two city council deputies, Valeriy Pavlyk (PR) and Oleh Bubych (KPU); and two members of the miners' trade union at the Rossiya mine, Oleksandr Vovk and Oleksandr Hurov, gathered at Museiko's house to discuss an upcoming trip to Dnipro. Two minibuses stopped nearby and discharged two dozen armed men, some of them in camouflage uniform, who stormed the house and seized all those present. Museiko recognized only two locals among the attackers.[117] The rest spoke with a noticeable North Caucasus accent and likely belonged to an undercover Russian contingent deployed from Chechnya.[118]

<hr>

114 Interview with Zaitsev, 2018.
115 Interview with Roman Mokhnyk, September 18, 2018.
116 "Znaishly tilo vbytoho separatystamy deputata vid Batkivshyny," *Ukrainska Pravda*, January 16, 2015: https://www.pravda.com.ua/news/2015/01/16/7055297/.
117 Interview with Kostiantyn Museiko, August 5, 2020; interview with Balinov, 2018.
118 Interview with Museiko, 2020.

All those captured were taken to Donetsk for interrogation. First, they were kept in the building of the oblast state administration in Donetsk and later were transferred to the TV and radio broadcasting center, controlled by militants from Oplot battalion. The interrogators asked about sources of funding, ties to the Right Sector, and any property that could be confiscated. Interrogations were accompanied by beatings and torture, including threats of execution. On the morning of May 7, after their disappearance became widely publicized in Ukrainian and international media, they were exchanged. Still, remaining separatist militants in Novohrodivka continued their assaults on pro-Ukrainian activists until the town returned under Ukraine's control.[119]

Following the initial use of selective violence against suspected Ukraine loyalists, militants turned to the arbitrary use of force. The final weeks of militancy in Lysychansk were marked by widespread looting of stores and companies, extortion of wealthy businessmen, kidnaping, and violence against residents suspected of supporting Ukrainian forces.[120] Dozens of men were rounded up for violation of curfew and taken to the militant base at the glass plant. Despite agreeing to hold joint patrols with the militants, the acting police head Vitaliy Petrenko ordered all criminal episodes recorded and reported them to Kyiv.[121] As a result, on the morning of July 8 he was kidnaped on his way to the office. His body was found two months later in the village outside of Lysychansk with a gunshot wound in his head.[122]

Violence became similarly widespread in the neighboring town of Sieverodonetsk, which was controlled by over one thousand militants, mainly Cossack units. Locals identified some of them as mercenaries from Russia since they spoke with a distinct accent and wore a different type of Cossack outfit.[123] Militants looted stores and businesses and abducted locals, often at the checkpoints outside the city.[124] According to the official police report, during militant control of Sieverodonetsk at least twenty-one people were killed and over sixty were detained, and over 160 cars were

---

[119] Interview with Lyudmyla Biletska, October 17, 2018.
[120] Tsentr Hromadianskyh Svobod, "'Khimichnyi trykutnyk' Luhanshyny pid chas okupatsii: Zaruchnyky, katuvannia ta pozasudovi straty," Kyiv, 2014.
[121] Interview with Mykhailo Vlasov, July 10, 2019.
[122] Tsentr Hromadianskyh Svobod, "'Khimichnyi trykutnyk.'"
[123] Interview with Dmytro Lipkevicius, June 13, 2019.
[124] Tsentr Hromadianskyh Svobod, "'Khimichnyi trykutnyk,'" 10.

stolen.[125] Officials at the local Tax Administration Office had to open their vaults and provide militants with cash collected from local businesses.[126] The basement of the SBU office was used for coercive interrogation of detained town residents.[127] The collapse of Ukrainian law enforcement became fully evident with the detention of the city's chief prosecutor Sergiy Grigorov—the only local top official who condemned the LNR as an illegal entity.[128] He was detained for several days and then released on condition that he leave the city. On June 23 militants captured the police department and the premises of the Department for Countering Organized Crime. All police were released from duty and offered a place in the militant ranks. In contrast to Grigorov, Police Chief Andriy Zhdanov reached an agreement with the militants that allowed the police to patrol the streets jointly with the separatists.[129] Violence and mayhem led to the mass exodus of residents from the city. One local remembered, "The city was half empty by the end of June and all expensive cars disappeared from the streets."[130]

From Hunters to Prey

In the first two months of the conflict, from late February to late April, the role of the local authorities in Donbas changed drastically. They led the initial anti-Maidan mobilization efforts in their towns and raised alarms about the threat that protests in Kyiv posed to residents. The first town-based self-defense groups operated under the patronage of the municipal authorities and in conjunction with law enforcement. The demands of local activists, however, quickly radicalized beyond anything that most mayors were ready to deliver. They, hence, had to walk a fine line between alienating their own communities and becoming outlaws in relations with Kyiv. But their belated efforts to dampen local discontent stumbled upon much larger geopolitical shifts. Once Russia demonstrated its expansionist ambitions in Crimea, the momentum behind secessionist demands in Donbas was far more difficult to contain.

---

[125] *Suspilne Donbas*, "Povernuty Donbas: Severodonetsk," YouTube, July 23, 2019, https://youtu.be/xiAZ4fcsPV4.
[126] Interview with Lishyk, 2019.
[127] Interview with Volodymyr Hrytsyshyn, June 12, 2019.
[128] Ibid.
[129] Interview with Svetikov, 2019.
[130] Interview with Lishyk, 2019.

Still, municipal leaders experienced a direct challenge to their authority only after Girkin's seizure of Sloviansk. That marked a turning point after which local elites either had to side with the separatist agenda or risk becoming a target of coercive pressure. As a result, not only political but also physical survival became their primary concern. The ensuing strategies of municipal leaders ranged from fleeing to cooperation and even resistance. As I demonstrate in the following chapters, their ultimate choices were conditioned by a combination of strength of the coercive presence of militant units and the capacity of local community members to counter them.

Chapter 6
Municipal Authorities

Between Collaboration and Exit

Kostiantyn Savinov, the first deputy mayor of Donetsk, who served between 2012 and 2014, never viewed the Gubarevs as a family of rebels. Yekaterina Gubareva, along with her husband, Pavel, were, in Savinov's words, "citizens full of initiative." He recalled how Yekaterina approached him with a proposal to build a children's playground in one of the city districts. After talking to his boss, Mayor Anatoliy Lukianchenko, he "reworked" her idea and constructed an open-air workout space instead. Unlike others in Donetsk, they were not "lobbying anyone's interests" or advancing their own business agenda. Instead, Yekaterina would "keep coming back with good ideas" for improving the city that Savinov considered worthwhile.[1]

When Pavel Gubarev suddenly transformed into a fiery and uncompromising leader of the new anti-Kyiv movement, Savinov viewed it in the context of his prior activism. Instead of dismissing him outright, the deputy mayor was willing to talk and listen. "They were renting an apartment near the city council, and we met several times," Savinov recalled. What did the Gubarevs want this time? "They invited me to join *them*, but I explained that we are elected representatives, and they should join *us*." Their goals were not necessarily at odds, but they diverged in their understanding of the sources of political power. For Pavel Gubarev, power sprang out of mass rallies and had to be seized by charismatic leaders like him. For Savinov, power emerged out of formal procedures and could be exercised only by those who followed them. He preferred to channel all the revolutionary energy into a city council resolution that would call on Kyiv to give the region financial and cultural autonomy. Gubarev, by contrast, wanted to dispense with the formalities and proclaim himself the "people's governor."

The dilemma that Savinov faced when dealing with Gubarev was common for most local administrators in Donbas. Their primary responsibilities

---

[1] Interview with Savinov, 2019.

Seize the City, Undo the State. Serhiy Kudelia, Oxford University Press. © Oxford University Press (2025). DOI: 10.1093/9780197795576.003.0007

were to maintain the town's infrastructure, distribute funds to public-sector employees and pensioners, sustain the operation of the town's economy, and keep public order. They also felt accountable to the communities they served. When community members suddenly started prioritizing political needs, municipal governments had to respond accordingly or risk losing the trust of their constituents.

This chapter examines how the local officials in Donbas responded to the rising separatist challenge. Embedded in the Party of Regions political machine, they first organized anti-Maidan rallies in their towns and sent locals to participate in pro-Yanukovych rallies in Kyiv. In the wake of the Yanukovych regime collapse, they formed self-defense units and endorsed the demands of pro-Russian activists. The annexation of Crimea, however, changed the calculus and behavior of local elites. Pro-Russian mobilization was no longer a shield against the new Ukrainian government, but a threat to their authority. Rather than gaining additional autonomy rights within a federalized Ukraine, local officials contended with the prospect of losing their jobs and dealing with violence in their towns. Due to these uncertainties, explicit collaboration by town mayors entailed significant risks and proved a rare choice. More common was collaboration of lower-level town officials, either deputy mayors or municipal department heads, who sought to capitalize politically on the rising chaos. Mayors, by contrast, were more likely to pursue a more cautious strategy of hedging. This meant cooperating on some technical matters of governance without publicly endorsing separatist goals or fully coordinating with their activities. When hedging was no longer sustainable, mayors more frequently withdrew or fled their towns rather than opt for full-scale collaboration.

Accommodation

The local administration in Donbas has long been tightly integrated into a patronage system of the Party of Regions. Almost all town mayors and their deputies in the region were members of the party, with backing from one of the local oligarchs or party bosses. The hierarchical nature of the PR pyramid meant that local administrations served the political goals of the party leadership and had to fulfill their instructions. With the start of the Euromaidan revolution, local officials in Donbas mobilized town workers or public employees for counterprotests staged in their town or oblast center or in Kyiv. In Bakhmut, the PR office was particularly active in recruiting locals for rallies in support of Yanukovych held near Mariinsky Park in Kyiv.[2] The city had long been under the patronage of Andriy Klyuev, at the time the head of Yanukovych's presidential administration. Along with his brother Serhiy, he owned three of the city's largest plants.[3] His protégé, Oleksandr Shynkarenko, a retired military officer and an Afghan war veteran, was the head of the PR faction on the city council. Once the Euromaidan revolution started, Shynkarenko personally accompanied hundreds of Bakhmut residents traveling for anti-Maidan rallies to Kyiv.

The first clashes between protesters and police in Kyiv indicated to local administrators that the instability in the capital could spill over into the regions. They also felt particularly threatened as members of Yanukovych's patronage network. "People's rage targeted Donbas, so this created a sense of threat for the entire Donetsk clan, and they started promoting aggressive rhetoric in return," argued a civic activist from Donetsk.[4] Shynkarenko remembered visiting Maidan in late February and witnessing the last clashes between the police and protesters near the Parliament building. The protest march to the Rada was advertised as Maidan's "peaceful offensive," but he observed protesters carrying sticks, chains, and petrol bombs. "They attacked the police in a provocative manner. I barely managed to get my guys out of there," he recalled.[5]

As pro-Russian rallies spread across Donbas, many representatives of local authorities shared resentments expressed by protest organizers. They also viewed popular mobilization as protection from the repressive backlash of the new authorities. This predisposed local elites to an accommodative stance, manifested in rhetorical support for protest demands, talks with rally organizers, and provision of resources to enable further activism.

The mayor of Bakhmut, Oleksiy Reva, spoke at the second major pro-Russian rally in town, on March 5. His meeting with the rally organizers was also broadcast on the local TV channel. Present at the meeting were all key city administrators, the police chief, and the head of the city council PR faction. The informal leader of the pro-Russian group was Maksym Zhyznevskiy, who later received an award from Girkin for his service.

---

[2] Interview with Shynkarenko, 2018.

[3] Prior to 2014 Kliuevs had control over Tsvetmet (a producer of nonferrous metals), the Artemovsk machine-building factory, and Vistek (a producer of metal chains and wire).

[4] Interview with Menendez, 2019.

[5] Interview with Shynkarenko, 2018.

Reva opened the meeting by praising anti-Kyiv demonstrators for their display of "patriotism and good sense."[6] He also endorsed demands to give greater powers to the regions so that local officials would "no longer humiliate" themselves with trips to Kyiv. He even agreed to form a local self-defense group and hold a "survey" of residents on the future of the region. A similarly accommodative stance was clear in the arguments of administrators from other towns. In Kostiantynivka, the city council secretary Yuri Rozumnyi addressed the first major rally, on March 1, channeling local grievances. He stressed how Maidan led to "humiliation of the dignity of Russian-speaking residents of Ukraine" and called on his listeners to "protect sacred religious objects" and "stop humiliating the historical past from Kutuzov to Lenin."[7] The Mayor Yuriy Khotlubei of Mariupol addressed rally participants on March 1 from the steps of the city council building. Rather than reassuring town residents, his address conveyed a sense of weakness and disorientation. He stressed that he had no leverage over the government in Kyiv since it controlled law enforcement and gave Mariupol funds to pay pensions and salaries. The only way to force Kyiv to make concessions, in his view, was "to take up arms and act like they did in Crimea." However, he admitted, "we have no arms or backing."[8]

Municipal officials of Kramatorsk, including City Council Secretary Andriy Borsuk, Deputy Mayor Andriy Pankov, and the head of the PR faction on the city council, Viktor Pankov, attended the pro-Russian rally on March 2. The resolution of the rally, which Viktor Pankov read on behalf of municipal authorities, condemned nationalism "in all its forms" and called on residents to defend the town's monuments.[9] It also demanded de facto economic autonomy for the region: "We ask to protect economic rights of Donbas residents. Those funds that we earned with our own hands need to be spent on the development of our cities. We insist on financial federalism!" However, to the surprise and consternation of some at the rally, the resolution ended with the assertion of Ukrainian unity: "We are for wealthy Ukraine! Glory to Ukraine!" Illustrative of this dual stance was the city

---

[6] Author's archived video from Bakhmut. See "Bakhmut 2014," Harvard Dataverse, https://doi.org/10.7910/DVN/JU9DSN.

[7] Author's archived video from Kostiantynivka, March 1, 2014. See "Kostiantynivka 2014," Harvard Dataverse, https://doi.org/10.7910/DVN/GMJEVH.

[8] Author's archived video from Mariupol, March 1, 2014. See "Mariupol 2014," Harvard Dataverse, https://doi.org/10.7910/DVN/4OBT5H.

[9] Author's archived video from Kramatorsk, March 2, 2014. See "Kramatorsk 2014," Harvard Dataverse, https://doi.org/10.7910/DVN/PAVEVZ.

council's deputy Ivan Polupan, who led the local youth wing of the PR. While advocating for closer ties with Russia, he also spoke against any separatist referendum since it risked "splitting Ukraine." Polupan later explained that the rhetoric of PR officials was intentionally aimed at "calming people down." The authorities, he recounted, were genuinely concerned that demonstrators could storm municipal buildings as they did in Donetsk the day before.[10] In the neighboring town of Druzhkivka, however, demonstrators did not even need to storm the council building to make symbolic gains. During the first rally there its mayor, Valeriy Gnatenko, ordered the Russian flag to be raised over the municipal council building and provided demonstrators with an office in the town's culture center.

Expressions of support from top local administrators were reinforced by collective resolutions of some city councils endorsing rally demands. The first example was set by the city council in Donetsk. Following a massive pro-Russian rally on March 1, council deputies gathered for an emergency session called by Mayor Lukianchenko. Their resolution supported "people's initiatives, such as holding the referendum on the future of Donbas," formation of "municipal police" to protect against "radical nationalists," keeping Russian as an "official language in Donetsk oblast," and recognizing Russia as a "strategic partner of Donbas."[11] After the vote, Lukianchenko personally came out to read the resolution to demonstrators. Mariupol city council similarly demanded that Kyiv subordinate municipal police to local authorities and refrain from imposing a "single historical narrative" on other regions. Although the resolution was adopted on March 2, even after Russia started its intervention in Crimea, it still called for establishing "friendly and good neighborly relations with the Russian Federation in political and economic spheres."[12] The resolution of Sieverodonetsk city council, adopted on March 18, was unusual due to its demands for autonomy in the financial sphere. It offered a long list of proposed changes to the tax code to allow local authorities to keep more of the tax revenues collected from individuals and businesses. For local elites everywhere across Donbas, anti-Kyiv rallies became a pretext to demand the expansion of their own authority, but still within the framework of the Ukrainian state.

---

[10] Interview with Ivan Polupan, September 2018. By an estimate of one local official, two-thirds of Kramatorsk residents at the time supported joining Russia. Interview with Andriy Bessonnyi, September 12, 2018.

[11] *Vecherniy Donetsk*, "Vneocherednaia sessia gorsoveta," March 4, 2014, 1.

[12] *Priazovskiy Rabochiy*, "Obrashenie deputatov Mariupolskogo gorodskogo soveta v Verkhovnuyu Radu Ukrainy, k zhyteliam Ukrainy i goroda Mariupolia," March 4, 2014, 1.

Of all assemblies, the Luhansk oblast council embraced the most radical rhetoric of the demonstrators. After adopting a moderate resolution on the morning of March 2, its deputies were forced back into the building by an angry crowd. Members of the separatist organization Lugansk Guard raised the Russian flag over the council building and forced deputies to vote on their own draft. Adopted with only two votes against and two abstentions, the new resolution recognized as "illegitimate all executive bodies formed by the Ukrainian Rada through violation of the law." It also raised the possibility of turning to "the brotherly people of the Russian Federation for assistance" if the authorities in Kyiv "ignored" people's demands or put "their livelihood at risk."[13] The council chairman, Valeriy Holenko, read the text of the resolution on the steps of the council building to a cheering crowd. When he got to the point on the possibility of requesting Russian assistance, the people exploded in chants of "Russia!"[14]

Some local observers believed that endorsements of protest actions by local administrators were simply a coordinated pressure tactic used against the new government in Kyiv. A sociologist from Luhansk, Illia Kononov, for example, called it a form of "blackmail" by the network of PR administrators seeking to compel post-Maidan elites in Kyiv to respect their informal powers.[15] Such coordination, however, did not exist. According to multiple independent firsthand accounts, municipal authorities in individual towns did not maintain contact with colleagues in neighboring towns, lacked any guidance from Kyiv, and usually decided on the appropriate response strategy themselves. As a result, the texts of city council resolutions varied substantially, while some councils refrained from adopting any resolutions altogether. "We were like kittens abandoned by their mother," the PR head in Bakhmut summarized.[16]

Such an isolated position of individual towns amid the severe sovereignty crisis was the result of several factors. Earlier, regional authorities acted as coordinators for municipal leaders. They organized their joint meetings through teleconferencing or in person in oblast centers. Elites in Donetsk

---

[13] *Vostochnyi Variant*, "1–2 marta v Luganskoi oblasti," March 2, 2014, https://v-variant.com.ua/ru/1-2-marta-v-luhanskoy-oblasty-oblsovet-shantazhyruet-tsentralnuiu-vlast-hubernator-otpravlen-v-otstavku-umvd-vozghlavyl-pomaranchev-y-heneral/.

[14] Author's archived video from Luhansk, March 2, 2014. See "Donbas Misc 2014," Harvard Dataverse, https://doi.org/10.7910/DVN/MKLMUF.

[15] Some Western scholars made similar arguments, that anti-Kyiv protests represented a form of bargaining by local political and business elites. See Arel and Driscoll (2022); Platonova (2021); Laryš and Souleimanov, "Delegated Rebellions as an Unwanted Byproduct of Subnational Elites' Miscalculation."

[16] Interview with Shynkarenko, 2018.

and Luhansk, in turn, followed instructions from Kyiv-based PR bosses, who set the overall agenda and their political objectives. The implosion of the PR and the flight of its main leaders to Russia unraveled long-existing informal hierarchies. The sense of chaos was exacerbated by uncertainty regarding the future of the party and lack of clarity regarding its new leadership. Several PR leaders either defected from the party to launch new political projects (e.g., Sergiy Tyhipko and Yuri Boiko) or engaged in the competition for a leadership position (e.g., Oleksandr Yefremov and Mykhailo Dobkin). Since municipal leaders outside Donetsk and Luhansk had no bearing on the outcome of the power struggles among remaining PR factions in Kyiv, they were largely left alone by the regional governors. Even local officials located next to each other, like the town officials in Sieverodonetsk and Lysychansk—two cities separated by a narrow river—saw no reason to communicate.[17] Some political actors certainly viewed protest mobilization in Donbas as an opportunity to settle scores with old rivals or gain leverage in dealing with elites in Kyiv. Still, for most municipal administrators the protests represented a nuisance that interfered with their daily administrative functions. Rather than a form of elite bargaining, the strategy of accommodation was a spontaneous attempt to dampen the intensity of protests through token concessions and rhetorical reassurances. This became particularly apparent as the intensity of anti-Kyiv protests began to wane.

Reversal

With the decline in frequency of and participation in rallies at the end of March, many mayors changed their rhetoric to emphasize their attachment to Ukraine. One of the strongest public endorsements of Ukrainian unity came from the Mayor Leonid Perebyinis of Lyman. Throughout the Euromaidan protests he was an adamant supporter of Yanukovych and even issued veiled secessionist threats against the opposition. When the protests prevailed, he took a more cautious stance and abstained from endorsing the formation of self-defense units in Lyman. This did not pass unnoticed among many locals. At the rally on March 10 he faced an angry crowd of about three hundred people who did not hide their contempt.

---

[17] These views were expressed in interviews with several administrators, including Rozumnyi (September 13, 2018) from Kostiantynivka; Tetiana Savchenko (September 18, 2018) from Bakhmut; and Vlasov (2019) from Lysychansk.

His appearance triggered a wave of public accusations of corruption and an excessively lavish lifestyle. One of the participants compared him to a spider that blanketed the entire town in his web and sucked money out of local entrepreneurs. Despite pressure from the crowd, however, Perebyinis refused to reject the legitimacy of the new Ukrainian authorities: "I am responsible for eighty percent of the people living here so that they can receive their wages and pensions on time. Do you want me to say that I don't recognize this government and then people would lose their income?" Instead, he now characterized Ukraine as a "powerful state" and warned that locals should not expect good treatment from Russia. But his mention of the capture of a Crimean town by Russian troops produced only shouts of "Hooray!" in response. Perebyinis seemed puzzled: "Why are you supporting this? You are Ukrainians and should not be giving away your motherland left and right." His rebuke triggered even louder chanting, this time of "Ro-si-ya!" (Russia!), and forced him off the stage.[18]

A similar reversal was clear in the rhetoric of Toretsk mayor Volodymyr Sleptsov. He expressed sympathy for pro-Russian demands at the first major rally, on March 1. Two weeks later, however, he staged a televised meeting with local officials in which he stressed the need to avoid confrontation with Kyiv and maintain unity: "I don't understand people who call to arms. . . . [A]ll issues need to be resolved diplomatically. . . . There are no differences between East and West and we must be together."[19] He also spoke against holding the regional separatist referendum, referencing the absence of a legal basis for such an initiative. His arguments were further reinforced by other officials in a carefully choreographed set of speeches. The chairman of the city court, Maslov, warned that if Donbas became part of Russia, it could end perks for the miners, endanger pension payments, and call into question real estate privatization results. "We have lived in independent Ukraine for twenty years and need to maintain it," he concluded. Shkiria, the city's representative in the Ukrainian Parliament, cautioned against replicating Maidan's violent tactics in Donbas: "Remember how we were furious about capture of the government buildings on Maidan? So why are we doing the same in Donetsk? We should show that Donbas can resolve issues in

---

[18] Author's archived video from Lyman, March 10, 2014. See "Lyman 2014," Harvard Dataverse, https://doi.org/10.7910/DVN/MCQ81K.

[19] Aleksandra Vostrikova, "Glavnoe—sokhranit' mir i soglasie," *Dzerzhynskiy Shakhter*, March 21, 2014, 2.

a civilized manner rather than with fists, sticks and threats." The front-page summary of the meeting in the municipal newspaper, *Dzerzhynskiy shakhter*, reflecting the position of local authorities, stressed the need to prevent a repetition of the Crimean referendum in Donbas and to counteract Russia's military aggression.[20]

Similar views were expressed by Mayor Gnatenko of Druzhkivka during a March 24 meeting of a "conciliatory council" with competing political parties. Despite participating in the town's pro-Russian rallies earlier, he now warned that further mass gatherings could steer Ukraine into civil war: "It is enough to take one shot and everything will lead to an armed conflict."[21] To avoid this, he proposed a moratorium on holding new rallies in Druzhkivka, cautioned against participating in political gatherings elsewhere, and refuted the possibility of holding a local referendum on secession.[22] "We were all born in Ukraine and have Ukrainian roots and see our future only in a united Ukraine," the mayor now asserted.[23]

Another prominent town leader, Mayor Shtepa of Sloviansk, had earlier called on men to start patrolling the streets to protect residents from Maidan activists. During a March 5 rally, organized by women's organizations under the slogan "For United Ukraine!," she suddenly declared that she did not want to see "separatism or extremism in our city" or hear calls "for splitting the country." She also tried to assure rally participants that the new Ukrainian authorities posed no threat: "The mayor of Lviv was willing to talk to us in Russian—he is against the language law. Our factories will keep trading with Russia—nothing will change."[24] Other mayors made even more direct statements against Russian meddling once the annexation campaign in Crimea was underway. During a city council session on March 5 the acting mayor of Pokrovsk, Halyna Havrylchenko, opened the discussion of political issues by declaring, "I am for partnering with Russia on economic issues, and for developing friendly cultural ties . . . but I oppose anyone—either Russia or us—who provokes war on the territory of our state. . . . We

---

[20] Ibid., 1.

[21] Evgeniy Fialko, "Gnatenko predlozhyl moratoriy na mitingi, no ne vse s nim soglasilis," *Nasha Druzhkovka*, March 26, 2014: https://nasha-druzhkovka.ru/gnatenko-predlozhil-moratorij-na-mitingi-no-ne-vse-s-nim-soglasilis/.

[22] Tatiana Volynets, "Situatsia v strane stala predmetom goriachei diskussii v ispolkome gorodskogo soveta," *Druzhkovka na Ladoniah plius*, March 26, 2014, 2, https://issuu.com/dnl_plus/docs/287_13.

[23] Fialko, "Gnatenko predlozhyl moratoriy."

[24] Author's archived video from Sloviansk, March 5, 2014. See "Sloviansk 2014," Harvard Dataverse, https://doi.org/10.7910/DVN/JU50BB.

need to find the 'golden middle' that will reconcile us—neither Putin nor Yanukovych can come to our town and ensure peace and harmony."[25]

For Sleptsov, Shtepa, Gnatenko, Havrylchenko, and other mayors of Donbas towns, anti-Kyiv mobilization posed a political challenge. The demands of pro-Russian activists gradually radicalized and included removal of old local elites—just as Maidan protesters weeks earlier sought to replace the local municipal authorities resistant to their claims. The annexation of Crimea also showed that Russian takeover might quickly elevate new leaders in positions of authority, like Aksionov in Simferopol and Chalyi in Sevastopol. Hence, the primary interest of municipal elites in Donbas was in restricting space for further public actions and advancing a counternarrative that would refute or downplay the main grievances of the activists.

Still, pro-Russian leaders who emerged during the first mobilization stage in March were not treated as intervening agents of a foreign power but rather as community activists who represented views of a large share of town residents. While capable of destabilizing their localities, they lacked resources to achieve their more radical goals. The accommodative response from local authorities did not empower them sufficiently to challenge the power holders directly. When Sloviansk mayor Shtepa addressed the crowd near the police station immediately after its capture on April 12, she described Girkin-led militants as "not some visitors from Western Ukraine, as we worried, but our Donbas guys who should keep negotiating [with Ukrainian authorities]."[26] Her initial reaction was typical of how other town administrators perceived local challengers. However, as the mayor's aide recalled, during a meeting in her office just three days later it became clear that neither Shtepa nor other local administrators had any power in Sloviansk.[27]

Elite Strategies I: From Hedging to Exit

The seizure of the Donetsk oblast administration on April 6 was the first clear sign that the escalation of separatist protest could seriously hamper the ability of municipal authorities to govern. The next day the mayor of

[25] Liubov Bastyreva, "Za mir v nashem gorode, regione, Ukraine," *Mayak*, March 6, 2014, 2.

[26] Author's archived video from Sloviansk, April 12, 2014. See "Sloviansk 2014," Harvard Dataverse, https://doi.org/10.7910/DVN/JU50BB.

[27] Interview with Denys Bihunov, December 10, 2014.

Kramatorsk, Henadiy Kostyukov, issued his sternest statement yet proclaiming that "all reasonable and law-abiding citizens should condemn separatist declarations and any illegal actions."[28] By then, such statements had little effect. When a pro-Ukrainian group tried to disperse those armed men who surrounded Kramatorsk police station on the evening of April 12, the group ultimately had to yield. As Police Chief Kolupai explained to a group member, the head of the Donetsk regional police office ordered them not to resist and to allow armed men inside the police station.[29] The next day a local separatist reported that, after reaching an agreement with the militants, the city police kept operating.[30]

The example of Kramatorsk showed that even when insurgents quickly acquired coercive dominance over a town, the local authorities could still fulfill their administrative tasks. A statement from Mayor Henadiy Kostyukov, in fact, produced an impression of government continuity: "Our task is to maintain order in communal property and preserve the lives of town residents."[31] This fully suited the interests of militant leaders with no knowledge of the town and no administrative skills to run it. The first militant commandant of Kramatorsk later recalled, "I wanted to keep the entire infrastructure of the city functioning. Naturally, also accounting for the defense needs of the city. . . . Obviously, any system can be easily broken into pieces, but what to do next? I could have removed the mayor of the city the very first day, but I had no connections or any personal acquaintances in the town [Kramatorsk]. So, instead, I started attracting these people to the side of the militia."[32]

Those town administrators who sought to continue their work but wanted to avoid the appearance of full-fledged support for the militancy adopted the strategy of hedging. On the one hand, they continued issuing instructions and addressing day-to-day administration problems. To do this, they abstained from making any critical statements regarding separatist rule and asserted their "apolitical" role. On the other hand, they emphasized their

---

[28] *Obshezhytie*, "Gorodskoi golova Gennadiy Kostyukov obratilsia k zhyteliam Kramatorska," April 7, 2014, https://obs.in.ua/news/novosti-kramatorska/5038-5038.

[29] Interview with Serhiy Borozentsev, September 10, 2018.

[30] Author's archived video from Kramatorsk, April 13, 2014. See "Kramatorsk 2014," Harvard Dataverse, https://doi.org/10.7910/DVN/PAVEVZ.

[31] Andrei Shtal' and Olga Semirazumenko, "'Donetskaia Respublika' v Kramatorske," *Kramatorskaia Pravda*, April 16, 2014, 5.

[32] ICORPUS, Interview with Ilovchenko (2014).

autonomy from the militants and self-sufficiency in decision-making. This enabled them to maintain working relations with the government agencies in Kyiv and avoid being charged with treason. Once militants in Kramatorsk fully seized the executive council building, municipal authorities moved their offices to another location. "They allowed us to take only documents, but no furniture," one of the local officials recalled.[33] In a tense exchange with Kostyukov inside the executive council room on April 13, one separatist activist tried to bargain: "Do you recognize the Donetsk People's Republic? If you accept us, you will stay in your position." Kostyukov immediately retorted, "Don't try to buy me! There are 157 thousand voters in the city, and you have only 500 people standing here."[34] In subsequent weeks, he refused to consult separatist leaders or invite them for staff meetings held in the community center. He also resisted attempts to submit to their authority and rejected any documents sent to him by the militants.[35] Most important, he blocked any attempts to channel city funds for separatist needs and rejected a proposal for a special account to finance separatist initiatives, such as a referendum.

Law enforcement, by contrast, was willing to widely publicize their cooperation with the militants. Following the referendum, the police department declared that it would now work closely with militia units. At a subsequent rally, the DNR-appointed police chief, Besproskurnyi, announced that policemen would replace Ukrainian state symbols on their uniforms with St. George's ribbons during their patrols with the militants. This gave militants full coercive control over the town, but with a defiant mayor they were still short of gaining full administrative control. Kramatorsk officials, however, quickly found themselves at the mercy of the militants. In the words of Deputy Mayor Andriy Bessonnyi, local officials felt "castrated" without police backing.[36] Municipal authorities could function only as long as the militants were willing to tolerate them.

Once separatist leaders concluded that Kostyukov had "no desire to deal with us," they used their coercive dominance to remove him.[37] At the end of May they entered his office and demanded his resignation, which he

---

[33] *Suspilne Donbas,* "Povernuty Donbas: Kramatorsk," July 5, 2019, https://youtu.be/CB4lbYgBk6Y.

[34] Ibid.

[35] Interview with Tsveloi, 2020.

[36] Interview with Bessonnyi, 2018.

[37] Interview with Tsveloi, 2020.

immediately submitted. Publicly, however, the circumstances of Kostyukov's departure were never revealed. During a city council session, the head of the PR faction, Viktor Pankov, explained Kostyukov's resignation as due to a sudden illness and praised him for his "political flexibility"—a precondition for "working peacefully and living peacefully, including with the self-defense of the Donetsk republic."[38] Kostyukov's deputy, Bessonnyi, similarly had to resign shortly afterward and even spent some time in militant detainment.

Kostyukov's replacement, City Council Secretary Borsuk, was an experienced and wily operator with ties to the town's largest machine-building factory, NKMZ. His appointment served the interests of its longtime director, Heorhiy Skudar, who maintained influence over local government by promoting former employees to government positions. Still, according to one former council deputy, militants sought to exercise much closer control over Borsuk's activities, and he was often seen "accompanied by armed men."[39] Ukrainian authorities, however, refused to recognize Kostyukov's resignation and stopped most financial transfers to Kramatorsk from the state treasury. At the end of June Borsuk also resigned and passed his responsibilities to Deputy Mayor Andriy Pankov, another local insider with NKMZ ties. Later Pankov explained his decision to take the job was so state funding would resume: "I was the only one with authorized access to the state treasury."[40] Some local officials were thus willing to cooperate with militants on some key aspects of town governance rather than withdraw completely.

In neighboring Kostiantynivka there was a similar divide, between top officials who chose to yield their powers in the face of separatist pressure and those who engaged in full-fledged collaboration. The mayor, Serhiy Davydov, was an owner of one of the city's largest enterprises, lead producer Svynets. His contribution to Yanukovych's presidential campaign earned him the president's endorsement in the mayoral election of October 2010. By several accounts, Davydov viewed the mayor's position as an opportunity to further his business and had limited involvement in the town's administration. In March Davydov disappeared from public view, and Council Secretary Rozumnyi addressed separatist rallies on behalf of the local authorities and cooperated with the local self-defense organization.

[38] Andrei Shtal, "Gennadiy Kostiukov podal v otstavku," *Kramatorskaya Pravda*, May 28, 2014, 1.
[39] Interview with Polupan, 2018.
[40] Interview with Andriy Pankov in *Suspilne Donbas*, "Povernuty Donbas: Kramatorsk."

Throughout April, when local militants joined ranks with Girkin, Rozumnyi expected he would remain in his position if he were responsive to their demands.[41] However, he also sought to abstain from full-fledged collaboration and, instead, hedge his risks. Rozumnyi agreed to call a city council meeting to discuss holding the secession referendum and endorsed it as the right "response to resident demands."[42] "There is not enough information on the Donetsk People's Republic, but it calls itself 'people's' so it should be able to get people's support," he observed during the council meeting. Still, he distanced himself from the separatist authorities and cautioned against allowing "the strongest person in camouflage with a gun" to prevail. In the end, his motion was to vote for the "people's initiative on the referendum" but to let DNR organizers "explain their objectives." Later Rozumnyi claimed that he drafted the resolution under duress—militants allegedly threatened him with the capture of the city council if the deputies refused to support the referendum. The adopted resolution expressed the deputies' support for the "people's initiative on holding a referendum on the territory of Donetsk oblast on the future of the Donetsk People's Republic." Rozumnyi reasoned that this intentionally vague wording made the resolution "empty" since it lacked explicit support for the actual referendum—asking only for the initiative to hold a referendum. The legalese, however, might have mattered only as possible protection against accusations of treason. Politically, the city council clearly sided with the separatist cause.[43]

Rozumnyi quickly realized that the hedging strategy was unsustainable. On April 28, a dozen armed men in camouflage entered and claimed control of the city council building and police headquarters. Several militants in balaclavas also entered Rozumnyi's office and demanded that he ordered a stop to any transfer of taxes from local businesses to the Ukrainian budget. Rozumnyi recalled how he called the police asking for assistance. But instead of sending a police unit they advised him to find a way to "rescue himself." The next day Rozumnyi packed his belongings, tendered his official resignation, and fled to Dnipro. As he explained, there was no point in pleading with Kyiv for help, but he also did not want to become a cover for separatist rule.[44]

⁴¹ Interview with Yuri Rozumnyi, September 13, 2018.
⁴² Author's archived video from Kostiantynivka, April 16, 2014. See "Kostiantynivka 2014," Harvard Dataverse, https://doi.org/10.7910/DVN/GMJEVH.
⁴³ Interview with Rozumnyi, 2018.
⁴⁴ Ibid.

Despite the absence of Mayor Davydov and Rozumnyi, the executive council in Kostiantynivka was working as usual. On May 7 it issued a statement confirming continued provision of basic services to residents. Full executive powers over the city were transferred to Deputy Mayor Svitlana Astakhova, who became the highest ranked city official to openly embrace the separatist cause. In an interview with a Russian media outlet on the day of city council's capture she asserted that a "referendum should be taking place" but objected to holding a presidential election in Donbas.[45] This was a clear sign of collaboration—a strategy of openly advancing the interests of separatist leaders. Rozumnyi attributed her decision to collaborate to her visit to Crimea in March 2014. After her return, he claimed that she became visibly supportive of the separatist movement.[46]

Astakhova played an essential role in staging the separatist referendum in Kostiantynivka. She directed her subordinates to set up polling stations and oversee ballot counting.[47] The head of the town election commission, Tamara Soinikova, who served in the same position before 2014, announced the results on behalf of the separatist authorities. Law enforcement also fully backed the militants. When the head of the local opposition party office noticed separatist flags flying over municipal buildings in Kostiantynivka, she decided to file an official complaint at the local police station.[48] Instead, police officers told her that they were all for the DNR and urged her to come to the referendum. In a May 28 interview with a pro-DNR newspaper, Police Chief Honcharov confirmed that the police were working closely with the militia to keep the criminal situation in the city under control.[49] The newspaper's editor, Averin, recalled how he personally asked Honcharov to remove the Ukrainian flag from the police station and launch joint patrols with the militants.[50] According to Honcharov, who later fled the city, about 90% of local police joined the ranks of the militants or aligned with them politically.[51]

Another town where local officials pursued a balancing act in response to the separatist challenge was Bakhmut. Oleksiy Reva has been mayor for

<hr>

[45] Rodion Shovkoshytnyi, "Interview with Svitlana Astakhova, KP.ru, April 28, 2014," YouTube, October 11, 2015, https://t.ly/EL4us.

[46] Ibid.

[47] Interview with Berezin, 2018.

[48] Interview with Buvailo, September 13, 2018.

[49] *Narodnaia Gazeta*, "V Konstantinovka kriminogennaia obstanovka ne uhudshylas," May 28, 2014, 4 (author's archive).

[50] Interview with Averin, 2020.

[51] Danko, "Vladimir Goncharov."

twenty-four years and won his fifth mayoral race in 2010 with 70% of the vote. Reva openly dismissed any possibility of separatist rule in Bakhmut, warning that it would cause a major disruption in town governance. In public remarks on April 15, he rejected the formation of alternative authority structures as damaging to the community since "no document signed by the people's mayor will be recognized." On the same grounds, he warned militants against capturing city council, which would put a stop to "financial transfers" from Kyiv. Reva also spoke adamantly against setting up checkpoints around town and even threatened to "close all schools and day cares and public transportation" if even one appeared. But he also admitted that he was talking to some separatist leaders to understand "what the DNR represents."[52]

In another sign of rising militant pressure, Reva agreed to raise a DNR flag in front of the city council building. When asked about this decision, he sternly responded, "What is more important to you—the Ukrainian flag or quiet in the city?"[53] In a further concession, municipal authorities provided separatists with an office just steps away from the city council office. Police Chief Bratkov explained that local authorities allowed "activists" to set up their office in return for "their assistance in protecting the city."[54] He later described militia members as "town residents who care about the fate of their region."[55] Their office became known as DNR headquarters in Bakhmut and functioned as the main recruitment center for local militia. Aspiring militants went there to receive DNR badges, clubs, and Molotov cocktails.[56]

According to a local journalist, it was already clear in March that Bratkov sympathized with the separatist cause.[57] Once the DNR was declared, Bratkov asked police personnel to take an oath of allegiance to the new "republic" and ordered them to form joint units with the militants for

[52] Author's archived video from Bakhmut, April 15, 2014. See "Bakhmut 2014," Harvard Dataverse, https://doi.org/10.7910/DVN/JU9DSN.

[53] *Vecherniy Bakhmut*, "Mer Artemovska: flag DNR nad gorsovetom—eto kompromiss," April 15, 2014, https://bahmut.com.ua/news/politics/1564-mer-artemovska-flag-dnr-nad-gorsovetom-eto-kompromiss.html.

[54] 06274, "Nachalnik Artemovskogo gorotdela obyasnil, pochemu aktivistam vydelil pomeshenie v zdanii MVD," April 18, 2014, https://www.06274.com.ua/news/518800/nacalnik-artemovskogo-gorotdela-obasnil-pocemu-aktivistam-vydelili-pomesenie-v-zdanii-mvd.

[55] *Vperiod*, "Sergei Bratkov: 'My davali prisiagu na vernost narodu. S narodom i ostanemsia!,'" April 16, 2014, 27.

[56] Verdict in court case N219/11331/15-K, Artemivsk city court, February 2, 2016, http://www.reyestr.court.gov.ua/Review/55585274.

[57] Interview with Vadym Mardian, September 18, 2018.

patrolling the streets.[58] Those who refused, like Serhiy Chrenyshev, were forcefully taken to Bezler and physically assaulted.[59] In late May, Bezler sent his unit to the police station to withdraw all the weapons stored there, but local deputies surrounded it and successfully pleaded with the militants to leave.[60] In a subsequent show of loyalty, the deputy head of the police, Ruslan Vitvytskyi, held a press conference with one of the militants at the prosecutor's office.[61] In his remarks Vitvytskyi stressed that both "police and militants were interested in maintaining order in the city." Police openly privileged cooperation with the militants over pro-Ukrainian activists.[62] Only separatists were allowed inside the police station freely. When a Ukrainian activist complained that DNR representatives broke into the territorial electoral commission offices and stole voting protocols, the police told her that those individuals were "ours."[63]

Despite increasingly open police collaboration, Bakhmut remained outside full coercive control of the insurgents. The Ukrainian military base located within town limits gave the Ukrainian state one last foothold in the city and attracted continuous military reinforcements. This might have influenced the decision of local authorities to stick to hedging instead of open collaboration. Their distancing from the militants became clear in the way municipal authorities responded to the separatist referendum and the presidential election. Reva dismissed the referendum initiative as illegal and avoided any direct participation in its organization.[64] As the deputy mayor explained, the opening of polling stations in schools and other buildings under municipal control occurred only following threats from the militants.[65] Some lower-level officials still willingly provided administrative support. One of them, Volodymyr Lytovchenko, chaired the emergency situations department of the executive council and an Afghan war veterans group. According to a local journalist, he used his administrative position

---

[58] Interview with Yelizaveta Honcharova, September 19, 2018.

[59] Interview with journalists of the newspaper *Sobytia*, September 18, 2018.

[60] Interview with Shynkarenko, 2018.

[61] *Vecherniy Bakhmut*, "Nachalnik kriminalnoi militsii Artemovska: militsia nikuda ne isparilas," June 6, 2014, https://bahmut.com.ua/news/society/1698-nachalnik-kriminalnoy-milicii-artemovska-miliciya-nikuda-ne-isparilas.html.

[62] Interview with Stanislav Tremasov, September 16, 2018.

[63] Interview with Honcharova, 2018.

[64] Interview with journalists of the newspaper *Sobytia*, 2018.

[65] Interview with Savchenko, 2018.

to ensure that voting on May 11 took place around the city, and the mayor agreed not to interfere with the process.[66]

Days later Reva spoke adamantly in favor of holding the Ukrainian presidential election on May 25, which militants opposed, and threatened with criminal prosecution those who would disrupt it. The militants, however, were hardly deterred. Two days before the scheduled election, an armed group from Horlivka sent by Bezler seized the city council building and removed the Ukrainian state emblem from the front of the building—the only remaining symbol of Ukraine's sovereign presence. Once militants successfully prevented the opening of any polling stations in Bakhmut, they withdrew from the city. Afterward the mayor rarely appeared in public and relied on his deputies for day-to-day governance.[67]

Elite Strategies II: From Hedging to Sabotage

In several towns, the municipal authorities, initially responsive to separatist demands, openly condemned separatist leaders once they resorted to violence. The authorities also sabotaged separatist initiatives and supported local initiatives to counter them. The largest of these cities was Mariupol, whose mayor, Yuriy Khotlubei, had been in office for sixteen years. On April 13, following the capture of the city council building, Khotlubei appeared on an evening news program on local television to explain the threat that separatists posed to local governance and public order. He also reiterated his commitment to Donbas remaining part of Ukraine: "If they talk about a federal system for Ukraine, why did they remove the Ukrainian flag [from the city council building]? If they raised the DNR flag, then there is no place here for Ukraine. . . . But we stand for remaining in Ukraine, for peace and stability."[68] Ten days later Khotlubei addressed the largest pro-Ukrainian rally organized to date in the city. Staged on the large square in front of the city's Drama Theater, it gathered over one thousand participants, including over one hundred members of the anti-separatist self-defense group Mariupol Patrol (Mariupolska Druzhyna). The presence of Khotlubei, as well as his

---

[66] Interview with Honcharova, 2018.

[67] Interview with Savchenko, 2018. They also received support from influential local businessmen who had to deal with militants to secure their assets. Interview with Ardash Dadashov, September 17, 2018.

[68] Author's archived video from Mariupol, May 1, 2014. See "Mariupol 2014," Harvard Dataverse, https://doi.org/10.7910/DVN/4OBT5H.

deputies and other local officials, signaled municipal authorities' consolidation behind Ukrainian statehood. The rally ended with the unfolding of a gigantic Ukrainian banner carried by dozens along the city streets.

The new police chief, Valeriy Andrushchuk, was known in Mariupol for his uncompromising anti-separatist stance. His unexpected appointment, announced on May 1, might have served to stop preparation for the secession referendum. Separatist leaders immediately responded by sending their supporters to the police station to demand his removal. Their public pressure worked. After hours of talks, Andrushchuk agreed to resign and put Deputy Police Chief Yuriy Gorustovich in charge. Gorustovich, the separatists' preferred candidate, came out to the crowd and pledged to let the referendum proceed: "We promise that there will be no use of force against the city council [held by militants at the time] and referendum commissions will operate as before."[69] Yet Andrushchuk made one final attempt to prevent voting on the referendum. On May 8 he led special police units to push separatists out of the city council building. In addition to the National Guard, dozens of armed men dressed in black uniforms surrounded the municipal building.[70] This was the first appearance of the volunteer battalion Dnipro-1, dispatched to Mariupol as a backup force from Dnipro by a billionaire businessman Ihor Kolomoiskiy. They fired warning shots at anyone who approached, which quickly turned the gathering on the square into a hostile rally. Militants also blocked nearby streets with tires to stop the movement of vehicles. After a five-hour standoff, the police and armed volunteers retreated, leaving the government building in the hands of the separatists.

The violent clashes on Mariupol streets on May 9, following the failed militant assault on the police station, resulted in almost complete withdrawal of Ukrainian military from the city. The militants now acquired temporary coercive control, which led their leader, Kuzmenko, to seek administrative control as well. During public talks with the mayor on May 13, he appealed for recognition of the DNR's authority: "This is a historical moment. We need to agree that today governance belongs to the DNR." As a compromise gesture, he agreed to keep the mayor in his position, but only to govern the town informally: "If we sit together with Yuri Yurievich [Khotlubei] and I

[69] Author's archived video from Mariupol, May 1, 2014. See "Mariupol 2014," Harvard Dataverse, https://doi.org/10.7910/DVN/4OBT5H.
[70] Author's archived video from Mariupol, May 8, 2014. See "Mariupol 2014," Harvard Dataverse, https://doi.org/10.7910/DVN/4OBT5H.

will tell him what to sign and what not to sign—that is how we can work." Otherwise, he explained to his more radical supporters, the Ukrainian government might suspend all financial transfers to Mariupol. Although still noncommittal, Khotlubei hinted that his stance might shift: "The referendum showed that city residents have a clear position. If I was elected by these people, I should be fulfilling their will."[71]

The actual candidate for the position of de facto mayor was Petr Ivanov, the head of the PR faction on city council and the key local ally of Dmitriy Sablin, the Russian politician involved in Crimean annexation. To gain formal authority over the city, Ivanov initiated an emergency city council session on May 20. By that time, many locals recognized that Kuzmenko and his disorganized supporters were not a credible alternative to the city's current administrators.[72] Despite the disarray in militant ranks, according to a local reporter, "influential people in the city believed that Mariupol would soon become part of Russia."[73] Khotlubei remained a major obstacle to these plans due to his repeated refusal to cooperate with the DNR. Ivanov, a prominent local politician, appeared to be a perfect replacement. To follow all formal procedures, however, Ivanov first had to become the secretary of the city council. Khotlubei's resignation would then automatically make Ivanov acting mayor.

By that time Khotlubei was aware of Ivanov's intention to take his place.[74] He first acted as if he did not object to the plan, and called a special meeting of the city council to confirm Ivanov's appointment as city council secretary. After announcing Ivanov's nomination, Khotlubei called for a short break in proceedings. Meanwhile, a group of armed men led by Kuzmenko entered the building to observe Ivanov's confirmation in person. Their presence was meant to intimidate the deputies and coerce them into voting for Ivanov. Its actual effect was the opposite.[75] Citing security concerns, most of the deputies left the session and refused to return. Khotlubei interpreted their departure as a signal from the most powerful businessman in the city, Rinat Akhmetov. The deputies who left the session were members of the PR faction headed by Ivanov, but also tied to the two factories owned by

---

[71] Author's archived video from Mariupol, May 13, 2014. See "Mariupol 2014," Harvard Dataverse, https://doi.org/10.7910/DVN/4OBT5H.

[72] Interview with Oleksandr Pankov, November 21, 2018.

[73] Ibid.

[74] Interview with Khotlubei, 2018.

[75] Lyudmila Kudrina, "Vchera posle poiavlenia vooruzhennyh liudei sessia gorsoveta byla dosrochno zakryta," *Priazovskiy Rabochiy*, May 21, 2014, 1–2.

Akhmetov. Their primary loyalties, hence, were to the oligarch. Their coordinated departure indicated Akhmetov's refusal to back a formal takeover of the city by Russia's proxies. He had an obvious business motive to undermine separatist plans. As he privately conveyed to one of his managers, if his factories were not affiliated with Ukraine, "they would not exist as a business at all."[76] Faced with a half-empty meeting room, Khotlubei announced the lack of a quorum for further deliberations and ended the session. This was the last attempt of the militants to establish full administrative control over Mariupol. Their defeat opened the path to holding the presidential election in the city on May 24. Mariupol became the only major city in Donbas that offered its residents an opportunity to vote for the next president of Ukraine.

Elite Strategies III: From Hedging to Collaboration

Initial hedging by municipal leaders also led to an even more cooperative stance: full collaboration. The mayor of Lyman, Leonid Perebyinis, is an example of such a shift. First elected mayor in 1994 and reelected four times, he initially voiced strong support for Ukraine's integrity. But when faced with an armed contingent of about a dozen militants who arrived from Sloviansk on April 12, Perebyinis quickly acquiesced to their demands. He agreed with the need to set up checkpoints around the town and announced that the town's only hotel, Zorya, located steps away from the police station, would be used as militant headquarters. The hotel belonged to Petro Tsymidan, the deputy of the oblast council and the town's major businessman, who leased agricultural equipment to local farmers. Tsymidan also owned the Tsaritsyne resort, which the militants turned into their second camp, with a checkpoint set up nearby.[77] At a rally held next to the hotel, the local separatist activist Yakovlev publicly credited Leonid Perebyinis with supporting the militants and affirmed they had no intention of removing him: "He ensured that the checkpoints had access to a power supply and made a deal with Tsymidan that we could be connected to his power grid. If we replace him with someone new, the entire infrastructure of the town would collapse."[78]

[76] Interview with Vadym Boichenko, November 19, 2018.
[77] Interview with Ruslan Denshikov, November 6, 2018.
[78] Author's archived video from Lyman, April 2014. See "Lyman 2014," Harvard Dataverse, https://doi.org/10.7910/DVN/MCQ81K.

Some evidence suggests that Perebyinis also assisted the militants in procuring weapons. As a major railway junction, Lyman had a specialized military guard meant to ensure the security of the tracks and carriages. On April 14 the commander of the unit, Igor Belousov, received a phone call from Perebyinis directing him to transfer all their weapons to the militants and document it formally.[79] Shortly afterward, a dozen armed men arrived at the guards' office demanding the surrender of weapons. According to one witness of the standoff, the police refused to interfere, while some members of the guard turned out to be on the side of the DNR.[80] Ultimately, the guard commander managed to hide eight operational machine guns and offered militants a collection of old revolvers from the early Soviet period.

The authority and administrative expertise of the mayor made him indispensable to the militants at the initial stage of Lyman's capture. Even though he refused to publicly advocate for the DNR cause, he exercised his influence to benefit militants behind the scenes. The hotel manager later testified that Perebyinis gave her personal orders to provide room and board to the militants and handed her cash to cover their food supplies.[81] According to a trade union leader at the railway depot, the mayor asked him to send some of his workers to the checkpoints and ensure the militants' food deliveries. Similarly, an agricultural inspector who participated in staff meetings of the executive council testified that Perebyinis appealed to his subordinates to raise funds for the militants and cited his own contributions as an example to follow.[82] Even the head of the town's public education department, Yuri Afonin, said that Perebyinis asked him to provide the militants with mattresses stored in some of the schools. Although some separatist activists accused Perebyinis of "playing both sides" for refusing to endorse the DNR in public, they admitted that he "suits us for now because he helps as much as he can."[83]

On April 30 Perebyinis called an emergency city council session to vote on the resolution in support of holding a separatist referendum. A dozen masked militants with automatic rifles entered the hall and remained in the aisles for the entire session. Meanwhile, militants outside surrounded the city council building with sandbags—supposedly a "protective measure" against possible Ukrainian attack. The unprecedented show of force

---

[79] Interview with Zaitsev, 2018.
[80] Ibid.
[81] Interview with Mateichenko, 2018.
[82] Ibid.
[83] Roman Punin, "Krasnyi Liman mitinguet v podderzhku Donetskoi Narodnoi respubliki," *Limanskaya Storona*, April 23, 2014, 6.

did have the desired effect. As one of the deputies present at the session recalled, seeing militants openly brandishing their guns had a chilling effect on everyone in the hall.[84] Privately, Perebyinis was telling his associates that he considered the referendum to be illegal but felt helpless to stop it. One of his associates said the mayor felt like "a hostage forced to cooperate with the militants to save the city."[85] Perebyinis also felt abandoned by the regional authorities. The local newspaper reported his public complaint that "there was not a single phone call from the governor or his deputies. . . . [T]he towns [in the Donetsk region] are left on their own."[86] So, during the council session the mayor called on council members to endorse the "people's initiative" and open polling stations where "people could support the DNR with their votes." The show of hands seemed to demonstrate unanimous support for the resolution. The vote, however, was coerced. Militants closely observed all deputies and forced out of the hall those opposed to the resolution.[87]

On May 11 thirty-eight polling stations were open across Krasnolymanskyi raion, including eleven in the city itself. Most were set up in schools and municipal buildings ordered to comply by city authorities. Local education chief Afonin authorized school principals and teachers to provide their facilities to the referendum, but many of them genuinely supported the DNR.[88] Electoral commissions were staffed by locals, most of whom had served there before. A privately owned city newspaper, *Limanskaya Storona*, reported on the euphoric feelings of referendum participants. It described residents "hurrying to vote" in the early morning hours with "smiles on their faces" and concluded that "they stopped being fearful and made their choices consciously." The article's headline was "To a Referendum As If to a Feast."[89]

The mayors of Druzhkivka and Toretsk offer even more clear-cut examples of collaboration. Both amassed considerable business influence in their towns through their relatives and proxies. The Mayor Gnatenko of

---

[84] Interview with Lomako, 2018.

[85] Ibid.

[86] Roman Punin, "Kiev ugrozhaet, oblastnaya vlast samoustranilas, gorodskaia militsia snova pri oruzhii," *Limanskaya Storona*, April 23, 2014, 2.

[87] Interview with Lomako, 2018.

[88] Interview with Zaitsev, 2018. The city council resolution also required municipal officials to provide space and ballot boxes for holding a referendum.

[89] Violetta Tsurkan, "Na referendum kak na prazdnik," *Limanskaia Storona*, May 14, 2014, 2–3. The newspaper reported 83.3% turnout with 96.7% of voters supporting DNR.

Druzhkivka, once the head of the local tax police, exercised informal control over town markets and production of street tiles, which received contracts from city government. He also maintained a patronage network of loyalists in schools, hospitals, and communal service companies.[90] On April 12, the day Girkin captured nearby Sloviansk, Gnatenko issued an appeal in support of both unified Ukraine and friendly relations with Russia. At the rally the next day, he agreed to raise the DNR flag over the executive council building. The special session of city council held shortly afterward signaled that the local authorities were now acting in sync with the militants. Thirty-five out of fifty deputies voted for the resolution authorizing the holding of a separatist referendum in Druzhkivka. The editor-in-chief of the city council newspaper, Borys Yuzhyk, even advocated asking people directly to recognize the Donetsk republic. Other council deputies rehashed grievances just like the ones expressed during pro-Russian rallies. Ashot Melikbegyan, a council member from the PR faction, asserted that Ukraine was "no longer an independent state" since its policies were "dictated from the West." Another council deputy, Vitaliy Podoprigora, whose brother organized the first self-defense groups in town, reiterated the threat posed from western Ukrainian nationalists, reminding everyone that "Farion [a nationalist MP from Lviv] said that they would kill us all."[91]

From the very beginning of the armed challenge, Gnatenko repeatedly justified the presence of militants in Druzhkivka. At a press briefing on April 15, Gnatenko publicly pledged to support the militants at the barricades with a power supply and trash bins. He stressed that they were all "locals" and would remain in town until the referendum was held. He also indicated that without him at the helm, the separatists would not be able to achieve their goals: "I can resign . . . but this would make it more difficult to organize the referendum since the Ukrainian government would block any financial transfers once the 'people's mayor' appears."[92] During a meeting with local officials on May 5 he suggested that police inaction was to blame for the emergence of armed self-defense groups. Still, he insisted that the groups provided a valuable public service by detaining drunk drivers and punishing

[90] Interview with Vitaliy Podoprigora, September 11, 2018.

[91] *Nasha Druzhkovka*, "Vneocherednaia sessia," April 15, 2014, http://nasha-druzhkovka.ru/vneocherednaya-sessiya/#more-14726.

[92] Tatiana Volynets, "Referendum dolzhen uspokoit liudei," *Druzhkovka na Ladoniah*, April 16, 2014, https://issuu.com/dnl_plus/docs/290_16.

those who sold alcohol illegally.[93] Meanwhile, mayor's deputy, Volodymyr Grigorenko, was helping to stage the separatist referendum six days later.

Militants received positive coverage in the town's private weekly, *Druzhkovka na Ladoniah*. Its owner, Viktor Gaiduk, had been the editor of the town's municipal newspaper and Gnatenko's subordinate. On May 21, it published an appeal from the "patriots" of Druzhkivka to join the self-defense units.[94] A report about the activities of one militant unit stressed the "good works" it was providing, such as detaining drunkards and protecting the cash supply to local banks. On June 4 it published an appeal from the town's military commander, calling on locals to avoid resisting the separatist armed groups operating in town.[95] An article in the same issue reported that militants were helping to end the drug trade and detain those involved in it.[96]

There were other indications that Gnatenko gained influence over the local separatists through members of his patronage network. Druzhkivka's self-proclaimed "people's mayor," Oleksandr Zinoviev, was a local entrepreneur who managed the town's largest food market. But the actual owner of the market allegedly was Gnatenko. Moreover, his mother, Lyudmyla Zinovieva, was the head of the public council, the body meant to consult municipal authorities and formed personally by the mayor. The municipal newspaper *Druzhkovskiy Rabochiy*, which functioned under the mayor's guidance, published a long interview with Zinoviev, where he was introduced as one of the organizers of the separatists in Druzhkivka.[97] He traced his political activism from participation in anti-Maidan actions in Donetsk in early 2014. In another interview, Zinoviev named reduction in crime and crackdown on corruption in law enforcement as two of the tangible achievements of the militants. In his view, the militants had effectively replaced the town police, who had stopped fulfilling their functions. He credited local entrepreneurs for financing the militants and other residents for tips on the

---

[93] Author's archived video from Druzhkivka, May 5, 2014. See "Druzhkivka 2014," Harvard Dataverse, https://doi.org/10.7910/DVN/ZURDUZ.

[94] *Druzhkovka na Ladoniah*, "Obrashenie patriotov Druzhkovki k zemliakam," May 21, 2014, https://issuu.com/dnl_plus/docs/295_21.

[95] *Druzhkovka na Ladoniah*, "Obrashenie Voennogo Komendanta Goroda Druzhkovki k Gorozhanam," June 4, 2014, https://issuu.com/dnl_plus/docs/297_23.

[96] *Druzhkovka na Ladoniah*, "Borba za Poriadok v Druzhkovke Prodolzhaetsia," June 4, 2014, https://issuu.com/dnl_plus/docs/297_23.

[97] Sergei Marintsev, "Opolchenie grozit prestupnikam i pomogaet bedstvuyushim," *Druzhkovskiy Rabochiy*, June 19, 2014, 2.

movement of Ukrainian troops. Gnatenko's behind-the-scenes cooperation with the militants to pressure businessmen to aid them was corroborated in interviews. When the militants detained a member of Parliament, Yevhen Konstantinov, he was told to appeal to Gnatenko for help.[98] And the building militants used as a detainment facility and a site of torture was located right next to the executive council and the mayor's office.

Gnatenko's rhetoric also amplified negative tropes used by the separatists against Kyiv. In a public address during the May 9 celebration Gnatenko claimed that "fascism is again emerging in our country" and warned against "neo-Nazis taking hold." Other local officials reinforced his narrative in their own speeches.[99] At the "rally of mothers" on May 29, held on the steps of the city council building with the mayor's participation, Valentina Lugov-aia, a school principal, characterized Ukrainian troops as "terrorists" and called on them to cease all military actions. Another speaker appealed to Russia to send peacekeepers to help "the new republic of Novorossia." The rally's slogan—"Save Donbas from the Ukrainian Army!"—was displayed on a large banner in front of the city council building and replicated separatist propaganda.[100]

Yet another town mayor who shifted from hedging to collaboration as militants gained full coercive control was Volodymyr Sleptsov in Toretsk. The takeover of neighboring Horlivka became an inflection point for Sleptsov. Following Bezler's capture of Horlivka, Sleptsov convened a special emergency session of the city council. Although only thirty-three of the forty-five deputies were present at the meeting, the assembly hall was overflowing with more than a hundred DNR supporters.[101] As the city council secretary recalled, this prevented normal deliberations and created enormous pressure on the deputies.[102] After opening the session, Sleptsov immediately gave the floor to a separatist activist, Lyudmyla Yeroshenko, who, in turn, introduced Pavel Skakun, a visitor from Donetsk who claimed to "represent the new DNR authorities." As a KPU member, Skakun ran for a seat in the Ukrainian Parliament from one of the districts in Donetsk in 2012 but lost

---

[98] Interview with Anatoliy Bashtovoi, September 2014.

[99] Author's archived video from Druzhkivka, May 9, 2014. See "Druzhkivka 2014," Harvard Dataverse, https://doi.org/10.7910/DVN/ZURDUZ.

[100] Author's archived video from Druzhkivka, May 29, 2014. See "Druzhkivka 2014," Harvard Dataverse, https://doi.org/10.7910/DVN/ZURDUZ.

[101] Author's archived video from Toretsk, April 15, 2014. See "Toretsk 2014," Harvard Dataverse, https://doi.org/10.7910/DVN/OSQ1SE.

[102] Interview with Yevsikov, 2018.

to PR candidate Oleksandr Bobkov.[103] The mayor not only recognized them both, but seated Skakun and Yeroshenko next to him in the presidium.

The separatists made their presence felt from the start of the meeting. First Yeroshenko demanded the removal of the national flag: "If you recognize the DNR, then the Ukrainian flag should not be placed here." Amid the applause of the activists and the silence of council deputies, the Ukrainian flag was quickly removed from the podium. Then Skakun took the floor and announced that the only item on the agenda was the endorsement of the May 11 referendum on the future of the DNR. Those few deputies who objected were immediately forced out. The rest were asked to stand on the stage outside the city council building and vote for the resolution facing a crowd of separatist sympathizers who gathered there. Predictably, no dissenters emerged on the stage. Then an unusual ritual ensued. Key city officials took turns to proclaim that they were "with the people." Among them were the mayor; Dmytro Zhytlyonok, the director of the town's mining company; and Police Chief Ivan Panasyuk. Zhytlyonok promised not to dismiss any miners who skipped work to guard the checkpoints or participate in the rallies and assist with holding a referendum. In conclusion, Yeroshenko announced the opening of the DNR office on the first floor of the city council building. Its task was to prepare the referendum and coordinate local participation in the militia. With the replacement of the Ukrainian with the DNR flag on the executive council building, the symbolic acquiescence of city leadership to the new separatist authorities was complete.[104]

In the run-up to the referendum, municipal authorities agreed to organize a rally in support of the DNR and provide buses to boost its attendance. The rally, held on May 4, was moderated by City Council Secretary Yevsikov and featured speeches from the mayor and the director of the largest mine, Dzerzhynska. Their rhetoric reinforced the key messages of DNR leaders, who accused Ukraine of unjust use of force against civilian population. Sleptsov appealed to Ukrainian armed forces to "stop killing unarmed people" in neighboring towns and pledged that he would organize local businessmen and enterprise directors to assist militia volunteers. Another rally at the end of May was organized with the mayor's active involvement. On May

---

[103] Bobkov also sided with the DNR and financed militant groups in Donetsk. See Kazansky and Vorotynskaia (2020).

[104] Based on author's archived videos from Toretsk, April 15, 2014. See "Toretsk 2014," Harvard Dataverse, https://doi.org/10.7910/DVN/OSQ1SE.

28 he arrived at the office of the city mining company to meet with its management and miners. He called for a one-day warning strike and appealed them to attend the rally: "Ukrainian TV channels are showing entertainment programming, while the Ukrainian army is killing its own people. . . . I want to make sure that workers from all communal enterprises and directors come to the square to support this protest action tomorrow morning. There should be at least ten thousand people on the square." Sleptsov then asked the directors of each mine to report on the number of miners they could send to the rally. Throughout the meeting he engaged himself in all aspects of planning. The signs, according to the mayor, had to state that "Donbas is against the genocide of its people." He insisted on choosing the best speakers from among the workers to address the rally "so that they don't lose track" and express themselves in "simple words but with fury." He even went into logistical details of group transportation to ensure maximum attendance. Also present at the meeting were several separatist leaders who praised the mayor as a role model for other officials.[105] The mayor's mobilization efforts paid off: the rally on May 29 attracted thousands of residents. It was moderated by Sleptsov's deputy, Serhiy Kulikov, who castigated Ukrainian authorities for killing two town residents: "Are they even human? They only need to extract shale gas from our land. They want to turn this into scorched earth." He asserted that city leadership was united in its rejection of Kyiv: "There is no one here who wants the junta to win and see these bloodsuckers do what they do. Neither mayor, nor the general director want that. We realize that if they [Ukraine] win we will be held responsible."[106] Kulikov became an adamant supporter of the DNR and left the city when Ukrainian troops arrived in late July.[107]

Some instances of collaboration were not as visible as in Druzhkivka and Toretsk, but still provided critical support in helping militants establish full administrative control. In Novohrodivka, a town close to Donetsk, both the mayor and his deputy engaged in behind-the-scenes collaboration with town separatists. The town's mayor was thirty-seven-year-old Oleksandr Antonenko, a former teacher of Ukrainian in a local school. Following the first pro-Russian rally in town, on April 15, Antonenko

---

[105] Author's archived video from Toretsk, May 28, 2014. See "Toretsk 2014," Harvard Dataverse, https://doi.org/10.7910/DVN/OSQ1SE.

[106] Author's archived video from Toretsk, May 29, 2014. See "Toretsk 2014," Harvard Dataverse, https://doi.org/10.7910/DVN/OSQ1SE.

[107] Interview with Yevsikov, 2018.

promptly called an emergency session to adopt the resolution in support of the separatist referendum. The draft text of the resolution was read to the deputies by DNR representative Volodymyr Podkolozin, the chief of the transportation department at the town's Rosiya mine.[108] Also present at the session were several militants in balaclavas who ensured that most deputies endorsed the resolution. Later, the two key local separatists, Podkolozin and Viktor Neier, a fifty-nine-year-old engineer in the town's water utility company, were seen attending the executive council meetings with Antonenko and his first deputy, Natalia Ivanova.[109] They also organized pro-DNR marches in the run-up to the referendum in which executive council members participated.[110] On July 3 soldiers from the Dnipro battalion abducted Deputy Mayor Ivanova, who was allegedly taken to Dnipropetrovsk for interrogation.[111] Her role in support of the militants was indirectly recognized by Bezler, who offered President Poroshenko to exchange the Ukrainian fighter pilot Nadia Savchenko for Ivanova's return.[112] Poroshenko never authorized the exchange, and Ivanova ultimately disappeared without a trace.

In Selydove, another mining town, the separatist presence was even weaker. The two leading pro-Russian activists were also well-known KPU members. The local officials, however, "never took them seriously" and viewed them as motivated by greed rather than ideological beliefs.[113] As one town resident observed, given their weakness, local separatists would never have been able to capture power.[114] However, the police still held joint patrols with local militants in town and wore St. George's ribbons with DNR insignia.[115] In the absence of a sizable separatist presence, the main coercive pressure over the authorities was exercised by armed militants from Donetsk, less than thirty miles away. Selydove's direct road to Donetsk allowed militants there to pay frequent visits to the town and meet locals to promote DNR. They were usually welcomed and accompanied by

[108] Interview with Museiko, 2018; interview with Biletska, 2018.

[109] Interview with Museiko, 2018. By several accounts, Ivanova was the real power-broker in the city tied to regional elites.

[110] The single polling station for the referendum was open in the building of the Culture Palace on the town's central square. Interview with Kukhliev, 2018.

[111] Interview with Biletska, 2018.

[112] UKROP, ""Korban na sudi rozpoviv pravdu pro pochatok ATO, obmin Savchenko i pomylky Poroshenka," YouTube, November 6, 2015, https://www.youtube.com/watch?v=HJ-IhysONIw&feature=emb_logo.

[113] Interview with Mykola Holubenko, October 17, 2018.

[114] Interview with Vitaliy Hrytsak, October 17, 2018.

[115] Ibid.

the members of the town's Cossack organization.[116] The permanent stage on the town's main square was also painted in DNR black-blue-and-red colors, but there were no frequent rallies held there in contrast to other towns. In the absence of visible local community pressure, the town's proximity to regional capital might have been one of the factors that induced collaboration of the town's officials.

Following the proclamation of the DNR in Donetsk in early April, Mayor Viktor Remizov of Selydove invited one of the KPU activists, Tetiana Stulova, to address a city council session. He endorsed the text of her proposed resolution to hold a referendum on the status of Donbas, adopted unanimously by council members, and provided her with an office in the executive council building.[117] This office was later used to distribute and count May 11 referendum ballots.[118] The polling stations for the referendum operated in six locations, including the municipal library, the technical college, and the culture palace, and were open under direct guidance from local authorities.[119] Stulova, who chaired the ad hoc electoral commission, was interviewed about the referendum results by the local television program *Info-tsentr*, where she announced that 98% of residents voted for DNR independence.[120] The official municipal newspaper, *Nasha Zoria*, published referendum results the next day. According to locals familiar with town media, this required direct authorization by the mayor.[121] In addition to propaganda efforts, municipal authorities assisted the DNR with revenue collection. Remizov called a meeting with local entrepreneurs to introduce Roman Shalamov, a self-described DNR deputy from Selydove.[122] Shalamov was a small entrepreneur running a local taxi service.[123] But now he claimed to represent the DNR government in Donetsk and asked the business owners to make contributions to the separatist cause. Deputy Mayor Dmytro Churchuk was allegedly put in charge of transferring the collected cash from to DNR authorities.[124]

[116] Interview with Oleksandr Tsakhiv, October 17, 2018.
[117] Interview with Hrytsak, 2018.
[118] Interview with Olha Khromenko, October 17, 2018.
[119] Ibid.
[120] Author's archived video from Selydove. See "Selydove 2014," Harvard Dataverse, https://doi.org/10.7910/DVN/1U1EAM.
[121] Interview with Khromenko, 2018.
[122] Interview with Hrytsak, 2018.
[123] Interview with Kruzhko, 2018.
[124] Interview with Khromenko, 2018.

The authorities in Selydove also took steps to prevent voting in the presidential election. The local PR branch refused to delegate its members to the election commissions.[125] Four days before the vote, city council issued an alarmist statement that emphasized the risks of holding an election: "Armed clashes in neighboring towns and villages further heighten social tensions in our town . . . . [P]eople are fearful of the uncontrolled use of firearms. . . . The current situation may lead to the breakdown of the presidential election in our town, people are refusing to participate in the work of the district electoral commissions."[126] The statement, published in the local press on the eve of the election, clearly served the separatist purpose of subverting the vote. Overall, only nine out of thirty polling stations in Selydove were open. But because the ballots were delivered to Selydove only thirty minutes before their official closure, only a handful of people managed to cast their votes.[127]

Everyone for Themselves

Local elites in Donbas shifted from relatively unified support for Yanukovych and accommodation of pro-Russian activists in February and March 2014 to a diverse set of strategies in response to a violent challenge from militants in April. Some, like the mayors of Lyman and Toretsk, engaged in full-fledged collaboration. Others, like the mayors of Kramatorsk and Bakhmut, remained in their positions but avoided endorsement of militant demands. Some of them opted to leave town altogether when balancing became untenable. Yet others, like the mayor of Mariupol, defied separatist rule and, later, sabotaged initiatives to strengthen local militants.

The lack of a unified response was the result of the crumbling of the administrative control system that subordinated municipal authorities to the PR leadership. This allowed town leaders to choose their strategy based on local circumstances and their own goals. The decisive factor in shaping elite choices was the extent of coercive control exercised over towns by the militants. In those cases where militants acquired full coercive control, the mayors had to either collaborate or flee. The example of Kostiantynivka

---

125 Ibid.

126 *Nasha Zoria*, "Obrashenie deputatov Selidovskogo gorodskogo soveta k Verkhovnoi Rade Ukrainy," May 23, 2014, 1.

127 Interview with Khromenko, 2018.

is indicative of this. While initially top local officials engaged in limited cooperation with local separatists, they had to resign from their positions when armed militants demanded more decisive support for separatist rule. By contrast, partial coercive control over Bakhmut and Mariupol allowed local officials to sabotage separatist initiatives. As a result, militants managed to establish administrative control only over those towns where they also maintained full coercive dominance. Most towns examined in this book were located in proximity to the Sloviansk and Horlivka agglomerations or Donetsk. By contrast, as I detail further, when militants lacked quick and direct access to a particular town, such as Dobropillia and Svatove, they had no means to establish a coercive presence and influence the administration.

Chapter 7
Governing under the Barrel of the Gun

On May 29, 2014, the deputies of Lysychansk city council gathered for a special session to elect a new council secretary slated to become the city's acting mayor. The only candidate for the position was thirty-three-year-old Tetiana Vynnyk, a city council deputy and schoolteacher with a family pedigree in communist activism. Her grandfather was a longtime local KPU office chief, while her husband represented KPU leader Petro Symonenko during the 2010 presidential elections. An awkward public speaker, Vynnyk rarely took the floor during city council meetings or addressed communist rallies.[1] Her sudden rise was even more unusual given that the Communists controlled only four seats in a forty-one-seat council, the rest allocated to the PR. However, Vynnyk became the new council secretary following a nearly unanimous vote.

The only council member who voted against Vynnyk's appointment was Mykhailo Vlasov, the very person she was about to replace in the secretary's chair. By then Vlasov realized that he could not continue governing the city. The outbreak of hostilities around Lysychansk in late May and the appearance of armed militants in government buildings had a paralyzing effect on the local authorities. According to one insider, they "withdrew from managing the city and left it to midlevel managers to make decisions."[2] In an interview at the time, Vlasov said he was informed that the town was "fully under control of the militants and on a war footing."[3] As his deputy Oleh Holub later recalled, "We were all shocked about what was happening. It was impossible to stop because people took up arms. Those who worked as drivers and locksmiths—they took up arms and we could not reverse it. They were all fired up."[4]

---

[1] Interview with Apryshkin, 2021.

[2] Ibid.

[3] *Lisichansk*, "Lisichansk nahoditsia pod zhestkim kontrolem narodnogo opolchenia," May 26, 2014, http://web.archive.org/web/20140701024928/https://lisichansk.com.ua/2014/05/29798.

[4] Interview with Oleh Holub, June 14, 2019.

Seize the City, Undo the State. Serhiy Kudelia, Oxford University Press. © Oxford University Press (2025).
DOI: 10.1093/9780197795576.003.0008

Acting Mayor Vlasov quickly became the prime target for separatists. The early indications of the likely governance collapse appeared in mid-May. ATMs started running out of cash; people rushed to stock up on basic food supplies; gas stations experienced gasoline shortages; and public transportation suffered major delays. The first altercations between the separatists and Ukrainian soldiers in the town's vicinity on May 22 further heightened the need to put local government decisively under separatist control. The town's KPU office had played an instrumental role in organizing rallies and opening polling stations for the secession referendum. So Vynnyk became a natural candidate for Vlasov's replacement. The morning after the vote, she arrived at the city council offices accompanied by men armed with assault rifles. "They started shouting that nationalists could take over, so they had to start ruling the town. They were all locals—the kind of people I could not imagine would be part of this," Holub recalled. While Vynnyk could seize government offices by force, she still lacked the formal basis to govern the town. This could be resolved only with further intervention by the militants.

In late May the newly arrived militant commander of the city, Oleksiy Mozgovoi, met with members of the town's executive council to bring them on board with the separatist rule.[5] Vlasov, however, was not invited to the meeting—the first sign that militants wanted him out. Hours later he was detained and taken to Mozgovoi's base at the town's glass-making plant. After hours of questioning and intimidation Vlasov agreed to sign a resignation letter that would formally enable his removal by the city council. The near unanimous council vote to appoint Vynnyk as new acting mayor became possible due to the efforts of Serhiy Barannyk, an influential PR member and one of the closest confidantes of the previous mayor, Dunaev. He mobilized enough votes of loyal council members to ensure that Vynnyk received a large majority support.[6]

Vynnyk represented a wider group of local officials in Donbas who sided with the militants and wished to govern on their behalf. They included incumbent mayors and deputy mayors, lower-level executive officials, and council members. Communist activists, as I will show, played a particularly vital role across the region in providing technical expertise and personnel. Other candidates for administrative roles came from the

<hr>

[5] Interview with Vlasov, 2019.
[6] Interview with Oleksandr Kustov, April 19, 2021.

milieu of separatist activists who emerged during the early mobilization phase. More often, however, militants lacked trusted and competent civilians to replace municipal leaders or sufficient power to remove incumbent authorities.

This chapter examines the contribution of local activists to separatist state building at its initial stage and outlines four governance systems that emerged under separatist control. In all towns fully or partially controlled by the militants they relied on preexisting institutions, such as the administrative apparatus, municipal agencies, and law enforcement, to maintain the provision of basic services.[7] In those localities where incumbent officials were sidelined or removed, *rebel governance* became the norm. While militants took responsibility for the provision of services there, they ordered existing civilian administrators to perform various governance tasks. The clearest cases of this model were the two major rebel strongholds—Sloviansk and Horlivka—as well as smaller nearby towns, like Lyman. The second mode was the system of *joint governance*, in which civilian and militant wings of the separatist movement governed side by side. The rest of the civilian administrators either served under their command or had to leave. Lysychansk, with its partnership between a communist leader and the militia chief, illustrates this governance type. Even there, however, separatists sought to take key positions within the existing formal hierarchy rather than create one from scratch.

The third model was a *parallel governance* system, in which local officials maintained their preponderant administrative role but had to coordinate some of their actions with local separatists or fulfill their requests. Under this mode, the separatists usually formed ad hoc councils or organizations, which acted as an alternative executive agency. As the case of Kramatorsk shows, municipal officials either had to remain responsive to separatist demands or risk replacement by more cooperative members of the local administration. Finally, under the *governance by default* model, the incumbent mayors remained in their positions, as in Sieverodonetsk and Druzhkivka, and continued performing their functions while militants exercised coercive control over their towns. This required municipal leaders' cooperative predisposition and the absence of alternative experienced candidates capable of performing governance roles.

---

[7] This corresponds with the hypothesis advanced by Mampilly in *Rebel Rulers*, that insurgencies in states with high penetration into society are "more likely to co-opt preexisting institutions and networks into its civil administration." See Mampilly, *Rebel Rulers*, p. 211.

Comrades in Arms

Communist Party activists formed the core of the new administrative personnel in multiple towns throughout the region. Due to their strong anti-Maidan stance in 2013–2014, many of them felt they had "no place in the future Ukraine" and so "nothing to lose."[8] Communist activists were hence willing to take higher risks that stopped many of their more pragmatic PR colleagues. As the deputy mayor of Lysychansk at the time recalled, "KPU was the driving force of the separatist movement."[9] Communists were the most natural opponents of the new Ukrainian government. Maidan leaders supported removal of the Lenin monument in central Kyiv in December 2013 and initiated *Leninopad* (demolition of Lenin monuments) across Ukraine. In response, Communists spearheaded the local counterorganizing aimed, initially, at protecting Lenin monuments across Donbas. Still, top officials within the Donetsk oblast KPU, including its head, Mykola Kravchenko, proved reluctant to challenge the Ukrainian state directly. As a result, the leading role within the separatist movement in the region was played by the less prominent sixty-year-old Boris Litvinov, who, at the time, was the head of the party office in Kirovskiy district in Donetsk. Litvinov was first elected as raion council deputy in 1979, at the peak of the stagnation era in the Soviet Union. He had since remained active in local politics as a Communist Party functionary but never rose to the top tier of party apparatchiks.

Litvinov's prior administrative experience, however, immediately elevated him among young neophytes in 2014. After the capture of the Donetsk oblast state administration on April 6 he drafted the two founding documents of the future self-proclaimed state—its Declaration of Sovereignty and the Act of State Independence.[10] Litvinov then shortly served as the chair of the DNR Parliament and later became one of the leaders of the new DNR Communist Party. In Luhansk, by contrast, key local KPU officials more readily embraced the separatist cause. The most prominent among them was Spiridon Kilinkarov, a member of the Ukrainian Parliament who coordinated the actions of local Communists in towns across Luhansk oblast.

---

[8] Interview with Apryshkin (2021).

[9] Interview with Holub (2019).

[10] *NewsFront*, "Lider kompartii DNR: Raskol v Donetskom obkome KPU ne pozvolil kommunistam vozglavit respubliku," June 20, 2021, https://news-front.info/2021/06/20/lider-kompartii-dnr-raskol-v-donetskom-obkome-kpu-ne-pozvolil-kommunistam-vozglavit-respubliku/.

His aides in Luhansk were oblast council deputy Yuri Khokhlov and the city council deputy Maksim Chalenko.[11] Later in June, the entire KPU faction of the oblast council, led by Aleksandr Adrianov, joined the so-called "people's council" of the LNR. Adrianov and Khokhlov became LNR deputies, while Kilinkarov moved to Moscow to become a commentator for Russian state media.

Prior experience with election campaigns allowed KPU officials to play a vital role in organizing the separatist referendum on May 11.[12] In Donetsk oblast they attracted up to twenty-one thousand volunteers to serve as commission members in close to two thousand polling stations. Illustrative of the KPU's role was the referendum preparations in Lysychansk. Local Communists organized a "Get Out the Vote" campaign across town and collected donations to cover administrative expenses. At the same time, they relied on the technical expertise of midlevel town officials, who provided access to voter rolls and set up voting booths and ballot boxes.[13] As one observer of voting in Lysychansk recalled, "All records with voter names and their addresses were listed accurately and voting booths were well prepared, which suggested that the authorities were behind the organization of the referendum."[14]

Rubizhne, a town just a dozen kilometers from Lysychansk, offered another example of the KPU's role in separatist mobilization. The town has long been a communist stronghold. In 2010 the KPU candidate Kostiantyn Koziuberda was elected mayor but was later removed by the PR majority of the city council for alleged misappropriation of city funds. The city council secretary, Oleksandr Khomenko, became the town's acting mayor. Local KPU leader and city council deputy Zadiraka quickly established an informal alliance with the PR and started cooperating with the acting city head.[15] Her son-in-law, thirty-two-year-old Dmitriy Khoroshylov, also served as a city council deputy and a KPU faction member. Together they addressed separatist rallies and channeled public outrage over the new Ukrainian authorities during city council meetings. They also engaged in continuous fundraising for the purposes of separatist organizing. At one of the rallies Zadiraka elaborated on the funding needs: "We are in a difficult

<hr>

[11] Kazansky and Vorotyntseva, *Yak Ukraina Vtrachala Donbas*, 227.
[12] Prokhanov, *Novorossia, kroviu umytaya*.
[13] Interview with Apryshkin, 2021.
[14] Interview with Antonida Melnykova, December 2014.
[15] Their cooperation became visible when Khomenko called a city council meeting to vote on Zadiraka's proposal to hold a referendum on May 11. Interview with Kharchuk, 2019.

position because Russia is not funding us, unfortunately, and we need to buy paper for posters et cetera. . . . We won't refuse Russia's help, but we are self-sustaining and appealing to you for help."[16]

Once the armed conflict started, communist activists in Rubizhne organized locals for nonviolent resistance against the Ukrainian armed forces. In mid-April Khoroshylov led a protest to prevent Ukrainian troops from passing through the town's railway juncture. Dozens of locals under his direction blocked railway tracks with tree trunks and other wooden barriers to stop what they regarded as an attempt to "unload military equipment" in Rubizhne destined for Luhansk.[17] With the outbreak of clashes between Ukrainian military and militants on May 22, Zadiraka also mobilized local civilians to block the movement of Ukrainian troops. When the troops were about to enter the city in late July, separatist leaders, including Zadiraka and Khoroshylov, fled to the LNR and later made successful political careers there. Zadiraka became the deputy of the LNR People's Council, while Khoroshylov was elected the council's deputy chairman.

Communists were also the driving force behind the organization of separatist rallies and the referendum in Sieverodonetsk. The first rally, on March 1, held on the central square under Russian flags, was organized and moderated by local KPU leader and city council deputy Pavel Korchagin. His namesake was a fictional communist hero from a bestselling novel by Arkady Ostrovsky, *How the Steel Was Tempered*, who died fighting for the newly founded Soviet state. Young and energetic, the real-life Korchagin was clearly trying to live up to his literary legend. He initially supported turning Ukraine into a federal state rather than the outright secession of Donbas. "We need to federalize the country, and all revenues should go to southeast Ukraine," Korchagin declared at one of the first rallies in the city.[18] His preferences quickly changed when the LNR was proclaimed and the preparation for a separatist referendum started.

Familiar with the local officials, Korchagin requested they assist with the referendum. Olga Lishyk, the head of the town's cultural department, supervised the operation of public fora, like the culture palace, where militants wanted to set up polling stations. Lishyk remembered that Korchagin along

---

[16] Author's archived video from Rubizhne. See "Rubizhne 2014," Harvard Dataverse, https://doi.org/10.7910/DVN/ONLPT3.

[17] Ibid.

[18] Author's archived video from Sieverodonetsk, March 1, 2014. See "Sieverodonetsk 2014," Harvard Dataverse, https://doi.org/10.7910/DVN/1KHPZE. KPU faction then drafted a resolution calling for a referendum on Ukraine's federal status, which was adopted by the city council in late March.

with several armed militants became enraged when she rebuffed their requests.[19] The top two officials who agreed to collaborate with the Communists were the city council secretary Andriy Havrilenko and deputy city head Sergiy Teryoshyn.[20] They had a reputation of being sympathizers of the "Russian World" ideology who viewed Ukraine as part of the Russian cultural sphere. Teryoshyn oversaw the educational sphere and, along with Havrilenko, instructed school principals to hold voting on school premises. When one principal refused to open the school for the referendum, Havrilenko threatened to call in the militants.[21] Following the referendum, local television station STV reported turnout of 78%, with 97% voting for "self-rule" of Luhansk oblast. Its news report featured only LNR supporters, who hailed the vote as a stepping stone to full integration with Russia.[22]

Rebel Governance

In the first months of separatist control, at least through July, most Donbas towns received regular financial transfers from Kyiv. Municipal heads used access to state funding as a bargaining chip with militant challengers to keep their positions. Still, some mayors preferred to yield their positions, taking a formal leave of absence and transferring their responsibilities to subordinates. Others were simply arrested before they could flee. Under these circumstances, de facto power over the city was often transferred to a militant leader, called a "commandant," or to an ad hoc separatist council. But militants also wanted to create a resemblance of legality of the new administrative order.

In Sloviansk separatist leaders sought to provide a legal basis for the two new institutions—"the people's mayor" and "the people's militia." They drafted a special statute for the "Sloviansk people's militia," described as

---

[19] Interview with Lishyk, 2019.

[20] Ibid.; interview with Nizhelska, 2019. Although Havrilenko remained in Sieverodonetsk after the arrival of the Ukrainian troops and was never prosecuted by Ukrainian authorities, he also stayed in the city when it was occupied by Russian troops in the summer of 2022 and participated in the meeting with the Russian-appointed mayor in July 2022. See photos from the meeting in Lugansk Information Center, "Eks-mer Brianki Became Acting Head of Sieverodonetsk Administration," July 7, 2022, https://lug-info.com/ru/news/eks-mer-bryanki-stal-ispolnyayushim-obyazannosti-glavy-administracii-severodonecka?preview=b71ab83aeaf5-d989-d6f4-bfa1-7923353b.

[21] Interview with Svetikov, 2019.

[22] Author's archived video from Sieverodonetsk, May 11, 2014. See "Sieverodonetsk 2014," Harvard Dataverse, https://doi.org/10.7910/DVN/1KHPZE.

a voluntary organization that was to cooperate with law enforcement and ensure public order.[23] The provision also stated that "the people's militia" functioned "in accordance with the Constitution of Ukraine," and its members had to "follow Ukrainian laws." It was adopted by city council on April 28 and signed by Mayor Nelia Shtepa, who was, at the time, already under house arrest on Girkin's orders. Meanwhile, the new "people's mayor," Ponomariov, replaced Shtepa as the head of the executive committee—again based on the council's vote. Two days later the city council met again to vote on transferring some of the city council offices to "the people's militia." This, in effect, legalized its seizure of the building two weeks earlier. Finally, the council voted to accept Shtepa's resignation based on her written request and designate her deputy, Oleh Tytianyn, to sign "financial documents" in her absence. These changes later allowed the separatist leaders to claim that they did not usurp power but received it from the hands of the only "legitimate" collective body elected by the people. At the very least, the pretense of legitimacy served their propaganda narrative, which contrasted their actions with the "illegality" of Maidan activists at the peak of the revolution.

Another element of the new separatist governance structure in Sloviansk was the formation of the Coordination Council on Self-Government, tasked with overseeing the local authorities. Its chairman was the head of the city's KPU office and the organizer of all anti-Kyiv rallies in town, Anatoliy Khmelyovyi. It also included three city council deputies from the leftist factions. Based on the example of Sevastopol, the council was to channel militant requests to the municipal bureaucracy and provide "the people's mayor" with a quasi-legal framework for decision-making. Their lack of administrative competence, however, prevented the council from having any tangible effect. According to one local official, "they would approach a head of the financial department with a demand to finance something, but it was all ridiculous—they had no idea how it all worked."[24] When fighting around the city escalated in late May, the Coordination Council and "the people's mayor" were removed from town governance, and all de facto executive authority over the city was concentrated within its militant wing, led by Girkin.[25] As one official recalled, "Local self-government agencies

<hr>

[23] 6262, "Kak deputaty Slavianskogo gorodskogo soveta Ukrainy predavali," September 24, 2015, https://www.6262.com.ua/news/973130/kak-deputaty-slavanskogo-gorodskogo-soveta-ukrainu-predavali.

[24] Cited in Oleh Protsenko, "Ne nashi khloptsi: Reaktsiya mistsevoi vlady na okupatsiyu," in *Misto, z yakoho pochalasia viyna*, ed. Anton Udovenko (Kyiv, Yamchynsky Publishing: 2020), 32.

[25] Interview with Denys Bihunov in *Suspilne Donbas*, "Povernuty Donbas: Sloviansk," YouTube, July 5, 2019, https://youtu.be/KZh6vcjfDPk.

functioned, police formally worked, but everything was controlled by men with guns."[26]

Rebel governance rested not only on full coercive control over a town but also on the willingness of local authorities to fully subordinate themselves to separatist forces. Hence, it was a rare arrangement in the first months of the armed conflict. Lyman was the only town in the agglomeration where the governance model resembled Sloviansk's. Following the referendum there, a local separatist activist named Yakovlev announced that the executive committee, led by the mayor, would now be overseen by a coordination council consisting of local DNR promoters. To convey its importance, the city council building was designated as the permanent seat for that new body. The expected change in power relations, which put separatists in control over a local executive, triggered an exodus of some local officials. The mayor went on medical leave, and his formal replacement, city council secretary Andriy Pshenychnyi, was rarely seen.[27] Later, militants claimed that they asked Mayor Leonid Perebyinis to resign, but he refused and disappeared.[28] Instead, they formed an "understanding" with Pshenychnyi, who participated in the executive council meetings jointly with the militants and "offered them his services."[29] Many local public servants, however, were wary of direct collaboration. A reporter who visited Lyman city council in mid-May noted the disappearance of names of department heads from office doors as well as of the mayor's photo at the entrance.[30] Although low-level officials remained in their places, the top brass of the city leadership was absent. The real decision-making power belonged to the Coordination Council, consisting of local separatists and the town "commandant" Grashchenko.

The successful subordination of town officials to Coordination Council was clearly demonstrated at a public gathering on the town square on May 24 where Council members appeared alongside several administrators.[31] Speakers included the director of the city pension fund, who discussed ongoing payments of retirement benefits; the head of the education department, who talked about school graduation plans and a summer camp program;

---

[26] Cited in Protsenko, "Ne nashi khloptsi," 32.

[27] Violetta Tsurkan, "Chto proskhodit v ispolkome?," *Limanskaya Storona*, May 21, 2014, 2.

[28] Author's archived video from Lyman, May 31, 2014. See "Lyman 2014," Harvard Dataverse, https://doi.org/10.7910/DVN/MCQ81K.

[29] Author's archived video from Lyman, May 24, 2014. See "Lyman 2014," Harvard Dataverse, https://doi.org/10.7910/DVN/MCQ81K.

[30] Tsurkan, "Chto proiskhodit v ispolkome?"

[31] Author's archived video from Lyman, May 24, 2014. See "Lyman 2014," Harvard Dataverse, https://doi.org/10.7910/DVN/MCQ81K.

and the representative of a public utility company, who addressed interruptions in the water supply. Their participation signaled their acquiescence to the militant authority and willingness to continue working under their supervision. This was particularly important a day before the presidential election in Ukraine, earlier banned in Lyman. In his brief remarks, Commandant Grashchenko promised to maintain order in the city and defend it despite the buildup of Ukrainian troops nearby. His words were echoed by the new police chief, Volodymyr Dubinin, who thanked the militants for conducting joint patrols with the police units. Earlier Dubinin served as deputy chief of Lyman's police department; he became its acting head after his boss left on medical leave in late April. Dubinin not only engaged militants in joint patrols but also provided them with personnel data and other internal police documents.[32]

The gathering in the square offered an occasion for promoting rebel governance in the local press. A report in an online outlet noted that "people appeared satisfied with the answers" and praised the DNR Coordination Council for its willingness to "maintain a dialogue with the population."[33] The official municipal newspaper, *Zorya*, featured photo of Grashchenko embracing an older woman, with the caption "Commandant Grashchenko ensures that the town remains calm."[34] As Lyman's example illustrates, the ability of militants to establish full administrative control rested on their clear coercive dominance and the mayor's willingness to cede his position to militants. Rebel governance also presumed that militants rather than their civilian sympathizers acquired a final say in all governance matters.

Shared Governance

While Lysychansk also fell under full coercive control of the militants, it exhibited a different governance model. Its commandant, Mozgovoi, had to administer the town alongside local elites led by city council deputy Vynnyk. Her prior record of separatist organizing made Vynnyk a reliable interlocutor from the standpoint of the militants. As someone integrated into the town's political milieu, she also became an acceptable mayoral candidate

---

[32] Criminal case N236/2050/15-K, https://reyestr.court.gov.ua/Review/61099436 (last accessed March 1, 2018).

[33] Roman Punin, "Pervyi otchet koordinatsionnogo soveta," *Limanskaya Storona*, May 28, 2014, 2.

[34] Evgeniy Frolenko, "Situatsia na krasnolimanshine stabilna," *Zoria*, May 28, 2014, 2.

for local elites interested in maintaining financing from Kyiv. Still, Vynnyk's bureaucratic and gradualist governing style often clashed with Mozgovoi's; he viewed himself as a revolutionary figure and sought immediate radical change. The shared governance structure—when civilian and militant leaders of the separatist movement had to coordinate their actions—often led to clashes between the two groups.

Mozgovoi, who enjoyed publicity, sought to demonstrate his decisive role in running the city using frequent appearances on local television. In his first TV address, on June 3, Mozgovoi was introduced as the leader of "people's militia of Luganshchina" (referring to the entire Luhansk region).[35] Wearing a camouflage uniform and a military cap, he stressed the role of militants in ensuring public order, limiting alcohol consumption, and cracking down on drug dealers. He made recruitment pitches and instructed locals on how to behave during bombings. He even made economic appeals. Central among them was the promise to resume operation of the oil-processing factory, the town's largest nonperforming industrial asset owned by the Russian state oil company Rosneft. This would bring "many new jobs" to town residents—one tangible value of reintegration with Russia. It was also something that only Mozgovoi could promise to achieve. According to one local official, "Mozgovoi presented himself as a direct channel of communication with Moscow—and only through direct orders from Putin could [the oil-processing factory] be relaunched."[36]

Most of Mozgovoi's promises, however, were patently unrealistic. Once the gas shortages started, for example, he promised to "nationalize" all gas stations allegedly belonging to billionaire oligarch Rinat Akhmetov and ensure that gasoline was supplied at a fixed price and in sufficient quantities.[37] He also lacked basic administrative competence to formulate any practical solutions to everyday governance challenges. A deputy mayor at the time remembered, "When he started speaking at the executive council meetings, I could not imagine how such men could decide anything."[38]

Vynnyk, on the other hand, had her own agenda for the city. According to her aide at the time, "Our task was not to bring new people, but to maintain continuity and legality."[39] This was particularly important to maintain

---

[35] Author's archived video from Lysychansk, June 3, 2014. See "Lysychansk 2014," Harvard Dataverse, https://doi.org/10.7910/DVN/R6HS13.
[36] Interview with Apryshkin, 2021.
[37] Ibid.
[38] Interview with Holub, 2019.
[39] Interview with Apryshkin, 2021.

access to financing from Kyiv. Her approach, however, angered Mozgovoi, who demanded that all ties with Ukraine be broken. As her aide explained, "When Vynnyk became the acting city head she had to act in the town's interests. And we had to maintain relations with Kyiv to prevent its collapse. But the radical part of the militia would not accept this—they wanted to see immediate changes."[40] A local KPU functionary, Anatoliy Yeremenko, took on the role of intermediary between militants and the new acting mayor: "He softened the edges in talks between the two sides."[41] Militants would also come to the city council and talk to local officials directly: "There were never emotional conversations or demands. They all made practical requests regarding day-to-day operations and asked to provide material assistance by legal means."[42]

The new LNR authorities in Luhansk also sought to influence executive decision-making in Lysychansk through "emissaries" who communicated LNR chief Valeriy Bolotov's desires to Vynnyk personally. One such demand was that city council recognize the LNR, which meant full subordination to the separatist rulers in Luhansk. For Vynnyk, however, this risked an immediate end to the town's economic relationship with Kyiv. She proposed instead a resolution that called merely for the recognition of the legality of the referendum on LNR independence and avoided any expression of support for its results. Even then PR council deputies refused to vote for it. One of them later recalled his reaction: "I thought it was stupid. Even though the referendum took place, why vote for its legality?"[43] After only four KPU deputies voted for the resolution, armed militants appeared in the council hall to compel the rest to support it. Their coercive pressure worked. The resolution was ultimately adopted with only one deputy—former acting mayor Vlasov—voting against it.

To the surprise of many, this recognition of the referendum did not lead to retaliation from the Ukrainian government. As Vynnyk's aide recalled, "Kyiv authorities accepted it—they pretended that they were still in control, and we pretended to be subordinate to them."[44] As a result, despite Lysychansk's falling under complete separatist control, the Ukrainian authorities did not severe its ties with the town. "Kyiv kept transferring funds. All banks were operating. All food supplies continued uninterrupted," recounted the deputy

---

[40] Ibid.
[41] Ibid.
[42] Ibid.
[43] Interview with Kustov, 2021.
[44] Interview with Apryshkin, 2021.

mayor at the time.[45] Meanwhile, the Ukrainian troops on the city's outskirts intensified the shelling, and skirmishes became a regular occurrence. This prevented Mozgovoi from exerting any consistent influence over the town's administration.[46] He also had to deal with a change in public attitudes in Lysychansk, which had turned against the militants. One local remembered, "People supported the militia until the first shots were fired. And then fear emerged and many were suggesting that militants should leave the city and fight their battles with Ukrainians somewhere in the open fields."[47] Public perception of the separatists also dimmed when pension payments were suspended due to disruption of the regional treasury office in Luhansk. This left local governments across the region without access to the electronic system of financial transfers and made many in Lysychansk afraid for their basic survival. "When it moved away from a political game of like or dislike to real-life effects, like shelling, killing, and cessation of payments, many changed their minds," a local official explained.[48]

Following the Ukrainian assault on a separatist checkpoint outside Lysychansk that killed twenty-three militants, Girkin summoned Mozgovoi to Donetsk and ordered him to retreat.[49] The withdrawal of Mozgovoi's units from Lysychansk on July 23 was as sudden and abrupt as their entry. Even some of the separatist administrators received no warning. One of them, Vynnyk's chief of staff Serhiy Apryshkin, had only hours to pack his belonging and flee before the arrival of Ukrainian troops on July 24. Years later, Apryshkin still took pride in his role in separatist governance: "We tried to avoid the chaos of transition. . . . We knew that ultimately representatives from Luhansk would take over our city, but there was this period between the old order, that already disappeared, and the new order, yet to arrive—this is when we worked."[50]

Parallel Governance

In Kramatorsk local separatist activists sought to establish their own shared governance structure, in which they would control the town on par with militants. However, they proved too weak to completely remove local elite

---

[45] Interview with Holub, 2019.
[46] Interview with Apryshkin, 2021.
[47] Ibid.
[48] Ibid.
[49] Zhuchkovskiy, *85 dnei Slavianska*, 70.
[50] Interview with Apryshkin, 2021.

groups tied to the town's major industrial groups. Militants also could not let town administrators continue ruling on their own. This produced a governing arrangement in which municipal authorities performed the basic administrative functions under militant supervision, while separatist activists operated through "parallel structures" to address new outstanding problems.

Separatist activists in Kramatorsk first organized themselves into an "initiative group" during a March 1 rally next to the city council building. Following the rally, about a dozen people participated in talks with the municipal officials on behalf of town residents. A leading member of the group was Pavel Tsveloi, the owner of a real estate company with no prior record of political activism. He resented Yanukovych's corruption and sympathized with Maidan protests at the start. But Tsveloi changed his mind when he saw more nationalist slogans and rising violence. His other major concern was the negative repercussions from severing ties with Russia. Tsveloi had attended a high school in Krasnoyarskiy krai in Russia for two years and still had relatives there. By his own admission, he "always viewed Russia as a homeland," and, therefore, "Ukraine detaching itself from Russia was painful to imagine."[51]

After militants seized Kramatorsk, Tsveloi became indispensable since all the militant leaders were outsiders unfamiliar with the town: "When I came to Ilovchenko [a militant commander] and told him that I knew how local administration functioned, he told me that they had no one to deal with civilian issues and I would be a perfect candidate." At the same time, Tsveloi recognized that his group lacked the necessary technical expertise to take charge of all aspects of city governance. Furthermore, the large industry concentrated in Kramatorsk depended on funds from Kyiv. As a result, the incumbent authorities had to remain in charge to keep the city afloat financially. As Tsveloi argued at the time, anyone interfering with the town's operation would "destroy our lives and social order."[52]

Tsveloi's goal was to oversee the executive in his new role of chair of the "anti-crisis council," a civic group recognized by the DNR government.[53] City administrators, however, felt strong animosity toward the Tsveloi-led council. They considered him and his fellow activists people "from nowhere"

[51] Author's interview with Pavel Tsveloi, June 28, 2020.
[52] Ibid.
[53] Ibid.

who were driven only by personal ambitions.[54] However, given the militant presence, the administrators had to invite the separatists to some of their staff meetings and even delegated someone to participate in the meetings of the "anti-crisis council."[55] Mayor Kostyukov also provided Tsveloi with an office inside the city council building where he could meet with residents.

Still, by his own admission, Tsveloi had no real power over the official paper flow and decision-making. His request to review draft resolutions before they were discussed and voted on by city council was completely ignored. One area where he managed to make a difference was local media. He demanded that the editor of the municipal newspaper, *Kramatorskaya Pravda*, submit all articles for his review before they went into print.[56] This gave him the kind of editorial control that only the mayor's office had had. In the ensuing months the paper published interviews with various DNR militants and offered an unabashedly positive account of their activities. Articles announced the militia's crackdown on gambling, drug trafficking, and moonshining as well as regular reports from Tsveloi's meetings with the locals and council initiatives.

Having pressured Mayor Kostyukov to resign, Tsveloi expected that the council would be more firmly in charge of town administration. In fact, the opposite happened. Due to internal squabbling, Tsveloi was charged with mishandling separatist funds and briefly jailed. Meanwhile, the influence of the anti-crisis council declined precipitously. After his release, Tsveloi was asked to submit fully to the militant authority and consult with them before taking any actions.[57] Although Girkin's representative Dubinskiy was de facto in charge of the armed unit stationed in Kramatorsk, publicly the role of commandant was performed by Gennadiy Kim. He was a fifty-five-year-old Kramatorsk native with Korean roots, who worked, by his own account, as a business coach and espoused "an internationalist worldview."[58] He graduated from the artillery school in Sumy and served in the army until his early retirement.

For a short three-week period, Kim acted as a convenient public front for the Russia-led separatists. He also dealt with city officials on behalf of

[54] Interview with Bessonnyi, 2018.

[55] City officials also gave access to updated voter registry for holding a referendum and authorized the opening of polling stations in municipal buildings. Interview with Tsveloi, 2020.

[56] Ibid.

[57] Ibid.

[58] Andrei Shtal, "Nachalnik shtaba kramatorskogo garnizona: 'Familiia Kim i ukrainskiy natsionalizm ne sopostavimy,'" *Kramatorskaia Pravda*, June 11, 2014, 4.

the militants. During a meeting with town administrators on June 13, Kim explained that his main task was to maintain public order. The municipal government, on the other hand, needed to ensure the continued supply of water, electricity, and provision of communal services.[59] "There are no professionals apart from you in the city," he admitted during the meeting with town administrators. In the presence of the acting mayor, Borsuk, Kim stressed that local officials should treat him as the final authority on all municipal matters: "I will now report to my commanders and DNR authorities that we are taking under control all matters related to the functioning of the city. If you support me in this, I will be grateful. If you don't manage, I will start putting together a new team." The report on the meeting in the town's newspaper featured Kim's photo under the headline "Kramatorsk Needs Stability."[60] This represented the militants' belated attempt to centralize decision-making in their hands.

Still, the town was administered from multiple centers operating in parallel to each other. It became particularly apparent after Kyiv stopped all financial transfers to Kramatorsk on May 18. This left public-sector employees and pensioners without their monthly income. Despite appeals from local businessmen, the Ukrainian government demanded full withdrawal of the militants from the city before payments would be resumed. At the same time, the "anti-crisis council" appealed to local businesses to stop paying taxes to Kyiv and send them to Donetsk instead. However, as they quickly learned, there was no mechanism yet to channel payments to the DNR.[61] Grievances over the wage and pension arrears were not expressed directly to the separatists. Tsveloi recalled seeing lines of "crying pensioners" who came to his office pleading for assistance. Unable to pay them, the separatist authorities started distributing food items. The newspaper report described food lines forming in the city center already in the morning. By the afternoon many "desperate people" packed the premises of the culture palace, the location of food distribution: "On June 11 people received macaroni and buckwheat. On June 12, according to people's patrol coordinator Maksim Vlasov, they planned to distribute potatoes, but of low quality," the paper reported.[62]

Only at the end of June did the DNR government provide Tsveloi with a lump sum of cash, which he personally brought from Donetsk. These funds,

---

[59] Author's archived video from Kramatorsk, June 13, 2014. See "Kramatorsk 2014," Harvard Dataverse, https://doi.org/10.7910/DVN/PAVEVZ.

[60] Andrei Shtal, "Kramatorsku nuzhna stabilnost," *Kramatorskaia Pravda*, June 18, 2014, 4.

[61] Interview with Tsveloi, 2020.

[62] Andrei Shtal, "Sotni gorozhan vystraivalis v ochered za gumanitarkoi," *Kramatorskaia Pravda*, June 18, 2014, 4.

about 1,200 UAH per person (equivalent to about 100 USD at the time), had to be distributed to local pensioners and "socially vulnerable" residents based on lists provided by local officials.[63] However, the militants refused to distribute these funds in the local government offices. This was another sign of the awkward coexistence of multiple governing structures, old and new. The cumbersome process by which individuals claimed their payments in a single separatist office allowed only very few to receive the money before militants withdrew from the city.

Overall, while militants maintained full coercive control over Kramatorsk for almost four months, they had difficulty running its administration. The actual militant commandant of the town, Dubinskiy, avoided interfering in administrative issues and abstained from replacing the town's municipal authorities. He also did not want to alienate the industrial bosses, whose cooperation militants needed for insurgent recruitment. As a result, local activists had to accept their limited influence over town governance, while Dubinskiy's public representative, Kim, lacked basic competence and proper staff to exercise day-to-day control.

Governance by Default

In cases of full collaboration with militants municipal leaders continue performing their duties without significant outsider interference. This produced a system of "governance by default," in which there were no visible changes in the composition of civilian authority despite coercive control by the militants. The prime examples of such a system were the two administrative capitals of the region—Donetsk and Luhansk. Their mayors, Anatoliy Lukianchenko and Serhiy Kravchenko, remained in their offices well into the summer despite the transformation of these cities into key rebel strongholds. As one DNR administrator recalled, when he arrived in Donetsk in July Lukianchenko was "in full control of the city, did not resist DNR in any way, and made constant concessions." Separatists tolerated his presence only because "he ensured continued transfers from the Ukrainian budget to pay pensions and cover other social needs."[64] Lukianchenko confirmed that "Borodai [self-proclaimed prime minister of the DNR] did not interfere in day-to-day governance" but helped with food deliveries across the border and protection from looters.[65]

<hr>

[63] Interview with Tsveloi, 2020.
[64] Pinchuk, *Kontur Bezopasnosti*, 53.
[65] Author's interview with Anatoliy Lukianchenko, December 2014.

Then deputy mayor of Donetsk Kostiantyn Savinov recalled that the interaction between municipal government and self-proclaimed DNR authorities was far more extensive. When he ran out of money to pay for street cleaning services, he turned to DNR deputy prime minister Oleksandr Kalyuskyi for funding. Even mundane tasks, such as regulating traffic lights, required approaching Borodai. This interaction, however, occurred discreetly. Publicly, town administrations remained subordinated exclusively to Kyiv. Only after Girkin approached Lukianchenko in mid-July with a request to start "working in the interests of the militants" did the mayor decide to leave the city. Nevertheless, he continued holding online meetings with the remaining city officials until September. According to Savinov, this ensured uninterrupted transfers from Kyiv to pay the salaries of public administration officials.[66]

Municipal authorities in Toretsk, led by Mayor Sleptsov, remained fully in charge of city governance despite the absence of police on the streets. Separatist leaders openly lauded him during the rallies. "There is stability in the city because DNR authorities and municipal authorities work in sync together," a prominent separatist activist Olena Geishtorova proclaimed. His deputy at the time explained the mayor's behavior as a product of his personality traits: he was "willful and ambitious" and could not "simply hide."[67] While ceding coercive control to the militants, Sleptsov had a busy administrative schedule even during the summer. He chaired executive council meetings and maintained regular visitor hours for city residents. He coordinated preparation of bomb shelters around Toretsk and worked on ensuring a continuous water supply following bomb damage to pipelines. In late June he chaired another city council session where he discussed measures to accommodate refugees from Sloviansk and inform city residents about civil defense measures. Following air strikes on the city in July he led an emergency response to ensure resumption of gas supplies and end power outages across the city.[68] After the Ukrainian troops forced militants out of Toretsk on July 21 Sleptsov chaired the city council meeting and praised local officials and utility services for successfully handling the "emergency situation" caused by the fighting.[69] This continuity in municipal government operation

[66] Interview with Savinov, 2019.

[67] Interview with S. Vynnyk, 2018. Meanwhile, militants used the city council building as recruitment and detention facility and for arms storage.

[68] For protocol of the meeting, see News.Toretsk.Online, "Beda prishla s vozdukha," July 16, 2014, https://www.dzerghinsk.org/news/beda_prishla_s_vozdukha/2014-07-16-5765.

[69] Denis Ksheminskiy, "Splotilis pered obshei bedoi," News.Toretsk.Online, August 1, 2014, https://www.dzerghinsk.org/news/splotilis_pered_obshhej_bedoj/2014-08-01-5785.

led one city official to acknowledge that, despite the lack of coercive control over town, he "never had a feeling that the Ukrainian state disappeared from the city."[70]

Mayor Valeriy Gnatenko of Druzhkivka also remained in his position and provided critical governance assistance to the insurgents. He pressured local stores and businessmen to avoid raising prices, ensured the smooth operation of communal services, provided housing for displaced residents of neighboring towns, and negotiated with Kyiv on access to financing.[71] Some locals even credited Gnatenko for ensuring that the city was largely spared during the most intense phase of fighting and hit with artillery only once. In contrast to Kramatorsk or Sloviansk, Druzhkivka received timely financial transfers from Kyiv.

Gnatenko's prior familiarity with militant leaders, who were all locals, allowed him to avoid jockeying for influence. Yet in June Gnatenko had to share power with a new separatist commander, Oleksandr Borovskiy (call sign "Vasilich"), who led the town's organization of Afghan veterans. Although Gnatenko was not removed from office, some indicated that he conducted meetings and received visitors together with Vasilich.[72] Once Ukrainian advances in the area quickened, Gnatenko took sick leave and left. He returned only after Ukrainian troops recaptured the town in July. Gnatenko continued running Druzhkivka for another five years. In the July 2019 parliamentary elections he won the seat in the Ukrainian Parliament and moved to Kyiv.[73]

"Governance by default" was similarly practiced in Sieverodonetsk, which was under full coercive control of the militants. Publicly, the municipal authorities continued holding regular meetings and reported on how they addressed the needs of town residents. Mayor Valentyn Kazakov and Secretary Havrilenko issued frequent statements, which usually started with the assurance that the city was "operating as normal." As if totally oblivious to the violence around them, they discussed funding for the repair of town roads and buildings, vacations for schoolchildren, and pension

---

[70] Interview with S. Vynnyk, 2018.

[71] Despite repeated requests, Gnatenko refused to be interviewed for this book. His activities at the time were extensively covered in the official town newspaper. See, for example, Vasiliy Ramishvili, "Proverka na prochnost," *Druzhkovskiy Rabochiy*, June 19, 2014, 6.

[72] Interview with Fialko, 2018.

[73] NV, "Sivoho i Kolesnikov—mymo: Mer Druzhkivky Gnatenko vyhrav vybory v okruzi Donetskoi oblasti," July 23, 2019, https://nv.ua/ukr/ukraine/politics/vibori-2019-sergiy-sivoho-i-boris-kolesnikov-prograli-meru-druzhkivki-50033632.html.

payments for retirees. The local media outlets controlled by Kazakov sought to preserve an illusion of normality with detailed reports from executive council meetings and no mention of militant violence.[74] At the same time, he openly condemned artillery strikes by "government forces" and enumerated the damage done to the town's infrastructure.[75] "Striking residential districts of the peacefully working city is unacceptable," Kazakov concluded in an official statement to the local press.

Behind the scenes, local authorities maintained close contact with militant leaders. According to one source, Havrilenko reported to Driomov and participated in meetings with him.[76] Later, Havrilenko claimed that the militants never seized power because "local government bodies were never fully replaced" by the new militant institutions: "All city council meetings happened on time and our decisions were purely administrative. Schools, day care centers, hospitals, transportation—all functioned as normal."[77] However, the local authorities also had to meet separatist demands. In early July, Kazakov agreed to provide Driomov's "Army of Southeast" with an office building near the city council building. His decision, he later explained, was based on his view of the LNR as a nongovernmental organization eligible to receive office space from local authorities.[78] As Ukrainian troops closed in on the city, Kazakov disappeared and did not return until several weeks after the raising of the Ukrainian flag over the city council building on July 22.

Bakhmut offers an example of governance by default that resulted not from collaboration but from the relative weakness of the militant presence and divisions among separatist leaders. During a city council session on May 28, a local separatist activist took the floor to complain that he saw "no tangible cooperation" between the municipal government and the DNR. A few minutes later, the town "commandant" Veles insisted that the incumbent authorities should continue in their positions: "I heard about these activists who demand to change things and remove power holders. Let the current executive council work! Otherwise, Ukraine will send troops here and they

---

[74] See, for example, *Severodonetski Visti*, "Valentin Kazakov: Nashy pervoocherednye zadachi—eto uluchshenie finansovogo snabzhenia goroda i podgotovka k zime," June 27, 2014, 1.

[75] *Severodonetski Visti*, "O sobytiah v Severodonetske 1 iyulia: Kommentariy gorodskogo golovy Valentina Kazakova," July 4, 2014, 1.

[76] Interview with Lishyk, 2019. Two city council members from PR faction, both major businessmen, also served as LNR representatives in town administration.

[77] Inteview with Andriy Havrilenko in *Suspilne Donbas*, "Povernuty Donbas: Severodonetsk," YouTube, July 23, 2019, https://youtu.be/xiAZ4fcsPV4.

[78] Interview with Svetikov, 2019.

will not be able to organize the city defense."[79] The meeting thus exposed the divergence between the interests of civilian organizers and militants. The former sought to replace local administrators or, at least, gain influence over them. The latter wanted to prevent any administrative rupture that would increase its vulnerability in confrontations with Kyiv. As a result, the deputy mayor at the time recalled, the local authorities never had any direct instructions or orders from militant leaders and felt that they were "still in charge."[80] Since there was no interruption of financing from Kyiv, public sector employees received salaries and town residents maintained access to basic services.[81]

Without a Template

The analysis of governance patterns across the Donetsk and Luhansk regions shows their significant variation across separatist-controlled towns at the initial stage of the conflict. The strength of coercive control influenced the strategies of top city officials. In towns under full militant control mayors had to either collaborate or flee. When militants and civilian separatists appeared fully in charge the result was rebel governance, as in Lyman and Sloviansk. When militants abstained from direct intervention in the administration, mayors usually kept their positions, producing governance by default, as in Bakhmut and Toretsk. Towns that had prior grass-roots separatist organizing, such as Kramatorsk, had parallel governance structures, when municipal elites and separatist representatives functioned side by side. Finally, under shared governance militants shared power with local separatist activists who town leadership, while the remaining municipal officials were fully subordinate to them. The variety of governance models adopted in the towns of Donbas at the conflict's onset suggests that its initial course was influenced by internal dynamics as much as external intervention. This becomes particularly clear from the analysis of towns that defied separatist control altogether.

---

[79] *Vecherniy Bakhmut*, "V Artemovske predstaviteli DNR prizvali mestnye vlasti ne sidet na dvukh stuliah," May 28, 2014, https://bahmut.com.ua/news/politics/1668-v-artemovske-predstaviteli-dnr-prizvali-mestnye-vlasti-ne-sidet-na-dvuh-stulyah.html.

[80] The only exception was the demand to collect taxes for DNR, which administrators rejected. Interview with Savchenko, 2018.

[81] Interview with Svitlana Ovcharenko, September 20, 2018.

Chapter 8
From Sabotage to Resistance

How Towns Fought Back

On the morning of April 9, 2014, a Ukrainian military column arrived in Dobropillia, a mining town on the border with the Dnipropetrovsk oblast. At least ten armored personnel carriers and over a hundred Ukrainian soldiers from the 25th Airborne Brigade unloaded at the town's railway station. As they started moving through the streets, they were quickly surrounded by dozens of angry civilians, mostly men, who tried to stop them. Once the squabbling erupted, another group of locals suddenly appeared and started pushing away the rabble-rousers to clear the path for the troops. The newly arrived brigade set up its base in the town's vicinity and helped to maintain order in Dobropillia in the next turbulent months. It could achieve this only through coordination with a few very determined local civilians.

Episodes of grassroots resistance to the rising separatist movement in the region occurred in many towns across Donbas between February and May 2014. They initially took predominantly nonviolent forms, such as participation in rallies under Ukrainian banners, staging pro-Ukrainian marches, and advocacy for Ukraine's integrity in the media and public fora. However, the space for pro-Ukrainian mobilization quickly shrank once armed men under Girkin's command emerged in Sloviansk and neighboring towns. The executions of several pro-Ukrainian activists, such as city council deputy Volodymyr Rybak in Horlivka, raised the costs of further public defiance. In Donetsk, the last pro-Ukrainian rally was held on April 17. An attempt to stage another march in the city under Ukrainian banners on April 28 ended with violent intervention by the militants. After that, it was no longer safe to hold public pro-Ukrainian gatherings in most towns across the region.

The only exceptions were the two towns of Donbas where pro-Ukrainian resistance gained in strength and visibility and acquired a clear organizational form in April and May. One was Dobropillia in the Donetsk oblast with a population of around thirty thousand people. Another was Svatove in the Luhansk oblast, an agricultural town of about twenty thousand

Seize the City, Undo the State. Serhiy Kudelia, Oxford University Press. © Oxford University Press (2025).
DOI: 10.1093/9780197795576.003.0009

located twelve miles from the Kharkiv oblast. In several larger cities, such as Pokrovsk and Mariupol, pro-Ukrainian activists were similarly prominent but not as strong or as well organized. This chapter shows how the location of Dobropillia and Svatove further away from the centers of militancy, but close to territory controlled by Ukraine, enabled the formation of anti-separatist units there. It examines the significance of three types of actors for defeating the separatist challenge: (1) elected mayors, (2) businessmen and entrepreneurs, and (3) volunteer battalions and regular armed units. In each case of successful resistance, at least two of these three actors were present to boost anti-separatist organizing. In Svatove, the initiative of the mayor accelerated the formation of pro-Ukrainian self-defense. The case of Dobropillia shows that even without direct municipal involvement the availability of resourceful activists could tip the power balance in Ukraine's favor. The chapter then extends this argument by examining the cases of Mariupol and Pokrovsk, where municipal and business elites also sided with the Ukrainian state. The evidence across these cases demonstrates that separatists failed to gain coercive dominance whenever they faced community resistance backed by the credible threat to use force.

When a Mayor Led

The core of the pro-Ukrainian self-defense groups in several towns across the region consisted of local businessmen and entrepreneurs who contributed personal funds to acquire equipment and ammunition. But Svatove and Dobropillia offer contrasting examples of how the initial self-defense organization started. In the former it was initiated by the town's mayor; in the latter it emerged as the initiative of local entrepreneurs, who then pressed local authorities to support their actions. The mayor of Svatove, Yevhen Rybalko, learned about the capture of Sloviansk almost immediately after the arrival of Girkin's unit there on April 12.[1] Fearful of the spillover of violence to neighboring towns, he called an emergency meeting of the executive council. In addition to local officials, he invited entrepreneurs and pro-Ukrainian activists, a total of about thirty people, to help him devise a strategy of the town's defense. As Rybalko explained, Svatove was located directly on the route from Sloviansk to the Russian border: "I realized that if

---

[1] Interview with Yevhen Rybalko, June 10, 2019. In the preceding weeks Rybalko publicly condemned separatism and rejected proposals to make Ukraine a federal state.

Girkin and the militants were forced out of the captured towns, they would be fleeing through Svatove and could possibly capture people here and take hostages."[2] The outcome of the meeting was the formation of Svatove's self-defense to prevent the entry of separatist militants into town.

The group was initially composed of executive council members, city council deputies, and wealthy local farmers. Its chairman was Leonid Privalov, owner of an agricultural business with a record of service in the Ukrainian National Guard in the 1990s. As an ethnic Russian born in Russia but a longtime Svatove resident, Privalov might have been a reassuring figure to those locals genuinely concerned about the threat of Maidan nationalists. One of the main financial contributors to the town's self-defense was an Armenian Ukrainian, Serhiy Avalyan, a major local grain trader and an owner of Zoryane farm.[3] He directed his workers to guard one of the two checkpoints set up by the self-defense group on the road to Starobilsk and provided food to maintain a round-the-clock sentry.[4] The second checkpoint was organized next to the police station and guarded jointly with the police. Uncertain about their loyalties, Rybalko warned them to immediately surrender their weapons and leave if they had any intention to yield to the separatists. "We knew that the police were all estimating their new salary if the town ended up under Russia," he explained.[5] Still, the local police chief, Serhiy Lukashov, proved to be a reliable supporter of the self-defense group and ensured police cooperation.

Given the strength of pro-Ukrainian sentiments among the town's wealthy residents, Svatove's self-defense group could have been organized through a bottom-up initiative. But the mayor proved essential for early coordination of all resourceful actors and ensuring a coherent response of the local government apparatus. This self-reliance was partially the result of his long independence from the clientelist network of the Party of Regions. Rybalko recalled that the regional bosses always treated him with suspicion and sought to undermine his authority. First elected as mayor of Svatove in 2002 at the age of thirty-seven, he became the head of raion state administration in 2005 and was elected as mayor again in 2010. Fast-talking, jocular,

---

[2] Ibid.

[3] Author's interview with Anatoly Kuzovenin, June 10, 2019. In 2020 Avalyan was recognized as one of the five richest people in Luhansk oblast. See *Depo*, "Top-5 samyh bogatyh lyudei Luganshiny," February 17, 2020, https://dn.depo.ua/rus/severodonetsk/tovstosumi-luganshchini-202002121112276.

[4] Interview with Kuzovenin, 2019.

[5] Interview with Rybalko, 2019.

and sharp-tongued, Rybalko owed at least part of his political success to the brazen way he ridiculed some of the most influential figures in the region.

Rybalko's first career steps were in the Soviet military. He served in the Far East and then studied in Leningrad Komsomol Institute to become a political officer in the Soviet army. After the fall of the USSR, Rybalko went to Donetsk to pursue business ventures and study economics at Donetsk University. His reputation as an outsider with a résumé of achievement outside his native town helped him to win his first mayoral race in Svatove in 2002. When he ran again in 2010, however, he was a known figure prone to squabbling with officials from the PR. He clinched victory over the PR-backed incumbent mayor in 2010 by a margin of just three hundred ballots, gaining 32.97% of the votes. This narrow victory positioned Rybalko to play a crucial role in thwarting separatist activities in the spring of 2014.

Along with forming a militia, Rybalko initiated an emergency session of the city council on April 14. By that time, most of the town's PR deputies had joined a new, nonpartisan group called Svatovchane (Residents of Svatove) and sided with the mayor. The council resolution offered support for the central government, a rare stance in Donbas, and condemned any attempts to "change the territorial composition of Ukraine by force."[6] The next day Rybalko ordered the first "emergency operation," in response to rumors that militants from Sloviansk could pass through Svatove. He ordered early closures of schools and day care facilities and sent members of the self-defense group to guard them. In a front-page interview with the local newspaper published on April 18, he explained that the events in Sloviansk and Kramatorsk forced him to act preemptively and minimize any potential danger posed by the militants.[7] In an emphatic address to town residents written in both Ukrainian and Russian, Rybalko dismissed claims about language restrictions or political prosecutions and called for unity "in the name of our Motherland."[8]

That same issue of the municipal newspaper first announced the formation of a city self-defense group by "patriotically minded residents."[9] The article claimed that 510 people with diverse professional backgrounds had already signed up to join the group. Its leader, Privalov, claimed in an

---

[6] *Holos Hromady*, "Zhyttediyalnist' mista zabezpechena," April 18, 2014, 2.

[7] Evgeniy Rybalko, "Zadumaemsia i sdelaem vyvody," *Holos Hromady*, April 18, 2014, 1.

[8] *Holos Hromady*, "Zvernennia Svativskogo miskogo holovy Y. V. Rybalka to zhyteliv Svativskoi terytorialnoi hromady," April 18, 2014, 1.

[9] *Holos Hromady*, "Svatovskaia samooborona," April 18, 2014, 2.

interview that checkpoints were guarded by "police, judges, Afghan veterans, entrepreneurs and Cossacks." In reality, there were never more than sixty-five people formally registered in the group.[10] One of them, Yuriy Irkha, believed that the actual number was even smaller: "If I say that there were thirty, I would be exaggerating a bit."[11] Rybalko later acknowledged that they intentionally inflated the numbers to create a "show of strength" and prevent any countermovement on the part of separatist sympathizers.

Rybalko's anti-separatist stance was unusual for the region. The clear counterexample was the behavior of local authorities in neighboring Staro-bilsk, a town just sixty kilometers east. Its pro-Ukrainian residents sought to form their own self-defense unit and emulate Svatove's residents. In mid-April they gathered in the town's stadium to discuss the response to a possible militant incursion. One of the meeting organizers was Oleksandr Paramonov, a local activist of the nationalist Svoboda Party. Another informal leader of the group was fifty-five-year-old former town police chief Oleksandr Zhurylov, who had to reassure local law enforcement that the group did not represent a threat to public order. The planning largely centered on ways in which locals could protect government buildings and the police station.[12] Still, the police chief at the time, Askiar Laishev, showed no enthusiasm for the initiative. He attended the gathering and warned that any attempt to use firearms during patrols or guarding of the checkpoints was illegal and would be prosecuted.[13] For many of those present this indicated that the police were on the separatist side: "We realized that our authorities would surrender and wanted to back them up and prevent the surrender. We offered to patrol the streets and raion state administration, but they refused."[14]

When Mayors Followed

Dobropillia offered an example of a successful self-defense organization based entirely on a grassroots initiative. At least thirty residents of the town participated in the founding meeting of the organization Patriots of Dobropillia at a local café in mid-April. They were mainly small and

[10] Interview with Rybalko, 2019.
[11] Interview with Yuriy Irkha, June 10, 2019.
[12] Interview with Yuriy Kahala, July 10, 2019.
[13] Interview with Petro Tsarevskyi, July 8, 2019.
[14] Interview with Kahala, 2019.

medium-size business entrepreneurs concerned with the future of their businesses in case separatists prevailed. One of the meeting organizers was Mykola Strepochenko, who had been running a large farm since the early 1990s. Until 2014 he had abstained from any political involvement and did not participate in Euromaidan.[15] However, the standoff over the movement of Ukrainian troops on April 9 pushed him to action. He was particularly furious that locals from the town's fringe circles, including petty criminals, positioned themselves as representative of the entire town. Their sudden appearance in spring of 2014 leading antigovernment protests compelled him to respond. Another group leader, Yevhen Chetveriov, felt similarly outraged. He learned that local separatists had compiled a list of local businesses slated for expropriation by DNR authorities. "We could lose everything—we already started packing bags," he recalled. Born in Russia, Chetveriov had long lived in Dobropillia and viewed it as his homeland: "As a private businessman, I don't like it when someone gets into my territory. I was defending not the state, but my family and friends."[16]

The mayor of Dobropillia, Viktor Deripaska, played no role at the initial organizing stage but provided important backing once the self-defense group was formed. On April 18 he held a meeting with local civic activists attended mainly by ardent Ukraine supporters. Pro-Russian activists were invited as well but, he explained, refused to appear. This was a sign that separatist activists already viewed the municipal authorities as unreliable. Pro-Ukrainian activists, by contrast, received lavish praise from the mayor as "genuine patriots" who ensured the town's "calm and order." Many of them, including Strepochenko and Chetveriov, were in the audience and used the opportunity to press further demands. Strepochenko asked Deripaska to ban the pro-Russian rally scheduled in Dobropillia for the following day. The mayor, however, argued it could no longer pose a threat: "If there are five hundred people who try to storm us and everyone who sits here will bring some of their friends, then we can have a thousand people and can resist them. . . . Today I see that these are patriots capable of defending the population of our town."[17] Deripaska then invited the two leaders of the self-defense group—Chetveriov and Strepochenko—to his office to plan a rally in response to the pro-Russian gathering. Staged the next day,

<hr>

[15] Interview with Mykola Strepochenko, October 26, 2020.

[16] Interview with Henadiy Chetveriov, October 16, 2018.

[17] Author's archived video from Dobropillia, April 18, 2014. See "Dobropillia 2014," Harvard Dataverse, https://doi.org/10.7910/DVN/MU1NF6.

it allowed the mayor to affirm that the "city council and executive council support Ukrainian unity."[18] Although it drew just several hundred people, its symbolism was hard to overstate. In most towns across Donbas a joint gathering of pro-Ukrainian activists and local authorities was no longer feasible.

In Pokrovsk, the largest town in Dobropillia's vicinity, separatist rallies had been taking place since early March. The most regular participants were young men in athletic gear who, allegedly, were on the payroll of the town's major businessman, Serhiy Andriychenko, tied to Oleksandr Yanukovych, the son of the deposed president.[19] At the rally organized a week after the capture of Sloviansk, local separatists issued an ultimatum to the acting mayor, Halyna Havrylchenko: endorse the DNR and assist with the separatist referendum or resign. They confronted her and other local officials directly during the city council meeting on April 23. A local thirty-five-year-old activist, Serhiy Kapkin, presented the council members with a collective letter signed, in his words, by over one hundred Pokrovsk residents. It contained a demand for city council to support a referendum on the status of the Donetsk oblast. Kapkin explained that the letter was to encourage council members to "adopt a legitimate resolution so that our town could then peacefully function."[20] His demand received an immediate pushback from one of the most influential local businessmen—the director of the town's largest mine, Zynoviy Pasternak. "One hundred and twenty people who signed this appeal decided to create their own republic. Now I want to talk to those people whom I represent to see what they think about it," asserted Pasternak, who also served on the oblast council. A female council member confronted Kapkin even more defiantly: "Who elected you? Ten thousand people at the rally by a show of hands? And millions elected us." When Kapkin again called for immediate action, saying that "people were fearful," another city council deputy, Anatoliy Zinchenko, cut him short. He pointed to the fate of Horlivka city council member Rybak, who was murdered by separatists days earlier: "He was abducted and killed in a barbarian manner. This is what we are fearful of.... This is *your* checkpoint standing there and *you* are intimidating people!" His vocal opposition illustrates how attitudes

---

[18] Author's archived video from Dobropillia, April 19, 2014. See "Dobropillia 2014," Harvard Dataverse, https://doi.org/10.7910/DVN/MU1NF6.

[19] Interview with Ruslan Trebushkin, November, 2018. The rallies in March also featured city council members from PR and KPU factions.

[20] Author archived video from Pokrovsk, April 23, 2014. See "Pokrovsk 2014," Harvard Dataverse, https://doi.org/10.7910/DVN/EUOZNV.

of some locals evolved. During the protests in Kyiv, Zinchenko refused to support Maidan because he "saw no point in replacing bandits with thieves conversant in English."[21] Still, he visited Donetsk when pro-Russian rallies began in March and saw the buses of people brought from neighboring Russian towns of Rostov and Taganrog. This was enough for him to understand that the conflict was no longer about political power but about Ukraine's future.

The rebuttal of separatist demands came not only from local council members but also from civic activists. One, Valentyn Pysarenko, read an appeal on the activists' behalf that condemned attempts to capture government buildings, raise separatist symbols, and elect "people's mayors." Now pro-Ukrainian activists defended the legality of Havrylchenko's rule and insisted on respecting her authority. The appeal reiterated that it represented the opinion of a majority of townspeople, who "overwhelmingly support Ukrainian unity." At the end of the council session Havrylchenko read a letter from a veteran miner who spoke on behalf of all miners of Pokrovsk: "We demand bringing order to the city where a group of people are raising flags of the occupying power. We are against federalization and referenda and any change in the country's system." The session revealed a clear pro-Ukrainian majority on city council, with no one willing to publicly endorse separatist demands.

The municipal newspaper *Mayak* was reflective of the anti-separatist stance of the local government in Pokrovsk. It abstained from circulating any DNR appeals and, instead, published educational articles on the Ukrainian history of Donbas and the true meaning of misused terms such as "federalism" and "fascism." One of its journalists, Oksana Vetoshko, explained that the paper purposefully waged a "quiet war" to counter Russian propaganda broadcast on television at the time.[22] Although Kapkin came to their office with requests to publish DNR materials, she said they managed to turn him away. Despite the newspaper's defiant stance, it never received any threats from local DNR activists. Still, separatist sympathizers remained visible. At the end of April hundreds of them, mainly young men, walked under DNR and NOD flags across Pokrovsk chanting "Referendum for Donbas!" That same day about two dozen Ukraine supporters protected by police gathered near the town's Shevchenko monument for a prayer.

<hr>

[21] Interview with Anatoliy Zinchenko, October 18, 2018.
[22] Interview with Oksana Vetoshko, October 18, 2018.

When Business Took the Lead

The only other major town in Donbas with a pro-Ukrainian resistance group was Mariupol. That group was formed following the assault by thugs under Russian banners on pro-Ukrainian demonstrators on April 13. Following the capture of Sloviansk, the resistance group gathered next to the police station in Mariupol to forestall a similar attack. Suddenly over one hundred young men, some carrying clubs, appeared on the street. They marched toward the two dozen pro-Ukrainian demonstrators with little to defend themselves. After the ensuing skirmishes, six pro-Ukrainian demonstrators were hospitalized, and many others were badly beaten. Following the assault some of the participants gathered in the office of the city council deputy Oleksandr Yaroshenko, the head of the opposition faction Front of Changes on the city council. During the meeting they decided to organize the Mariupol Patrol (Mariupolska Druzhyna; MD) to counter the separatist militia and provide protection to pro-Ukrainian demonstrations.[23] The financial backing for the initiative came from Oleksandr Taruta, an elder brother of the newly appointed Donetsk oblast governor.[24] He was the co-owner of a major construction company, Azovintex, headquartered in Mariupol. One of the leaders of MD, Oleksandr Pyrha, oversaw security in Taruta's company.[25] The new organization also reached out to police veterans led by the town's police chief Valeriy Androshchuk to form the backbone of the organization.

By that time Androshchuk was already holding meetings with former police officers and discussing ways of neutralizing the rising separatist threat. According to one participant, police veterans saw former convicts leading pro-Russian rallies and felt insulted that they could capture power.[26] Another source of backing for a pro-Ukrainian group was the local soccer ultras formed around the city club Illichiovets. About two dozen young men had already tried to act as a "shield" for pro-Ukrainian demonstrators at previous rallies. Now they sought special training to act more forcefully in response to likely attacks.[27] Both ultras and some members of MD attended training sessions at the Ukrainian military base outside the city. During subsequent rallies they appeared in uniform with helmets and

---

[23] Interview with Eduard Kolesov, November 20, 2018; interview with Viktoria Pridushchenko, November 19, 2018.
[24] Interview with Kolesov, 2018.
[25] Interview with Pridushchenko, 2018.
[26] Interview with "Ares," November 21, 2018.
[27] Ibid.

masks, short-wave radios, and pepper spray. Later, the ultras also collected intelligence for the volunteer battalions stationed outside the city. Although MD remained small, it demonstrated a local capacity for self-organization in defense of the Ukrainian state and became an additional pressure point for the separatists.

One clear example of this was a successful but short-lived retaking of the city council building on April 24. Early in the morning several dozen young men from MD and soccer ultras clubs entered the occupied building and clashed with pro-Russian activists inside. Once they forced most of them out of the building, the police units took control of the entrance. Still, there were only about thirty pro-Ukrainian activists inside the city council building at the time, and they were quickly surrounded by newly arrived separatist supporters: "We had to leave because if they blocked us in the city council building it could have become a 'second Odessa.'"[28] Another organizer of the raid confirmed, "We had no capacity to keep the building—this was a police task."[29] However, after short talks between local separatist leader Denis Kuzmenko and one of the police chiefs, the police units withdrew from their positions and the building returned under separatist control.

Beginning in mid-May separatists faced sudden pushback from the personnel of the two major metallurgical enterprises—Azovstal and Ilyicha—owned by Rinat Akhmetov. Initially their respective directors—Enver Tskitishvili and Yuri Zinchenko—sought an accommodation with separatist leaders and even issued a joint statement calling on Ukrainian troops to withdraw from the city. Following the May 11 referendum, they signed the memorandum on "order and security" with the mayor, the police chief, and Kuzmenko. Its text called on the Ukrainian authorities to remove military checkpoints surrounding the city and transfer control over public safety to municipal police and militia.[30] However, just a week later the stance of the two largest companies fully reversed in response to continued intimidation tactics by the militants. When factory directors announced a march for peace with workers' participation, militants threatened them with violence. This led Akhmetov to break with conciliatory rhetoric and issue an unusually harsh statement, published on the front page of the

---

[28] Interview with Kolesov, 2018.

[29] Oleksandr Hladkyi cited in Kateryna Hladka et al., eds., *Dobrobaty* (Kharkiv: Folio, 2018), 184.

[30] *Priazovskiy Rabochiy*, "Mariupolskie metallurgi, gorodskaia vlast, obshestvennost Mariupolia i lider DNR podpisali Memorandum o poriadke i bezopasnosti," May 17, 2014, 1.

town newspaper. He accused separatists of "fighting against the people of Donbas" and characterized their actions as "genocide." He also went after DNR leaders, calling them "a bunch of con-men who terrorize the people of Donbas."[31]

The directors of the two enterprises followed Akhmetov's lead. Speaking on local television they described the consequences of separatism for Mariupol in dire terms, warning that it would produce an "economic abyss" and "tens of thousands of city residents would lose their jobs and appear unable to feed their families."[32] They also attacked separatist authorities. Azovstal director Tskitishvili lamented that the true face of the DNR was "the face of a terrorists" whose only idea was "to grab and split [power] between themselves." Zinchenko, the director of the Ilyich factory, described pro-DNR locals as "bandits" who came to "break rather than build." He observed that they used to have "more supporters in the city, but turned people away with terrorism and banditry." Zinchenko predicted that "the circus will soon leave, but they can still shed blood and bring grief and horror to the towns of Donbas." Only the presidential elections scheduled for May 25, he argued, could prevent this outcome by establishing "legitimate authorities recognized all around the world."[33]

The top managers also addressed the factory workers directly. Since employees and families accounted for about a third of the city's population, management believed that they could have a decisive effect on the developments in the city.[34] In mid-May factory management started distributing daily news briefs aimed at discrediting the DNR. Vadym Boichenko, at the time the personnel director at Ilyicha factory, recalled, "At every factory shop we gathered up to three thousand people and showed photos of some DNR activists and how they were looting the city."[35] Factory management also prepared a slideshow for workers which emphasized the costly consequences of separatist victory: enterprises shut down, loss of income, rampant crime, regional isolation, and the paralysis of normal town life. "You will be the one making the decision!!!" declared the final slide. Boichenko admitted that only about a third of the workers believed pro-Ukrainian

---

[31] *Priazovskiy Rabochiy*, "Ekstrennoe zaiavlenie Rinata Akhmetova v sviazi s situatsiei v Donbasse," May 21, 2014, 1.

[32] Author's archived video from Mariupol. See "Mariupol 2014," Harvard Dataverse, https://doi.org/10.7910/DVN/4OBT5H.

[33] Ibid.

[34] Interview with Boichenko, 2018.

[35] Ibid.

appeals, while the rest were "either for DNR or against Ukraine." Still, in his view, the anti-DNR campaign might have persuaded at least some workers to avoid separatist rallies.[36]

By the end of May two forces competed for control of the city. Akhmetov and the management of his two factories mobilized over ten thousand workers for daily city patrols and paid workers for participation.[37] They set the tone of the news coverage in local media. They communicated directly with the central government in Kyiv on behalf of embattled local authorities who received personal threats from the separatists.[38] On the other side were over one hundred armed separatists who controlled several buildings in the city center and surrounded them with concrete blocks and wire. They issued appeals to locals to join them, and also engaged in frequent marauding and extortion of local businesses. However, their presence in the city was felt by only one neighborhood, where they established their base. Indicative of the ambiguity that emerged in Mariupol at the time, one pro-Ukrainian activist suggested that "there was never a feeling that the city fell in separatist hands."[39]

Deterring Collaboration

Resistance groups, which emerged in Svatove, Dobropillia, and, later, Mariupol, relied both on visible public actions and undercover coercive pressure. Pro-Ukrainian activists in Dobropillia made their first group appearance on the very day Girkin led the seizure of the police station in Sloviansk. One of the activists received a tip from a former policeman that two minibuses with DNR militants were moving from Donetsk to Dobropillia to emulate the actions in Sloviansk. He was concerned that the local police would surrender just as they did in Sloviansk: "Our police had a salary of two thousand hryvnias [~250 USD in early 2014], and in Russia they would receive five times that, so they were ready to betray their motherland."[40] Faced with the prospect of police defection, activists decided to defend the police station themselves. In a matter of hours hundreds of people surrounded the

---

[36] Author's presentation copy provided by Vadym Boichenko. See "Mariupol 2014," Harvard Dataverse, https://doi.org/10.7910/DVN/4OBT5H.

[37] Interview with Vladimir Khabarov, November 21, 2018.

[38] Interview with Khotlubei, 2018.

[39] Interview with Kolesov, 2018.

[40] Interview with Strepochenko, 2020.

building. Someone brought a truck full of tires and unloaded them near the entrance. When about thirty local DNR supporters arrived expecting to hold talks with the police chief exclusively, they had to overcome the pro-Ukrainian activists first. After angry exchanges, it became clear that the pro-DNR side's plan had failed. As a result, the two minibuses with supporters from Donetsk turned around near the village of Rodynske, about ten miles from Dobropillia. In Strepochenko's view, DNR militants avoided entering his town not out of fear of the Patriots, but because they "did not want to fight with town residents and expected locals to capture the police themselves."[41] Any confrontation with pro-Ukrainian supporters would have exposed local divisions and undermined separatist narratives about the unanimity of anti-Kyiv views among town residents.

A group in Svatove made themselves visible by driving around town in two dozen automobiles flying Ukrainian flags to signal to potential separatist sympathizers that there were "many people capable of action." Still, some locals showed their disapproval and shouted obscenities at the procession.[42] A self-defense member from Svatove, Anatoliy Kuzovenin, agreed that many had "negative views of self-defense and wanted to see Russia come to Svatove."[43] Still, there were no attempts to push back against pro-Ukrainian mobilization. Another local activist recalled that the power balance favored the pro-Ukrainian side: "Those who would have liked to come out under a Russian flag realized that it would not end to their benefit."[44] One local KPU member, who would later be prosecuted by the Ukrainian government on separatist charges, admitted that he felt intimidated by the emergence of self-defense in Svatove and feared that it could lead to violence.[45]

The only time pro-Ukrainian activists in Svatove were ready to use force was on May 7, when about thirty separatist militants led by Oleksiy Mozgovoi arrived at the district administration.[46] Mozgovoi was a native of the nearby village of Duvanka, where his parents still lived. Earlier he had worked in Svatove's military enlistment office and performed in its folk music ensemble. Rybalko knew Mozgovoi personally and remembered him as an impulsive man who often got into brawls and led a tumultuous life.[47] By early May, Mozgovoi commanded one of the largest battalions in Luhansk

[41] Ibid.
[42] Interview with Irkha, 2019.
[43] Interview with Kuzovenin, 2019.
[44] Interview with Irkha, 2019.
[45] Interview with Oleksandr Tsymbal, July 10, 2019.
[46] Interview with Kuzovenin, 2019.
[47] Interview with Rybalko, 2019.

and had established high-level political connections in Moscow. Although not yet stationed in Lysychansk, he started traveling across the region to mobilize local separatists in preparation for the referendum.

Despite little separatist activity in Svatove, there were dozens of active separatist supporters in town allegedly waiting for orders from Mozgovoi.[48] Rybalko was afraid that they would use the day of Mozgovoi's arrival to capture the police station and the city council building. In cooperation with the self-defense group, he set up small armed groups around the town center to counter the possible assault.[49] Self-defense members knew that Mozgovoi had an advantage in firepower, so they could not stop him on the town's outskirts.[50] Some even thought of creative ways they could disperse the welcoming crowd, like opening a beehive full of bees next to the rally.[51] Ultimately there was no need to engage in crowd control. Mozgovoi appeared without any prior coordination with his supporters. One communist activist recalled that he was making calls to his colleagues that day and found them in complete disbelief about Mozgovoi's arrival.[52]

Rybalko met Mozgovoi in the office of the head of the district council, a longtime member of PR sympathetic to Russia. The militant leader made two predictable requests: to assist with the holding of the referendum in Svatove and to raise LNR flags over municipal buildings. In response, Rybalko did not mince words: "I told Mozgovoi that he should remember what guerrilla warfare is and that any separatist flags would be immediately removed."[53] The district council head was less categorical but similarly refused to take any steps before receiving authorization from the council members.[54] This joint rebuttal might have compelled Mozgovoi to avoid putting any further pressure on the local authorities. Before departure, he even jokingly promised the police chief that he would not attempt to capture the police station since his militants "had enough weapons already." In hindsight, Rybalko believed that "the rumors of eight hundred people drafted in Svatove's self-defense could have deterred the militants from using violence."[55] Separatists drew their strength from creating an impression of grassroots support. Any violent altercations with the locals that day would have ruined that.

<hr>

48 Ibid.
49 Interview with Irkha, 2019.
50 Interview with Kuzovenin, 2019.
51 Interview with Irkha, 2019.
52 Interview with Tsymbal, 2019.
53 Interview with Rybalko, 2019.
54 Interview with Kuzovenin, 2019.
55 Interview with Rybalko, 2019.

Starobilsk, a town just an hour's drive from Svatove, illustrates how the absence of an assertive mayor could quickly induce collaboration by municipal authorities. At the time, the town was governed by the head of the district state administration, Valeriy Harkavyi. He had presided over the region since the 1990s and recently worked as a director of Starobilsk Community College. On the morning of May 7, he observed from his office a large crowd gathering outside. Several men entered the building, climbed up the stairs, took down the Ukrainian flag, and threw it from the roof. Amid the cheering crowd, one person picked it up from the ground and carried it away. This was Volodymyr Vynnyk, a former Security Service officer known in town for his pro-Ukrainian views. Vynnyk identified signs that the rally was tightly planned: some of the participants came on minibuses from the neighboring villages, and people with handheld radios were coordinating the activity. In Vynnyk's view, the rally could have been carried out only with the assistance of former local administrators and businessmen: "Our authorities through local oligarchs, large landowners, ordered criminals to organize the capture of the administration. Since many of them lived off the smuggling of goods to Russia they were not interested in any change."[56]

The overall purpose of this staged gathering became clear when Mozgovoi, wearing a green uniform and accompanied by two armed guards, appeared at the entrance of the building. "Are they from Luhansk? Are they Right Sector?" anxious voices shouted, the crowd unable to recognize any militant leader.[57] "They must be ours!" someone responded. When a rally moderator proclaimed, "These are the defenders of the people," the crowd erupted in a wild cheer. Meanwhile, one of the local separatist leaders, Illia Monachenko, appealed to Mozgovoi to attack pro-Ukrainian activists: "You need to remove those who would interfere with the holding of the referendum … I know that there will be provocations since I spoke to pro-Ukrainian forces here and they told me that they would not allow any referendum." "This is why we are here," Mozgovoi sternly replied.

When Harkavyi appeared in front of the crowd he was immediately struck by its size: "I never saw this many people gathering for a rally in Starobilsk, and I lived there for most of my life."[58] With the public on his side, Mozgovoi read appeals from "the LNR people's council" and from the "presidium of

---

[56] Interview with Volodymyr Vynnyk, July 9, 2019. Weeks earlier Vynnyk's grocery story was put on fire in a reprisal for his pro-Ukrainian activism.

[57] Author's archived video from Starobilsk, May 7, 2014. See "Starobilsk 2014," Harvard Dataverse, https://doi.org/10.7910/DVN/LJFHAG.

[58] Interview with Valeriy Harkavyi, July 10, 2019.

Luhansk oblast council" to prepare for a referendum. When Harkavyi tried to object, Mozgovoi issued an ultimatum: "You need to pick one position—either you continue supporting Kyiv or you side with the people. . . . And if you disagree with the people you need to resign." After a brief exchange, Mozgovoi turned to the crowd: "I am Aleksei Mozgovoi, people's militia of Luhanshchina. We just delivered the resolution of the presidium of Luhansk oblast council on holding a referendum. And now your head of administration will make a statement that he will support it, right?" Harkavyi stepped forward and shouted in a high-pitched voice, "About twenty minutes ago we agreed that you will have ballot boxes. Once your initiative group sends an appeal to the authorities I will assist with the referendum. What else do you want from me?" With apparent satisfaction, Mozgovoi turned to the crowd: "Please do not seize the administration building. They need to keep on working. Otherwise, only bricks will remain." He then glanced at the police chief: "As to the police, they need to make a choice." Standing in a plain shirt with several uniformed police behind him, Chief Askar Liaishev declared, "The police are with the people of Starobelsk!"[59] Mozogovoi's mission was over—the civilian administrators and law enforcement had pledged to cooperate with the separatists. In a few minutes, he left Starobilsk never to return.

Harkavyi later explained that even that brief visit by Mozgovoi was sufficient to convince him that separatists had the upper hand, primarily because he felt no support from law enforcement: "I thought we had the police and SBU, but they were not doing anything—seventy to eighty percent of policemen were ready to join the other side."[60] Vynnyk and other pro-Ukrainian activists who watched the rally believed that Harkavyi could have responded differently: "He could have openly objected or left town and refused to participate in the rally. But he became their collaborator."[61] Harkavyi, however, explained that without organized grassroots support his defiance was senseless: "Imagine I would tell Mozgovoi to fuck off . . . and they would then take me to the basement in Luhansk. Who would take care of me? Our activists were standing right in the middle of the crowd—just observing."[62] The

---

[59] After Russian troops occupied Starobilsk on March 2, 2022, Askar Liaishev collaborated with the Russian occupying forces and was assassinated on August 12, 2022. NV, "Poiavilos videos momenta podryva avot mestnogo kollaboranta v Starobelske," August 26, 2022, https://nv.ua/ukraine/events/askyar-layshev-moment-vzryva-mashiny-kollaboranta-v-starobelske-popal-na-video-50265946.html.

[60] Interview with Harkavyi, 2019.

[61] Interview with V. Vynnyk, 2019. One pro-Ukrainian activist, however, believed that "it was senseless to resist them" because "the crowd was too emotional." Interview with Kahala, 2019.

[62] Interview with Harkavyi, 2019.

district head also felt abandoned by the regional and national authorities: "There were no specific instructions prior to the referendum, neither from Kyiv nor from Luhansk." Even his deputy told him openly that he supported Russia and refused to work with him if he sided with Kyiv. As a result, Harkavyi allowed separatist activists to take the official ballot boxes and instructed personnel to let them inside the polling stations. On the day of the referendum, all the polling stations in Starobilsk but one were open.

Selective Violence

By mid-May the pro-Ukrainian self-defense group in Dobropillia was divided into "coercive" and "humanitarian" wings.[63] While the "humanitarian" group was responsible for nonviolent advocacy of the Ukrainian cause, those on the "coercive" side were preparing for a targeted pressure campaign against separatist sympathizers. They complied a special registry of pro-Russian activists using tips from town residents. Sarcastically titled "The Mean Separatists of Our Town," it included the main organizers of separatist actions and those who traveled to Donetsk for instructions.

The use of coercive tactics became possible due to a newly found ally: Governor Ihor Kolomoiskiy of the Dnipropetrovsk oblast. His deputy and business partner, Henadiy Korban, visited Dobropillia on May 11, the day of the separatist referendum, to meet with group leaders. Strepochenko recalled that he was not aware of Korban's views at the time and was surprised by his offer to assist with the voting. Their cooperation, however, allowed the Patriots to respond to local separatists more forcefully. Korban agreed to provide local activists with hunting rifles at a discounted price, which Strepochenko brought from Dnipro to Dobropillia in the trunk of his car. They received at least twenty rifles at the price of around 1,200 USD each and had to bribe police to expedite the issuing of permits.[64] The firearms were then distributed among members of the organization and used during coercive attacks on separatist activists.

In late May the coercive wing of the Patriots launched a series of abductions of separatist supporters, some of whom were transported to Dnipro for further interrogation.[65] About a dozen residents were abducted in this

---

[63] Interview with Chetveriov, 2018.
[64] Author's meeting with the members of Patriots of Dobropillia, October 3, 2018.
[65] Ibid.

manner, and at least four were transferred to Dnipro. At the request of SBU operatives, a prominent separatist supporter, Lyudmila Vinogradskaya, was abducted and transferred to the base of the volunteer battalion Dnipro-1 several times.[66] Still, to the surprise of many Patriots members, Ukrainian security officers ultimately released all those suspected of supporting separatism. According to one group member, the goal of such action was not to punish separatist sympathizers but to intimidate them: "If we saw that a particular separatist activist was gaining popularity among *vata* [a derogatory term for separatists], we would take him out of town or warn them to flee. If these leaders followed our orders, then their followers would get quiet as well."[67]

Despite the dubious legality of such actions, even local activists suspicious of the true motives of the Patriots accepted their use. One activist said, "The violent methods of Patriots were the only ones possible since everything was happening very quickly, and local authorities distanced themselves from everything."[68] A local resident estimated that about 80% of Dobropillia's residents supported the DNR. Being in the minority, Patriots needed to act in a particularly forceful manner to deter further separatist mobilization.[69] City council secretary Viktor Dreval, on the other hand, recalled that he was concerned about Patriots' intimidating tactics, particularly as a potential trigger for retaliations. "I did not want to see the war here," he said. Still, he recognized that these coercive resources ultimately allowed Patriots to come out on top: "They prevailed because they were the ones who had weapons and could exercise full control over town."[70] As Strepochenko observed, "Every person is moved most powerfully by two emotions—love and fear. We did not have time to make them love us, but we certainly made them fearful."[71]

Subverting the Referendum

Despite the evidence of pro-Ukrainian resistance in several towns in Donbas, pro-Russian activists still sought to force the referendum process there by setting up voting booths or polling stations. In Svatove the referendum

---

[66] Ibid.
[67] Ibid.
[68] Interview with Volodymyr Oros, October 3, 2018.
[69] Ibid.
[70] Interview with Viktor Dreval, October 3, 2018.
[71] Interview with Strepochenko, 2019.

organizers were the KPU city council deputies. Chief among them was Vitaliy Pryn, a teacher in the local school and a "genuine believer in the LNR."[72] Pryn and his wife, a town library director, fled to Russia shortly after the referendum. The only separatist polling in Svatove was conducted in the open square next to the city council building. Despite the public visibility, it attracted a relatively large crowd, revealing hundreds of active supporters of the LNR among town residents. One supporter recalled that the people felt "euphoric" and expected that "regional autonomy would secure them from chaos in Kyiv."[73] Ultimately, about 1,200 ballots were cast in Svatove on May 11, which represented close to 10% of the town's adult population.[74] Self-defense members abstained from interfering with the polling but decided to document the vote count afterward. Several of them went to the Communist Party office as observers, with the intention of preventing fraud and recording those involved in the counting.[75] Ultimately, two communist officials who remained in Svatove were convicted by the Ukrainian courts and served time in jail for their role in the referendum.

In Dobropillia, the separatist referendum received an indirect challenge from the local pro-Ukrainian activists. During a meeting with DNR representatives from Donetsk the mayor insisted on the impossibility of holding a referendum. Among the reasons he cited were the absence of legal grounds, the lack of funds, and restricted access to voter rolls controlled by the Central Election Commission.[76] On the day of the referendum, local authorities refused to open any municipal buildings for polling but allowed referendum organizers to set up tents in the central square. In response, Patriots launched an "alternative referendum" across the street under the slogan "For peace, order, unity!" Their ballot question was about the possible merger of Dobropillia district with neighboring Dnipropetrovsk oblast. This was an open trolling of the separatists since Governor Kolomoiskiy of the Dnipropetrovsk oblast was a vocal supporter of Ukraine's integrity. The counterinitiative exposed a major disparity in attitudes among town residents. "There were three hundred sixty people who participated in our referendum and about three thousand who voted in the DNR referendum," one of the organizers admitted.[77] Still, the very presence of pro-Ukrainian

---

[72] Interview with Kuzovenin, 2019.

[73] Interview with Tsymbal, 2019.

[74] Interview with Irkha, 2019.

[75] Ibid.

[76] Iana Ruban, "V Dobropolie snova protestuyut," *Dobropolie na Ladoniah*, April 30, 2014, 2, https://issuu.com/dnl_plus/docs/418_18.

[77] Author's interview with members of Patriots of Dobropillia, 2018.

activists undermined the impression of unanimity behind the separatist project conveyed by DNR polling in other towns. The local newspaper clearly pointed this out: "Those who voted in [an anti-separatist] survey saw no future in the DNR or Russia, did not want to return to the 1990s and believed that the Donbas economy would collapse in the case of its secession."[78] The following day, when pro-DNR activists wanted to hold a celebratory motorcade in Dobropillia, Patriots in black balaclavas and with gun replicas in their hands blocked their movement and forced them to disperse.[79]

The separatist referendum in neighboring Pokrovsk was the only one in Donbas which pro-Ukrainian groups managed to subvert, but not without bloodshed. It became a turning point in the escalating confrontation between the separatists and pro-Ukrainian paramilitaries in this town. The largest makeshift polling station was set up outside the city council building with cardboard boxes used to collect ballots. The organizers had no voter rolls, so women sitting behind round plastic tables had to copy names of individual voters from their passports onto blank pages.[80] The lines of people waiting for their turn to cast DNR ballots formed early in the morning. In the afternoon, however, referendum organizers learned about several vehicles with armed men inside moving from the Dnipropetrovsk oblast to Pokrovsk.[81] The two green vans had the logo of Privatbank, a Kolomoiskiy-owned bank, on their side panels. The arrival of the Dnipro-1 battalion had been organized by the oligarch a few weeks earlier, after repeated requests of local city council deputies. One of them, Zinchenko, traveled to Dnipropetrovsk and met with Kolomoiskiy's associates to persuade them to send battalion members to Pokrovsk.[82] In anticipation of a possible attack, the referendum organizers hid all the ballot boxes and released commission members.

When the vans reached the city about thirty men in black uniforms armed with machine guns jumped out and rushed to the entrance of the city council building. Several took firing positions around the square in front of the building and near the police station. A crowd of DNR supporters who came

[78] *Dobropolie na Ladoniah*, "Referendum sostoialsia—a chto zhe dal'she?," May 14, 2014, 2, https://issuu.com/dnl_plus/docs/420_20.

[79] Author's archived video of an interview with Aleksandr Sergeyev, press-secretary of "Patriots of Dobropillia," May 14, 2014. See "Dobropillia 2014," Harvard Dataverse, https://doi.org/10.7910/DVN/MU1NF6.

[80] Author's archived video from Pokrovsk. May 11, 2014. See "Pokrovsk 2014," Harvard Dataverse, https://doi.org/10.7910/DVN/EUOZNV.

[81] Interview with Oleksandr Aladin, August 18, 2020.

[82] Interview with Zinchenko, 2018.

to vote observed these movements with open resentment. Despite repeated warnings, they refused to disperse, and some kept shouting insults at the paramilitary troops. When several men came out of the crowd, soldiers fired a series of warning shots and disappeared behind the doors of the city council building. Two men left bleeding on the ground were a forty-eight-year-old miner, Yuriy Mykolenko, and thirty-nine-year-old local resident Vadym Khudych. Both died where they fell. Another wounded man had his leg amputated. Hours later the entire armed unit withdrew, leaving many residents in shock and seething with anger.

All officials immediately sought to distance themselves from the incident. The police statement claimed, "We don't know who they were or who they support or don't support, and we don't know why they left."[83] Kolomoisky's administration denied that the Dnipro-1 battalion was in Pokrovsk on referendum day, contradicting earlier public claims by the unit commander.[84] Mayor Havrylchenko later issued a statement expressing her condolences and dismissing rumors that the armed group arrived at the invitation of local authorities.[85] However, coordination between the armed unit and local officials was obvious. Upon arrival, the armed men freely gained access to the executive council building and used it as their operational base. Moreover, according to one local insider, Kolomoiskiy agreed to send his battalion to Pokrovsk in return for the promise of political benefits from local authorities.[86] Six months later, Yevhen Geller, a businessman affiliated with Kolomoiskiy, won a seat from Pokrovsk district in the parliamentary election amid numerous allegations of election fraud.[87]

In hindsight, violence on referendum day was a tipping point for Pokrovsk. It deterred many DNR supporters from taking any further actions and ended all separatist rallies in town.[88] The town's separatist leader Oleksandr Aladin recalled that a few days later he had a chance encounter with

[83] Sabra Ayres, "Chaos and Fear Grip Residents in Eastern Ukraine after Referendum," *Aljazeera America*, May 12, 2014, http://america.aljazeera.com/articles/2014/5/12/chaos-and-fear-gripeastukraineafterthereferendum.html.

[84] One of the Dnipro-1 soldiers, Volodymyr Parasiuk, confirmed that battalion commander Yuriy Bereza sent a platoon to Pokrovsk to "liberate the city from the separatists." See Hladka et al., *Dobrobaty*, 253.

[85] *Mayak*, "Zaiavlenie i.o. Krasnoarmeiskogo gorodskogo golovy G. A. Gavrilchenko," May 16, 2014, 1.

[86] Interview with Zinchenko, 2018.

[87] *Nashi Hroshi*, "Kassir Partii regionov peremetnulsia v lager Kolomoiskogo,: November 4, 2014, http://nashigroshi.org/2014/11/04/kassyr-partyy-rehyonov-peremetnulsya-v-laher-kolomojskoho/.

[88] Interview with Lilia Borovaia, October 16, 2018.

a man wounded on referendum day. Instead of a demand to avenge the violence, Aladin heard the man's emotional plea to refrain from setting up checkpoints or engaging in further separatist activities.[89] After this, Aladin decided to leave town for good. He first joined Girkin's unit in Sloviansk and later moved to Yenakievo, where he served under Bezler's command. The Dnipro battalion returned to Pokrovsk on May 24 to guard the polling stations during the presidential election. Shortly afterward, the Ukrainian military and National Guard units set up checkpoints on all roads leading into Pokrovsk and finalized their control over the city.

Presidential elections were held in all towns where pro-Ukrainian resistance groups were present. Svatove district had 93% of their polling stations open for the election—the highest share in Donbas. In Mariupol, the largest town in Donbas where the presidential election took place, the election became possible following Akhmetov's intervention. The management of his two factories played a crucial role in helping to secure the ballots and ensure the operation of most electoral commissions despite separatist threats. They provided vehicles and protection to deliver ballots to the electoral commissions and sent groups of factory worker observers to each polling station.[90] According to Mariupol mayor at the time, Yuriy Khotlubei, "There were fifty to sixty workers gathered at each polling station to prevent the possible attack."[91] In the end, 202 out of 216 polling stations in the city were opened for voting, and about 15% of registered voters participated in the election.[92]

In Dobropillia, local authorities turned to Patriots for help organizing the presidential election.[93] By that time the 95th Air Assault Brigade was redeployed to the vicinity of Sloviansk, so Patriots requested military reinforcements to prevent any subversion on the part of the separatists. The Kolomoiskiy-sponsored Dnipro-1 battalion arrived in Dobropillia on May 22. On election day its armed volunteers blocked all streets near the district election commission building, while snipers took positions on roofs in case of a separatist attack. In the end, seventy-seven of the one hundred polling stations in the district were open for voting. By then all separatist actions in Dobropillia had subsided. Several DNR supporters left for Donetsk or

---

[89] Interview with Aladin, 2020.
[90] Interview with Boichenko, 2018.
[91] Interview with Khotlubei, 2018.
[92] Based on the data of the Central Election Commission of Ukraine, https://www.cvk.gov.ua/vibory_category/vibori-prezidenta-ukraini/pozachergovi-vibori-prezidenta-ukraini-25-travnya-2014-roku.html# (last accessed: May 15, 2022).
[93] Interview with Strepochenko, 2020.

Sloviansk, where they joined Girkin's unit.[94] Others withdrew from all political activism as the failure of the DNR to establish a presence in town became clear. Still, some undercover DNR supporters remained and managed to stage a revenge attack on the self-defense leaders. On the morning of July 22, Chetveriov went to Strepochenko's house and noticed a brick-shaped juice box lying near the entrance. The moment he picked it up, the object exploded, tearing away his fingers and leaving him virtually deaf for the next several months.[95]

Signaling Coercive Capacity

One of the factors that encouraged the formation of pro-Ukrainian resistance groups in Dobropillia was the stationing of Ukrainian armed forces or volunteer units nearby. The organizers of the self-defense group there agreed that the early stationing of the 25th Airborne Brigade from the Dnipropetrovsk oblast in the town's vicinity had a reassuring effect. They now believed that the power balance could tip in their favor. As Chetveriov later suggested, had there been no Ukrainian military presence near Dobropillia he likely would have gone to Kyiv and joined a volunteer battalion there instead of organizing a self-defense group locally.[96] The capture of Sloviansk and Kramatorsk increased hesitation among some activists on whether further participation in self-defense was worth the risk. So the deployment of the brigade became the focal point for local pro-Ukrainian organizing and reassured those who hesitated.

Later in April another military convoy of armored vehicles from the 95th Air Assault Brigade appeared outside Dobropillia. Strepochenko shared his contacts with the commander and quickly received a phone call from one of the officers regarding "uninvited guests" detained by the soldiers.[97] When he arrived at the brigade's temporary base, he saw nine men and one woman lying on the ground with their hands tied. They were detained for obstructing the movement of the convoy and hurling insults at the soldiers. Eight of them turned out to be from Druzhkivka, a separatist-controlled town an hour away, while the other two were from a nearby village. Strepochenko

---

[94] Interview with Dreval, 2018.
[95] Interview with Chetveriov, 2018.
[96] Ibid.
[97] Interview with Strepochenko, 2020.

even recognized one of the locals. What struck him, however, was the decisive response of the commanders. Rather than engaging in talks, as was common in similar episodes earlier, they quickly arrested the separatists.

Strepochenko realized that the military units could help demonstrate Ukraine's preponderance of force to those sympathetic to the DNR. Patriots repeatedly asked the commanders to send their soldiers and vehicles to guard the police and city streets. On April 30, when separatist supporters planned to stage a motorcade demonstration under DNR flags in Dobropillia, a military convoy of two trucks, four Humvees, and one armored personnel carrier arrived at the police station to "meet the new police chief." The following day, when DNR supporters held a rally to agitate for the referendum, the Ukrainian soldiers cordoned off the central part of town and prevented cars from traveling the main streets.[98] Military checkpoints were also set up at the entrances to the town and all vehicles were inspected. The show of force was intentionally designed to signal the preeminence of Ukraine's coercive capacity.

The proximity of Ukrainian military forces was crucial in keeping militants out of Rubizhne. Although, until July, it was designated a separatist-controlled territory on Ukrainian official maps, there was no visible militant presence or checkpoints on the streets. Rather, the town became a contested area. The stationing of units from the 30th Mechanized Brigade near Krasnianka village, just five miles from Rubizhne, led some locals to bring them food and other material supplies.[99] Their presence also encouraged denunciations, which enabled the soldiers to conduct targeted raids into Rubizhne to capture some of the militants.[100]

In addition to the regular military, the volunteer battalions also had a demobilizing effect on the separatists. Pro-Ukrainian self-defense forces in Starobilsk, which failed to organize in April due to the reluctance of local authorities, suddenly received a boost from the volunteer battalion deployed in the area. Its name, Aidar, came from the river that flows from the Russian-Ukrainian border through Starobilsk and further south to Luhansk. Battalion commander Serhiy Melnychuk, who earlier failed to establish a base in Svatove, found an alternative location just sixty kilometers further east.

---

[98] Author's archived video from Dobropillia, May 1, 2014. See "Dobropillia 2014," Harvard Dataverse, https://doi.org/10.7910/DVN/MU1NF6.

[99] *Suspilne Donbas*, "Povernuty Donbas: Rubizhne."

[100] Interview with Artyukh, June 13, 2019. When a local businessman received a tip that militants were looting his house, he called Ukrainian soldiers nearby to interfere and detain the intruders. Interview with Kharchuk, 2019.

Despite the successful holding of the referendum in Starobilsk, separatist activists made no further attempt to establish their authority over the town. There was no sign of them patrolling the streets or guarding government buildings. After the referendum, Starobilsk turned into what some locals called a "gray zone"—a contested territory over which neither side could claim full control. As a local activist Volodymyr Hryhorenko explained, "If one walked around town in early May, they wouldn't understand which authorities were here. Despite the LNR flag flying over the state administration building, most of the district was 'no man's land.'" Hryhorenko remembered how he traveled to a neighboring village with the Ukrainian flag displayed on top of his car and faced no pushback. He concluded that separatists were "not capable of organizing here."[101] Another local activist agreed: "They could not organize any serious militancy in Starobilsk because they were too weak here—they just did not have enough supporters."[102] This allowed Melnychuk's newly formed Aidar battalion to reestablish Ukraine's coercive preponderance there. Upon arrival, he distributed firearms to about sixty local self-defense members and pro-Ukrainian activists. One of them recalled receiving arms—a gun and two grenades each—under the legal pretext of staging special "field exercises" for reserve soldiers.[103] But they were allowed to keep their weapons for as long as they served in the battalion.

The stationing of Aidar battalion in the abandoned meat factory on the outskirts of Starobilsk empowered other pro-Ukrainian organizers to act. Two days after the referendum, on May 13, a dozen of them went to the district administration building and removed the LNR and red Communist Party flags. Separatist supporters tried to interfere but failed to stop them. A day later, Aidar fighters raided the separatist office, where all the referendum ballots were stored, and took down the last LNR flag.[104] They also set up checkpoints on the roads around the town. When some locals obstructed a military convoy moving through town on May 17, several cars and a yellow minibus with two dozen Aidar fighters soon arrived. Dressed in casual athletic outfits or shorts and sandals and brandishing guns and automatic rifles, they fired into the air and quickly apprehended several protesters.[105] A dozen police present at the scene were pushed aside. "Someone was

---

[101] Interview with Hryhorenko, 2019.
[102] Interview with V. Vynnyk, 2019.
[103] Interview with Tsarevskyi, 2019.
[104] Ibid.
[105] Author's archived video from Starobilsk, May 2014. See "Starobilsk 2014," Harvard Dataverse, https://doi.org/10.7910/DVN/LJFHAG.

wounded in the leg. So local separatists got scared and lay low after that," an Aidar volunteer recalled.[106] In the view of one local, the quick defeat of the separatists in Starobilsk resulted from the absence of an armed wing: "If Mozgovoi left about fifty rifles to our locals they would have showed greater confidence."[107] Others argued that separatist leaders counted on the sheer indifference of Starobilsk residents in planning the consolidation of their rule: "Without Aidar's arrival in mid-May the contact line [dividing Ukraine and separatist-controlled areas] would have been along the Kharkiv oblast."[108]

Volunteer battalions were also crucial for restoring Ukraine's control over Mariupol. By early May the Ukrainian armed forces were already based on its outskirts. They used small mobile units composed of volunteers to conduct raids into the city to collect data and capture individual militants. One of the participants recalled, "There was total chaos in the city, and local law enforcement could not control anything—all the scoundrels from the police defected to the militant side, while the rest put on civilian clothes and stayed at home, waiting to see how it would all end."[109] The main hub of the Ukrainian coercive presence was Mariupol Airport. Located on the eastern side of the city, five miles away from the center, it served as the base for several Ukrainian units: the 72nd Mechanized Brigade deployed from the Kyiv region, volunteers from the Dnipro battalion, National Guard units, and the newly formed Azov battalion. Azov was officially created on May 5 by Andriy Biletskyi, the leader of an ultranationalist organization, Patriot of Ukraine. It immediately attracted not just the members of the organization but also Maidan activists and even foreigners who shared Biletskyi's far-right ideology.[110] In addition, fifty members of MD joined the Azov ranks.[111] As a result, Azov's membership grew from several dozen fighters in early May to 150 by mid-June.[112]

Azov made its first appearance on the streets of Mariupol along with the volunteer battalion Dnipro-1 on the evening of May 6 in an attempt to clear the city council building. On May 9 Azov fighters also came to defend the police station captured by the militants. This operation ended with the burning of the police building and withdrawal of all remaining Ukrainian

[106] Interview with Kahala, 2019.
[107] Interview with Hryhorenko, 2019.
[108] Interview with 2019.
[109] Mykola Kravchenko, ed., *Vyzvolennia Mariupolia* (Kyiv: Orientyr, 2018), 36.
[110] Ibid., 124.
[111] Interview with Pridushchenko, 2018.
[112] Kravchenko, *Vyzvolennia Mariupolia*, 24.

troops from the city. Despite initial setbacks, Azov established its training base in Berdiansk, a neighboring town in the Zaporizhzhia region on the Azov Sea and forty-five miles from Mariupol. According to one recollection, nationalist beliefs made Azov fighters better motivated than regular troops.[113] Hence, Ukrainian authorities turned to Azov to lead the operation against separatist militants in Mariupol.[114] Biletskyi and his deputy, Vadym Troian, became regular participants in meetings with the National Guard commander Stepan Poltorak, who planned the operation to retake the city.[115]

By early June separatists realized that they were far outnumbered by Ukrainian forces and could not offer an effective resistance given the absence of new recruits. The reconnaissance assault on a separatist position by Azov fighters on May 26 resulted in a fierce gun battle on city streets. This led a new militant commander, Andriy Borisov, to publicly lament the lack of tangible support from the locals: "We don't have real men here. On Zello [a push-to-talk communication app] there are thousands of people discussing things . . . but when there is an attack, they get silent."[116] While Ukrainians were aware of the dwindling numbers of separatist fighters, they were still preparing for intense street battles and postponed the assault until mid-June. In the early morning hours of June 13, the Ukrainian forces launched a joint operation which ended with the capture of separatist-held buildings and the raising of Ukrainian flags over all municipal buildings. The operation was conducted jointly by Azov, Dnipro, and the National Guard units and lasted about five hours.[117] Azov spearheaded the assault, while Dnipro participated in the cleanup operation. National Guard soldiers had to provide outer security to capture fleeing militants. One of the soldiers remembered, "The city was in deep silence, the streets were deserted. There were no cars on the road except our truck."[118] Several Azov fighters admitted that they were surprised by the lack of serious resistance on the part of the separatists.[119] The operation ended with no fatalities on the Ukrainian side; only five soldiers were wounded by detonations of improvised explosive devices. On the separatist side, at least seven were reported killed and several dozen captured

---

[113] Ibid., 45.

[114] Murlykina, *Mariupol. Posledniy Forpost*, 221.

[115] Ibid., 223.

[116] Author's archived video from Mariupol, May 27, 2014. See "Mariupol 2014," Harvard Dataverse, https://doi.org/10.7910/DVN/4OBT5H.

[117] Kravchenko, *Vyzvolennia Mariupolia*, 30.

[118] Ibid., 66.

[119] Ibid., 37.

in subsequent house searches. As it turned out, Borisov and most local separatist activists had fled the city hours before the Ukrainian attack.[120]

Fighting Fire with Fire

The examples of Dobropillia and Svatove—two towns located on opposite ends of Donbas—suggest that the fall of the entire region under separatist control was hardly an inevitable outcome. Even though each town had a large share of locals who embraced separatist goals, they were unable to organize and impose their demands on the municipal authorities in the absence of sizable armed militant units. When towns were located far from the militant strongholds, such as Sloviansk and Horlivka, separatists there usually lacked any coercive resources. Pro-Ukrainian self-defense groups there were particularly effective in tilting the power balance in favor of the Ukrainian state.

The coordination dilemmas of local Ukrainians in Donbas were resolved either by local officials who would set the anti-separatist agenda or wealthy businessmen willing to invest resources in launching and sustaining self-defense efforts. The proximity of regular Ukrainian troops or volunteer battalions served as a further boost for self-defense. Their coordinated actions in several towns signaled that coercive preponderance was on the government's side. In each town where Ukrainian self-defense groups were organized, activists could either apply direct coercive pressure against separatists or credibly threaten the use of force. This proved sufficient to deter seizure of government buildings or collaboration of the local authorities and left these towns outside the separatists' reach.

---

[120] Ibid., 81.

Chapter 9

Beyond Donbas

Why Separatism Failed in Kharkiv and Odesa

On March 1 thousands of people gathered on major squares in Kharkiv and Odesa to protest the new post-Maidan government. These protests resembled similar rallies organized that day across Donbas. There were numerous Russian flags; some of the rally participants were wearing masks and helmets; the speakers called for federalization of Ukraine and for holding a referendum on the country's future; the crowds responded with the usual cheer: "Russia!" In Kharkiv, hundreds of Russian citizens arrived from the neighboring Belgorod oblast to increase the rally size.[1] In Odesa, Russian actors monitored the rally, coordinated actions of pro-Russian activists, and reported back to Moscow.[2] It seemed that the wave of separatist activism, backed by Russian special operation forces and adventurists, was about to engulf not only one region but also two of the country's largest cities outside the capital. Eight weeks later, however, just as militants in Donbas were preparing for the fateful referendum, most of the separatist leaders either fled Kharkiv and Odesa or found themselves behind bars. Meanwhile, popular mobilization behind the pro-Russian agenda dissipated there almost completely.

This chapter compares the background conditions in Donbas, on the one hand, and Kharkiv and Odesa, on the other, including prevalent identity and historical narratives, electoral politics, and Russia's influence. It then examines the reasons for demobilization of pro-Russian protests outside Donbas and the failure of local separatist leaders there to implement elements of the secessionist strategy used in Crimea and, later, in Donetsk and Luhansk. Three variables that proved significant in keeping some of the

---

[1] Interview with Oleksandr Fisun, May 24, 2019.

[2] Embassy of Ukraine to the United Kingdom of Great Britain and Northern Ireland, "Ukraine's Prosecutor's General Office Materials of the Criminal Proceedings against Russian Officials," September 13, 2016, https://uk.mfa.gov.ua/en/news/50778-ukraines-prosecutors-general-office-materials-of-the-criminal-proceedings-against-russian-officials.

Seize the City, Undo the State. Serhiy Kudelia, Oxford University Press. © Oxford University Press (2025). DOI: 10.1093/9780197795576.003.0010

Table 9.1 Types of Response to Pro-Russian Mobilization in Donetsk, Luhansk, Kharkiv, and Odesa, March–May 2014

	Donetsk	Luhansk	Kharkiv	Odesa
Pro-Ukrainian self-defense groups	No	No	Yes	Yes
State coercive response	No	No	Yes	No
Elite opposition	No	No	Yes	Yes

towns in Donbas, like Svatove and Dobropillia, outside separatist control also appeared decisive in defeating separatist challenges in Kharkiv and Odesa (Table 9.1).

First, following the victory of the Euromaidan revolution, both towns witnessed an increase in pro-Ukrainian popular mobilization as well as a rise in pro-Russian activism. Collective actions of local supporters of a unitary Ukraine and of separatist alternatives revealed a more even distribution of preferences there than in towns of Donbas. Second, the state demonstrated a stronger coercive presence in Kharkiv and Odesa and applied force more consistently to quell separatist challenges. This disrupted the plans of separatist leaders and deterred their supporters from pursuing escalation. Third, key local elite actors sabotaged and even openly resisted attempts to impose a separatist agenda on the cities. They sided decisively with the new Ukrainian government and, in some instances, supported pro-Ukrainian civic movements.

The combined effect of these three variables precluded the successful formation of quasi-state entities outside Donbas and the spillover of large-scale violence beyond the region.

Background Conditions

The two cities shared with Donetsk and Luhansk a history of pro-Russian organizing, active support of the Russian state for local civic initiatives, and political dominance of the Party of Regions prior to 2014. However, compared to Donbas, they had greater ethnic and linguistic diversity at the regional level, more political pluralism, and tenuous, largely opportunistic, elite connections to the PR political machine.

Political Practices

Ideological diversity in the political arenas of the two cities was already visible in the early 1990s. Odesa's first mayoral election, in 1994, produced a close victory for forty-six-year-old Eduard Gurvits, the son of a dissident economist jailed under Stalin. He campaigned on anticommunist slogans and openly sympathized with the national-democratic forces. In 1998 Gurvits lost reelection to a former local communist official, Ruslan Bodelan, but in 2005 he returned to the mayor's office as a member of President Viktor Yushchenko's team. Five years later he was replaced by PR candidate Oleksiy Kostusev. Hence, over the course of sixteen years, Odesa had three mayors representing competing political forces and holding divergent ideological views. While Gurvits embraced a nationalist agenda and sought to rename some city streets for nationalist heroes, Bodelan and Kostusev advocated for cultural rights of Russian speakers and called for closer relations with Russia.

Kharkiv's first mayor, Yevhen Kushnariov, became a vocal proponent of integration with Russia and even called for a referendum on forming a separate "southeastern republic." By contrast, his successor, Volodymyr Shumilkin, sided with the national-democratic forces and endorsed Yushchenko during the 2004 elections. The local elite confrontation became particularly intense after 2006, when Mykhailo Dobkin, a Yanukovych supporter, was elected mayor. His political opponent was a major businessman, Arsen Avakov, appointed by Yushchenko to head the regional administration. Their conflicts involved disputes over symbolic issues, like Russian-language rights, and over practical governance issues, like management of state-owned enterprises and land control.[3] Between 2007 and 2009 they engaged in intense political fights using court appeals, protest actions, and no-confidence votes initiated in the local councils.

The PR first acquired a majority of seats on Kharkiv city and oblast councils in 2006, when Dobkin won the mayoral race. Four years later, the PR party list received only plurality support in the city and in Kharkiv oblast, but retained a majority of seats on the two councils by winning the most of individual races.[4] The competitive nature of local politics was more clearly revealed in a mayoral race in which PR-backed Henadiy Kernes defeated his

---

[3] Platonova (2021), 137.

[4] The PR party list received 31.53% in the city of Kharkiv and 40.21% in Kharkiv oblast. See Central Election Commission of Ukraine, https://www.cvk.gov.ua/pls/vm2010/wp0011.html.

opponent, Avakov, by less than one percentage point. Given Avakov's affiliation with Yushchenko's party, this would have been an impossible outcome for any major town in Donbas.

In Odesa, PR gained a majority of seats in the city and oblast councils only in 2010, but its party list fell well short of a majority.[5] Although Kostusev, the city's new mayor, was also endorsed by PR, he had long been a fixture in local politics, so his victory cannot be attributed solely to PR backing. Overall, while the PR gained control over local assemblies in Kharkiv and Odesa, support for the opposition parties in the two cities was substantially higher than in Donetsk and Luhansk (see Table 9.2).

The dominance of the PR in the two cities also belied a more tenuous connection that local elite actors had to the party leadership. While business and political elites in Donbas participated in the founding of the PR in the late 1990s and used it for a political comeback after the 2004 Orange Revolution, elite actors in Kharkiv and Odesa jumped on the PR bandwagon only later and for opportunistic reasons. As a result, they often brought their own resources to the party and maintained autonomy from the party's Donbas-centered clientelist network. Kharkiv's Kushnariov was the leader of his own New Democratic Party. In late 2005 he merged it with PR after receiving one of the top spots on the PR party list. Dobkin was previously a member of another pro-Russian party, the Social-Democratic Party (United) led by Viktor Medvedchuk, and defected to the PR after the party lost access to administrative backing. In Odesa, Kostusev was similarly a leader of the small pro-Russian party Union. He agreed to merge with PR in 2005

Table 9.2 Results of 2012 Elections to the Ukrainian Parliament in Donetska, Luhanska, Kharkivska, and Odeska Oblasts Based on Party List Votes (in %)

	Donetska	Luhanska	Kharkivska	Odeska
Opposition parties (Batkivshyna, Ukrainian Democratic Alliance for Reforms (UDAR), Svoboda)	11.2	11.5	31.9	32.6
Pro-government parties (PR, KPU)	83.9	82.2	61.8	60.1

Source: "Parlamentski Vybory 2012: Rezultaty Holosuvannia v Bahatomandatnomu Okruzi," Datatowel.In.Ua, https://datatowel.in.ua/elections/parliamentary2012.

[5] The PR party list received 30.4% in the city of Odesa: https://dumskaya.net/news/_160-009470/.

in exchange for becoming a member of PR's governing bureau. Another wealthy businessman and future city mayor, Henadiy Trukhanov, was affiliated with the centrist People's Party until 2010, when he got elected to the city council on the PR list. Eventually, Trukhanov became the head of the PR faction in 2010 and thus the second most influential city official after the mayor.

Another distinct feature of local politics in the two cities prior to 2014 was a wide pro-Russian organizational network funded by the Russian government. In Kharkiv, there were dozens of small pro-Russian organizations, often with just a handful of members. They promoted Russian culture and language rights but also advocated for stronger political and economic ties with the Russian state. For example, an organization named For Cultural-Linguistic Equality included among its goals the "need to counter falsification of the history of Russian civilization . . . and propaganda of Russian-Ukrainian integration projects, protection of the image of Russia and Russian Orthodox Church."[6] Among its activities in 2012, it listed roundtables in support of Ukraine's Eurasian integration, rallies near the Russian consulate endorsing Vladimir Putin, antinationalist and antifascist marches, and press publications criticizing the government for slow implementation of its pro-Russian agenda. These activities, however, involved only a handful of people and failed to develop deeper ties to the local community. In the words of one insider, pro-Russian groups were "mainly fictional organizations" which sought only to "show themselves off in front of the Russian sponsors."[7]

In Odesa, by contrast, some pro-Russian activists managed to gain far greater influence and visibility—even compared to their counterparts in Crimea and Donbas. This was achieved by using a popular media platform and joining a new political party, Rodina (Motherland). The party was organized by local businessman Igor Markov, whose foray into politics began in 2006 with the launch of the television channel ATV. Its programming consisted mainly of commentary and opinion that attacked the pro-Western policies of President Yushchenko. The channel positioned itself as the primary advocate for the rights of the Russophone majority of

---

[6] Ravnopravie, "Otchet o deiatelnosti KhGOO 'Za kulturno-iazykovoe ravnopravie' i koordinatsyonnogo soveta russkikh organizatsiy Vostoka Ukrainy 'Russkoe Veche, 2011–2012,'" https://www.ravnopravie.org/news/stati/otchet_o_deyatelnosti_hgoo_za_kulturno-yazykovoe_ravnopravie_i_koordinacionnogo_soveta_russkih_organizacij_vostoka_ukrainy_russkoe_veche_konec_2011-12_god.html.

[7] Interview with Andriy Borodavka, May 22, 2019.

Odesa. This messaging quickly paid off—despite stiff competition from several dozen local television outlets, ATV turned into one of the most watched channels in Odesa.[8] The party Rodina, formed a year later, sought to capitalize on the success of this media project.[9] ATV's founders—Aleksandr Vasiliev and Igor Dmitriev—became party ideologues, while Markov emerged as the party leader. Ten years later Vasiliev drew direct parallels between the stances of the party and those of the European populists: "We were against the Ukrainian establishment . . . against Ukrainian nationalism, but we appealed to human rights, multiculturalism and showed that one can protect the Russian language with liberal instruments . . . We advocated for Eurasian integration initiated by Putin. We tried to borrow both from Russian politics and Western antiglobalism."[10] One of Vasiliev's mentors, Odesa University professor Aleksandr Prigarin, still emphasized the Russo-centric nature of the party, suggesting that Vasiliev and others in the party "viewed Ukraine as part of the Russian project."[11]

History, Urbanization and Ethnocultural Composition

The political pluralism of the Kharkiv and Odesa regions was, partially, a reflection of their greater ethnocultural diversity and particular historical background. The Odesa region has two large ethnic minority groups—Bulgarians and Moldovans—residing mainly in the southern part of the province, along the border with Romania.[12] The majority in three of its southern districts—Izmail, Reni, and Bolgrad—are native Bulgarian and Moldovan speakers.[13] The region's other major urban center—Podilsk—is located close to the Vinnytsia oblast and has been predominantly Ukrainian-speaking. Such ethnic heterogeneity produced three distinct linguistic areas within the Odesa region: the southern, with substantial non-Russian minorities; the northern, with a Ukrainian majority; and the central, with Odesa largely divided between Russian and Ukrainian speakers. While the Kharkiv region does not have large ethnic minorities, the use of the

[8] Interview with Aleksandr Prigarin, June 26, 2019.
[9] Interview with Mykhailo Shmushkovych, June 22, 2019.
[10] Interview with Aleksandr Vasiliev, July 24, 2019.
[11] Interview with Prigarin, 2019.
[12] Based on 2001 census results, Bulgarians constituted 6.1%, while Moldovans constituted 5% of the region's population. See http://2001.ukrcensus.gov.ua/results/general/nationality/odesa/.
[13] Bulgarians constituted 60% of the residents of the Bolgrad region; Moldovans constituted 49% of the Reni region; in the Izmail region 27.6% were Moldovans and 25.7% were Bulgarians. Ibid.

Ukrainian language is far more prevalent there than in Donbas.[14] Apart from Kharkiv, the only two other towns where Ukrainian speakers constituted a minority in 2014 were Chuhuiv and Pervomaiskiy.[15] In the rest of the areas, particularly in the more agricultural western and southern parts, Ukrainian speakers predominated. The two regions also differed from Donbas in their population settlement patterns. Both have a much lower urbanization level and no urban agglomerations outside the two regional capitals.[16] The lower population density and greater dispersal of urban centers made the two regions far more difficult to capture and control for an outside actor.

The regional centers, Kharkiv and Odesa, have also been historically shaped by varied cultural influences, which produced competing myths about their political belonging. From its founding by Catherine the Great, Odesa had a strong historical connection to the Russian imperial past, but its nineteenth-century history was also closely tied to Western Europe. French aristocrats were among its first governors, while many European architects designed its iconic buildings.[17] Odesa residents, for most of the city's history, represented a multicultural blend of visitors and settlers from different parts of the Russian Empire and the European continent. To quote a local city historian: "Odesa was never a Soviet city. It has been a merchant city. Odesa is always scheming. It is a transactional city... Odesa has also never been a Russian city. For 200 years it has been built by newcomers and migrants."[18] In early 2014 these historical roots provided "usable past" narratives for the two antagonistic groups of pro-Russian and pro-Ukrainian activists. Their marches would often symbolically intersect near the monuments to the Russian empress and the French noble, located steps from each other.

Kharkiv, in turn, evolved historically as a city with a predominantly ethnic Ukrainian population. Founded as a Cossack settlement, its growth in the nineteenth century resulted from its location at the intersection of major trading routes. Contemporary chroniclers noted the common Ukrainian

---

[14] In 2001 census, 53.8% of Kharkiv region residents identified Ukrainian as their native language, compared to 24.1% in Donetsk oblast and 30% in Luhansk oblast. See http://2001.ukrcensus.gov.ua/results/general/language.

[15] Data from Oleksandr Fisun and Anton Aksentyev, "Kharkiv's patronal politics: Pro-Maidan vs anti-Maidan rivalry and competing power pyramids," in *Ukraine and Its Regions: Societal Trends and Policy Implications*, ed. Ryhor Nizhnikau and Arkady Moshes (Helsinki: FIIA Report, 2020), 64.

[16] Hamilton, *Ukraine - Urbanization Review*.

[17] Charles King, *Odessa: Genius and Death in a City of Dreams* (New York: Norton, 2012).

[18] Cited in Maks Gordienko, *Odessa-2014: Krakh ruzzkoi vesny* (Kharkiv: Folio, 2022), 134–135.

way of speaking and distinguished it from the speech of Odesa.[19] Its vibrant cultural and university life attracted prominent Ukrainian writers and scholars, who turned it into "the capital of Ukrainian national culture."[20] It also became the site for the formation of the Ukrainian revolutionary party—the first political force in eastern Ukraine which advocated for Ukraine's self-determination.

Still, Kharkiv's location on the Russian-Ukrainian frontier made the city essentially bicultural—about two-thirds of its residents identified Russian as their native language in the 2001 census.[21] The city's emergence as the major industrial center of the Soviet Union and its status as the "first capital" of Soviet Ukraine also tied it more closely to the communist past. The Soviet legacy is particularly visible in its monumental constructivist-style buildings around Freedom Square and broad boulevards lined with neoclassical architecture—all built during Stalin's reign. As Kharkiv historian Volodymyr Kravchenko noted, the regional media discourses combined both recognition of Soviet history, particularly the memory of World War II, and Ukrainian national symbols and narratives.[22] Kharkiv's version of the Ukrainian historic paradigm emphasized its "organic continuity" with the Soviet past, which, in contrast to Donbas, did not stand in contradiction to the new Ukrainian statehood.[23]

Overall, these differences in historical legacies, settlement patterns, ethnocultural composition, and political practices already suggested that any separatist challenge in Odesa and Kharkiv regions would face substantial hurdles.

Behind Pro-Russian Mobilization

Just as in Donbas in early 2014, at the forefront of pro-Russian movements in the cites of Kharkiv and Odesa were little-known activists backed by thousands of sympathetic locals. They also questioned the legitimacy of the new authorities, exploited animosity toward Euromaidan, and stoked distrust of the West. Still, in contrast to Donetsk and Luhansk, pro-Russian

---

[19] Vladimir Kravchenko, *Kharkov/Kharkiv: Stolitsa Pogranichia* (Vilnius: EGU, 2010), 163.

[20] Ibid., 166.

[21] Kharkovska Miska Rada, "Pro rosiysku movu u Kharkovi," June 3, 2006, https://www.city.kharkiv.ua/uk/document/pro-rosiysku-movu-v-m-harkovi-1910.html.

[22] Kravchenko, *Kharkov/Kharkiv*, 304.

[23] Ibid., 301.

mobilization in these two cities was less representative of local preferences and had no broader support across the region. Its various factions competing for outside resources and publicity never managed to reconcile their interests, agree on a single goal, or join forces to seize the initiative from the government.

In Odesa, the movement under pro-Russian slogans was highly eclectic ideologically and had no clear leadership structure. Its core consisted of two quasi-militant groups created in January 2014 in response to the Euromaidan revolution. People's Militia (Narodnaia Druzhyna; PM) was led by twenty-eight-year-old Anton Davidchenko, who had prior ties to the leftist Rodina. He led many of the initial rallies and marches. Another group, the Odesa Militia (Odesskaia Druzhyna; OM), was launched by local far-right activist Dmitriy Odinov. His organization, Slavic Unity (Slavianskoe Yedinstvo), earlier staged annual Russian nationalist marches under Russian black-yellow-white imperial flags. The two groups differed not only in terms of ideology but also in their funding sources. While Davidchenko was rumored to have received funds from the Russian consulate in Odesa and oligarchs like Medvedchuk, Odinov relied on funding from Russian nationalist sympathizers.[24] Stylistically, both groups resembled Maidan self-defense groups. They wore helmets, covered their faces with black balaclava masks, and paraded with baseball bats. One local journalist recalled, "It looked comical—they were marching with sticks and helmets while the other side already had firearms and was more experienced in fighting."[25] Another tactic borrowed from Maidan was the formation of a tent city on the square next to the trade union building, once the office of the Odesa oblast Communist Party committee. The square became the site for all pro-Russian rallies held between February and May 2014, while the movement became synonymous with its name: Kulykovo Field.

In late February 2014 Davidchenko became the most recognizable face of the pro-Russian movement in Odesa due to his ubiquitous presence in local media. But despite his visibility, he seemed out of his depth when he suddenly confronted issues of national significance. He was ridiculed even by some within the movement, who viewed him as a "caricature of the civic activist" and suspected him of pursuing personal benefit rather than genuine political change.[26] One local journalist relayed a widespread rumor that with

[24] Interview with Serhiy Dibrova, June 24, 2019.
[25] Interview with Yuriy Tkachev, June 28, 2019.
[26] Interview with Shmushkovych, 2019.

the start of protests Davidchenko "acquired several bodyguards and a new Mercedes," suggesting access to external funding.[27]

By all accounts, the only serious ideologue in the movement was city council member Vasiliev. He prepped Davidchenko before some of his public appearances and drafted the first Kulykovo Field manifestos. However, Vasiliev quickly realized that the movement lacked sufficient resources to achieve anything tangible.[28] Later in the spring, when he learned that Ukrainian authorities had opened a criminal case against him, Vasiliev fled Odesa, never to return. With his disappearance, according to one insider, the movement "lost its brain trust."[29] While the rallies and marches continued, the movement relied on increasingly fringe figures. Following Davidchenko's arrest, his younger brother tried to play the part of an urban revolutionary but proved even less compelling. This opened up a space for extremists from Odesa Militia, like Odinov or the former policeman Sergei Dolzhenkov, to gain more visibility and provoke violent clashes that led to dozens of deaths on the streets of Odesa on May 2.

In Kharkiv the most visible speakers of the pro-Russian movement were Yuriy Apukhtin from the organization Great Rus' (Velikaia Rus) and Anton Gurianov, affiliated with the neo-Soviet Russia-based organization Essence of Time (Sut' Vremeni). The gray-haired sixty-six-year-old Apukhtin represented the older generation, nostalgic for the Soviet era. According to a personal acquaintance, Apukhtin was "a real Ukrainophobe who denied the existence of the Ukrainian nation and language."[30] Tall and bespectacled Gurianov, on the other hand, had just turned forty and signaled that pro-Russian ideas could have a broader appeal. Prior to 2014 he worked as an economics professor at a local college, but he also became a permanent feature of all pro-Russian gatherings. On November 24, 2013, three days after the start of the Euromaidan revolution in Kyiv, Gurianov and Apukhtin staged an anti-EU rally on the central square of Kharkiv attended by barely several dozen residents.[31] In two months, as Euromaidan protests gained revolutionary scale, Gurianov created a new organization, named, in a clear nod to Russia's irredentist desires, The Russian East (Russkiy Vostok). Apukhtin, Gurianov, and several other activists, including the communist member

[27] Interview with Dibrova, 2019.
[28] Interview with Vasiliev, 2019.
[29] Interview with Dibrova, 2019.
[30] Interview with Borodavka, 2019.
[31] Author's archived video from Kharkiv, November 24, 2013. See "Kharkiv 2014," Harvard Dataverse, https://doi.org/10.7910/DVN/1KOXU0.

of Parliament Alla Aleksandrovska, formed one wing of the pro-Russian movement in Kharkiv consisting of longtime activists.

The other "nonsystemic" or outsider wing emerged in the first two weeks of protests in March 2014 around figures without a prior history of activism. Most prominent among them were Sergei Yudaev and Yegor Logvinov, both in their forties, who positioned themselves as "Kharkov Defenders." They were less polished as speakers and lacked political experience but illustrated the new phenomenon of "leaders from the masses," personified by the emergence of Pavel Gubarev as the "people's governor" in Donetsk. Their demands were often more direct and radical, while their pro-Russian sympathies were often provocatively articulated. "We will be shouting 'Russia—Help!' and this is our right to do this," Logvinov argued during a press conference.[32] They also attracted some militants who arrived from Russia. A notorious Russian fighter, Arseniy Pavlov (call-sign Motorolla), a member of Girkin's unit in Donbas, was first spotted next to Logvinov at a rally near the Russian consulate in Kharkiv on March 16.[33]

The rivalry between the two wings came out in the open during a rally on March 30, when Logvinov accused Apukhtin of paying only lip service to the pro-Russian cause. "They give out promises, but do nothing," Logvinov asserted as Apukhtin sought to cut him short.[34] As an alternative, they announced the formation of Ukrainian Eastern Bloc and demanded "economic independence" of the Kharkiv region followed by full sovereignty and ascension to Russia. The new organization's two leaders—Logvinov and Yudaev—led the storming of the state administration building on April 6, which became the grounds for their arrest two days later. Both remained behind bars in Ukraine for several years. Apukhtin and other leaders from their rival groups, by contrast, continued holding much smaller rallies until May.

Why Did Russia Abstain?

The organizational drivers of the pro-Russian mobilization in Kharkiv in early 2014 were individuals who had long operated in the city under

---

[32] Author's archived video from Kharkiv, February 2014. See "Kharkiv 2014," Harvard Dataverse, https://doi.org/10.7910/DVN/1KOXU0.

[33] Author's archived video from Kharkiv, March 16, 2014. See "Kharkiv 2014," Harvard Dataverse, https://doi.org/10.7910/DVN/1KOXU0.

[34] Author's archived video from Kharkiv, March 30, 2014. See "Kharkiv 2014," Harvard Dataverse, https://doi.org/10.7910/DVN/1KOXU0.

patronage from the Russian state. In the years prior, they received funds to stage events aligned with Russia's agenda. But in spring of 2014, as Gurianov later explained, they needed substantially more funding to "organize trainings for young people who could participate in street skirmishes, rent office space for their organizations and publish propaganda materials."[35] The fractured nature of the pro-Russian organizational milieu in Kharkiv, however, hindered transparent distribution of available funds and, instead, encouraged internal competition and squabbling. Given the lack of any external oversight, embezzlement became the dominant motive for many of its members.[36] The greed of separatist leaders, one analyst quipped, might have preserved the Ukrainian sate in Kharkiv.[37]

In Odesa, there was at least the potential for a more consolidated action due to the existence of the strong pro-Russian party. Already in early March, activists tied to Rodina met to plot the capture of the local council.[38] They viewed the regional council meeting, scheduled for March 3, as an opportunity to follow Crimea's example and adopt the resolution to call a referendum on the status of Odesa oblast. However, they also recognized that the passing of such a resolution would require pressuring council deputies through mass action. One meeting participant recalled, "We started looking at our power resources, men who could blockade the council building et cetera. We also contacted police and SBU to understand how law enforcement would react. We even considered a potential candidate for 'people's governor,' but ultimately we realized that we had insufficient resources to implement this." One of the key factors that stopped a more radical scenario, according to Vasiliev, was uncertainty regarding the broader response of Odesa residents: "In Donetsk and Luhansk people were bringing food and forming live shields around the building.... We realized that we could gather ten to fifteen thousand people for a rally, but we did not believe that we could survive there for a week without major public support."[39]

Another factor was inability to shift from civic to armed resistance: "Later in Donbas we saw what people could achieve by fighting the Ukrainian army. But we did not realize it then. We were professional politicians and did not know how to act outside legal space."[40] As a result, pro-Russian groups

---

[35] Anton Gurianov, "Ya absolutno uveren v pobede sil soprotivlenia v Kharkove: Eto lish vopros vremeni," *Nakanune*, August 23, 2016, https://www.nakanune.ru/articles/112013/.

[36] Interview with Borodavka, 2019.

[37] Interview with Anton Aksentyev, May 24, 2019.

[38] Interview with Vasiliev, 2019.

[39] Interview with Vasiliev, 2019.

[40] Ibid.

only managed to stage a rally near the council building, clashed with the police, and sent their leader, Davidchenko, inside to address the deputies. His appearance, however, elicited a skeptical response from the council members. Some of them even tried to chase him away from the hall. In an emotional appeal to the deputies, Davidchenko warned that protesters gathered outside could storm the council if the deputies fail to support them.[41] His words, however, had no desired effect. Just fourteen deputies voted for the resolution to hold a referendum on the autonomy of Odesa oblast, while the majority of those present abstained (six) or voted against it (thirty-nine).

The events on March 3 turned into a major defeat for the pro-Russian groups in Odesa. Some of their leaders, including Davidchenko, were arrested, while wavering elite members were convinced to stay away from the movement. Although pro-Russian rallies and marches still brought thousands of city residents to the streets, they could not articulate any clear political goals. After March 3 nobody among movement insiders could seriously discuss the possibility of proclaiming an Odesa People's Republic or adopting the "Crimean scenario."[42] Even their sympathizers felt that "there was an absence not just of the program, but of any sense in their actions."[43]

One reason for the early defeat and subsequent demobilization of pro-Russian groups in Odesa was the reluctance of Moscow to offer any support beyond rhetorical encouragement. Its involvement in Kharkiv and Odesa was substantially smaller in scale than in Donbas. Activists in both Odesa and Kharkiv initially communicated with the Russian side through Crimean officials. Vasiliev had known the Crimean separatist leader Sergei Aksionov well before 2014 and even contemplated creating a joint political force with him based in the Rodina party.[44] He reached out to Aksionov on March 1 with a request for assistance in the run-up to the oblast council meeting. Aksionov demurred, stating that he could "barely manage" himself. Two weeks later Vasiliev traveled to Crimea to observe the so-called referendum and meet with the Russian security personnel behind the capture of the peninsula. He inquired about possible Russian intervention from Transnistria, but quickly saw that the Russian side had no interest in a coercive takeover of Odesa province: "The person who was related to military or

---

[41] Author's archived video from Odesa, March 3, 2014. See "Odesa 2014," Harvard Dataverse, https://doi.org/10.7910/DVN/DLPG6I.

[42] Interview with Moris Ibragim, June 27, 2019.

[43] Interview with Prigarin, 2019.

[44] Interview with Vasiliev, 2019.

intelligence, widely known now, he told me that we have no contacts with the authorities in Transnistria or security officials there. Once I heard this, I realized that the 'coercive scenario' or capture of power by force is out of the question."[45] Girkin, a likely interlocutor of Vasiliev, confirmed that he discussed the possibility of a raid on Odesa instead of Donbas prior to his incursion. However, he dismissed it at the time as unrealistic: "I was asked to go to Odesa. But how should I go there? By sea? . . . Going there without access to the rear is pure adventurism without any chance of success. There should have been at least a theoretical opportunity of support from the 'big land' [Russia]. So we decided to go to Donetsk instead."[46] In the absence of any direct coercive intervention, there was no chance for Moscow to place Odesa under its control. Even those who publicly led the pro-Russian movement in Odesa ultimately did not believe in its success.[47]

Just like Vasiliev, Yudaev from Kharkiv made three trips to Crimea in March and April for meetings with Aksionov's representatives.[48] He also met Aksionov's advisor from Moscow, most likely Aleksandr Borodai, who consulted him on the proper course of action in Kharkiv. From him Yudaev learned about the planned operation on April 6, when activists in Donetsk and Luhansk would simultaneously seize government buildings. But it also became clear to Yudaev that Moscow prioritized Donetsk and Luhansk over Kharkiv. His request for "arms and a group or two of 'green men'" to assist with the capture of government buildings went unmet.[49] Even though Yudaev's group managed to seize the regional state administration building on the evening of April 6, they remained inside for less than forty-eight hours. The declaration of the Kharkiv People's Republic on April 7 turned out to be premature since, as Yudaev later explained, the separatists "had no weapons and resources to defend it." A special National Guard unit cleared the building on the morning of April 8 in under twenty minutes using only stun grenades. None of over sixty men inside tried to resist, and no firearms were found. Just like the aborted seizure of the regional council in Odesa on March 3, the short-lived takeover of the regional state administration in Kharkiv quickly deflated the city's pro-Russian movement.

---

[45] Ibid.

[46] Zhabin, "Igor Strelkov..", 2021.

[47] Interview with Shmushkovych, 2019.

[48] Sergei Yudaev, *Protivostoianie-2*, LiveJournal, November 18, 2015, https://gruzd22.livejournal.com/36966.html.

[49] Ibid.

Russia attracted not only local activists, however, but also key elite actors from Kharkiv, such as Kernes and Dobkin. Together they flew to Moscow for consultations immediately after the Euromaidan victory. The very fact of their brief visit to the Russian capital, allegedly for a meeting with Putin's advisor Vladislav Surkov, suggested the need to consult, if not to coordinate, with Russian officials. Although the exact nature of their conversations remains unknown, their quick return and reversal of their stance—now in support of Ukraine's unity—was an indirect sign that they had received no firm assurances from Moscow. This was also the moment when, in the words of one local journalist, the two "decided to give up the big game."[50]

Russia's apparent disinterest in providing coercive backing to activists in Odesa and Kharkiv or co-opting local elites might have been motivated by several factors. First, given that the operation in Donbas had to be conducted covertly, Moscow might have decided to concentrate its efforts on the region where such tactics could have had the highest likelihood of success. It also might have decided to intervene only in Donbas because doing so required fewer resources. After all, since March the pro-Russian mobilization was underway in the entire region and not just in two regional capitals. By contrast, there were no pro-Russian rallies in any of the smaller towns in the Kharkiv or Odesa regions. An additional constraint in the case of Odesa, as Girkin made clear, was the lack of a shared border with Russia. Although pro-Ukrainian activists there feared the possibility of military intervention from Russia-controlled Transnistria, sustained covert military assistance to Odesa would have been much harder to organize.

The End of Pro-Russian Mobilization

Despite the relative weakness of pro-Russian organizations in Kharkiv and Odesa, they still posed a challenge to Ukraine's control over the two cities. The unprecedented spike in political violence that the regional capitals experienced throughout spring 2014 was a clear evidence of the destabilizing potential of such organizations. Pro-Russian groups launched violent actions in the two cities almost immediately after the start of the Euromaidan revolution. The very first assault against the peaceful pro-Maidan demonstration in Kharkiv occurred on December 2. It was conducted by a

---

[50] Interview with Borodavka, 2019.

group of young men tied to a local pro-Russian organization, Oplot (Bulwark). The organization had informal backing of Mayor Kernes and was led by a former policeman, Yevhen Zhylin. Many of Oplot's members came from the police ranks and were recruited for their strong ideological affinity with Russia.[51] Its militant wing had about two hundred members, who were often sent to Kyiv to assault Maidan supporters. In Odesa pro-Maidan activists received anonymous threats and suffered damage to their property.[52] The most serious assault during the three months of protests occurred on February 19. Hundreds of young men dressed in black outfits, wearing helmets or balaclavas, and carrying wooden sticks encircled a small group of pro-Maidan protesters next to the regional state administration building. They threw some of the protesters on the ground, beat them, and chased those who sought to escape. Dozens of protesters as well as several reporters received serious injuries and left the square with bruises or wounds gushing blood.

The similar public beating and humiliation of Maidan activists on Freedom Square in Kharkiv on March 1 marked a clear shift from earlier covert attacks by Oplot. That day hundreds of men, some with sticks, surrounded and stormed the regional state administration building earlier seized by Euromaidan supporters. Their stated goal was to clear the building of protesters. When dozens of Euromaidan activists, some covered in blood, were pushed out onto the street, they were not allowed to flee. Instead, they were dragged onto the stage in front of a cheering crowd. Young men were put on their knees and asked to repent while enduring slurs and violence from onlookers. This was also the first time the Russian flag was raised in front of Kharkiv's regional administration building.

The confrontation between the two camps in Kharkiv quickly escalated to gunfights two weeks later. On the evening of March 14, hundreds of pro-Russian militants, some with clubs and firearms, surrounded the office of the Right Sector, which they accused of an attack hours earlier. In subsequent clashes, two pro-Russian militants were killed. Mayor Kernes held late-night negotiations with enraged militants to ensure a safe exit for the RS activists hiding inside the building. Another major assault on pro-Ukrainian demonstrators happened on April 6 next to the Shevchenko monument. The small rally under Ukrainian flags was immediately surrounded and attacked with

[51] Interview with Dmytro Bulakh, May 21, 2019.
[52] Interview with Ostapenko, 2019.

stones and clubs. While most of the rally participants managed to escape, a dozen young men were captured and forced to crawl through the crowd. In Odesa, violence turned lethal on May 2 when Odesa Militia members opened fire on Ukrainian Unity march participants, triggering retaliation by pro-Ukrainian demonstrators. In the ensuing clashes forty-eight people lost their lives.[53]

Three factors contributed to the rapid demobilization of separatist groups in Odesa and Kharkiv after weeks of public confrontation: (1) the demonstrated capacity of pro-Ukrainian groups for countermobilization, (2) the reassertion of a coercive monopoly by the state, and (3) resistance and sabotage by local elites.

"One for All"

In Kharkiv, the pro-Ukrainian self-defense group emerged from the milieu of Maidan activists in early 2014. According to one activist, they had "arms and a militant wing with young people who would later join volunteer battalions and go to the front [in Donbas]."[54] Some were members of local soccer ultras club, while others belonged to the far-right organization Patriot of Ukraine, which later formed the core of the Azov battalion. The capacity of pro-Ukrainian militants to fight back became particularly evident during a violent showdown at the RS office on March 14, when they first used arms for self-defense. Pro-Ukrainian mobilization continued in Kharkiv in April and played an especially visible role following the capture of the state administration building by pro-Russian activists on April 6. The next morning, a sizable pro-Ukrainian protest gathered on the square across from the building, with young men and women singing Ukrainian songs and waving national flags. In Donetsk, by contrast, a similar counterprotest under Ukrainian banners next to the captured state administration building was no longer possible.

The formation of a pro-Ukrainian self-defense group in Odesa happened in response to an assault by local anti-Maidan thugs on February 19. Given the inaction of the police, local Euromaidan supporters met later that day to organize their own self-defense unit.[55] Over one hundred people

---

[53] Anna Hryniv, "Odesskaia tragedia: Piat let. Znaem li my bolshe?," BBC News Ukraine, May 2, 2019, https://www.bbc.com/ukrainian/features-russian-48131691.

[54] Interview with Volodymyr Chystylin, May 23, 2019.

[55] Interview with Vitaliy Kozhuhar in Gordienko, *Odessa-2014*, 88–96.

immediately volunteered to join the group. It accompanied the city's first major demonstration for Ukrainian unity on March 2. In addition, a smaller group of several dozen people started meeting at the abandoned factory for firearm training.[56] They formed a new battalion, named Shtorm (Storm), led by Ruslan Forostiak, a native of Lviv who stayed in Odesa after graduating from the naval college. Its initial objective was to "prepare small tactical groups for moving around the city under the emergency conditions and secure its vital targets."[57]

In mid-April many Shtorm members started guarding the checkpoints that pro-Ukrainian supporters had established around Odesa. Altogether there were seventeen checkpoints, each guarded by seven to ten people, some of them armed. They controlled and monitored traffic movement in and out of the city to prevent the entry of Russian undercover militants. They stopped and inspected vehicles and provided daily reports to law enforcement. Although Forostiak recognized that they could not repel a large-scale military attack, he expected them to have a "psychological" effect on the residents and demonstrate the dominance of pro-Ukrainian forces in the city.[58] One of the local journalists, Aliona Balaba, thought that they served exactly this purpose: "Checkpoints persuaded anti-Maidan activists that we did not just march around the city, but could mobilize and fight back."[59]

Initially, the parity of power between pro-Ukrainian and pro-Russian groups in Odesa even encouraged cooperation between them in joint planning of march routes.[60] Many members of both groups had a shared record of activism and had known each other for some time. One scholar familiar with the parties remembered, "They would accuse each other publicly, but then would go and drink vodka together afterwards."[61] Still, with the escalation of separatist actions in Donbas in mid-April the relationship between the two camps became more confrontational. The most contested site was the pro-Russian tent camp on Kulykovo Field, viewed by the pro-Ukrainian side as a threat to the city. On April 17, a group of pro-Ukrainian activists picketed Odesa's main police station, demanding removal of the tents. "Why do they hold rallies with the Russian artists and Russian television broadcasts? Why did they march under Russian flags on the day

---

[56] Ibid.
[57] Interview with Ruslan Forostia in Gordienko, *Odessa-2014*, 68–87.
[58] Ibid.
[59] Interview with Aliona Balaba in Gordienko, *Odessa-2014*, 190–195.
[60] Interview with Dibrova, 2019.
[61] Interview with Prigarin, 2019.

of Odesa's liberation from the Nazis?" one female participant probed.[62] In response, Police Chief Dmytro Fuchedzhy required a court order before he would do anything about it.

On May 2, Kulykovo Field became the place of the worst violence in Odesa since World War II. In response to an earlier attack, pro-Ukrainian demonstrators and soccer ultras burned down the tent city and attacked the trade union building with Molotov cocktails. Forty-two people (thirty-four men, seven women, and a boy) hiding inside died because of the fire—due to asphyxiation or fatal jumps.[63] This tragedy acquired major symbolic significance for both sides. For the pro-Ukrainian activists, the events of May 2 became, in the words of Serhiy Pashynsky, then head of the Presidential Administration, "the inflection point, after which the revival of Ukraine began."[64] For the pro-Russian side, by contrast, it showed the futility of any expectations about Russian intervention or a public uprising. One city resident recalled, "After May 2 I felt that everyone would wake up and say 'Yes!,' but instead people became afraid."[65] The founder of the local self-defense group, Vitaliy Kozhuhar, had a similar impression: "Odesa was in a state of shock. We [pro-Ukrainian forces] were afraid to achieve victory at such a price, while they were afraid that we would finish them off."[66] As a result, the staunchest pro-Russian supporters left to fight in Donbas, while the rest withdrew from all public activity.[67] The cycle of popular mobilization, unprecedented in scale for Odesa, ended abruptly.

The State Strikes Back

While the level of pro-Ukrainian civic mobilization was weaker in Kharkiv than in Odesa, it compensated with a stronger coercive response from the state. The government's operation was led by the two city locals—Arsen Avakov and Stepan Poltorak—who, following Maidan's victory, became the interior minister and the commander of interior troops, respectively.

---

[62] Author's archived video from Odesa, April 17, 2014. See "Odesa 2014," Harvard Dataverse, https://doi.org/10.7910/DVN/DLPG6I.

[63] Matilad Bogner, "7 Years with No Answers: What Is Lacking in the Investigation of Events in Odesa on 2 May 2014?," UN OHCHR, April 30, 2021, https://ukraine.un.org/en/126054-7-years-no-answers-what-lacking-investigations-events-odesa-2-may-2014.

[64] Gordienko, *Odessa-2014*, 232.

[65] Interview with Prigarin, 2019.

[66] Gordienko, *Odessa-2014*.

[67] Interview with Tkachev, 2019.

The simultaneous capture of state administration buildings by pro-Russian groups on April 6 led the Ukrainian government to dispatch its representatives to Kharkiv, Donetsk, and Luhansk. In the case of Kharkiv the delegation was led by Avakov, a city native widely known locally and familiar with regional politics. As Avakov later recalled, he arrived in Kharkiv on April 7 ready to use force: "We had an obligation to liquidate the threat—any talks with terrorists or compromises through dialogue regarding Ukraine's sovereignty were unacceptable."[68] He was confident that only a minority of locals shared the goals of pro-Russian activists.[69] However, there were few reliable forces at his disposal capable of acting against the separatists. Two days after the seizure of the administration building, in the early morning of April 8, Avakov ordered mobilization of all main policing units in the city, including Berkut and the Security Service units. However, he recalled, "none of them arrived at the set time to participate in the storming."[70] As a backup, Avakov also ordered about two hundred soldiers to be transferred from the "Jaguar" special unit of the National Guard stationed in Vinnytsia, a city in central Ukraine which largely supported Maidan. They led the clearing of the building. Even though Avakov authorized the use of deadly force in case of resistance, special forces relied only on stun grenades and completed their task in under an hour.

The successful removal of pro-Russian demonstrators from the regional administration building empowered local law enforcement to act more decisively as well. In the following weeks SBU detained hundreds of separatist activists. Some were taken outside Kharkiv for what one operative called "prophylactic conversations."[71] Local businessmen who witnessed the effectiveness of coercive tactics decided to pay for the equipment of three volunteer police battalions created by the Interior Ministry. According to Avakov's advisor Anton Gerashchenko, the authorities made the decision to "distribute arms to pro-Ukrainian activists who could then ensure that no scum would come to the region."[72] When the final skirmishes occurred between pro-Russian militants and soccer ultras on April 27, police units removed the tent city near the Lenin monument and banned any further gatherings on the square. The government's timely coercive intervention in

[68] Arsen Avakov, *2014: Myttevosti kharkivskoi vesny* (Kharkiv: Folio, 2020), 177.
[69] Ibid., 190.
[70] Ibid., 193.
[71] Daria Bura and Yuri Butusov, *Bytva za Kharkiv* (Kharkiv: Folio, 2023), 256.
[72] Ibid., 273.

Kharkiv prevented the type of uncontrolled violent escalation witnessed in Odesa.

The Game of Local Elites

One factor behind protest demobilization common to Kharkiv and Odesa was active sabotage of and even resistance to the pro-Russian movement by key elite actors. This was expressed in consistent advocacy of the unity of Ukraine, challenges to separatist speakers and dismissal of their demands, subversion of the pro-Russian movement from within, and support for civic resistance efforts against them. This was particularly surprising in Kharkiv given that prior statements by Kernes and Dobkin suggested that they would decisively oppose a post-Maidan government.[73] In February they launched the Ukrainian Front of anti-Maidan militia groups.[74] Kernes even suggested that he would not recognize "an unconstitutional power capture in Kyiv."[75] As part of their anti-Maidan coalition building, Kernes and Dobkin initiated a congress of local officials from the regions of southeastern Ukraine, which drew parallels to the first "separatist" gathering of local officials in Sieverodonetsk in 2004. This led some pro-Russian activists to conclude that, once Maidan prevailed in Kyiv, "Kharkiv could have become a temporary capital of Ukraine."[76] Immediately prior to the congress, however, Kernes received a public warning from a billionaire oligarch Ihor Kolomoiskiy: "You can make separatist statements only if you plan to send your son on a tour not to Maldives, but to Dagestan or a railway station in Volgograd.... Mr. Kernes, if you start playing with the fates of millions of people, your difficult life will become even harder."[77] In his speech at the congress, Kernes asserted his loyalty to Ukraine: "I receive hundreds of threats every day and even one main Jew, Kolomoiskiy, an oligarch, called me a separatist. I am for a united country, and Kharkov was, is, and will remain part of Ukraine."[78] Privately, Kernes was far less confident in his own future.

---

[73] Interview with Aksentyev, 2019.

[74] Maria Zubova, "Vmeste my—sila!," *Kharkovskie Izvestia*, February 4, 2014, 6.

[75] *Kharkovskie Izvestia*, "Gennadiy Kernes: V Kharkove est zakonnaia, a ne samozvannaia vlast," February 11, 2014, 3.

[76] *Rus Triedinaia*, "K piatiletiyu 'Russkoi vesny'—Kharkovskoe soprotivlenie bylo podavleno zhestokimi metodami," 2019, https://dzen.ru/a/YtalFXstEg02gLxO.

[77] LB, "Kolomoiskiy obratilsia k Kernesu s prizyvom ne razvalivat Ukrainu," February 22, 2014, https://rus.lb.ua/news/2014/02/22/256603_kolomoyskiy_obratilsya_kernesu.html.

[78] Author's archived video from Kharkiv, February 22, 2014. See "Kharkiv 2014," Harvard Dataverse, https://doi.org/10.7910/DVN/1KOXU0.

So later the same day he flew to Geneva to meet with Kolomoiskiy personally. Kolomoiskiy later recalled, "I had to calm him down and explain that nothing would happen. You are an elected mayor, you gave an oath as a state official, so follow the oath, serve Ukraine and everything will be fine."[79]

Upon returning to Kharkiv, Dobkin and Kernes signaled their opposition to separatist appeals. On February 24 Dobkin announced his intention to participate in early presidential elections; two days later Kernes stopped demonstrators who tried to raise the Russian flag in front of the mayoral office. Both appeared on the square for a large rally on March 1 and described all those calling for radical actions against the Ukrainian government "provocateurs." They pledged to remain within the Ukrainian legal framework and defend the city's interests in their current positions. None of the separatists was allowed to take the stage. In an interview with the city newspaper on March 4, Kernes expressed confidence that "the overwhelming majority" of the city's residents supported Ukrainian statehood. He also reiterated the difference between Crimea and Kharkiv: "This is an autonomous republic with its own Constitution. And we live and work according to the laws of Ukraine. So, if we are law-abiding citizens and avoid following emotions, we will not let our rallies turn into the seizure of power for Russia's benefit."[80]

Despite a clear change in the tone of their public statements, the Ukrainian government took further steps to put the two Kharkiv leaders on a "shorter leash."[81] This was likely a response to the severe beatings of Maidan supporters in front of the state administration building following the March 1 rally. On March 10, Dobkin was detained on charges of undermining Ukraine's territorial integrity and taken to Kyiv, where the local court ordered him to jail. On March 14, the same court ordered Kernes to be put under temporary house arrest—a much softer sanction that indicated an intimidation tactic meant to deter rather than punish him. This did not prevent Kernes from interfering to stop the assault of pro-Russian militants on the RS office later the same day. The mayor's involvement on behalf of the nationalist group drew anger from the city's pro-Russian milieu. When he appeared at a rally near the Lenin monument the next day he was no longer allowed to speak.[82]

[79] Dmitriy Gordon, "Interview with Igor Kolomoiskiy," *V Gostiah u Gordona*, December 20, 2018, https://t.ly/bRr0.

[80] *Kharkovskie Izvestia*, "Interview with Gennadiy Kernes," March 4, 2014.

[81] Interview with Borodavka, 2019.

[82] Author's archived video from Kharkiv, March 15, 2014. See "Kharkiv 2014," Harvard Dataverse, https://doi.org/10.7910/DVN/1KOXU0.

"Please stop escalation!" Kernes pleaded amid loud booing from the crowd. "Shame!" the crowd roared as Kernes was leaving the square.

The final and decisive face-off between Kernes and pro-Russian demonstrators happened on April 13, after thousands surrounded the city council building and threatened to seize it. One of their leaders, Anton Gurianov, later explained, "We planned to adopt the initial decrees, already drafted, on self-determination, formation of militia and defense of the new state."[83] The actions of Kernes and his supporters proved critical in undermining this scenario. As hundreds of people pushed through police lines into the backyard of the council building, he went right into the crowd with offers for protest leaders to come inside for talks. Wearing a baseball cap and a black shirt, Kernes resembled the demonstrators rather than a city official. His security personnel also looked more like the thugs often spotted at pro-Russian rallies. His informal demeanor and rough conversational manner suggested that he could speak the language of the crowd. He also knew many of the protest leaders personally. One was Konstantin Dolgov, who had once worked for Kernes as a political consultant. Well-known for his fiery addresses at the pro-Russian rallies, he now vouched for Kernes in front of an angry crowd: "He is an elected mayor and asked us not to humiliate him." With a police officer by his side, Kernes then pledged to act in the interests of the protestors: "I just talked to some of your leaders and [I am] ready to speak to others. I agree that it was not right to stop the broadcasting of the Russian TV channel. . . . I am ready to support people who are in jail . . . and I am ready to ensure that you can hold your rallies on the square and receive coverage on local TV . . . but I will not take any illegal steps."[84]

While Kernes was seeking to diffuse tension with his conciliatory rhetoric, numerous men suddenly started calling on everyone to leave. One man shouted through a loudspeaker, "Nobody is going to storm the building. Please move out and voluntarily. I am speaking on behalf of Kharkov resistance." Another shouted from the roof, "We need to disperse because otherwise they will put us down. . . . They already arrested more than sixty people!" A man in a black hat insisted on not seizing the building since "we won't be able to hold it." These men were all part of Kernes's entourage trying to sow confusion in the absence of clear leadership among

---

[83] Gurianov, "Ya absolutno uveren v pobede sil soprotivlenia v Kharkove."

[84] Author's archived video from Kharkiv, April 13, 2014. See "Kharkiv 2014," Harvard Dataverse, https://doi.org/10.7910/DVN/1KOXU0.

the demonstrators.[85] Through co-optation of some separatist leaders and insertion of his undercover loyalists into the crowd, Kernes managed to subvert the assault on the city council building without seeking help from Avakov's police.

Gurianov, who initially sought to enter the city council building, was now apathetically observing the commotion near the entrance. When a journalist asked him to describe his next steps, he replied that Kernes refused to let demonstrators inside. "So we will now hold the meeting of the deputies [of the self-proclaimed people's council] elsewhere," Gurianov said resignedly.[86] Several hours later, after the failed march on the city council building, Gurianov packed his belongings and left Kharkiv for good. "I fled using backroads and already understood that I would, most likely, never return to Kharkiv again," he remembered.[87] In a video issued a few days later Gurianov described Kernes as "the main enemy of protests," citing his actions to undermine them.[88] Gurianov's rushed departure from the city represented an end to the separatist movement. Although smaller pro-Russian rallies continued, they no longer posed a direct challenge to Ukraine's sovereign control of the city. Kernes, however, paid a price for playing his part in quelling the separatist uprising. On the morning of April 28, he was critically wounded following an assassination attempt, from which he never fully recovered. Winning another mayoral race in 2015, Kernes spent the final six years of his life in a wheelchair.

In Odesa, local elites resorted to similar sabotage. The central unifying figure for different elite groups there was the head of the PR faction in the city council and a successful businessman, Henadiy Trukhanov. In contrast to Kernes, however, he eschewed publicity and acted largely behind the scenes. The first and only time Trukhanov addressed pro-Russian demonstrators on Kulykovo Field was during the first rally there, on March 1. In his barely two-minute address he promised that "the city council would not be working for the sake of Kyiv authorities, but for the residents of the city." Trukhanov's main appeal, however, was to "avoid any clashes" and resolve any differences "in a tolerant manner."[89] This call for civic

[85] Interview with Borodavka, 2019.

[86] Author's archived video from Kharkiv, April 13, 2014. See "Kharkiv 2014," Harvard Dataverse, https://doi.org/10.7910/DVN/1KOXU0.

[87] Gurianov, "Ya absolutno uveren v pobede sil soprotivlenia v Kharkove."

[88] Soiuz Grazhdan Ukrainy i Rossii, "Obrashenie predsedatelia soveta narodnyh deputatov KhNR—Antona Gurianova," YouTube, April 18, 2014, https://t.ly/vZMM-.

[89] Author's archived video from Odesa, March 1, 2014. See "Odesa 2014," Harvard Dataverse, https://doi.org/10.7910/DVN/DLPG6I.

order contradicted more boisterous and radical attitudes prevalent among pro-Russian activists at the time. He made no mention of the key demands widely repeated by the speakers, such as calls for federalization or referendum. The crowd responded to his speech with heckling and disapproval. This public resentment as well as his earlier experience visiting Maidan protests in Kyiv influenced the way Trukhanov viewed the separatist challenge in Odesa.[90] When Vasiliev approached Trukhanov during the rally with the suggestion that Trukhanov lead the movement, the businessman spoke of "the fear he felt when he saw people on Maidan ready to attack MPs." In Trukhanov's view, pro-Russian activists in Odesa "underestimated the strength of the opposite force." "He told me that he experienced several scary days in Kyiv," Vasiliev remembered.[91]

Despite Trukhanov's opposition to Euromaidan, its outcome cleared the path for him to take the vacant position of mayor. In late February, the Ukrainian Parliament voted to schedule the mayoral election in Odesa for May 25. According to a pro-Maidan activist, "When we talked to Trukhanov, he was not interested in politics or ideology—he wanted to control the city."[92] The first polls showed that Trukhanov was the favorite to win the election, with his main rival, Gurvits, well behind.[93] This gave Trukhanov a clear reason to support the Ukrainian state despite his opposition to the new leaders. His lead also reassured those midlevel town officials who sought to maintain their positions without joining the pro-Maidan side. As Vasiliev recalled, when he earlier asked several PR deputies to adopt a resolution condemning the coup in Kyiv, they appeared more concerned about Gurvits becoming mayor again: "This fear was paralyzing them. They were afraid to lose contracts, land, and other benefits."[94] By contrast, in the words of one local reporter, Trukhanov offered "a quiet lagoon for PR members who wanted to maintain face."[95] This allowed him to draw endorsements from the chairs of all district administrations who could mobilize administrative resources for his election.[96] Two other prominent city politicians—PR MP Serhiy Kivalov and Rodina party leader Igor Markov—also joined Trukhanov's campaign. In Vasiliev's view, if these three politicians—Trukhanov, Kivalov,

[90] Interview with Vasiliev, 2019.
[91] Ibid.
[92] Interview with Ostapenko, 2019.
[93] Interview with Tkachev, 2019.
[94] Interview with Vasiliev, 2019.
[95] Ibid.
[96] Valeria Ivashkina, "Odeski vybory: Pidkylymni intryhy i viyna kompromativ," *Tyzhden*, May 24, 2014, https://tyzhden.ua/odeski-vybory-pidkylymni-intryhy-i-vijna-kompromativ/.

and Markov—made a deal to support the pro-Russian movement "they would have taken Odesa to the Russian Federation."[97] The opportunity to gain formal power through the mayoral election led at least some of them to prefer that Odesa remain inside Ukraine. Still, like Kernes earlier, Trukhanov reached out to Kolomoiskiy for informal assurances. At the time, the Dnipropetrovsk region governor sought to secure control over the Odesa region through his business partners. Their meeting in one of Odesa's restaurants in April allegedly led to a division of influence: the city remained under Trukhanov, while the rest of the region had to come under Kolomoiskiy's control.[98]

The top political leaders in Odesa and Kharkiv—Trukhanov and Kernes—had similar motives to remain loyal to Ukraine. They had a clear vision of their political prospects based on their relative popularity in the city and informal bargains they reached with the new authorities through Kolomoiskiy. They viewed the pro-Russian movement as consisting of fringe actors whom they did not trust or respect. They lacked significant influence over some of its leaders who maintained ties with Moscow through various Russian operatives. As longtime entrepreneurs, Trukhanov and Kernes were also motivated by their business interests. Their business empires required influence over municipal government. One local activist said of Kernes, "He understood that if Russians arrived, he would turn into nothing, so instead he opted to remain a small feudal lord."[99] Similarly, if separatists succeeded, Odesa was likely to become "the second Transnistria"—a poor peripheral territory without proper international recognition and sanctioned by major powers. That meant asset devaluation and loss of key revenue streams that enriched local elites up until 2014. As a result, the interests of all major businessmen in Odesa were "linked to the survival of the Ukrainian state."[100]

A Bridge Too Far

The Kharkiv and Odesa regions lacked several structural preconditions that allowed for the separatist uprising in Donbas to occur. Both regions were more diverse ethnically and linguistically than Donbas and far less

[97] Interview with Vasiliev, 2019.

[98] Interview with Dibrova, 2019. Kolomoiskiy's business partner Ihor Palytsia was appointed head of the state administration of Odesa oblast on May 6, 2014, and remained in this position until May 30, 2015.

[99] Interview with Chystylin, 2019.

[100] Interview with Dibrova, 2019.

urbanized. Both lacked a single unifying regional identity framed in pro-Russian terms. As a result, in both regions significant pro-Russian street mobilization in March occurred in only the two capital cities, but immediately faced a strong pro-Ukrainian countermovement. Russia initially showed interest in destabilizing both regions and encouraged separatist activists there. By early April, however, Moscow was no longer willing to commit substantial resources to assist them. A covert military intervention in the two regions was untenable to Russia due to the absence of internal support bases outside the two largest cities and, in the case of Odesa, lack of access to external supply routes.

As a result, one could argue that the separatist movement in both cities was, from the start, doomed to failure. However, if pro-Russian organizers were buttressed by local political and business elite groups, the movement could have, at the very least, lasted much longer. Quite possibly it could have triggered either a change in the status of these regions or a more intense and lethal conflict. Hence, quick suppression of separatist challenges in Odesa and Kharkiv was the result of both structural factors that impeded a large-scale separatist uprising and agency-level choices that prevented pro-Russian actors from gaining strength and momentum.

Conclusion

Reassessing 2014 . . . and 2022

In the early morning of August 24, 2014, when Ukraine marked its twenty-third anniversary of independence, the chief of the Ukrainian General Staff General Viktor Muzhenko received first reports about thousands of Russian regular troops with dozens of armored vehicles moving inside eastern Ukraine. These initial reports were first dismissed as false by Ukraine's top military commanders.[1] After four months of asymmetric warfare against local militants and Russian mercenaries, the Ukrainian leadership doubted Moscow could openly deploy the large contingent of its regular troops in Donbas. However, a day later these reports were impossible to ignore.

In total, eight battalion-tactical groups of the Russian armed forces crossed the Ukrainian border in the last week of August—four moving to Donetsk and four others moving to Luhansk.[2] Ukrainian army soldiers and volunteer battalions entered into intense battles with the Russian forces at multiple locations in the vicinity of Donetsk. The largest group of over one thousand Ukrainian troops found itself quickly trapped in the town of Ilovaisk, located on the road leading from Donetsk to the Russian border. In the ensuing retreat, at least 366 Ukrainian soldiers were killed and 429 wounded under a barrage of fire from the Russian positions—the single largest loss of life in the war at that time.[3] Close to four hundred soldiers were taken prisoner.[4] The videos of battered Ukrainian POWs were circulated online to demonstrate the severity of the Ukrainian defeat.

This was an abrupt reversal for the Ukrainian troops, which conducted successful offensive operations for most of the summer. After two months

---

[1] Michael Cohen, "Ukraine's Battle at Ilovaisk, August 2014: The Tyranny of Means," *Army Press Online Journal*, APOJ 16-25, February 4, 2016; Ukrainian Helsinki Union for Human Rights, "Ilovaiska Trahedia 2014: Podii ta Vidpovidalnist," September 5, 2016, https://www.helsinki.org.ua/wp-content/uploads/2016/09/Yllowaysk_UGSPL-1.pdf.

[2] Ukraine Ministry of Defense, "Analiz vedennia antyterrorystychnoi operatsii ta naslidkiv vtorhnennia Rosiyskoi Federatsii v Ukrainu u serpni-veresni 2014 roku," August 2015, https://www.mil.gov.ua/content/other/anliz_rf.pdf.

[3] Office of the United Nations High Commissioner for Human Rights, "Human Rights Violations and Abuses and International Humanitarian Law Violations Committed in the Context of Ilovaisk Events in August 2014," August 1, 2018, https://www.ohchr.org/en/documents/country-reports/human-rights-violations-and-abuses-and-international-humanitarian-law.

[4] Serzh Marko, *Khronika hibrydnoi viyny* (Kyiv: Alterpress, 2016), 124.

Seize the City, Undo the State. Serhiy Kudelia, Oxford University Press. © Oxford University Press (2025).
DOI: 10.1093/9780197795576.003.0011

of fighting the Ukrainian forces liberated most of the separatist-controlled areas. The largest militant contingent from the Sloviansk agglomeration withdrew to Donetsk in early July. Ukrainian troops then took back Bakhmut, Lysychansk, Sieverodonetsk, Toretsk, and many smaller towns. The low density of insurgent presence outside urban centers allowed Ukrainian troops to surround town-based pockets of resistance and force militants to flee.[5] One of the Ukrainian officers recalled feeling "euphoric" about the August offensive: "Every day we seized a new town. . . . [T]hey had one or two cannons against our entire batteries—we erased their check-points to the ground and they had to flee leaving only their weapons behind."[6] There were no records of continued insurgent activity or civilian resistance in any of the liberated areas of Donbas. Instead, there were numerous reports of desertion from among the militant ranks.[7] There was also a strong sense that the separatist republics now survived on borrowed time. Their leaders—Girkin, Borodai, and Bolotov—had fled to Russia by mid-August. Those who replaced them were no longer capable of providing civilians with most basic services or protection and faced massive breakdown of administrative order. There were constant reports of water shortages, electricity blackouts, and shelling of infrastructure. Donetsk and Luhansk were almost completely encircled and small Ukrainian units already entered these cities with reconnaissance raids.[8] Complete seizure of the two regional capitals was expected in a matter of days or weeks.[9]

The surprise incursion of Russian troops quickly reversed the battlefield dynamics. Now Ukrainian troops were on the retreat, surrendering the localities they had fought so hard to retake. The Ukrainian leadership grappled with the real prospects of mounting casualties and new territorial losses. The signing of the Minsk Protocol on September 5, the agreement that led to de facto freezing of the conflict along the existing contact line, became Kyiv's

[5] A Russian military analyst suggested that the lack of a contiguous front line across the entire region was one of the main characteristics of the initial stage of the conflict. See Tsyganok, *Donbas*, 407–408.

[6] Serhiy Hlotov et al., *U vohnianomy kiltsi. Oborona Luhanskoho Aeroportu* (Kharkiv: Folio, 2018), 455.

[7] Andrew Kramer, "Ukraine Says Army Controls Center of a Rebel City," *New York Times*, August 17, 2014, https://www.nytimes.com/2014/08/18/world/europe/ukraine.html.

[8] On August 17 Ukrainian officials even claimed that the Ukrainian flag was raised over the central police station in Luhansk. See ibid.

[9] Interview with Ukraine's defense minister Stepan Poltorak by Artem Shevchenko in Hladka et al., *Dobrobaty*, 278.

desperate measure to stop further Russian advances.[10] It also created breathing space for the shrinking separatist enclave. The representatives of the two self-proclaimed republics, Oleksandr Zakharchenko and Igor Plotnitskiy, both Donbas-based commanders of large separatist battalions, added their signatures to the Minsk Protocol and were instantly elevated to the level of international diplomacy. Their quasi-state entities were now recognized by the Protocol as "special districts in Donetsk and Luhansk Oblasts" and received the right to have a special "system of self-governance" along with immunity for those who fought on their behalf. The second Minsk Agreement, signed in February 2015 following another Russia-led incursion around Debaltseve, dictated the need to guarantee the special status of these areas under the Ukrainian Constitution.

Over the next seven years the issue of de facto autonomous status of the two "republics" became one of the key stumbling blocks in all talks between Russia, Ukraine, and the West. Meanwhile, separatist formations produced their own symbols, myths, ideological narratives, and institutional framework; their political leadership turned into Moscow's proxies fully subordinated to the Kremlin's wishes.[11] On February 21, 2022, after years of shunning their requests, Putin signed the decrees recognizing the DNR and LNR as independent states. Three days later he used them as a pretext to announce a new, open military assault on Ukraine.

What Enabled the Conflict?

The centrality of the Donbas conflict in Russia's justifications for a full-scale invasion makes the understanding of its origins particularly vital. Russia initiated the formation of these quasi-state entities and aided in their institutional development, ensured their survival, and used them to further undermine Ukraine—first economically and diplomatically, then militarily. The evidence presented in this book points categorically to this conclusion. However, as this book also demonstrates, Russia's efforts might have failed in the early stages of the conflict without the cooperation of a variety of

---

[10] Sevhil Musayeva, "Petro Poroshenko: V mene, na zhal, ye za sho prosyty probachennia v Hospoda," *Ukrainska Pravda*, August 1, 2019, https://www.pravda.com.ua/articles/2019/08/1/7222417/.

[11] International Crisis Group, "Rebels without a Cause: Russia's Proxies in Eastern Ukraine," Report N254, July 16, 2019, https://www.crisisgroup.org/europe-central-asia/eastern-europe/ukraine/254-rebels-without-cause-russias-proxies-eastern-ukraine.

local actors. Analysis of the overall success of Russia's covert intervention thus takes us from considering public predispositions and insurgent tactics to examining elite responses and structural characteristics of the region.

Public preferences. None of the Ukrainian regions had a clear majority support for secession or Russia's irredentist campaign. However, apart from Crimea, Donbas showed the highest demand for various degrees of autonomy from Kyiv. Moreover, the backing of autonomous status in Donbas was not limited to the two capital cities but spread relatively evenly across the region. This became apparent in early March, when rallies in support of the referendum on self-determination were staged in the region's large and small towns. The autonomy drive was also linked to a strong supranational, regional identity that emphasized the industrial might of Donbas and its historical cultural and economic ties to Russia. It also appealed to those who prioritized regional attachment over loyalty to the Ukrainian state. Their prevalence allowed demonstrations in support of Ukraine to be suppressed and the separatist agenda to be imposed on most of the region. Yet in those few towns of Donbas where pro-Ukrainian activists managed to form alliances with business or political actors and engaged in visible resistance, they succeeded despite sizeable opposition.

Coercion. A shift in mass public sentiment was a background condition for the loss of Ukraine's sovereign control over Donbas. But it was achieved by a handful of individuals capable of removing symbols of the Ukrainian state by force. As the book shows, the initial assaults on key coercive state agencies produced a powerful contagion across the region, replicated by separatist sympathizers in neighboring towns. The shift in sentiment also shaped expectations of local officials, police, and civilians; conditioned municipal elite responses; influenced patterns of civilian recruitment into the militancy; and encouraged police defection. The armed challenge to the Ukrainian government in Donbas also prevented it from suppressing the separatist uprising more decisively from the start. Where Ukraine could show its coercive dominance, it had the advantage. Even limited deployment of Ukrainian troops and volunteer battalions in contested areas of control shifted the power balance in favor of local pro-Ukrainian actors. The ability of Ukrainian forces to prevail in violent skirmishes or quickly reverse separatist gains encouraged separatist sympathizers to flee to areas where militants still had the upper hand.

Topography. The spatial context of the insurgency in Donbas is critical for understanding its initial success in taking over a large territory despite its small scale. The high density of urban agglomerations helped separatist control quickly spread across the region. It served as a force amplifier for small numbers of militants with high mobility. This, in turn, enabled them to exert coercive pressure over local officials and civilians suspected of pro-Ukrainian loyalties. It also encouraged local sympathizers in neighboring towns to emulate their tactics and so acquire extra leverage in dealing with local officials. Towns with favorably predisposed residents acted as a shield for militants. They limited the type of arms that the Ukrainian armed forces could use and created additional operational obstacles, and the potentially high cost of urban warfare discouraged quick frontal assaults.

Municipal elites. The choices and strategies of town-level elite actors have been at the center of the book's analysis. While collaboration has not been the dominant strategy in towns reviewed here, many local officials hedged their risk by cooperating with the militants. This proved critical for achieving the key tasks of the separatist rulers, from organizing a region-wide referendum to ensuring continuity in towns' administration. Elites were also essential for separatist propaganda efforts. Top local officials amplified their grievances and endorsed their demands in official speeches, ensured favorable coverage of militants in local media, raised funds and provided office space for their needs, and replaced state symbols with separatist imagery. However, municipal elites were not just passive targets of coercive pressure. In some cases, mayors proactively delegated their proxies to run town-based militant groups. In others, they formed alliances and used their influence to mobilize residents for rallies on behalf of separatist authorities. Yet others exercised agency by subverting militant efforts to take full control of a town's administration or by leading locals to quash separatist challenges.

Governance. The demand for self-rule rested on the expectation of higher living standards once the region became autonomous. Militants exploited these expectations by adding anti-oligarchic and social justice themes to their messages. So it was essential for them to prevent any rupture in the provision of services and payments during the secession process. They proved highly strategic in allowing local officials to continue fulfilling their roles and elevating those who were willing to collaborate with them. The examples of Sloviansk and Horlivka, where mayors were detained and rebel leaders took on administrative responsibilities, were exceptions. More common were governing arrangements whereby local officials either remained fully in control or had to share some of their power with separatist representatives.

This legitimized separatist rule and minimized costs that the secessionist process would have otherwise imposed on residents.

2022 in Light of 2014

Their experience with instigating the conflict in Donbas in 2014 should have given the Russian leaders reasons for both optimism and caution. On one hand, the capacity to trigger pro-Russian mobilization outside Donbas was limited even in 2014—and became minimal in subsequent years.[12] Cognizant of this, many senior Ukrainian policymakers and analysts expressed skepticism about Western warnings that Russia could launch an offensive.[13] Two weeks before the attack, the former defense minister of Ukraine, Andriy Zahorodnyuk, claimed that the amount of Russian troops concentrated on Ukrainian borders was "far from sufficient" for the "apocalyptic scenario" of a full-scale invasion. "It would be a senseless adventurism if they try it," he concluded.[14]

For the Russian leadership, however, the experience of covert takeover of Donbas might have offered a different lesson. It showed that minimal coercive pressure from a handful of militants could induce defection of local law enforcement and the cooperation of local officials. It also might have demonstrated that a minority of vocal supporters among civilians could overpower the silent opposing majority intimidated by possible violent reprisals. As a result, a large enough number of local collaborators and a vocal minority combined with the show of military force might have been viewed in Moscow as sufficient for the quick capture of new Ukrainian regions bordering Russia. One report published weeks before the 2022 invasion and based on Ukrainian intelligence sources suggested that the Russian security agency had a detailed map of potential local collaborators in different regions of Ukraine.[15] They were expected to help Russian troops secure key infrastructural objects, take government buildings, neutralize opponents, and run the occupation regime. Given the extent of cooperative behavior

[12] John O'Loughlin, Gerard Toal, and Vladimir Kolosov, "The Rise and Fall of 'Novorossiya': Examining Support for a Separatist Geopolitical Imaginary in Southeast Ukraine," *Post-Soviet Affairs* 33, no. 2 (2017): 124–144.

[13] Dmitriy Gordon, "Interview with Minister of Foreign Affairs of Ukraine Dmytro Kuleba," *V Gostiah u Gordona*, August 15, 2022, https://www.youtube.com/watch?v=vleLiygfw2A&ab_channel=OpenUkraine.

[14] Zahorodnyuk, "Public Remarks at the Kyiv Security Forum."

[15] Jack Watling and Nick Reynolds, "The Plot to Destroy Ukraine," *RUSI Special Report*, February 15, 2022, 10.

of local elites in 2014, it was not unrealistic to believe that this experience might be replicated in 2022.

In the early morning hours of February 24, 2022, Russian troops entered a very different Ukraine. Instead of lacking legitimate leadership, the country's president had the strongest popular mandate of any of his predecessors.[16] Instead of acquiescing, local authorities, even formerly pro-Russian mayors, like the ones in Odesa, Kharkiv, and Kryvyi Rih, suddenly emerged at the forefront of organizing the defense of their cities.[17] And instead of an indifferent or welcoming local population, Russian soldiers encountered unprecedented grassroots resistance, ranging from public defiance to subversion.[18] Although there were a handful of instances of collaboration among town officials, as in Rubizhne in the Luhansk region and Kupiansk in the Kharkiv region, the scale of defection of local officials was much smaller than in 2014. Instead, many municipal leaders openly defied the Russian military presence and encouraged nonviolent protests. They kept Ukrainian flags flying over government buildings and used social media to make regular public appeals and reassert their loyalty to Ukraine. The challenge that such a defiant stance posed to Moscow became clear when, several weeks into the invasion, Russian forces started abducting local administrators to coerce them into collaboration.[19] While some were ultimately released and forced to flee their towns, several disappeared or were confirmed killed.

Ironically, what made the local response to the Russian invasion so different were the institutional and societal changes triggered by Russia's earlier intervention in 2014. In response to demands for regional autonomy, the Ukrainian government had introduced far-reaching decentralization reforms that empowered municipal authorities. They left more of the locally generated revenues with the communities and gave community-elected leaders greater discretion in setting spending priorities. This led to noticeable improvement in the quality of public services and delivery of

[16] In the run-off for the 2019 presidential election, Zelensky received a larger share of votes (73.22%) than any of the winning candidates of the previous presidential elections in Ukraine.

[17] For an account of the role of municipal authorities in organizing town defenses, see Andrew Harding, *A Small, Stubborn Town: Life, Death and Defiance in Ukraine* (London: Ithaka Press, 2023).

[18] *The Economist*, "Technology Is Deepening Civilian Involvement in War," July 3, 2023, https://www.economist.com/special-report/2023/07/03/technology-is-deepening-civilian-involvement-in-war.

[19] Council of Europe, "Congress President Condemns the Continuing Abduction of Ukrainian Local Elected Representatives," September 5, 2022, https://www.coe.int/en/web/congress/-/congress-president-condemns-the-continuing-abduction-of-ukrainian-local-elected-representatives (last accessed: December 21, 2023).

new public goods. One municipal survey showed that over half of respondents in the eleven largest municipalities were satisfied with the activities of their mayors.[20] The second change was the accelerated nation-building that increased the sense of attachment to the state and the feeling of national pride. A growing number of Ukrainians identified Ukraine as their homeland (an increase of 11% between 2012 and 2015).[21] Despite continued divisiveness in Ukrainian politics, in two presidential elections in a row (2014 and 2019) society could coalesce around a new political leader despite cultural or regional differences. One implication of the rising civic attachment was the strengthened cross-regional commitment to defend Ukraine against full-scale Russian attack. As reports on a pending Russian invasion intensified, the share of Ukrainians willing to engage in armed resistance grew from 33.3% in December 2021 to 37.3% in February 2022.[22] And weeks prior to the assault, over half of respondents across Ukraine (57%) suggested that they were willing to resist by any means possible.

Finally, there has been a clear shift in public attitudes to Russia and its role in the Donbas conflict. By 2021 two-thirds (72%) of Ukrainians viewed Russia as an enemy state, while the share of those who described their attitudes to Russian people as "warm" declined from 47% in May 2018 to 30% in April 2021.[23] Moreover, Russia came to be viewed as the main culprit in the ongoing armed conflict in Donbas. In 2020, 61% of Ukrainians agreed that the conflict was due to "Russian aggression with the use of local militants," and only 21% still argued that it was a civil war.[24] Russian aggression was the instigator in the opinion of most respondents in all regions of Ukraine except for the East, where a plurality (42.2%) of respondents still considered it to be an "internal conflict." This attitudinal change helped to produce

[20] International Republican Institute, "Annual Municipal Survey of Ukraine Reveals Satisfaction with Local Government," September 15, 2022, https://www.iri.org/resources/annual-municipal-survey-of-ukraine-reveals-satisfaction-with-local-governments/.

[21] Grigore Pop-Eleches and Graeme Robertson, "Identity and Political Preferences in Ukraine—before and after the Euromaidan," *Post-Soviet Affairs* 34, nos. 2–3 (2018): 111.

[22] Survey of 2004 respondents conducted by Kyiv International Institute of Sociology, February 5–11, 2022, https://www.kiis.com.ua/?lang=ukr&cat=reports&id=1099&page=1. By contrast, in April 2014 only 11.9% of respondents in Donetska and 10.7% in Luhanska were willing to use force against Russian aggression. See Kyiv International Institute of Sociology survey conducted April 8–16, 2014, https://www.kiis.com.ua/?lang=rus&cat=reports&id=302&page=7.

[23] *Slovo i Dilo*, "Yak zminyvalos stavlennia ukraintsiv do rosii I rosian," March 10, 2023, https://www.slovoidilo.ua/2023/03/10/infografika/suspilstvo/yak-zminyuvalosya-stavlennya-ukrayinicziv-rosiyi-ta-rosiyan.

[24] Survey of 2022 respondents conducted in Ukraine September 14–19, 2020, by Razumkov Center, https://detector.media/infospace/article/181066/2020-09-29-yak-zminylys-upodobannya-ta-interesy-ukraintsiv-do-zasobiv-masovoi-informatsii-pislya-vyboriv-2019-r-ta-pochatku-pandemii-covid-19/.

broad consensus among Ukrainians in March 2022 on the actual goals of a full-scale Russian invasion. Only 6% of respondents in the East and 1% in all other regions viewed the war as, in Putin's terms, an attempt to protect the Russian-speaking population.[25] Instead, majorities in all regions (56% on average across Ukraine) interpreted Moscow's goal in starkly existential terms, as "full annihilation of the Ukrainian people."[26]

Ultimately, Putin's decision to launch an open assault on Ukraine reflected his recognition that Russia had failed to achieve any of the longer-term goals behind its initial covert intervention in Donbas. It did not produce a large-scale civil war—in fact, Ukraine-controlled Donbas remained stable and peaceful. The separatist sentiments did not spill over into neighboring regions but dissipated with the rise in civic pride. Ukraine withstood the pressure to federalize or create autonomous enclaves; instead, it decentralized power responsibly and with effective results. It did not experience a democratic reversal; rather, it conducted democratic elections that produced a peaceful turnover in ruling elites. And Ukraine's economy did not crumble under the burden of new military expenses; its GDP had been growing at an average annual rate of 2% since 2015, and individual incomes were on the rise. But Putin's decision also, and conclusively, revealed that even if Ukraine's state-building could be derailed by a few dozen armed men, it could no longer be stopped, even by Russia's entire military might.

[25] Survey of 1,200 respondents conducted March 12–13, 2022, by Rating sociological company, https://ratinggroup.ua/research/ukraine/chetvertyy_obschenacionalnyy_opros_ukraincev_v_usloviyah_voyny_12-13_marta_2022_goda.html. By contrast, in April 2014 almost half of respondents in Donetska (47%) and Luhansk (44%) oblasts and a third of respondents (32.6%) in all southeastern regions said that Russia was justly protecting the interests of Russian speakers in Ukraine. See Mostovaya and Rakhmanin, "Yugo-Vostok: Vetv Dreva Nashego."

[26] Survey of 1,200 respondents conducted March 12–13, 2022, by Rating sociological company, https://ratinggroup.ua/research/ukraine/chetvertyy_obschenacionalnyy_opros_ukraincev_v_usloviyah_voyny_12-13_marta_2022_goda.html.

Appendix

Initial Fatalities of the Armed Conflict in Donetsk and Luhansk Regions, April 11–May 5, 2014

Date of Fatality[*]	Government Side	Insurgent Side	Civilians
April 13	Henadiy Bilichenko	Ruben Avanesian	
April 16		Oleksandr Averbakh	
		Andriy Guzhva	
April 17	Yuri Popravka		
	Yuri Diakovskyi		
	Volodymyr Rybak		
April 20	Mykhailo Stanislavenko	Pavlo Pavelko	
		Serhiy Rudenko	
		Oleksandr Siganov	
April 24		Oleksandr Lubenets	
April 27		Anatoliy Lastovchenko	
May 2	Ruslan Plohod'ko	Valeriy Pavlov	
	Oleksandr Sabada	Sergei Zhurikov	
	Serhiy Rudenko	Andriy Afonin	
	Mykola Topchiy		
	Ihor Hrishyn		
	Serhiy Panasiuk		
	Petro Kovalenko		
May 3			Yulia Izotova
May 5	Oleksandr Anishenko	Viacheslav Rudakov	
	Ruslan Luzhevskyi	Oleksandr Parkhomenko	
	Viktor Dolinskyi	Valeriy Parsegov	
		Volodymyr Kukhno	
		Kostiantyn Ivanov	

[*] Dates may reflect the day of confirmed disappearance.
Note: Table lists only fatalities that resulted from direct engagements of the warring sides.
Sources: Memory Book, "Knyha pamiati polehlyh za Ukrainu" (Memory book of those who died for Ukraine). Website launched on July 22, 2014. Last Accessed October 8, 2024. https://memorybook.org.ua/index1.htm; Ukrainian Wikipedia, "Vtraty prorosiyskyh syl u rosiysko-ukrainskiy viyni z 2014 roku" (The losses of pro-Russian forces in Russian-Ukrainian war 2014). Last edited on September 27, 2024. Last Accessed on October 8, 2024. https://t.ly/UzuD1; Zhuchkovskiy *85 dnei Slavianska*.

Bibliography

Primary Sources

List of Interviews (with affiliation in spring 2014)

Anonymous 1: civic activist in Severodonetsk (Severodonetsk, June 13, 2019).

Anonymous 2: entrepreneur/owner of a trading company in Severodonetsk (online, June 10, 2021).

Anonymous 3: judge (Svatove, June 10, 2019).

Anonymous 4: local entrepreneur (Svatove, July 10, 2019).

Anonymous 5: political consultant (Moscow, July 23, 2019).

"Ares": member of soccer ultras club FC Ilichyvets (FK Mariupol)/pro-Ukrainian activist (Mariupol, November 21, 2018).

Journalists of Bakhmut newspaper *Sobytia* (Bakhmut, September 18, 2018).

Patriots of Dobropillia members (Dobropillia, October 3, 2018).

Aksentyev, Anton: political analyst (Kharkiv, May 24, 2019).

Aladin, Oleksandr: head of Russian Bloc party office in Pokrovsk (online, Pokrovsk, August 18, 2020).

Apryshkin, Serhiy: chief of staff of acting city mayor of Lysychansk (online, May 4, 2021).

Artyukh, Oleksiy: journalist (Rubizhne, June 13, 2019).

Avakyan, Gayane: journalist (Bakhmut, November 4, 2018).

Averin, Volodymyr: editor of separatist newspaper *People's Newspaper* in Kostiantynivka (online, May 28, 2020).

Balinov, Oleksandr: entrepreneur/city council deputy of Novohrodivka (Novohrodivka, October 18, 2018).

Barabash, Mykhailo: city council deputy in Rubizhne/head of energy department Rubizhanskiy Krasitel (Rubizhne, June 13, 2019).

Bashtovyi, Anatoliy: director of Druzhkivka Community College (Druzhkivka, September 11, 2018).

Batozskyi, Kostiantyn: ex-advisor to the head of Donetsk oblast state administration Serhiy Taruta (Kyiv, December 2014).

Berezin, Volodymyr: civic activist/journalist (Kostiantynivka, September 20, 2018).

Besarab, Serhiy: civic activist in Myrnohrad (Myrnohrad, October 16, 2018).

Bessonnyi, Andriy: deputy city mayor of Kramatorsk (Kramatorsk, September 12, 2018).

Bihunov, Denys: Sloviansk city council official (Sloviansk, December 10, 2014).

Biletska, Lyudmyla: city council deputy of Novohrodivka (Novohrodivka, October 17, 2018).

Bohach, Vasyl (Ivan Bohdan): SBU officer, director of SBU division on counterterrorism and threats to national statehood in Mariupol (Mariupol, November 19, 2018).

Boichenko, Vadym: personnel director on MMK Illicha (Mariupol, November 19, 2018).

Boiko, Volodymyr: Bakhmut city council deputy/KPU faction (September 19, 2018).

Borodavka, Andriy: journalist (Khariv, May 22, 2019).

Borova, Lilia: journalist in Pokrovsk (Kramatorsk, October 16, 2018).

Borozentsev, Serhiy: lawyer/civic activist (Kramatorsk, September 10, 2018).

Brazhnikov, Dmytro: head of Novodonetsk-Service (Dobropillia, October 3, 2018).

Bredykhin, Anton: civic activist/Cossack researcher (Moscow, July 22, 2019).

Bukharkova, Tetian: head of Batkivshchyna office in Druzhkivka (Druzhkivka, September 11, 2018).

Bulakh, Dmytro: civic activist (Kharkiv, May 21, 2019).

Buvailo, Svitlana: head of Batkivshyna office in Kostiantynivka (Kostiantynivka, September 13, 2018).

Chetveriov, Henadiy: entrepreneur (Dorbropillia, October 3/October 16, 2018).

Chystylin, Volodymyr: civic activist/coordinator of Kharkiv Euromaidan (Kharkiv, May 23, 2019).

Dadashov, Ordash: Donetsk oblast city council deputy/entrepreneur (Bakhmut, September 17, 2018).

Denshikov, Ruslan: entrepreneur/Svoboda party office head in Lyman (Lyman, November 6, 2018).

Denyshchenko, Denis: entrepreneur/civic activist in Luhansk (Severodonetsk, June 14, 2019).

Dibrova, Serhiy: journalist at online newspaper *Dumskaya* (Odesa, June 24, 2019).

Dreval, Viktor: secretary of Dobropillia city council (Dobropillia, October 3, 2018).

Dudnyk, Petro: pastor (Sloviansk, December 10, 2014).

Fialko, Yevhen: editor-in-chief of *Nasha Druzhkovka* (Druzhkivka, September 11, 2018).

Firsov, Yegor: member of Ukrainian Parliament (Kyiv, December 2014).

Fisun, Oleksandr: professor of political science, Karazin Kharkiv National University (Kharkiv, May 24, 2019).

Harkavyi, Valeriy: head of Starobilsk raion state administration (Starobilsk, July 10, 2019).

Holub, Oleh: deputy mayor of Lysychansk (Severodonetsk, June 14, 2019).

Holubenko, Mykola: city council secretary/Selydove city council deputy (Selydove, October 17, 2018).

Honcharova, Elizaveta: journalist (Bakhmut, September 19, 2018).

Hrudkin, Andriy: lawyer in Dzerzhynskvuhol/civic activist (Toretsk, November 7, 2018).

Hryhorenko, Volodymyr: former police officer/entrepreneur/pro-Ukrainian activist (Starobilsk, July 8, 2019).

Hrytsak, Vitaliy: IT administrator (Selydove, October 17, 2018).

Hrytsyshyn, Volodymyr: Severodonetsk mayor 1994–2010 (Severodonetsk, June 12, 2019).

Ibrahim, Moris, deputy head of KPU city office (Odesa, June 27, 2019).

Irkha, Yuriy: entrepreneur (Svatove, June 10/July 10, 2019).

Ivanov, Vasiliy: Druzhkivka city council member (Druzhkivka, September 20, 2018).

Kabchenko, Vitalina: deputy of Bilozersk city council (October 3, 2018).

Kahala, Yuriy: construction worker/Aidar battalion volunteer (Starobilsk, July 10, 2019).

Khainus, Aleksandr: entrepreneur (Chasiv Yar, September 19, 2018).

Khabarov, Volodymyr: worker at MMK Illicha/pro-Russian activist (Mariupol, November 21, 2018).

Kharchuk, Valeriy: Rubizhne city council deputy/entrepreneur (Rubizhne, June 13, 2019).

Khotlubei, Yuriy: mayor of Mariupol (Mariupol, November 20, 2018).

Khromenko, Olga: head of Batkivshyna party Selydove office (Selydove, October 17, 2018).

Kolesov, Eduard: Mariupol fire rescue department/civic activist (Mariupol, November 20, 2018).

Kononets, Dmytro: local entrepreneur/civic activist (Bakhmut, September 17, 2018).

Kononov, Illia: professor of sociology at Luhansk National University (Ivano-Frankivsk, August 3, 2019).

Kopatko, Yevhen: sociologist and political consultant (Kyiv, December 16, 2014).

Kormiltsev, Oleksiy: assistant to member of parliament (Dobropillia, October 3, 2018).

Kruzhko, Bohdan: news photographer (Selydove, October 17, 2018).

Ksheminskiy, Denis: editor-in-chief of Toretsk municipal newspaper *Dzershynskiy Shakhter* (Toretsk, November 8, 2018).

Kuhliev, Anton: manager at Culture Palace in Novohrodivka/civic activist (October 17, 2018).

Kustov, Oleksandr: head of youth wing of the Party of Regions in Lysychansk (online, April 19, 2021).

Kuzovenin, Anatoliy: entrepreneur/Svatove raion Cossack chief (Svatove, June 10, 2019).

Ladyka, Oleksiy: reporter for regional newspaper *Vostochnyi Ekspress* (Kramatorsk, September 12).

Lishyk, Olha: head of culture department in Severodonetsk city administration (Severodonetsk, June 12, 2019).

Lomako, Oleksandr: city council deputy/principal of Lyman Gymnasium (Lyman, November 7, 2018).

Luhova, Valentyna: Druzhkivka school principal (Druzhkivka, September 11, 2018).

Lukianchenko, Anatoliy: Donetsk mayor (Kyiv, December, 2014).

Lysohor, Mykola: journalist (Mariupol, November 20, 2018).

Malanchuk, Yaroslav: deputy head of Svoboda party office in Kostiantynivka (Kostiantynivka, September 13, 2018).

Mardian, Vadym: editor-in-chief of Bakhmut newspaper *Sobytia* (Bakhmut, September 18, 2018).

Mateichenko, Kostiantyn: commander of Artemivsk battalion (Kyiv, November 9, 2018).

Menendez, Enrique: civic activist in Donetsk (Kyiv, July 6, 2019).

Milakovsky, Brian: USAID expert (Severodonetsk, June 11, 2019).

Mokhnyk, Roman: city council deputy of Soledar/Batkivshchyna faction (Soledar, September 18, 2018).

Murlykina, Anna: political reporter of Mariupol online portal 0629 (Mariupol, November 21, 2018).

Museiko, Kostiantyn: city council deputy/entrepreneur (online, August 5, 2020).

Nemyria, Hryhoriy: member of the Ukrainian Parliament (Kyiv, December 16, 2014).

Nesterova, Viktoria: manager of Chasiv Yar Culture Palace (Chasiv Yar, September 19, 2018).

Nizhelska, Olena: personnel department of Lysychansk NPZ/pro-Ukrainian activist (Severodonetsk, June 14, 2019).

Opanasenko, Olha: mayor of Chasiv Yar (Chasiv Yar, September 19, 2018).

Oros, Volodymyr: civic activist (Dobropillia, October 3, 2018).

Osovskiy, Maksym: pro-Ukrainian activist/video streamer in Luhansk (Kyiv, June 6, 2019).

Ostapenko, Oleksandr: Odesa city council deputy/Front of Changes faction (Odesa, June 24, 2019).

Ovcharenko, Svitlana: editor-in-chief of Bakhmut newspaper *Vpered* (Bakhmut, September 20, 2018).

Pankov, Oleksandr: political reporter at *Priazovskiy Rabochiy* (Mariupol, November 21, 2018).

Podoprigora, Vitaliy: Druzhkivka city council member/entrepreneur (Druzhkivka, September 11, 2018).

Podybailo, Maria: lecturer at Mariupol State University/pro-Ukrainian activist (Mariupol, November 20, 2018).

Polishuk, Vasiliy: Odesa city council deputy/KPU faction (Moscow, July 24, 2019).

Polupan, Ivan: city council deputy/leader of youth branch of Party of Regions in Kramatorsk (Kramatorsk, September 10, 2018).

Pridushchenko, Viktoria: civic activist from Mariupol Druzhyna (Mariupol, November 19, 2018).

Prigarin, Aleksandr: professor at Odesa National University (Odesa, June 26, 2019).

Priheba, Hryhoriy: entrepreneur/pro-Ukrainian activist in Luhansk (Severodonetsk, June 13, 2019).

Punin, Roman: journalist for *Limanskaya Storona* (Lyman, November 6, 2018).

Romankiv, Dmytro: priest of Ukrainian Autocephalous Orthodox Church Pokrovy in Svatove (Svatove, June 10, 2019).

Romantsova, Maryna: civic activist in Kramatorsk (Kramatorsk, September 10, 2018).

Rozputko, Mykhailo: editor-in-chief of newspaper *Provintsia* (Kostiantynivka, September 13, 2018).

Rozumnyi, Yuriy: secretary of city council of Kostiantynivka (Kostiantynivka, September 13, 2018).

Rybalko, Yevhen: mayor of Svatove (Svatove, June 10, 2019).

Samarskyi, Serhiy: Severodonetsk city council deputy/journalist (Severodonetsk, June 3, 2015).

Savchenko, Tetiana: deputy mayor of Bakhmut (September 18, 2018).

Savinov, Konstantin: deputy mayor of Donetsk (Moscow, July 23, 2019).

Shapovalov, Andriy: oblast council deputy/journalist in Luhansk (Severodonetsk, July 14, 2019).

Shmushkovych, Mykhailo: Odesa oblast council deputy/Party of Regions faction (Odesa, June 22, 2019).

Shtal, Andriy: political reporter for *Kramatorskaya Pravda* (Kramatorsk, September 12, 2018).

Shvedov, Viktor: lawyer/pro-Ukrainian activist (Lysychansk, June 12, 2019).

Shynkarenko, Oleksandr: city council deputy and head of the Party of Regions factions.

Sivkovich, Vitaliy: worker at Chasiv Yar plant (Chasiv Yar, September 19, 2018).

Strepochenko, Mykola: farmer/pro-Ukrainian activist in Dobropillia (online, October 20, 2020).

Svetikov, Oleksiy: journalist (Severodonetsk, June 11, 2019).

Tkachev, Yuriy: editor-in-chief of online newspaper *Timer* (Odesa, June 28, 2019).

Trebushkin, Ruslan: mayor of Myrnohrad (November 2018).

Tremasov, Stanislav: entrepreneur/pro-Ukrainian activist in Bakhmut (Bakhmut, September 20, 2018).

Tsakhiv, Oleksandr: Selydove city treasury department official (Selydove, October 17, 2014).

Tsarevskyi, Petro: farmer/deputy of Starobilsk raion council (Starobilsk, July 8, 2019).

Tsveloi, Pavel: entrepreneur/head of anti-crisis council/pro-Russian activist in Kramatorsk (online, June 28, 2020).

Tsymbal, Oleksandr: deputy of Svatove raion council (Svatove, July 10, 2019).

Vasiliev, Aleksandr: Odesa city council deputy/lecturer at Odesa National University (Moscow, July 24, 2019).

Vetoshko, Oksana: editor-in-chief of Pokrovsk municipal newspaper *Mayak* (Pokrovsk, October 18, 2018).

Vlasov, Mykhailo: secretary of Lysychansk city council (Severodonetsk, July 10, 2019).

Vodolazskyi, Anatoliy: pro-Ukrainian activist (Druzhkivka, September 20, 2018).

Vynnyk, Serhiy: head of communal services department in Toretsk town administration (Toretsk, November 8, 2018).

Vynnyk, Volodymyr: former SBU officer/deputy of Starobilsk city council/entrepreneur (Starobilsk, July 9, 2019).

Yermolchenko, Oleksandr: worker at NKMZ (Kramatorsk, September 10, 2018).

Yevsikov, Yuri: Toretsk city council secretary (Toretsk, November 8, 2018).

Zaitsev, Viktor: instructor of military guard of the Donetsk railway in Lyman (Lyman, November 6, 2018).

Zinchenko, Anatoliy: Pokrovsk city council deputy (Pokrovsk, October 18, 2018).

Secondary Sources

Anderson, Noel. "Competitive Intervention, Protracted Conflict, and the Global Prevalence of Civil War." *International Studies Quarterly* 63, no. 3 (2019): 692–706.

Aratyunyan, Anna. *Hybrid Warriors: Proxies, Freelances and Moscow's Struggle for Ukraine.* London: Hurst, 2022.

Arel, Dominique. "Language, Status, and State Loyalty in Ukraine." *Harvard Ukrainian Studies* 35, nos. 1–4 (2017–2018): 233–263.

Arel, Dominique, and Jesse Driscoll. *Ukraine's Unnamed War: Before the Russian Invasion of 2022.* Cambridge: Cambridge University Press, 2022.

Arjona, Ana. *Rebelocracy: Social Order in the Colombian Civil War.* Cambridge: Cambridge University Press, 2016.

Arjona, Ana, Nelson Kasfir, and Zachariah Mampilly, eds. *Rebel Governance in Civil War.* Cambridge: Cambridge University Press, 2015.

Arslan, Mehmet, David Cunningham, Kristian Skrede Gleditsch, and Idean Salehyan."Trends in Civil War Data: Geography, Organizations, and Events." In *What Do We Know about Civil Wars?*, edited by T. David Mason and Sara McLaughlin Mitchell. Lanham, MD: Rowman & Littlefield, 2023: 249–262.

Ayres, Sabra. "Chaos and Fear Grip Residents in Eastern Ukraine after Referendum." *Aljazeera America,* May 12, 2014. http://america.aljazeera.com/articles/2014/5/12/chaos-and-fear-gripeastukraineafterthereferendum.html.

Balcells, Laia, and Stathis Kalyvas. "Does Warfare Matter? Severity, Duration, and Outcomes of Civil Wars." *Journal of Conflict Resolution* 58, no. 8 (2014): 1390–1418.

Baranets, Viktor. *Spetsoperatsiya Krym 2014.* Moscow: Komsomolskaia Pravda, 2019.

Barkov, Aleksandr. *Novorossia v moem serdtse.* Moscow: Izdatelskie Reshenia, 2018.

Bastyreva, Liubov. "Za mir v nashem gorode, regione, Ukrainye." *Mayak,* March 6, 2014.

BBC News Ukraina. "Minoborony opublikuvalo analiz boyu pid Ilovaiskom." October 19, 2015. https://www.bbc.com/ukrainian/politics/2015/10/151019_ilovaysk_report_vs.

BBC Ukraina. "Regiony ukrepliayutsia i gotoviatsia k provokatsiyam." January 28, 2014. https://www.bbc.com/ukrainian/ukraine_in_russian/2014/01/140128_ru_s_regional_protests.

Beall, Jo, Tom Goodfellow, and Dennis Rodgers. "Cities and Conflict in Fragile States in the Developing World." *Urban Studies* 50, no. 15 (November 2013): 3065–3083.

Beissinger, Mark. *Revolutionary City: Urbanization and the Global Transformation of Rebellion.* Princeton, NJ: Princeton University Press, 2022.

Beissinger, Mark. "Structure and Example in Modular Political Phenomenon: The Diffusion of Bulldozer/Rose/Orange/Tulip Revolutions." *Perspective on Politics* 5, no. 2 (June 2007): 259–276.

Bellingcat. "'A Birdie Is Flying towards You': Identifying the Separatists Linked to Downing of MH17." June 2019. https://www.bellingcat.com/app/uploads/2019/06/a-birdie-is-flying-towards-you.pdf.

Bellingcat. "Identifying the Separatists Linked to the Downing of MH17." June 19, 2019. https://www.bellingcat.com/news/uk-and-europe/2019/06/19/identifying-the-separatists-linked-to-the-downing-of-mh17/.

Bellingcat. "JIT Indictments and Reactions: Analyzing New Evidence Linking Separatists and Russian Officials to MH17." July 17, 2019. https://www.bellingcat.com/

news/uk-and-europe/2019/07/17/jit-indictments-and-reactions-analyzing-new-evidence-linking-separatists-and-russian-officials-to-mh17/.

Bellingcat. "The Role of Sergey Dubinsky in the Downing of MH17." March 2, 2017. https://www.bellingcat.com/news/uk-and-europe/2017/03/02/the-role-of-sergey-dubinsky-in-the-downing-of-mh17/.

Bogner, Matilad. "7 Years with No Answers. What Is Lacking in the Investigations of the Events in Odesa on 2 May 2014?" UN OHCHR, April 30, 2021. https://ukraine.un.org/en/126054-7-years-no-answers-what-lacking-investigations-events-odesa-2-may-2014.

Bohdan, Ivan. *Mariupol 2014*. Mariupol: KIT, 2016.

Bohdan, Ivan. *Patriotv'yazni*. Mariupol: KIT, 2018.

Bondar, N. "Davaite Zhyty Myrno." *Visnyk Starobilshyny*. Nos. 35–36. May 2, 2014.

Bovdunov, Aleksandr. "Kogda my horonim nashyh rebiat, groby nakryvaem trikolorom." *Voennoe Obozrenie*, August 26, 2014. https://topwar.ru/56789-kogda-my-horonim-nashih-rebyat-groby-nakryvaem-trikolorom.html.

Bowen, Andrew. "Coercive Diplomacy and the Donbas: Explaining Russian Strategy in Eastern Ukraine." *Journal of Strategic Studies* 42, nos. 3–4 (2019): 312–343.

Bratkov, Sergei. "My davali prisiagu na vernost narodu: S narodom i ostanemsia!" *Vperiod*, April 16, 2014.

Brik, Tymofiy. "Ukraine's 'Type 4' Conflict: Why Is It Important to Study Terminology before Changing It?" Policy Memo No. 575. Washington, DC: PONARS Eurasia, February 2019. https://www.ponarseurasia.org/wp-content/uploads/attachments/Pepm575_Brik_Feb2019-1.pdf.

Buckholz, Quentin. "The Dogs That Didn't Bark: Elite Preferences and the Failure of Separatism in Kharkiv and Dnipropetrovsk." *Problems of Post-Communism* 66, no. 3 (2019): 151–160.

Bukey, Evan Burr. *Hitler's Austria: Popular Sentiment in the Nazi Era*. Chapel Hill: University of North Carolina Press, 2000.

Bura, Daria, and Oleksandr Krasovytskyi. *Khronika Viyny 2014–2020: Vid Maidanu do Ilovaisku*. Kharkiv: Folio, 2020.

Burns, William. *The Back Channel: A Memoir of American Diplomacy and the Case for Its Renewal*. New York: Random House, 2019.

Büscher, Karen. "African Cities and Violent Conflict: The Urban Dimension of Conflict and Post Conflict Dynamics in Central and Eastern Africa." *Journal of Eastern African Studies* 12, no. 2 (2018): 193–210.

Byman, Daniel, Peter Chalk, Bruce Hoffman, William Rosenau, and David Brannan. *Trends in Outside Support for Insurgent Movements*. Santa Monica, CA: RAND, 2001.

Cederman, Lars-Erik, Seraina Rüegger, and Guy Schvitz. "Redemption through Rebellion: Border Change, Lost Unity, and Nationalist Conflict." *American Journal of Political Science* 66, no. 1 (2022): 24–42.

Censor. "Putin, Bog, i Surkov—sviataia troitsa glavaria terroristov atamana Kozitsyna." November 13, 2014. https://censor.net/ru/video_news/311820/putin_bog_i_surkov_svyataya_troitsa_glavarya_terroristov_atamana_kozitsyna_video.

Charap, Samuel. "NATO Honesty on Ukraine Could Avert Conflict." *Financial Times*, January 13, 2022. https://www.ft.com/content/74089d46-abb8-4daa-9ee4-e9e9e4c45ab1.

Charap, Samuel, and Timothy J. Colton. *Everyone Loses: The Ukraine Crisis and Ruinous Contest for Post-Soviet Eurasia*. London: IISS, 2017.

Charap, Samuel, et al. *Russia's Military Intervention: Patterns, Drivers, and Signposts*. Research Report. Santa Monica, CA: RAND, 2021.

Chazan, Naomi. "Conclusion: Irredentism, Separatism, and Nationalism." In *Irredentism and International Politics*, edited by Naomi Chazan. Boulder, CO: Lynne Rienner, 1991: 139–152.

Chekinov, Sergei, and Sergei Bogdanov. "O kharaktere i soderzhanii voiny novogo pokolenia." *Voennaia Mysl'*, no. 10 (2013): 13–24.

Cohen, Michael. "Ukraine's Battle at Ilovaisk, August 2014: The Tyranny of Means." *Army Press Online Journal*, APOJ 16-25, February 4, 2016.

Collier, Paul, and Anke Hoeffler. "Greed and Grievance in Civil War." *Oxford Economic Papers* 56, no. 4 (October 2004): 563–595.

Council of Europe. "Congress President Condemns the Continuing Abduction of Ukrainian Local Elected Representatives." September 5, 2022. https://www.coe.int/en/web/congress/-/congress-president-condemns-the-continuing-abduction-of-ukrainian-local-elected-representatives.

Constitution of Ukraine. 2013. https://www.justice.gov/sites/default/files/eoir/legacy/2013/11/08/constitution_14.pdf.

Conway, M. A., et al. "The Formation of Flashbulb Memories." *Memory & Cognition* 22 (1994): 326–343.

Costalli, Stefano, and Andrea Ruggeri. "Emotions, Ideologies, and Violent Political Mobilization." *PS: Political Science & Politics* 50, no. 4 (October 2017): 923–927.

Court of the Hague. "Judgement against Leonid Volodymyrovych Kharchenko." November 17, 2022. https://uitspraken.rechtspraak.nl/inziendocument?id=ECLI:NL:RBDHA:2022:12218&showbutton=true&keyword=ECLI%3aNL%3aRBDHA%3a2022%3a12218/.

Coynash, Halya. "Tortured to Death for Defending Ukraine: The First War Crimes Russia Brought to Donbas." Kharkiv Human Rights Protection Group, April 17, 2019. https://khpg.org/en/1555269923.

Crawford, Timothy. "Moral Hazard, Intervention and Internal War: A Conceptual Analysis." *Ethnopolitics* 4, no. 2 (2005): 175–193.

D'Anieri, Paul. *Ukraine and Russia: From Civilized Divorce to Uncivil War*. Cambridge: Cambridge University Press, 2023.

Danko, V. "Vladimir Goncharov: Chest pod formoi menta."' *Provintsia*, July 16, 2014. https://www.konstantinovka.com.ua/newspaper/chelovek-i-zakon/vladimir-goncharov-chest-pod-formoy-menta.

Datatowel.In.Ua. "Parlamentski Vybory 2012: Rezultaty Holosuvannia v Bahatomandatnomu Okruzi." https://datatowel.in.ua/elections/parliamentary2012.

DeBenedektis, Kent. *Russian "Hybrid Warfare" and the Annexation of Crimea: The Modern Application of Soviet Political Warfare*. London: I. B. Tauris, 2021.

Democratic Initiatives Foundation. "Dva misiatsi protestive v Ukraini: Sho dali?" January 21, 2014. https://dif.org.ua/article/dva-misyatsi-protestiv-v-ukraini-shcho-dali.

Depo. "Top-5 samyh bogatyh lyudei Luganshiny." February 17, 2020. https://dn.depo.ua/rus/severodonetsk/tovstosumi-luganshchini-202002121112276.

Detektor.Media. "Yak zminylos upodobannia ta interesy ukraintsiv do zasobiv masovoi informatsii pislia vyboriv 2019 roku ta pochatku pandemii COVID-19." September 2020. https://detector.media/infospace/article/181066/2020-09-29-yak-zminylys-upodobannya-ta-interesy-ukraintsiv-do-zasobiv-masovoi-informatsii-pislya-vyboriv-2019-r-ta-pochatku-pandemii-covid-19/.

Dobropolie na Ladoniah. "Referendum sostoialsia—a chto zhe dal'she?" May 14, 2014. https://issuu.com/dnl_plus/docs/420_20.

Dobrov, Aleksei. "Chelovek Surkova u istokov DNR." *Realna Gazeta.* July 30, 2015. https://realgazeta.com.ua/chelovek-surkova-v-lnr/.

Donets'ka oblasna derzhavna administratsiia. "17 kvitnia—Den' vilnyh lyudei u Kramatorsku." April 17, 2022. https://dn.gov.ua/news/17-kvitnya-2014-roku-den-vilnih-lyudej-u-kramatorsku.

Dorogan, Aleksina. "Razvedka s ikonami: Kak v 2014 Rossiya rabotala v Krymu pod prikrytiem Moskovskogo patriarkhata." *Radio Svoboda,* March 1, 2021. https://ru.krymr.com/a/razvedka-krym-2014-russia-okkupatsiya-pod-prikrytiem-tserkvi/31124680.html.

Driscoll, Jesse. "Ukraine's Civil War: Would Accepting This Terminology Help Resolve the Conflict?" Policy Memo No. 572. Washington, DC: PONARS Eurasia, February 2019. https://www.ponarseurasia.org/ukraine-s-type-4-conflict-why-is-it-important-to-study-terminology-before-changing-it/.

Druzhkovka na Ladoniah. "Borba za Poriadok v Druzhkovke Prodolzhaetsia." June 4, 2014. https://issuu.com/dnl_plus/docs/297_23.

Druzhkovka na Ladoniah. "Obrashenie patriotov Druzhkovki k zemliakam." May 21, 2014. https://issuu.com/dnl_plus/docs/295_21.

Druzhkovka na Ladoniah. "Obrashenie Voennogo Komendanta Goroda Druzhkovki k Gorozhanam." June 4, 2014. https://issuu.com/dnl_plus/docs/297_23.

Druzhkovskiy Rabochiy. "Kliuchevoi moment." February 27, 2014. https://issuu.com/dzhulianochka/docs/09_fe8940fe2c27dd.

Dubovoi, Gennadiy. "Legendarnye podrazdelenia ot Gennadia Dubovogo." YouTube, March 15, 2019. https://t.ly/RIcn.

Dugin, Aleksandrd. *Russkaia Vesh: Ocherki natsional'noi filosofii.* Vol. 1. Moscow: Arktogeia-tsentr, 2001.

Dzerzhynskiy Shakhtior. "My khotim zhyt', sozidat', trudit'sia bez revoliutsiy i kataklizmov." February 18, 2014.

Dzerzhynskiy Shakhtior. "Obrashenie k gromade goroda Dzerzhynska." February 25, 2014.

The Economist. "Technology Is Deepening Civilian Involvement in War." July 3, 2023. https://www.economist.com/special-report/2023/07/03/technology-is-deepening-civilian-involvement-in-war.

Elfversson, Emma, and Kristine Höglund. "Are Armed Conflicts Becoming More Urban?" *Cities* 119 (2021): 1–10.

Embassy of Ukraine to the United Kingdom of Great Britain and Northern Ireland. "Ukraine's Prosecutor's General Office Materials of the Criminal Proceedings against Russian Officials." September 13, 2016. https://uk.mfa.gov.ua/en/news/50778-ukraines-prosecutors-general-office-materials-of-the-criminal-proceedings-against-russian-officials.

Ermishyna, Lyudmila and Aleksandr Pankov. "Na den pobedy armia unichtozhyla iz pushek i avtomatov gosupravlenie militsii i streliala po bezoruzhnym gorozhanam." *Priazovskiy Rabochiy*. No. 67. May 13, 2014. https://issuu.com/priazrab/docs/67___2014.

Ermishyna, Lyudmila, and Ekaterina Svistun. "Na referendume v Mariupole vystraivalis' mnogotysichanye ocheredi." *Priazovskiy Rabochiy*, no. 67. (May 13, 2014): 2.

Fang, Chuanglin, and Danlin Yu. "Urban Agglomeration: An Evolving Concept of an Emerging Phenomenon." *Landscape and Urban Planning* 162 (2017): 126–136.

Fearon, James D., and David D. Laitin. "Ethnicity, Insurgency and Civil War." *American Political Science Review* 97, no. 1 (2003): 75–90.

Fialko, Evgeniy. "Gnatenko predlozhyl moratoriy na mitingi, no ne vse s nim soglasilis." *Nasha Druzhkovka*, March 26, 2014. https://nasha-druzhkovka.ru/gnatenko-predlozhil-moratorij-na-mitingi-no-ne-vse-s-nim-soglasilis/.

Financial Times. "Vladislav Surkov: An Overdose of Freedom Is Lethal to a State." June 18, 2021. https://www.ft.com/content/1324acbb-f475-47ab-a914-4a96a9d14bac.

Finkel, Eugene. *Intent to Destroy: Russia's Two-Hundred-Years Quest to Dominate Ukraine.* New York: Basic Books, 2024.

Fisun, Oleksandr, and Anton Aksentyev. "Kharkiv's Patronal Politics: Pro-Maidan vs Anti-Maidan Rivalry and Competing Power Pyramids." In *Ukraine and Its Regions: Societal Trends and Policy Implications*, edited by Ryhor Nizhnikau and Arkady Moshes. Helsinki: FIIA Report, 2020: 57–72.

ForPost. "Faces of the City: Basov Gennadiy Anatolevich." https://sevastopol.su/faces/basov-gennadiy-anatolevich.

ForPost. "Kazachiy Ataman Bebniov: Yesli Yanukovich Poteriaet Vlast, My Shturmom Vozmem MVD, SBU, i Voinskie Chasti Ukrainy v Sevastopole." February 20, 2014. https://sevastopol.su/news/kazachiy-ataman-bebnev-esli-yanukovich-poteryaet-vlast-my-shturmom-vozmem-mvd-sbu-i-voinskie.

ForPost. "Krymskiy deputat nazval Krym 'russkoi avtonomiei' i prosit zashity u Rossii." February 4, 2014. https://sevastopol.su/news/krymskiy-deputat-nazval-krym-russkoy-avtonomiey-i-prosit-zashchity-u-rossii

ForPost. "Vybory-2010: Offitsialnye rezultaty golosovania po vyboram v Sevastopolskiy gorodskoi sovet." November 5, 2010. https://sevastopol.su/news/vybory-2010-oficialnye-rezultaty-golosovaniya-po-vyboram-v-sevastopolskiy-gorodskoy-sovet.

Freedman, Lawrence. *Ukraine and the Art of Strategy.* Oxford: Oxford University Press, 2019.

Fridman, Ofer. *Russian Hybrid Warfare: Resurgence and Politicisation*. Oxford: Oxford University Press, 2018.

Frolenko, Evgeniy. "Situatsia na krasnolimanshine stabilna." *Zoria*, May 28, 2014.

Ghelbach, Scott, Roger Myerson, and Tymofiy Mylovanov. "A Way Forward for Ukraine." *New York Times*, March 19, 2014: https://www.nytimes.com/2014/03/20/opinion/a-way-forward-for-ukraine.html.

Gleditsch, Kristian Skrede. "Transnational Dimensions of Civil War." *Journal of Peace Research* 44, no. 3 (2007): 293–309.

Gonacharenko, Aleksei. "Gorlovskaia militsia perehodit pod okkupantov." YouTube, April 14, 2014. https://t.ly/Xk-c.

Gordienko, Maks. *Odessa-2014: Krakh ruzzkoi vesny*. Kharkiv: Folio, 2022.

Gordon, Dmitriy. "Interview with Igor Girkin." *V Gostiah u Gordona*, May 18, 2020. https://t.ly/41KEE.

Gordon, Dmitriy. "Interview with Igor Kolomoiskiy." *V Gostiah u Gordona*, December 20, 2018. https://t.ly/bRr0.

Gordon, Dmitriy. "Interview with Minister of Foreign Affairs of Ukraine Dmytro Kuleba." *V Gostiah u Gordona*, August 15, 2022. https://t.ly/-nKzb.

Grant, Thomas D. "Annexation of Crimea." *American Journal of International Law* 109, no. 1 (2015): 68–95.

Gromova, Elena. "Dushman: Moi dom nahoditsia na okkupirovanoi territorii." *Voennoe Obozrenie*, July 14, 2015. https://topwar.ru/78732-dushman-moy-dom-nahoditsya-na-okkupirovannoy-territorii.html.

Gubarev, Pavel. *Fakel Novorossii*. Moscow: Piter, 2016.

Gurianov, Anton. "Ya absolutno uveren v pobede sil soprotivlenia v Kharkove: Eto lish vopros vremeni." *Nakanune*, August 23, 2016. https://www.nakanune.ru/articles/112013/.

Haer, Roos, Johannes Vüllers, and Nils Weidmann. "Studying Micro Dynamics in Civil Wars: Introduction." *Zeitschrift für Friedens und Konfliktforschung* 8 (2019): 151–159.

Hamilton, Delphine Alberta. *Ukraine – Urbanization Review*. Washington, DC: World Bank Group, 2015.

Harding, Andrew. *A Small, Stubborn Town: Life, Death, and Defiance in Ukraine*. London: Ithaka Press, 2023.

Hasova, Lenka, and Levi Wolf. "Proximity and Distance Decay." In *The Geographic Information Science & Technology Body of Knowledge*, edited by John P. Wilson. (2022 edition). https://doi.org/10.22224/gistbok/2022.2.3.

Hauer, Roos, Johannes Vüllers, Nils B. Weidmann. "Studying Micro Dynamics in Civil Wars: Introduction." *Zeitschrift für Friedens- und Konfliktforschung* 8 (2019): 151–159.

Hauter, Jakob. "Delegated Interstate War: Introducing an Addition to Armed Conflict Typologies." *Journal of Strategic Studies* 12, no. 4 (2019): 90–103.

Hauter, Jakob. "Forensic Conflict Studies: Making Sense of War in the Social Media Age." *Media, War & Conflict* 16, no. 2 (2023): 153–172.

Hepp, U., A. Gamma, G. Milos, D. Eich, V. Ajdacic-Gross, W. Rössler, J. Angst, and U. Schnyder. "Inconsistency in Reporting Potentially Traumatic Events." *British Journal of Psychiatry* 188 (2006): 278–283.

Hinnat, Lori, Vasilisa Stepanenko, Sarah El Deeb, and Elizaveta Tilna. "Russia Scrubs Mariupol's Ukraine Identity, Builds on Death." Associated Press, December 22, 2022. https://apnews.com/article/russia-ukraine-war-erasing-mariupol-499dceae43ed77f2ebfe750ea99b9ad9.

Hladka, Kateryna, et al., eds. *Dobrobaty*. Kharkiv: Folio, 2018.

Hlotov, Serhiy, et al., eds. *U vohnianomu kiltsi: Oborona Luhanskoho aeroportu*. Kharkiv: Folio, 2018.

Holos Hromady. "Svatovskaia Samooborona." April 18, 2014.

Holos Hromady. "Zhyttediyalnist' mista zabezpechena." April 18, 2014.

Holos Hromady. "Zvernennia Svativskogo miskogo holovy Y. V. Rybalka to zhyteliv Svativskoi terytorialnoi hromady." April 18, 2014.

Horbatenko, Serhiy. "Kontroliruemyi ad Bezlera: Ukraina, nakonets, gotova sudit rossiyskogo ofitsera za pytki." *Radio Svoboda*. August 4, 2021. https://www.radiosvoboda.org/a/bezler-bes-sud/31391687.html.

Horbatenko, Serhiy. "8 chasov v zdanii, po kotoromu biot tank: Kak VSU osvobozhdali Toretsk." *Radio Svoboda*, November 11, 2019. https://www.radiosvoboda.org/a/30261723.html.

Horowitz, Donald. "Patterns of Ethnic Separatism." *Comparative Studies of Society and History* 23, no. 2 (1981): 165–195.

Horowitz, Donald L. "Irredentas and Secessions: Adjacent Phenomena, Neglected Connections." In *Irredentism and International Politics*, edited by Naomi Chazan. Boulder, CO: Lynne Rienner, 1991: 9 – 22.

Hromadske. "Yuzivska Vesna: Yak my borolysia za Donetsk." April 28, 2016. https://t.ly/IRqS.

Hryniv, Anna. "Odesskaia tragedia. Piat let. Znaem li my bolshe?" BBC News Ukraine, May 2, 2019. https://www.bbc.com/ukrainian/features-russian-48131691.

Huang, Reyko. *The Wartime Origins of Democratization: Civil War, Rebel Governance, and Political Regimes*. Cambridge: Cambridge University Press, 2016.

ICORPUS. "Interview with the Head of the 2nd Department of GRU DNR Leonid Kharchenko." YouTube. April 11, 2015. https://www.youtube.com/watch?v=7a2WJGvADPY&ab_channel=ICORPUS.

ICORPUS. "Interview with Vadim Ilovchenko." YouTube. October 31, 2014. https://www.youtube.com/watch?v=mlzqSiDqU-M&ab_channel=ICORPUS.

Ignatius, David. "What We Learned in Crimea." *Washington Post*, March 18, 2014. https://www.washingtonpost.com/opinions/david-ignatius-russias-military-delivers-a-striking-lesson-in-crimea/2014/03/18/c1273044-aed7-11e3-9627-c65021d6d572_story.html.

Insider. "Marashall Malofeyev: Kak rossiyskiy reider zakhavtil Yugo-Vostok Ukrainy." May 27, 2014. https://theins.ru/politika/796.

International Crisis Group. "Rebels without a Cause: Russia's Proxies in Eastern Ukraine." Report No. 254. July 16, 2019. https://www.crisisgroup.org/europe-central-asia/eastern-europe/ukraine/254-rebels-without-cause-russias-proxies-eastern-ukraine.

International Foundation for Electoral Systems. "Public Opinion in Ukraine 2014: Findings from the IFES 2014 Survey in Ukraine." Washington, DC, IFES: 2014.

International Republican Institute. "Annual Municipal Survey of Ukraine Reveals Satisfaction with Local Government." September 15, 2022. https://www.iri.org/resources/annual-municipal-survey-of-ukraine-reveals-satisfaction-with-local-governments/.

International Republican Institute. "Public Opinion Survey of Residents of Ukraine." March 14–26, 2014. https://www.iri.org/wp-content/uploads/2014/04/201420April205201RI20Public20Opinion20Survey20of20Ukraine2C20March2014-262C202014.pdf.

ITV. "Priniali Prisiagu." YouTube. September 13, 2015. https://t.ly/acnhi.

Ivashkina, Valeria. "Odeski vybory: Pidkylymni intryhy i viyna kompromativ." *Tyzhden*, May 24, 2014. https://tyzhden.ua/odeski-vybory-pidkylymni-intryhy-i-vijna-kompromativ/.

Izborskiy Klub. "Ukraina mezhdu Zapadom i Rossiei: Predvaritelnyie Itogi Ukrainskogo Perevorota." April 25, 2014. https://izborsk-club.ru/3069.

Jackson, Jaime, Belgin San-Akca, and Zeev Maoz. "International Support Networks and the Calculus of Uprising." *Journal of Peace Research* 57, no. 5 (2020): 632–647.

Johnny Mnemonic. "Spetsnaz Strelkova." YouTube, June 12, 2014. https://www.youtube.com/watch?v=x1cJGxO414Y.

Justice for Peace in Donbas. "Prisons and Torture Houses of Horlivka: The MoI Basement." April 14, 2016. https://www.jfp.org.ua/rights/porushennia/violation_categories/nezakonni-mistsia-nesvobody/rights_violations/tiurmy-ta-kativni-horlivky-pidval-mu-hu-mvs?locale=en.

Justino, Patricia, Tilman Brück, and Philip Verwimp. *A Micro-Level Perspective on the Dynamics of Conflict, Violence, and Development.* Oxford: Oxford University Press, 2013.

Kalyvas, Stathis. *The Logic of Violence in Civil War.* Cambridge: Cambridge University Press, 2006.

Karaulov, Andrei. Interview with Igor Girkin. 2020. Archived at "Russian Actors 2014." Harvard Dataverse. https://doi.org/10.7910/DVN/7DBNNB.

Kasfir, Nelson, Georg Frerks, and Niels Terpstra, "Introduction: Armed Groups and Multi-layered Governance." *Civil Wars* 19, no. 3 (2017): 257–278.

Kashyn, Oleg. "The Most Dangerous Man in Ukraine Is an Obsessive War Reenactor Playing Now with Real Weapons." *The New Republic*, July 22, 2014. https://newrepublic.com/article/118813/igor-strelkov-russian-war-reenactor-fights-real-war-ukraine.

Kasianov, Georgiy. *Memory Crash: Politics of History in and around Ukraine, 1980s–2010s.* Budapest: CEU Press, 2022.

Kasianov, Georgiy. *Past-Continuous: Istorychna polityka 1980-h–2000-h. Ukraina ta susidy.* Kyiv: Antropos-Logos-Film, 2018.

Katchanovski, Ivan. "The Separatist War in Donbas: A Violent Break-up of Ukraine?" *European Politics and Society* 17, no. 6 (2016): 473–489.

Kazansky, Denys, and Maryna Vorotyntseva. *Yak Ukraina Vtrachala Donbas*. Kyiv: Chorna Hora, 2020.

Kharkivska Miska Rada. "Pro rosiysku movu u Kharkovi." June 3, 2006. https://www.city. kharkiv.ua/uk/document/pro-rosiysku-movu-v-m-harkovi-1910.html.

Kharkovskie Izvestia. "Gennadiy Kernes: V Kharkove est zakonnaia, a ne samozvannaia vlast." February 11, 2014.

Kharkovskie Izvestia. "Interview with Gennadiy Kernes." March 4, 2014.

Kholmogorov, Yegor. "Goroda Geroi—nachalo Russkoi Vesny." *Live Journal*, February 24, 2014. https://holmogor.livejournal.com/6161827.html.

Kholmogorov, Yegor. "Vozdukh russkoi vesny." *Vzgliad*, April 10, 2014. https://vz.ru/ columns/2014/4/10/681367.html.

Kholodyuk, Anatoliy. "Imperskiy oskolok na Dnestre: Vospominania soldata." *Proza*, April 5, 2020. https://proza.ru/2020/05/04/1925.

Khronika 'Russkoi Vesny.' "Biografia Igoria Ivanovicha Strelkova." February 23, 2016. https://istrelkov.ru/9-biografiya-igorya-ivanovicha-strelkova.html.

King, Anthony. *Urban Warfare in the Twenty-First Century*. London: Polity, 2021.

King, Charles. *Odessa: Genius and Death in a City of Dreams*. New York: Norton, 2012.

Kofman, Michael. "Russian Hybrid Warfare and Other Dark Arts." *War on the Rocks*, March 11, 2016. https://warontherocks.com/2016/03/russian-hybrid-warfare-and-other-dark-arts/.

Kofman, Michael, et al. *Lessons from Russia's Operations in Crimea and Eastern Ukraine*. Santa Monica, CA: RAND, 2017.

Kommersant. "Blok NATO razoshelsia na blokpakety." April 7, 2008. https://www. kommersant.ru/doc/877224.

Kononov, Illia. "Donbas v Etnokulturnyh Koordynatah Ukrainy (Sociological Analysis)." PhD dissertation. Taras Shevchenko Luhansk National Pedagogical University, 2005.

Kononov, Illia, and Svitlana Khobta. 2014. Zvit za Resul'tatamy Doslidzhennia "Zhyttevi Svity Skhodu i Zahodu Ukrainy." Taras Shevchenko Luhansk National Pedagogical University.

Kopstein, Jeffrey, and Jason Wittenberg. *Intimate Violence: Anti-Jewish Pogroms on the Eve of the Holocaust*. Ithaca, NY: Cornell University Press, 2018.

Kosarev, Valeriy. *Krymskiy Vybor*. Moscow: Algoritm, 2018.

Kotyhorenko, Viktor, et al., eds. *Donbas v ethnopolitychnomu vymiri*. Kyiv: Kuras Institute of Political and Ethnonational Studies, 2014.

Kravchenko, Mykola, ed. *Vyzvolennia Mariupolia*. Kyiv: Orientyr, 2018.

Kravchenko, Vladimir. *Kharkov/Kharkiv: Stolitsa Pogranichia*. Vilnius: EGU, 2010.

Ksheminskiy, Denis. "Splotilis pered obshei bedoi." News.Toretsk.Online. August 1, 2014. https://www.dzerghinsk.org/news/splotilis_pered_obshhej_bedoj/2014-08-01-5785

Kudelia, Serhiy. "When Numbers Are Not Enough: The Strategic Use of Violence in Ukraine's 2014 Revolution." *Comparative Politics* 50, no. 4 (2018): 501–521.

Kudelia, Serhiy, and Johanna van Zyl. "In My Name: The Impact of Regional Identity on Civilian Attitudes in the Armed Conflict in Donbas." *Nationalities Papers* 47, no. 5 (2019): 801–821.

Kudrina, Lyudmila. "Vchera posle poiavlenia vooruzhennyh liudei sessia gorsoveta byla dosrochno zakryta." *Priazovskiy Rabochiy*. May 21, 2014.

Kuromiya, Hiroaki. *Freedom and Terror in the Donbas: A Ukrainian-Russian Borderland, 1870s–1990s*. Cambridge: Cambridge University Press, 1998.

Kushnirenko, Mykhailo. "Znachenie sotsiologicheskikh obsledovaniy v gradostroitel-non proektrirovanii na uroven gorodskoi i raionnoi planirovki Donbassa." *Dosvid ta Perpspektyvy Rozvytku Mist Ukrainy*, no. 25 (2013): 60–75.

Kuzio, Taras. *Putin's War against Ukraine:Revolution, Nationalism, and Crime*. Independently Published: CreateSpace, 2017.

Kvavilashvili, L., J. Mirani, S. Schlagman, K. Foley, and D. Kornbrot. "Consistency of Flashbulb Memories of September 11 over Long Delays: Implications for Consolidation and Wrong Time Slice Hypothesis." *Journal of Memory and Language* 61 (2009): 556–572.

Kyiv International Institute of Sociology. "Dumky ta pohliady zhyteliv pivdenno-skhidnykh oblastei Ukrainy: Kviten 2014." April 20, 2014. https://kiis.com.ua/?lang=ukr&cat=reports&id=302&page=1&y=2014&m=4.

Kyiv International Institute of Sociology. "Dynamika Stavlennia Naselennia Ukrainy do Rosii ta Naselennia Rosii do Ukrainy, Yakyh Vidnosyn z Rosieyu Khotily b Ukraintsi." March 4, 2014. https://kiis.com.ua/?lang=ukr&cat=reports&id=236.

Kyiv International Institute of Sociology. "Nastroenia Ukrainy—Rezultaty sovmestnogo issledovania KMIS i SOCIS." February 7, 2014. https://www.kiis.com.ua/?lang=rus&cat=reports&id=227&page=1&y=2014&m=2.

Kyiv International Institute of Sociology. "Otnoshenie v Ukraine i Rossii k aktsiyam protesta v Ukraine." February 28, 2014. https://www.kiis.com.ua/?lang=rus&cat=reports&id=231&page=1&y=2014&m=2.

Ladyka, Aleksei. "V Kramatorske do sih por ishut lyudei, propavshyh eshe vnachale konflikta." *Radio Svoboda*, May 26, 2016. https://www.radiosvoboda.org/a/27747739.html.

Laryš, Martin, and Emil Souleimanov. "Delegated Rebellions as an Unwanted Byproduct of Subnational Elites' Miscalculation: A Case Study of Donbas." *Problems of Post-Communism* 69, no. 2 (2022): 155–165.

LB. "Kolomoiskiy obratilsia k Kernesu s prizyvom ne razvalivat Ukrainu." February 22, 2014. https://rus.lb.ua/news/2014/02/22/256603_kolomoyskiy_obratilsya_kernesu.html.

Lewis, Janet. *How Insurgency Begins: Rebel Group Formation in Uganda and Beyond*. Cambridge: Cambridge University Press, 2020.

Liga 360. "Voenna doktryna Ukrainy." Approved on June 15, 2004. https://ips.ligazakon.net/document/view/u648_04?an=234&ed=2005_04_21.

Lipskiy, Andrei. "Predstavliaetsia pravilnym initsiirovat prisoedinenie vostochnyh oblastei Ukrainy k Rossii." *Novaya Gazeta*, February 25, 2015. https://novayagazeta.ru/articles/2015/02/24/63168-171-predstavlyaetsya-pravilnym-initsiirovat-prisoedinenie-vostochnyh-oblastey-ukrainy-k-rossii-187.

Lisichansk. "Lisichansk nahoditsia pod zhestkim kontrolem narodnogo opolchenia." May 26, 2014. http://web.archive.org/web/20140701024928/https://lisichansk.com. ua/2014/05/29798.

Loyle, Cyanne E., et al. "New Directions in Rebel Governance Research." *Perspectives on Politics* 21, no. 1 (March 2023): 264–276.

Lugansk Information Center. "Eks-mer Brianki Became Acting Head of Severodonetsk Administration." July 7, 2022. https://lug-info.com/ru/news/ eks-mer-bryanki-stal-ispolnyayushim-obyazannosti-glavy-administracii- severodonecka?preview=b71ab83aeaf5-d989-d6f4-bfa1-7923353b.

Lytvyn, Mykola. *Linia Rozmezhuvannia.* Kyiv: Hamzyn, 2019.

Malyarenko, Tetyana, and Stefan Wolff. *The Dynamics of Emerging De-Facto States: Eastern Ukraine in the Post-Soviet Space.* New York: Routledge, 2019.

Malyarenko, Tetyana, and Stefan Wolff. "The Logic of Competitive Influence-Seeking: Russia, Ukraine, and the Conflict in Donbas." *Post-Soviet Affairs* 34, no. 4 (2018): 191– 212.

Mampilly, Zachariah. *Rebel Rulers: Insurgent Governance and Civilian Life During War.* Ithaca, NY: Cornell University Press, 2011.

Marintsev, Sergei. "Opolchenie grozit prestupnikam i pomogaet bedstvuyushim." *Druzhkovskiy Rabochiy,* June 19, 2014.

Mariupol News. "V Mariupol prokhodit referendum." May 11, 2014. https://web.archive. org/web/20200812142553/http://mariupolnews.com.ua/news/view/v-mariupole- prohodit-referendum.

Marko, Serzh. *Khronika hibrydnoi viyny.* Kyiv: Alterpress, 2016.

Matsuzato, Kimitaka. "The Donbas War and the Politics in Cities on the Front: Mariupol and Kramatorsk." *Nationalities Papers* 46, no. 6 (2018): 1008–1027.

Matsuzato, Kimitaka. "The Donbass War: Outbreak and Deadlock." *Demokratizatsiya: The Journal of Post-Soviet Democratization* 25, no. 2 (Spring 2017): 175–200.

Matveeva, Anna. *Through Times of Trouble: Conflict in Southeastern Ukraine Explained from Within.* London: Lexingon Books, 2017.

Mayak. "Zaiavlenie i.o. Krasnoarmeiskogo gorodskogo golovy G. A. Gavrilchenko." May 16, 2014.

Mazzuca, Sebastian. *Latecomer State Formation: Political Geography and Capacity Failure in Latin America.* New Haven, CT: Yale University Press, 2021.

Mearsheimer, John. "Why the Ukraine Crisis Is the West's Fault: The Liberal Delusions That Provoked Putin." *Foreign Affairs* 93, no. 5 (2014): 77–127.

Medium. "Breaking Down the Surkov Leaks." October 25, 2016. https://medium.com/ dfrlab/breaking-down-the-surkov-leaks-b2feec1423cb.

Meduza. "Nikto ne veril, chto eto vserioz." March 27, 2014. https://meduza.io/feature/ 2017/03/21/nikto-ne-veril-chto-eto-vseriez.

Melnikova, Kristina. "Desiat' let my gotovilis i verili: Kak nachinalas Russkaia vesna na Donbasse." *Eurasia Daily,* July 4, 2016. https://eadaily.com/ru/news/2016/07/04/ desyat-let-my-gotovilis-i-verili-kak-nachinalas-russkaya-vesna-na-donbasse.

Memory Book. "Knyha pamiati polehlyh za Ukrainu" (Memory book of those who died for Ukraine). https://memorybook.org.ua/index1.htm.

Menon, Rajan, and Eugene Rumer. *Conflict in Ukraine: The Unwinding of the Post–Cold War Order*. Cambridge, MA: MIT Press, 2005.

Mostovaya, Yulia, and Sergei Rakhmanin. "Yugo-Vostok: Vetv Dreva Nashego." *ZN*, April 18, 2014. https://zn.ua/internal/yugo-vostok-vetv-dreva-nashego-_.html.

Murlykina, Anna. *Mariupol. Posledniy Forpost*. Mariupol: Poligraf UA, 2018.

Musayeva, Sevhil. "Petro Poroshenko: V mene, na zhal, ye za sho prosyty probachennia v Hospoda." *Ukrainska Pravda*, August 1, 2019. https://www.pravda.com.ua/articles/2019/08/1/7222417/.

Mykhed, Oleksandr. *"Ya zmishayu tvoyu krov iz vuhilliam": Zrozumity ukrainskyi Skhid*. Kyiv: Nash Format, 2021.

Mykhnenko, Vlad. "Causes and Consequences of the War in Eastern Ukraine: An Economic Geography Perspective." *Europe-Asia Studies* 72, no. 3 (April 2020): 528–560.

Narodnaia Gazeta. "Pogib nash drug: Pogib, zashishaya rodnoi gorod." June 4, 2014.

Narodnaia Gazeta. "V Konstantinovka kriminogennaia obstanovka ne uhudshylas." May 28, 2014.

Nasha Druzhkovka. "Vneocherednaia sessia." April 15, 2014. http://nasha-druzhkovka.ru/vneocherednaya-sessiya/#more-14726.

Nasha Zoria. "Obrashenie deputatov Selidovskogo gorodskogo soveta k Verkhovnoi Rade Ukrainy." May 23, 2014.

Nashi Hroshi. "Kassir Partii regionov peremetnulsia v lager Kolomoiskogo." November 4, 2014. http://nashigroshi.org/2014/11/04/kassyr-partyy-rehyonov-peremetnulsya-v-laher-kolomojskoho/.

Nedal, Dani, Megan Stewart, and Michael Weintraub. "Urban Concentration and Civil War." *Journal of Conflict Resolution* 64, no. 6 (2020): 1146–1171.

News.Toretsk.Online. "Beda prishla s vozdukha." July 16, 2014. https://www.dzerghinsk.org/news/beda_prishla_s_vozdukha/2014-07-16-5765

NewsFront. "Lider kompartii DNR: Raskol v Donetskom obkome KPU ne pozvolil kommunistam vozglavit respubliku." June 20, 2021. https://news-front.info/2021/06/20/lider-kompartii-dnr-raskol-v-donetskom-obkome-kpu-ne-pozvolil-kommunistam-vozglavit-respubliku/.

Newsweek. "Russia's Medvedev Threatens Ukraine with Pre-emptive Nuclear Strike." May 26, 2023: https://www.newsweek.com/russia-medvedev-ukraine-nuclear-strike-weapons-west-putin-1802829.

Nitsova, Silviya. "Why the Difference? Donbas, Kharkiv and Dnipropetrovsk after Ukraine's Euromaidan Revolution." *Europe-Asia Studies* 73, no. 10 (2021): 1832–1856.

North Atlantic Treaty Organization. Bucharest Summit Declaration. April 3, 2008. https://www.nato.int/cps/en/natolive/official_texts_8443.htm.

North Atlantic Treaty Organization. Charter on a Distinctive Partnership between the North Atlantic Treaty Organization and Ukraine. July 8, 1997. https://www.nato.int/cps/en/natohq/official_texts_25457.htm.

Novorossia TV. "Internatstional'noe dvizhenie Donbassa: U istokov politicheskoi sub'ektnosti regiona." November 19, 2019. https://t.ly/kzSx.

Novosti Pridnestrovia. "K 70-letiyu Vladimira Antyufeeva MGB vypustilo film o sozdatele organov gosbezopasnosti PMR." February 21, 2021. https://novostipmr .com/ru/news/21-02-21/k-70-letiyu-vladimira-antyufeeva-mgb-vypustilo-film-o-sozdatele.

Novyi Den'. "'Russkoe edinstvo': Rezultat vyborov v Krymu—eto ne pobeda, no i ne porazhenie." November 16, 2010. https://newdaynews.ru/crimea/309146.html/amp/.

Novyi Put. "Resolution of Lysychank City Council." January 29, 2014.

NV. "Poiavilos video s momenta podryva avot mestnogo kollaboranta v Starobelske." August 26, 2022. https://nv.ua/ukraine/events/askyar-layshev-moment-vzryva-mashiny-kollaboranta-v-starobelske-popal-na-video-50265946.html.

NV. "Sivoho i Kolesnikov—mymo: Mer Druzhkivky Gnatenko Vyhrav Vybory v Okruzi Donetskoi Oblasti." July 23, 2019. https://nv.ua/ukr/ukraine/politics/vibori-2019-sergiy-sivoho-i-boris-kolesnikov-prograli-meru-druzhkivki-50033632.html.

Obshezhytie. "Gorodskoi golova Gennadiy Kostyukov obratilsia k zhyteliam Kramatorska." April 7, 2014. https://obs.in.ua/news/novosti-kramatorska/5038-5038.

Office of the United Nations High Commissioner for Human Rights. "Accountability for Killings in Ukraine from January 2014 to May 2016." 2016. https://www.ohchr.org/sites/default/files/Documents/Countries/UA/OHCHRThematicReportUkraine Jan2014-May2016_EN.pdf.

Office of the United Nations High Commissioner for Human Rights. "Human Rights Violations and Abuses and International Humanitarian Law Violations Committed in the Context of Ilovaisk Events in August 2014." August 1, 2018. https://www.ohchr.org/en/documents/country-reports/human-rights-violations-and-abuses-and-international-humanitarian-law.

Office of the United Nations High Commissioner for Human Rights. "Report on the Human Rights Situation in Ukraine, July 15, 2014." July 28, 2014. https://www.ohchr.org/sites/default/files/Documents/Countries/UA/HRMMUReport15June2014.pdf.

Official Website of the President of the Russian Federation. "Poslanie Prezidentu Ukrainy Viktoru Yushchenko." August 11, 2009. http://www.kremlin.ru/catalog/countries/UA/events/5158.

Official Website of the President of Russian Federation. "Zaiavlenia dlia pressy i otvety na voprosy zhurnalistov po okonchanii peregovorov s Prezidentom Ukrainy Viktorom Yushchenko i vtorogo zasedania Rossiysko-Ukrainskoi mezhgosudarstvennoi komissii." February 12, 2008. http://www.kremlin.ru/events/president/transcripts/24833.

O'Loughlin, John, Gerard Toal, and Vladimir Kolosov. "The Rise and Fall of 'Novorossiya': Examining Support for a Separatist Geopolitical Imaginary in Southeast Ukraine." *Post-Soviet Affairs* 33, no. 2 (2017): 124–144.

Osipian, Ararat, and Alexandr Osipian. "Why Donbas Votes for Yanukovych: Confronting the Ukrainian Orange Revolution." *Demokratizatsiya: The Journal of Post-Soviet Democratization* 14, no. 4 (2006): 495–517.

Ostrov. "Vyshedshyi iz podvala DNR eks-sekretar Donetskogo gorsoveta Bogachev." October 29, 2018. https://www.ostro.org/general/politics/news/557491/.

Ostrovsky, Simon. "Pro-Russian Protesters Attempt to Seize Airfield: Russian Roulette. Dispatch 27." *Vice News*, April 18, 2014. https://www.youtube.com/watch?v=8mywTyAhlJM.

Pearlman, Wendy. "Emotions and the Microfoundations of the Arab Uprisings." *Perspectives on Politics* 11, no. 2 (June 2013): 387–409.

Petersen, Roger D. *Resistance and Rebellion: Lessons from Eastern Europe.* Cambridge: Cambridge University Press, 2001.

Petersen, Roger. *Western Intervention in the Balkans: The Strategic Use of Emotion in Conflict.* Cambridge: Cambridge University Press, 2011.

Petersen, Scott. "A Ukrainian Murder Mystery Ensnares a Church in Former Rebel Stronghold." *Christian Science Monitor*, August 12, 2014. https://www.csmonitor.com/World/Europe/2014/0812/A-Ukrainian-murder-mystery-ensnares-a-church-in-former-rebel-stronghold.

Pettersson, Therese. "UCDP/PRIO Armed Conflict Dataset Codebook v 24.1 (https://ucdp.uu.se/downloads/)." 2024.

Pidhrushnyi, Hryhoriy, and Oleksandr Vrublevskyi. "Miski Aglomeratsii Donbasu." In *Aglomeratsii: Mizhnarodnyi Dosvid, Tendentsii, Vysnovky dlia Ukrainy. Analitychna Zapyska*, edited by Nina Natalenko, 81–103. Kyiv: Instytut Hromadianskoho Suspilstva, 2017.

Pifer, Steven. *The Eagle and the Trident: U.S.-Ukraine Relations in Turbulent Times.* Washington, DC: Brookings Institution Press, 2017.

Pinchuk, Andrei. *Kontur Bezopasnosti.* Moscow: Algoritm, 2017.

Platonova, Daria. *The Donbas Conflict in Ukraine: Elites, Protest, and Partition.* New York: Routledge, 2021.

Plinskiy, Evgeniy. "Nellia Shtepa: 'Ia vyshyla na lifchike imia i datu rozhdeniya—chtoby opoznali telo, esli menia vyrbosiat kuda-to mertvoi.'" LB, October 29, 2015. https://rus.lb.ua/society/2015/10/29/319648_nelya_shtepa_ya_vishila_lifchike_imya.html

Politie. "The Witness Appeal June 2019: Chain of Responsibility in the Russian Federation 4 (8)." YouTube, June 18, 2019. https://www.youtube.com/watch?v=hPGmFJH2ZO8.

Politie. "Update on Criminal Investigation of MH17 Disaster." YouTube, June 19, 2019. https://www.youtube.com/watch?v=Kq-L72slP18&t=1042s&ab_channel=Politie.

Politie. "Witness Appeal 11 '19—Possible Russian Influence on Appointments in the DPR." YouTube, November 13, 2019. https://www.youtube.com/watch?v=eahMvdRoC-g&ab_channel=Politie.

Politie. "Witness Appeal November 2019—Conversation Surkov and Borodai; Reinforcements from Russia." YouTube, November 13, 2019. https://www.youtube.com/watch?v=RpE0YMivLu0.

Polukhina, Yulia. "Vsyo poshlo po klanu." *Novaya Gazeta*, October 5, 2015.

Pomerantsev, Peter. "The Hidden Author of Putinism: How Vladislav Surkov Invented the New Russia." *The Atlantic*, November 7, 2014. https://www.theatlantic.com/international/archive/2014/11/hidden-author-putinism-russia-vladislav-surkov/382489/.

Ponomariov, Viacheslav. "Narodnyi mer Slavianska o nachale voiny, Girkine i razved-chukakh NATO." WarGonzo, April 2021. https://rutube.ru/video/6909618ed094237 02161773bf3e88a30/.

Pop-Eleches, Grigore, and Graeme Robertson. "Identity and Political Preferences in Ukraine—before and after the Euromaidan." *Post-Soviet Affairs* 34, nos. 2–3 (2018): 107–118.

Priazovskiy Rabochiy. "Ekstrennoe zaiavlenie Rinata Akhmetova v sviazi s situatsiei v Donbasse." May 21, 2014.

Priazovskiy Rabochiy. "Mariupolskie metallurgi, gorodskaia vlast, obshestvennost Mariupolia i lider DNR podpisali Memorandum o poriadke i bezopasnosti." May 17, 2014.

Priazovskiy Rabochiy. "Obrashenie deputatov Mariupolskogo gorodskogo soveta v Verkhovnuyu Radu Ukrainy, k zhyteliam Ukrainy i goroda Mariupolia." March 4, 2014.

Prokhanov, Aleksandr. "Beseda Aleksandra Prokhanova s Nikolaem Kozitsynym." *Zavtra*, December 11, 2014. https://ru-prokhanov.livejournal.com/333947.html.

Prokhanov, Aleksandr. *Novorossia, kroviu umytaya: Peredovitsy.* Moscow: Knigovek, 2016.

Prokhanov, Aleksandr. "Oruzhie! Daite Oruzhie!" *Zavtra*, June 5, 2014. https://pub.wikireading.ru/156241.

Prokhanov, Aleksandr. "Russkie idut." Rodina, March 7, 2014. https://rodina.ru/novosti/Aleksandr-Proxanov-Russkie-idut.

Protsenko, Oleh. "Ne nashi khloptsi: Reaktsiya mistsevoi vlady na okupatsiyu." In *Misto, z yakoho pochalasia viyna*, edited by Anton Udovenko. Kyiv: Yamchynsky Publishing, 2020. 15–42.

Provintsiya. "V Konstantinovke novyi nachalnik militsii." March 28, 2014. https://www.konstantinovka.com.ua/newspaper/sluzhba-103-soobschaet/v-konstantinovke-novyy-nachalnik-milicii.

Punin, Roman. "Kiev ugrozhaet, oblastnaya vlast samoustranilas, gorodskaia militsia snova pri oruzhii." *Limanskaya Storona*, April 23, 2014.

Punin, Roman. "Krasnyi Liman mitinguet v podderzhku Donetskoi Narodnoi respubliki." *Limanskaya Storona*, April 23, 2014.

Punin, Roman. "Pervyi otchet koordinatsionnogo soveta." *Limanskaya Storona*, May 28, 2014.

Quinlivan, James. "Burden of Victory: The Painful Arithmetic of Stability Operations." *RAND Review* 27, no. 2 (Summer 2003): 28–29.

Radio Krym. "Golosa krymskoi vesny: Vadim Ilovchenko." February 21, 2022. https://crimea-radio.ru/program/golosa-krimskoy-vesni/21-02-2022-vadim-ilovchenko/.

Raleigh, Clionadh. "Urban Violence Patterns across African States." *International Studies Review* 17 (2015): 90–160.

Ramishvili, Vasiliy. "Istoria vershytsia na glazah." *Druzhkovskiy Rabochiy*, March 6, 2014, 2. https://issuu.com/dzhulianochka/docs/10.

Ramishvili, Vasiliy. "Proverka na prochnost." *Druzhkovskiy Rabochiy*, June 19, 2014.

Rasler, Karen. "Internationalized Civil War: A Dynamic Analysis of the Syrian Intervention in Lebanon." *Journal of Conflict Resolution* 27, no. 3 (1987): 421–456.

Rating Group. "Nostalgia za SRSR ta stavlennia do okremyh postatei." May 2014. https://ratinggroup.ua/files/ratinggroup/reg_files/rg_historical_ua_052014.pdf.

Ravnopravie. "Otchet o deiatelnosti KhGOO 'Za kulturno-iazykovoe ravnopravie' i koordinatsyonnogo soveta russkikh organizatsiy Vostoka Ukrainy 'Russkoe Veche, 2011-2012." https://www.ravnopravie.org/news/stati/otchet_o_deyatelnosti _hgoo_za_kulturno-yazykovoe_ravnopravie_i_koordinacionnogo_soveta_russkih_ organizacij_vostoka_ukrainy_russkoe_veche_konec_2011-12_god.html.

RBC. "Malofeev rasskazal o svoem uchastii v prisoedinenii Kryma." November 13, 2014. https://www.rbc.ru/politics/13/11/2014/54647847cbb20f11b6a74400.

Regan, Patrick. "Interventions into Civil War: A Retrospective Survey with Prospective Ideas." *Civil Wars* 12, no. 4 (2010): 456–476.

Regan, Patrick, and M. Scott Meachum. "Data on Interventions during Periods of Political Instability." *Journal of Peace Research* 51, no. 1 (2014): 127–135.

Regionalnye Vesti. "Obrashenie Novogrodovskogo gorodskogo golovy A. V. Antonenko k zhyteliam Novogrodovki." February 28, 2014.

Regionalnye Vesti. "Volna Mitingov i Protestov." March 7, 2014.

RF State Duma. "Stenogramma zasedania 25 dekabria, 1998 goda." December 25, 1998. http://transcript.duma.gov.ru/node/2445/.

RF State Duma. "Transcript of the Proceedings." April 2, 2008. http://transcript.duma. gov.ru/node/570/.

RIA Novosti. "Biografia Igoria Bezlera." August 28, 2014. https://ria.ru/20140828/ 1021803991.html.

Rice, Condoleezza. *No Higher Honor: A Memoir of My Years in Washington.* New York: Crown, 2011.

Rodina. "Prokhanov ob Ukraine: Na nashyh glazah proiskhodit chudovishnoe deistvie." February 26, 2014. https://rodina.ru/novosti/Proxanov-ob-Ukraine-Na-nashix-glazax-proisxodit-chudovishhnoe-dejstvie.

Roeder, Phillip. *Where Nation-States Come From: Institutional Change in the Age of Nationalism.* Princeton, NJ: Princeton University Press, 2006.

Rotberg, Robert I., ed. *When States Fail: Causes and Consequences.* Princeton, NJ: Princeton University Press, 2004.

Ruban, Iana. "V Dobropolie snova protestuyut." *Dobropolie na Ladoniah,* April 30, 2014. https://issuu.com/dnl_plus/docs/418_18.

Russian Ministry of Foreign Affairs. "Zaiavlenie MID Rossii v sviazi s antirossiskimi proiavleniyami na Ukraine." December 14, 2007. https://mid.ru/ru/foreign_policy/ news/1644533/.

Russkoe Edinstvo. "Etapy stanovlenia Russkoi obshiny Kryma." September 3, 2018. http://www.ruscrimea.ru/etapy-stanovleniya-russkoj-obshhiny-kryma.

Rus Triedinaia. "K piatiletiyu 'Russkoi vesny'—Kharkovskoe soprotivlenie bylo podavleno zhestokimi metodami." 2019. https://dzen.ru/a/YtalFXstEg02gLxO.

Ruzhynskiy, Sergei. "Sergei Pashynskiy: My perestali byt natsiei rabov. My stali silnoi, dinamichnoi, russko-ukrainoiazychnoi natsiei." iPress, June 27, 2014. https://ipress.ua

/ru/articles/sergey_pashynskyy_mi_perestaly_bit_natsyey_rabov_mi_staly_sylnoy_dynamychnoy_russkoukraynoyazichnoy_natsyey_72025.html.

Rybalko, Yevgeniy. "Zadumaemsia i sdelaem vyvody." *Holos Hromady*, April 18, 2014.

Saideman, Stephen. "Explaining the International Relations of Secessionist Conflicts: Vulnerability versus Ethnic Ties." *International Organization* 51, no. 4 (1997): 721–753.

Sakadynskiy, Sergei. *Luganskiy Razlom*. Izdatelskie Reshenia, 2016.

Sakharov, Vasilii. *Zapiski Dobrovoltsa*. Last edited online July 5, 2018. http://samlib.ru/s/saharow_w_i/zapiskidobrowolxca.shtml.

Sakharov, Vasilii. *Zapiski Dobrovoltsa - 2*. Last edited online August 31, 2015. http://samlib.ru/s/saharow_w_i/zapiski-2.shtml.

Salehyan, Idean. *Rebels without Borders: Trasnational Insurgencies in World Politics*. Ithaca, NY: Cornell University Press, 2009.

Salo, Olena. Police Interrogation Report. September 13, 2014.

Sambanis, Nicholas, Stergios Skaperdas, and William Wohlforth. "External Intervention, Identity, and Civil War." *Comparative Political Studies* 53, no. 14 (2020): 2155–2182.

San-Akca, Belgin. *States in Disguise: Causes of State Support for Rebel Groups*. Oxford: Oxford University Press, 2016.

Sassen, Saskia. "When the City Itself Becomes a Technology of War." *Theory, Culture & Society* 27, no. 6 (2010): 33–50.

Scott, James C. *The Art of Not Being Governed: An Anarchist History of Upland Southeast Asia*. New Haven, CT: Yale University Press, 2009.

Seddon, Max. "Documents Show Rebel Justice in East Ukraine Was Bureaucratic, Swift and Merciless." *BuzzFeed News*, July 10, 2014. https://www.buzzfeednews.com/article/maxseddon/documents-show-rebel-justice-in-east-ukraine-was-bureaucrati.

Semionova, E. V., ed. *Na Perednem Kraye: Bitva za Novorossiyu v Memuarakh Eyo Zashitnikov*. Moscow: Traditsiia, 2017.

Semyonova, Elena. *Dobrovol'tsy: Vek XXI. Bitva za Novorossiyu v portretah eyo geroev*. Moskva: Traditsiya, 2015.

Setdikova, Dinara. "Vezhlivye kazaki pribyli v Antratsyt." *Radio Svoboda*, May 6, 2014. https://www.svoboda.org/a/25374732.html.

Severodonetsk.Info. "Ukrainskogo muzykanta iz Rubezhnogo, kotorogo priviazali k derevu, mogut eshe posadit na 5 let." April 22, 2014. http://sever.lg.ua/2014-04-22-ukrainskogo-muzykanta-iz-rubezhnogo-kotorogo-privyazyvali-k-derevu-mogut-eshche-i-posadit.

Severodonetski Visti. "O sobytiah v Severodonetske 1 iyulia: Kommentariy gorodskogo golovy Valentina Kazakova." July 4, 2014.

Severodonetski Visti. "Valentin Kazakov: Nashy Pervoocherednye Zadachi—Eto Uluchshenie Finansovogo Snabzhenia Goroda i Podgotovka k Zime." June 27, 2014.

Sharafutdinova, Gulnaz. *Red Mirror: Putin's Leadership and Russia's Insecure Identity*. Oxford: Oxford University Press, 2020.

Shargorodskiy, Andrei. "Pogibshye i propavshye: Zhertvy 'beskrovnoi' anneksii Kryma." *Radio Svoboda*, March 18, 2020. https://ru.krymr.com/a/zhertvy-beskrovnoj-anneksii-kryma/30495796.html.

Sheremet, Mikhail. "'Krymskaia vesna': Ka eto bylo. Instina." TRK Millet, February 19, 2021. https://trkmillet.ru/program-episode/mikhail-sheremet-krimskaya-vesna-kak-ye/.

Shevchenko, Artem. *Sloviansk. Pochatok Viyny*. Kharkiv: Folio, 2020.

Shovkoshytnyi, Rodion. "Interview with Svitlana Astakhova, KP.ru, April 28, 2014." YouTube, October 11, 2015. https://t.ly/EL4us.

Shtal, Andrei. "Gennadiy Kostiukov podal v otstavku." *Kramatorskaya Pravda*, May 28, 2014.

Shtal, Andrei. "Kramatorsku nuzhna stabilnost." *Kramatorskaia Pravda*, June 18, 2014.

Shtal, Andrei. "Nachalnik shtaba kramatorskogo garnizona: 'Familiia Kim i ukrainskiy natsionalizm ne sopostavimy.'" *Kramatorskaia Pravda*, June 11, 2014.

Shtal, Andrei. "Sotni gorozhan vystraivalis v ochered za gumanitarkoi." *Kramatorskaia Pravda*, June 18, 2014.

Shtal, Andrei, and Olga Semirazumenko. "'Donetskaia Respublika' v Kramatorske." *Kramatorskaia Pravda*, April 16, 2014.

Shtohrin, Iryna. "Chomu ne vtrymaly Krym: Stenohrama RNBO vid 28 lyutoho 2014 roku." *Radio Liberty Ukrainian Service*, February 27, 2019. https://www.radiosvoboda.org/a/29794488.html.

Siruk, Mykola. "Yevhen Marchuk: Na Shliakhu do NATO." *Den'*, nos. 205–206 (2016). https://day.kyiv.ua/uk/article/den-planety/yevgen-marchuk-na-shlyahu-do-nato.

6262. "Kak Deputaty Slavianskogo Gorodskogo Soveta Ukrainy Predavali." September 24, 2015. https://www.6262.com.ua/news/973130/kak-deputaty-slavanskogo-gorodskogo-soveta-ukrainu-predavali.

Slavgord. "V sotsialnyh setia slaviantsev prizyvayut." February 27, 2014. https://slavgorod.com.ua/news/article/447/.

Slovo I Dilo. "Yak zminyuvalos stavlennia ukraintsiv do rosii I rosian." March 10, 2023. https://www.slovoidilo.ua/2023/03/10/infografika/suspilstvo/yak-zminyuvalosya-stavlennya-ukrayincziv-rosiyi-ta-rosiyan.

Snyder, Timothy. "A Fascist Hero in Democratic Kiev." *New York Review of Books*, February 24, 2010: https://www.nybooks.com/online/2010/02/24/a-fascist-hero-in-democratic-kiev/.

Snyder, Timothy. "Putin's Case for Invading Ukraine Rests on Phony Grievances and Ancient Myths." *Washington Post*, January 28, 2022. https://www.washingtonpost.com/outlook/2022/01/28/putin-russia-ukraine-myths/.

Sobchak, Ksenia. "Interview with Aleksandr Borodai." TV Dozhd, November 12, 2014. https://tvrain.tv/teleshow/sobchak_zhivem/aleksandr_borodaj_strelkov_pytalsja_stat_politiche-378007/.

Soiuz Grazhdan Ukrainy i Rossii. "Obrashenie predsedatelia soveta narodnyh deputatov KhNR—Antona Gurianova." YouTube, April 18, 2014. https://t.ly/vZMM-.

Sossa, Santiago. "The Micro-dynamics of Conflict and Peace: Evidence from Colombia." *International Interactions: Empirical and Theoretical Research in International Relations* 49, no. 2 (2023): 163–170.

Staniland, Paul. "Cities on Fire: Social Mobilization, State Policy, and Urban Insurgency." *Comparative Political Studies* 43, no. 12 (2010): 1623–1649.

Staniland, Paul. "States, Insurgents, and Wartime Political Orders." *Perspectives on Politics* 10, no. 2 (2012): 243–264.

Staniland, Paul. *Networks of Rebellion: Explaining Insurgent Cohesion and Collapse.* Ithaca, NY: Cornell University Press, 2014.

Supreme Council of Ukraine. "Zakon Ukrainy pro Holodomor 1932–1933 rokiv v Ukraini." November 28, 2006. https://zakon.rada.gov.ua/laws/show/376-16.

Surkov, Vladislav. *Teksty 97–07: Stati i vystuplenia.* Moscow: Evropa, 2008.

Sushko, Oleksandr. "After the Ukraine-Russia War: Is There a Sustainable Solution?" Policy Memo No. 356. Washington, DC: PONARS Eurasia, September 2014.

Suspilne Donbas. "Povernuty Donbas: Kramatorsk." YouTube, July 5, 2019. https://youtu. be/CB4lbYgBk6Y.

Suspilne Donbas. "Povernuty Donbas: Rubizhne." YouTube, July 21, 2019. https://youtu. be/LNPayf18vbA.

Suspilne Donbas. "Povernuty Donbas: Severodonetsk." YouTube, July 23, 2019. https://youtu.be/xiAZ4fcsPV4.

Suspilne Donbas. "Povernuty Donbas: Sloviansk." YouTube, July 5, 2019. https://youtu. be/KZh6vcjfDPk.

Syrotenko, A., ed. *Voenni Aspekty Protydii "Hibrydnii" Ahresii.* Kyiv: National Defense University of Ukraine, 2020.

Tilly, Charles. "Mechanisms in Political Processes." *Annual Review of Political Science* 4 (2001): 21–41.

Toal, Gerard. *Near Abroad: Putin, the West, and the Contest over Ukraine and the Caucasus.* Oxford: Oxford University Press, 2017.

Toft, Monica Duffy. "Indivisible Territory, Geographic Concentration, and Ethnic War." *Security Studies* 12, no. 2 (2002): 82–119.

Tokarskiy, Nikolai. "Referendum proshel. Chto dalshe?." *Priazovskiy Rabochiy*, no. 68. (May 14, 2014).

Toukan, Mark. "International Politics by Other Means: External Sources of Civil War." *Journal of Peace Research* 56, no. 6 (2019): 812–826.

Treisman, Daniel. "Why Putin Took Crimea: The Gambler in the Kremlin." *Foreign Affairs* 96, no. 3 (May–June 2016): 47–54.

Tretiakova, Marina. "Referendum o federalizatsii Donbassa: 20 let bor'by." *Aktualnye Kommentarii*, December 9, 2014. https://actualcomment.ru/referendum-o-federalizatsii-donbassa-20-let-borby.html.

Tsentr Hromadianskyh Svobod. "'Khimichnyi trykutnyk' Luhanshyny pid chas okupatsii: Zaruchnyky, katuvannia ta pozasudovi straty." Kyiv, 2014.

Tsurkan, Violetta. "Chto proskhodit v ispolkome?" *Limanskaya Storona*, May 21, 2014.

Tsurkan, Violetta. "Na referendum kak na prazdnik." *Limanskaia Storona*, May 14, 2014.

Tsygankov, Andrei. "Vladimir Putin's Last Stand: The Sources of Russia's Ukraine Policy." *Post-Soviet Affairs* 31, no. 4 (2015): 279–303.

Tsyganok, Anatoliy. *Donbass: Neokonchennaia voina. Grazhdanskaia voina na Ukraine (2014–2016): Russkiy vzgliad.* Moscow: AIRO-XXI, 2017.

Turchynov, Oleksandr. "Zapadnye diplomaty ne verili, chto my vystoim." *Babel*, August 23, 2021. https://babel.ua/ru/texts/68499-zapadnye-diplomaty-ne-verili-chto-my-vystoim-aleksandr-turchinov-rasskazyvaet-kak-vesnoy-letom-2014-goda-zanyal-vse-vysshie-posty-v-ukraine-zanovo-stroil-vlast-i-nachal-ato.

Ukraine Ministry of Defense. "Analiz vedennia antyterrorystychnoi operatsii ta naslidkiv vtorhnennia Rosiyskoi Federatsii v Ukrainu u serpni-veresni 2014 roku." August 2015. https://www.mil.gov.ua/content/other/anliz_rf.pdf.

Ukraine Ministry of Defense. *The White Book of Anti-Terrorist Operation in the East of Ukraine in 2014–2016.* Kyiv: Ukraine Ministry of Defense, 2017.

Ukraine Ministry of Defense. "*Zbroini Syly Ukrainy.*" White Paper. Kyiv: Ukraine Ministry of Defense, 2015.

Ukraine Ofis Heneralnoho prokurora. "Dokazy prychetnosti vlady RF do posiahannia na terytorialny tsilisnist Ukrainy." August 23, 2016. https://t.ly/8d62.

Ukrainian Helsinki Union for Human Rights. "Ilovaiska Trahedia 2014: Podii ta Vidpovidalnist." September 5, 2016. https://www.helsinki.org.ua/wp-content/uploads/2016/09/Yllowaysk_UGSPL-1.pdf.

Ukrainian Wikipedia. "Vtraty prorosiyskyh syl u rosiysko-ukrainskiy viyni z 2014 roku" (The losses of pro-Russian forces in Russian-Ukrainian war 2014). Last accessed October 2, 2024. https://t.ly/UzuD1.

Ukrainska Pravda. "Medvedev obvinil Yushchenko v antirossiyskom kurse." August 11, 2009. https://www.pravda.com.ua/rus/news/2009/08/11/4498008/.

Ukrainska Pravda. "Militsia prosyt' ne ity na mitynhy v Donetsku cherez 'radykaliv.'" April 17, 2014. https://www.pravda.com.ua/news/2014/04/17/7022751/.

Ukrainska Pravda. "Znaishly tilo vbytoho separatystamy deputata vid Batkivshyny." January 16, 2015. https://www.pravda.com.ua/news/2015/01/16/7055297/

UKROP. "Korban na sudi rozpoviv pravdu pro pochatok ATO, obmin Savchenko i pomylky Poroshenka." YouTube. November 6, 2015. https://www.youtube.com/watch?v=HJ-Ihys0NIw&feature=emb_logo.

UNIAN. "Vystuplenie Vladimira Putin na sammite NATO." April 18, 2008. https://www.unian.net/politics/110868-vyistuplenie-vladimira-putina-na-sammite-nato-buharest-4-aprelya-2008-goda.html.

United Nations. "Treaty on Friendship, Cooperation and Partnership between Ukraine and the Russian Federation." Signed on May 31, 1997. https://treaties.un.org/Pages/showDetails.aspx?objid=08000002803e6fae.

UN News. "Backing Ukraine's Territorial Integrity, UN Assembly Declares Crimea Referendum Invalid." March 27, 2014. https://news.un.org/en/story/2014/03/464812.

U.S. National Security Archive. "Summary Report on the One-on-One Meeting between Presidents Clinton and Yeltsin." May 10, 1995. https://nsarchive.gwu.edu/document/16825-document-04-summary-report-one-one.

Vasiliev, Aleksandr. "Predstaviteli LNR zaiavili o sebe v biznes-klube 'Evropeiskiy vybor' v Severodonetske." *Severodonetsk.Info*, May 14, 2014. http://sever.lg.ua/2014-05-14-predstaviteli-lnr-zayavili-o-sebe-v-biznes-klube-evropeiskii-vybor-v-severodonetske.

Vchasno. "Deviat klasiv osvity ta lyubov do radianshyny." June 25, 2022. https://vchasnoua.com/donbass/72867-deviat-klasiv-osvity-ta-liubov-do-radianshchyny-u-sievierodonetsku-okupantamy-pryznacheno-mera.

Vecherniy Bakhmut. "Mer Artemovska: Flag DNR nad gorsovetom – eto kompromiss." April 15, 2014.

Vecherniy Bakhmut. "Nachalnik kriminalnoi militsii Artemovska: militsia nikuda ne isparilas." June 6, 2014. https://bahmut.com.ua/news/society/1698-nachalnik-kriminalnoy-milicii-artemovska-miliciya-nikuda-ne-isparilas.html.

Vecherniy Bakhmut. "Trebuem zhestkih i reshytelnyh deistviy." January 30, 2014. https://bahmut.com.ua/news/politics/1344-trebuem-zhestkih-i-reshitelnyh-mer-artemovskie-deputaty-prinyali-obraschenie-k-prezidentu.html.

Vecherniy Bakhmut. "V Artemovske predstaviteli DNR prizvali mestnye vlasti ne sidet na dvukh stuliah." May 28, 2014. https://bahmut.com.ua/news/politics/1668-v-artemovske-predstaviteli-dnr-prizvali-mestnye-vlasti-ne-sidet-na-dvuh-stulyah.html.

Vecherniy Donetsk. "Vneocherednaia sessia gorsoveta." March 4, 2014.

Verwimp, Philip, Patricia Justino, and Tilman Brück. "The Analysis of Conflict: A Micro-level Perspective." *Journal of Peace Research* 46, no. 3 (2009): 307–314.

Vlashenko, Natasha. *Krazha ili Beloe Solntse Kryma.* Kharkiv: Folio, 2017.

Vogt, Manuel, Kristian Skrede Gleditsch, and Lars-Erik Cederman. "From Claims to Violence: Signaling, Outbidding, and Escalation in Ethnic Conflict." *Journal of Conflict Resolution* 65, nos. 7–8 (2021): 1278–1307.

Volynets, Tatiana. "Referendum dolzhen uspokoit liudei." *Druzhkovka na Ladoniah,* April 16, 2014. https://issuu.com/dnl_plus/docs/290_16.

Volynets, Tatiana. "Sergei Novikov: 'Spokoistvie Druzhkovchan—pod pristalnym kontrolem.'" *Druzhkovka na Ladoniah Plius,* March 26, 2014. https://issuu.com/dnl_plus/docs/287_13.

Volynets, Tatiana. "Situatsia v strane stala predmetom goriachei diskussii v ispolkome gorodskogo soveta." *Druzhkovka na Ladoniah plius,* March 26, 2014. https://issuu.com/dnl_plus/docs/287_13.

Vostochnyi Variant. "1–2 marta v Luganskoi oblasti." March 2, 2014. https://v-variant.com.ua/ru/1-2-marta-v-luhanskoy-oblasty-oblsovet-shantazhyruet-tsentralnuiu-vlast-hubernator-otpravlen-v-otstavku-umvd-vozghlavyl-pomaranchev-y-heneral/.

Vostochnyi Variant. "Preizidium oblsoveta obratilsia k Yanukovichu." February 18, 2014. https://v-variant.com.ua/ru/prezydyum-oblsoveta-obratylsia-k-yanukovychu-prosiat-vvesty-chp-a-takzhe-zahovoryly-o-federalyzatsyy-ukrayn-obnovleno/.

Vostrikova, Aleksandra. "Glavnoe—sokhranit' mir i soglasie." *Dzerzhynskiy Shakhter,* March 21, 2014.

Watling, Jack, and Nick Reynolds. "The Plot to Destroy Ukraine." *RUSI Special Report,* February 15, 2022.

Way, Lucan. *Pluralism by Default: Weak Autocrats and the Rise of Competitive Politics.* Baltimore: Johns Hopkins University Press, 2015.

Weidmann, Nils. "Geography as Motivation and Opportunity: Group Concentration and Ethnic Conflict." *Journal of Conflict Resolution* 53, no. 4 (2009): 526–543.

Wiegrafe, Klaus. "The Day the War Really Began." *Der Spiegel,* September 25, 2019. https://www.spiegel.de/international/europe/ukraine-how-merkel-prevented-ukraine-s-nato-membership-a-der-spiegel-reconstruction-a-c7f03472-2a21-4e4e-b905-8e45f1fad542.

Wilson, Andrew. "The Donbas in 2014: Explaining Civil Conflict Perhaps, but Not Civil War." *Europe-Asia Studies* 68, no. 4 (2016): 631–652.

Wilson, Andrew. "Elements of a Theory of Ukrainian Ethno-national Identities." *Nations and Nationalism* 8, no. 1 (2002).

World Bank Group. *Cities in Europe and Central Asia: Ukraine.* Washington, DC: World Bank Group, 2013.

Yudaev, Sergei. *Protivostoianie-2.* LiveJournal. November 18, 2015. https://gruzd22.livejournal.com/36966.html.

Yuga. "Kak kazaki v Krymu Voevali: Vosmoninania Uchastnikov Operatsii." March 18, 2015. https://www.yuga.ru/articles/society/7135.html.

Zahorodnyuk, Andriy. "Public Remarks at the Kyiv Security Forum." YouTube, February 11, 2022. https://www.youtube.com/watch?v=vleLiygfw2A&ab_channel=OpenUkraine.

Zaraz. "Lisichanskiy zavod RTI unichtozhaetsia kak Donetskiy aeroport, no bez voiny." October 20, 2017. https://zaraz.info/lisichanskij-zavod-rti-unichtozhaetsya-kak-donetskij-aeroport-no-bez-vojny-foto/.

Zelensky, Volodymyr. "Address in a Joint Meeting of the US Congress." Official Website of the President of Ukraine, December 22, 2022. https://www.president.gov.ua/en/news/mi-stoyimo-boremos-i-vigrayemo-bo-mi-razom-ukrayina-amerika-80017.

0629. "V Mariupole zahvacheno zdanie gorodskogo soveta." April 13, 2014. https://www.0629.com.ua/news/514955/v-mariupole-zahvaceno-zdanie-gorodskogo-soveta-obnovlaetsafoto.

06274. "Nachalnik Artemovskogo gorotdela obyasnil, pochemu aktivistam vydelil pomeshenie v zdanii MVD." 06274.com.ua, April 18, 2014.

Zhabin, Aleksei. "Igor Strelkov: 'Voevat ia ne sobiralsia.'" *News,* December 28, 2021. https://news.ru/cis/intervyu-igorem-strelkovym/.

Zhuchkovskiy, Aleksandr. *85 dnei Slavianska.* Nizhniy Novgorod: Chernaia Sotnia, 2018.

Zhuchkovskiy, Aleksandr. *Mozgovoi.* Nizhniy Novgorod: Chernaya Sotnia, 2020.

Zhukov, Yuri. "Trading Hard Hats for Combat Helmets: The Economics of Rebellion in Eastern Ukraine." *Journal of Comparative Economics* 44, no. 1 (2016): 1–15.

Zhyrokhov, Mikhail. *Bitva za Lugansk.* Kiev: Patriot Book, 2019.

Zhyrokhov, Mikhail. "Piat' shtrumov artemovskoi bazy." Liga. https://project.liga.net/projects/shturm_artemovska/.

Zimmer, Kerstin. "Trapped in the Past Glory: Self-Identification and Self-Symbolisation in the Donbass." In *Re-constructing the Post-Soviet Industrial Region: The Donbass in Transition,* edited by Adam Swain. London: Routledge, 2007: 97 – 121.

Zubok, Vladislav. *Collapse: The Fall of the Soviet Union.* New Haven, CT: Yale University Press, 2021.

Zubova, Maria. "Vmeste my—sila!" *Kharkovskie Izvestia,* February 4, 2014.

Index

For the benefit of digital users, indexed terms that span two pages (e.g., 52–53) may, on occasion, appear on only one of those pages.